ies
TEST
PREP

SAT®
READING:
History Passages

✔
ADVANCED
PRACTICE
SERIES

- ◆ **50 History Passages**
- ◆ **500 SAT Questions**
- ◆ **2000 Answer Explanations**

Authors
Khalid Khashoggi, Co-Founder IES Test Prep
Arianna Astuni, Co-Founder IES Test Prep

Editorial
Christopher Carbonell, Editorial Director
Megan Caldwell, Editor
Hannah Thorpe, Editor
Cassidy Yong, Editor

Design
Christopher Carbonell
Sophia Wang

Contributors
Anna Binkovitz   Hannah Thorpe
Megan Caldwell   Rajvi Patel
Christopher Carbonell   Shweta Sharma
Elizabeth Crisman   Jazmyn Wang
Johnna Landau   Cassidy Yong

• •

Published by IES Publications
www.IESpublications.co
© IES Publications, 2020

ON BEHALF OF

Integrated Educational Services, Inc.

355 Main Street

Metuchen, NJ 08840

www.iestestprep.com

We would like to thank the IES Publications team as well as the teachers and students at IES Test Prep who have contributed to the creation of this book.

The SAT® is a registered trademark of the College Board, which was not involved in the production of, and does not endorse, this product.

ISBN-13: 9798618218191
QUESTIONS OR COMMENTS? Visit us at iestestprep.com

TABLE OF CONTENTS

Dear Student,

We at IES Test Prep are thrilled to bring you this book as a way to help you intensely practice the SAT History (Global Conversation) Passage. This book contains fifty SAT reading comprehension passages that focus on the struggle for civil and human rights as seen from various points of view and within different political contexts.

During the development of this body of work—from early 2019 to February 1, 2020—we have striven for objectivity and adherence to the standards of the SAT by conducting student trials and incorporating each passage into the curriculum of our verbal courses. This material has been consulted by 8 teachers and tested on over 1,000 students, a process which has shed light on problematic questions and allowed us to make the necessary edits to ensure consistency with official SAT material.

Recognizing students' widespread frustration with the SAT history passage, we hoped to provide a resource that features the typical material tested by the College Board. Though some of the language in these passages may appear distasteful according to today's standards, it reflects the values and conventions of society during the time period in which it was written. Understanding these historical periods will not only further your progress on the SAT, but will also prove valuable for a more nuanced view of the past and its enduring consequences.

Wishing you all the best in your test taking endeavors!

—Khalid Khashoggi

INTRODUCTION

The SAT history (global conversation) passage will be excerpted from a speech, book, or essay written by a prominent intellectual, political, or economic figure throughout modern history. These excerpts will reflect one or more of the following themes—Unity, Democracy, Women's Rights, African-American Rights, Imperialism, Economic Equality, and Tolerance—all of which have provided both the fuel for global conflict and the impetus for societal progress.

Unity

Passages that explore the theme of unity are often written in response to a political, economic, or social crisis and highlight the importance of solidarity, collaboration, and sacrifice. Throughout these passages, the authors will encourage their audience to feel pride in a culture or a way of life and invoke a sense of duty to protect the country that embodies such principles.

Examples:
Sinews of Peace (Iron Curtain) by Winston Churchill
The Three Principles of the People by Sun Yat-Sen
A Crisis of Confidence by Jimmy Carter

Democracy

Passages that explore the theme of democracy are often written in response to a challenge to the balance of power within a constitutional democracy or to a threat from a foreign government. The authors of these passages will cite the separation of powers among the branches of government, the freedoms afforded to citizens in times of conflict, and the tension between the authority of the federal government and that of the states.

Examples:
Statement on the Articles of Impeachment by Barbara Jordan
Hayne-Webster Debate by Robert Hayne and Daniel Webster
Free Speech in Wartime by Robert M. La Folette

Women's Rights

Passages that explore the theme of women's rights are often written in response to the persistent inequality with respect to the opportunities afforded on the basis of gender. The authors of these passages will offer their perspectives on such issues as women's suffrage, the role of women in society, and the potential effects of greater education and economic mobility for women.

Examples:
Disappointment is the Lot of Women by Lucy Stone
Woman Man's Equal by Reverend Thomas Webster
The Crisis by Carrie Chapman Catt

African American Rights

Passages that explore the theme of African American rights are often written in response to the longstanding subjugation and exploitation of Black Americans under the system of slavery and subsequently under discriminatory Jim Crow laws. The authors of these passages will address the momentous impacts of the abolitionist and civil rights movements, as well as the need for jobs and education for newly freed African Americans.

Examples:
The Hypocrisy of American Slavery by Frederick Douglass
Dissenting Opinion on Plessy v. Ferguson by Justice John Marshall Harlan
Address at the National Convention of 1843 by Henry Highland Garnet

Anti-Imperialism

Passages that explore the theme of anti-imperialism are often written in response to egregious acts of tyranny or subjugation under rule by a foreign power. Throughout these passages, the authors will address the hypocrisy and injustice of colonialism and contemplate the necessity of rebellion in order to achieve national sovereignty.

Examples:
Vietnam Veterans Against the War Statement by John Kerry
Common Sense by Thomas Paine
Appeal to China, the United States of America, the Soviet Union, and Great Britain by Ho Chi Minh

Economic Equality

Passages that explore the theme of economic equality are often written in response to the growing income gap that usually accompanies industrial development and urbanization. Authors of these passages will examine the relative advantages of different economic systems, evaluating the need for government intervention as a way of alleviating poverty.

Examples:
Progress and Poverty by Henry George
Cross of Gold by William Jennings Bryan
A Square Deal by Theodore Roosevelt

Tolerance

Passages that explore the theme of tolerance are often written in response to the social marginalization and discrimination of a minority group. Authors of these passages will encourage the protection, acceptance and understanding of those with stigmatized conditions or identities, as well as warn of the danger that could occur from failing to do so.

Examples:
A Whisper of AIDS by Mary Fisher
Speech on a Visit to Washington, D.C by Chief Joseph
I Express My Shame by Gerhard Schröder

Chapter
One

Questions 1-10 are based on the following passage.

1.1

This passage is adapted from Dr. Sun Yat-Sen, San Min Chu I: The Three Principles of the People, translated by Frank W. Price.

As revolutionary ideas have spread through the East, the word "liberty" has come too. But since the word has been brought to China, only a few of the
Line intelligentsia have had time to study and to understand
5 it. If we should talk to the common people of China in the villages or on the streets about "liberty," they would have no idea of what we meant. So we may say that the Chinese have not gotten anything yet out of the word: even the new youth and the returned students,
10 those who have paid some attention to Western political affairs, have a very hazy conception of what it signifies. No wonder that foreigners criticize the Chinese, saying that their civilization is inferior and their thinking immature, that they even have no idea
15 of liberty and no word with which to express the idea, yet at the same time criticizing the Chinese for being disunited as a sheet of loose sand.

These two criticisms are ridiculously contradictory. What do foreigners mean when they
20 say that China is a sheet of loose sand? Simply that every person does as he pleases and has let his individual liberty extend to all phases of life; hence China is but a lot of separate sand particles. Take up a handful of sand; the particles will slip about without
25 any tendency to cohere—that is loose sand. But if we add cement to the loose sand, it will harden into a firm body like a rock, in which the sand has lost its power to move about freely. Liberty, to put it simply, means the freedom to move about as one wishes
30 within an organized group. Because China does not have a word to convey this idea, everyone has been at a loss to appreciate it. We have a phrase that suggests liberty—"running wild without bridle," but that is the same thing as loose sand—excessive liberty for the
35 individual. So foreigners who criticize us do not realize that it is everybody's liberty which is making us a sheet of loose sand and that if all are united in a strong body we cannot be like loose sand. These critics are "holding their spear against their own shield."
40 As the revolutionary ferment of the West has lately spread to China, the new students, and many earnest scholars, have risen up to proclaim liberty. They think that because European revolutions, like the French Revolution, were struggles for liberty,
45 we, too, should fight, for liberty. This is nothing but

"saying what others say." They have not applied their minds to the study of democracy or liberty and have no real insight into their meaning. There is a deep significance in the proposal of our Revolutionary
50 Party that the Three Principles of the People, "Min-ts'u, Min-ch'uan, Min-sheng" (People's Nationalism, People's Sovereignty, People's Livelihood), rather than a struggle for liberty, should be the basis of our revolution. The watchword of the French Revolution
55 was "Liberty"; the watchword of the American Revolution was "Independence"; the watchword of our Revolution is the "Three Principles of the People." We spent much time and effort before we decided upon our watchword; we are not merely imitating others. Why
60 do we say that our new youth's advocacy of liberty is not the right thing, while the Europeans' cry of liberty was so fitting? I have already explained: when we propose an objective for a struggle, it must be relief from some suffering that cuts deep under the skin if
65 we want all the people eagerly to take part in it. The peoples of Europe suffered so bitterly from despotism that as soon as the banner of liberty was lifted high, millions with one heart rallied about it.

Therefore the aims of the Chinese Revolution are
70 different from the aims in foreign revolutions, and the methods we use must also be different. Why, indeed, is China having a revolution? To put the answer directly, the aims of our revolution are just opposite to the aims of the revolutions of Europe. Europeans rebelled
75 and fought for liberty because they had had too little liberty. But we, because we have had too much liberty without any unity and resisting power, because we have become a sheet of loose sand and so have been invaded by foreign imperialism and oppressed by
80 the economic control and trade wars of the Powers, without being able to resist, must break down individual liberty and become pressed together into an unyielding body like the firm rock which is formed by the addition of cement to sand. Chinese today are
85 enjoying so much freedom that they are showing the evils of freedom. This is true not merely in the schools but even in our Revolutionary Party. The reason why, from the overthrow of the Manchus until now, we have not been able to establish a government is just this
90 misuse of freedom.

CONTINUE →

1

The primary purpose of the passage is to

A) juxtapose the concept of revolution in the East and West so as to underscore the efficacy of Chinese methods.

B) respond to criticisms of the Chinese Revolution by highlighting its formidable nature.

C) contend that China's unique struggles necessitate a new guiding principle of revolution.

D) chronicle the rise of revolutionary ideas in the East and identify the advent of the notion of liberty.

2

What does Sun Yat-Sen identify as foreigners' primary criticism of the Chinese?

A) They fail to recognize the democratic value of the struggle for liberty.

B) They do not understand the meaning of liberty and therefore lack unity.

C) They have not dedicated adequate time to the study of Western ideals.

D) They have yet to educate their masses about revolutionary concepts.

3

Which choice provides the best evidence for the answer to the previous question?

A) Lines 5-7 ("If we...meant.")

B) Lines 14-17 ("that they...sand.")

C) Lines 43-45 ("They think...liberty.")

D) Lines 46-48 ("They have...meaning.")

4

Over the course of the passage, Sun Yat-Sen's rhetoric is notable for its use of

A) didactic language, which furthers the agenda of Chinese revolutionaries and intellectuals.

B) parallel structures, which create a contrast between the China of the past and that of the future.

C) extended metaphor, which underscores a deficiency and clarifies the impetus for revolution.

D) historical anecdotes, which prove the merit of governmental acceptance of unprecedented ideas.

5

Ultimately, why is liberty an inadequate watchword for the Chinese Revolution?

A) It has become a vice that is rampant among the country's intellectuals.

B) It does not have a direct Chinese translation and thus is not considered a virtue.

C) It is incomprehensible even to the Chinese youth who have studied abroad.

D) It does not galvanize action as it is not a right that is being suppressed.

6

Which choice provides the best evidence for the answer to the previous question?

A) Lines 2-5 ("But since...it.")

B) Lines 30-32 ("Because China...it.")

C) Lines 63-65 ("it must...it.")

D) Lines 84-87 ("Chinese today...Party.")

7

As used in line 54, "watchword" most nearly means

A) truism.

B) motto.

C) adage.

D) idiom.

8

According to the passage, revolution is necessary because China has suffered from a lack of

A) national cohesion, which has inadvertently allowed the encroachment of outside forces.

B) cultural autonomy, which has created a dearth of support and solidarity among citizens.

C) fervent nationalism, which has resulted in societal and governmental mimicry of the West.

D) self-initiative, which has paved the way for foreign incursion into China's economic affairs.

CONTINUE

9

As used in line 90, "misuse" most nearly means

A) waste.

B) misapplication.

C) excess.

D) exploitation.

10

It can most reasonably be inferred from the passage that Sun Yat-Set would disagree with which approach to revolution?

A) Emulating past revolutions without thoroughly considering the local applicability of their objectives and methods.

B) Heralding freedom and independence as the aims of a revolution while neglecting the importance of other values.

C) Launching a revolution that fails to eradicate the specific suffering of the country at issue and thus escalates its grievances.

D) Overhauling the local understanding of morality by pursuing a revolution based on ideals that are irrelevant to those concerned.

CONTINUE

Questions 1-10 are based on the following passage.

1.2

The following passage is adapted from an address by Henry Highland Garnet, read at the National Convention held at Buffalo, N.Y., in 1843.

Brethren and Fellow Citizens:
Your brethren of the north, east, and west have been accustomed to meet together in National
Line Conventions, to sympathize with each other, and to
5 weep over your unhappy condition. In these meetings, we have addressed all classes of the free, but we have never until this time sent a word of consolation and advice to you. We have been contented in sitting still and mourning over your sorrows, earnestly hoping that
10 before this day your sacred liberties would have been restored. But, we have hoped in vain. Years have rolled on, and tens of thousands have been borne on streams of blood and tears to the shores of eternity. While you have been oppressed, we have also been partakers with
15 you; nor can we be free while you are enslaved. We therefore write to you as being bound with you.
Many of you are bound to us, not only by the ties of a common humanity but by the more tender relations of parents, wives, husbands, children,
20 brothers, sisters, and friends. As such we most affectionately address you.
Slavery has fixed a deep gulf between you and us, and while it shuts out from you the relief and consolation which your friends would willingly render,
25 it afflicts and persecutes you with a fierceness which we might not expect to see in the fiends of hell. But still, the Almighty Father of Mercies has left to us a glimmering ray of hope, which shines out like a lone star in a cloudy sky. Mankind are becoming wiser,
30 and better; the oppressor's power is fading, and you, every day, are becoming better informed and more numerous. Your grievances, brethren, are many. We shall not attempt, in this short address, to present to the world all the dark catalogue of this nation's sins,
35 which have been committed upon an innocent people. Nor is it indeed necessary, for you feel them from day to day, and all the civilized world look upon them with amazement.
Two hundred and twenty-seven years ago, the
40 first of our injured race were brought to the shores of America. They came not with glad spirits to select their homes in the New World. They came not with their own consent to find an unmolested enjoyment of the blessings of this fruitful soil. The first dealings which

45 they had with those calling themselves Christians exhibited to them the worst features of corrupt and sordid hearts, and convinced them that no cruelty is too great, no villainy and no robbery too abhorrent, for even enlightened men to perform, when influenced by
50 avarice and lust. Neither did they come flying upon the wings of Liberty to a land of freedom. But they came with broken hearts from their beloved native land, and were doomed to unrequited toil and deep degradation. Nor did the evil of their bondage end at
55 their emancipation by death. Succeeding generations inherited their chains, and millions have come from eternity into time, and have returned again to the world of spirits, cursed and ruined by American Slavery.
The propagators of the system, or their immediate
60 ancestors, very soon discovered its growing evil, and its tremendous wickedness, and secret promises were made to destroy it. The gross inconsistency of a people holding slaves, who had themselves "ferried o'er the wave" for freedom's sake, was too apparent to
65 be entirely overlooked. The voice of Freedom cried: "emancipate your Slaves." Humanity supplicated with tears for the deliverance of the children of Africa. Wisdom urged her solemn plea. The bleeding captive plead his innocence, and pointed to Christianity who
70 stood weeping at the cross. But all was vain. Slavery had stretched its dark wings of death over the land. Its throne is established, and now it reigns triumphantly.
Nearly three million of your fellow citizens are prohibited by law, and public opinion, from reading
75 the Book of Life. Your intellect has been destroyed as much as possible, and every ray of light they have attempted to shut out from your minds. The oppressors themselves have become involved in the ruin. They have become weak, sensual, and rapacious. They have
80 cursed you—they have cursed themselves—they have cursed the earth which they have trod. In the language of a Southern statesman, we can truly say, "even the wolf, driven back long since by the approach of man, now returns after the lapse of a hundred years, and howls amid the desolations of slavery."

CONTINUE

1

What is a central claim of the passage?

A) Although slavery is mostly harmful to the slave, its destructiveness has spread throughout American life.

B) Although the South supports slavery, there are signs of a growing abolitionist movement in the North.

C) Although slavery was once a profitable institution, its growing unpopularity makes it unsustainable.

D) Although slavery is beginning to fall out of favor, its legacy of irreparable damage cannot be overcome by abolition.

2

With which choice would the author most likely agree about the bond between the free and the enslaved?

A) There can be no meaningful bonds between the two groups as long as slavery exists.

B) All Americans, whether free or enslaved, are bound by common Christian values.

C) Many free Americans have close familial ties with those who are enslaved.

D) The future prospects for free Americans are inextricably tied to the fate of the enslaved.

3

Which choice provides the best evidence for the answer to the previous question?

A) Lines 13-15 ("While you … enslaved")

B) Lines 17-21 ("Many of...you")

C) Lines 39-41 ("Two hundred...America")

D) Lines 44-50 ("The first...lust")

4

As used in line 22, "fixed" most nearly means

A) solved.

B) solidified.

C) set.

D) mended.

5

Throughout the fourth paragraph (lines 22-38), the main focus shifts from

A) a lamentation of the indifference of the world toward slavery to an appeal for global sympathy.

B) a depiction of the animosity between slaves and free African-Americans to the urging that such a divide be closed.

C) a recognition of the destructiveness of slavery to the promise of a possible reprieve.

D) a statement about slaves' ignorance of their plight to a recognition of their gradual enlightenment of their condition.

6

Garnet indicates that many of the slaves who were first taken from Africa as slaves

A) had children in the Americas who were born into slavery.

B) died from the harsh conditions on the trip to the Americas.

C) eventually escaped to freedom in the North.

D) returned to Africa after securing their freedom.

7

Which choice provides the best evidence for the answer to the previous question?

A) Lines 42-44 (" They came … soil")

B) Lines 51–54 ("But they … degradation")

C) Lines 55-58 ("Succeeding generations...Slavery")

D) Lines 68-70 ("The bleeding...cross")

8

As used in line 49, "influenced" most nearly means

A) motivated.

B) manipulated.

C) inspired.

D) tempted.

16

CONTINUE

9

What is the "inconsistency" to which Garnet alludes in lines 62-65 ("The gross...overlooked.")?

A) That many American slaves were told that they would be free in America, only to be enslaved upon arriving.

B) That a country founded by immigrants seeking freedom should allow other "immigrants" to be held in bondage.

C) That some American slaveowners were once slaves themselves.

D) That many American slaves are not, in fact, American by birth, as they were born in Africa.

10

Garnet indicates that slavery has produced which effect on slaveholders?

A) It has put them in the position to avoid facing the injustice of their actions.

B) It has allowed them to lead empty lives of hedonism and immorality.

C) It has artificially raised their socio-economic position to one above Africans.

D) It has maintained their privilege so that they are ignorant of others' suffering.

CONTINUE

[handwritten annotations in top margin: "T: Woman's rights / T: Negative / W - Do not break th / 6000 tradition of / domestic sphere. At most, men / men sh... important in the domestic / in the domestic / T! / T! / W:"]

Questions 1-11 are based on the following passage.

1.3

In July 1848, the Women's Rights Convention was launched in Seneca Falls, NY, which set the foundation for what was to become the Women's Suffrage movement. Passage 1 is from an article published in Mechanic's Advocate. Passage 2 is adapted from an 1848 editorial by Frederick Douglass in his paper, *The North Star*.

Passage 1

We are sorry to see that the women in several parts of this State are holding what they call "Woman's Rights Conventions," and setting forth a formidable
Line list of those Rights in a parody upon the Declaration of
5 American Independence. The papers of the day contain extended notices of these Conventions. Some of them fall in with their objects and praise the meetings highly; but the majority either deprecate or ridicule both.

10 The women who attend these meetings, no doubt at the expense of their more appropriate duties, act as committees, write resolutions and addresses, hold much correspondence, make speeches, etc. They affirm, as among their rights, that of unrestricted
15 franchise, and assert that it is wrong to deprive them of the privilege to become legislators, lawyers, doctors, divines, etc.; and they are holding Conventions and making an agitatory movement, with the object in view of revolutionizing public opinion and the laws of the
20 land, and changing their relative position in society in such a way as to divide with the male sex the labors and responsibilities of active life in every branch of art, science, trades, and professions.

Now, it requires no argument to prove that this
25 is all wrong. Every true hearted female will instantly feel that this is unwomanly, and that to be practically carried out, the males must change their position in society to the same extent in an opposite direction, in order to enable them to discharge an equal share of the
30 domestic duties which now appertain to females, and which must be neglected, to a great extent, if women are allowed to exercise all the "rights" that are claimed by these Convention-holders. Society would have to be radically remodeled in order to accommodate itself to
35 so great a change in the most vital part of the compact of the social relations of life; and the order of things established at the creation of mankind, and continued six thousand years, would be completely broken up.

But this change is impracticable, uncalled for, and
40 unnecessary. If effected, it would set the world by the

ears, make "confusion worse confounded," demoralize and degrade from their high sphere and noble destiny, women of all respectable and useful classes, and prove a monstrous injury to all mankind. It would
45 be productive of no positive good, that would not be outweighed tenfold by positive evil. It would alter the relations of females without bettering their condition. Besides all, and above all, it presents no remedy for the real evils that the millions of the industrious, hard-
50 working, and much suffering women of our country groan under and seek to redress.

Passage 2

One of the most interesting events of the past week, was the holding of what is technically styled a Woman's Rights Convention at Seneca Falls.
55 The speaking, addresses, and resolutions of this extraordinary meeting were almost wholly conducted by women; and although they evidently felt themselves in a novel position, it is but simple justice to say that their whole proceedings were characterized by marked
60 ability and dignity.

In this meeting, there were frequent differences of opinion and animated discussion; but in no case was there the slightest absence of good feeling and decorum. Several interesting documents setting forth
65 the rights as well as grievances of women were read. Among these was a Declaration of Sentiments, to be regarded as the basis of a grand movement for attaining the civil, social, political, and religious rights of women.
70 We should not do justice to our own convictions, or to the excellent persons connected with this infant movement, if we did not in this connection offer a few remarks on the general subject which the Convention met to consider and the objects they seek to attain. In
75 doing so, we are not insensible that the bare mention of this truly important subject in any other than terms of contemptuous ridicule and scornful disfavor, is likely to excite against us the fury of bigotry and the folly of prejudice. A discussion of the rights of animals would
80 be regarded with far more complacency by many of what are called the wise and the good of our land, than would be a discussion of the rights of women. Many who have at last made the discovery that the negroes have some rights as well as other members
85 of the human family, have yet to be convinced that women are entitled to any. Eight years ago, a number of persons of this description actually abandoned the anti-slavery cause, lest by giving their influence in that direction they might possibly be giving countenance to
90 the dangerous heresy that woman, in respect to rights,

18

CONTINUE →

stands on an equal footing with man. It is perhaps
needless to say, that we cherish little sympathy for such
sentiments or respect for such prejudices. Standing
as we do upon the watch-tower of human freedom,
95 we cannot be deterred from an expression of our
approbation of any movement, however humble, to
improve and elevate the character of any members of
the human family.

    While it is impossible for us to go into this
100 subject at length, we are free to say that in respect to
political rights, we hold woman to be justly entitled
to all we claim for man. We go farther, and express
our conviction that all political rights which it is
expedient for man to exercise, it is equally so for
105 woman. All that distinguishes man as an intelligent
and accountable being, is equally true of woman;
and if that government only is just which governs
by the free consent of the governed, there can be no
reason in the world for denying to woman the exercise
110 of the elective franchise, or a hand in making and
administering the laws of the land. Our doctrine is
that "right is of no sex." We therefore bid the women
engaged in this movement our humble Godspeed.

1

As used in line 6, "notices of" most nearly means

A) warnings about.
B) proclamations of.
C) articles on.
D) news about.

2

The main issue that the author of Passage 1 takes with the
women's suffrage movement is that

A) forming committees and writing addresses are
unwomanly activities that are a waste of time
B) allocating equal rights to women would necessarily
encroach upon those of men and force unnatural
adaptation.
C) the movement's main proclamation is a frivolous and
disrespectful attempt to emulate the Declaration of
Independence.
D) the movement's demand for the radical upheaval of
gender roles would be devastating to the order of
society.

3

In line 32, the author of Passage 1's use of quotations
has which effect?

A) It calls attention to the discomfort true-hearted
women would experience if those rights were
granted.
B) It underscores the irony of women who attempt to
secure rights they do not understand.
C) It distances the author from the idea that rights should
be extended to women.
D) It alludes to the author's description of the rights for
which women are advocating.

4

What relationship does the author of Passage 2 see
between the movement for women's rights and that for
African-American rights?

A) He views the struggles as parallel and deserving of
reciprocal respect and support.
B) He sees the movement for women's rights as a
catalyst for African-American rights.
C) He believes that African American activists are
undermining the struggle for women's rights.
D) He laments the lack of intersectionality and
inclusivity in the women's suffrage movement.

5

Which choice provides the best evidence for the answer
to the previous question?

A) Lines 83-86 ("Many who...any")
B) Lines 86-91 ("Eight years...man")
C) Lines 95-98 ("we cannot...family")
D) Lines 99-102 ("While it...man")

6

As used in line 74, "objects" most nearly means

A) ends.
B) items.
C) focus.
D) privileges.

CONTINUE ➡

7

Which choice best identifies a key difference in how the author of Passage 1 and the author of Passage 2 view the Declaration of Sentiments?

A) The author of Passage 1 suggests that it is a joke that deserves extensive ridicule, whereas the author of Passage 2 argues it is a serious declaration that requires analysis and animated discussion.

B) The author of Passage 1 perceives it as a laughable imitation of the Declaration of Independence, whereas the author of Passage 2 views it as a fascinating document of a worthy movement.

C) The author of Passage 1 sees it as an attempt to divide the labors and responsibilities of the sexes, whereas the author of Passage 2 argues that it strives to enumerate the civil and religious rights of women.

D) The author of Passage 1 insists that it is impractical and entirely uncalled for, whereas the author of Passage 2 believes it is dignified and should be regarded with complacency.

8

By positioning himself "on the watch-tower of human freedom" (line 94), Douglass maintains that

A) Those furthering the abolitionist cause are the most clear-sighted and morally upstanding.

B) Those who guard and praise the freedom of one group must persevere in guarding and praising the freedom of all.

C) Those who watch and wait are those who are most cognizant of the true pains of inequality.

D) Those promoting freedom must cherish their allies and not be deterred by bigotry and hate.

9

The author of Passage 1 would most likely view the sentiment expressed in lines 79-82 ("A discussion… women") with

A) strong disagreement, since the comparison degrades the high sphere of womanhood.

B) reluctant acceptance, since women's rights are impractical and unnecessary.

C) complete agreement, since animal rights are less societally incendiary.

D) justified hesitation, since the statement questions those who are wise and good.

10

Which choice provides the best evidence for the answer to the previous question?

A) Lines 33-36 ("Society would...life")

B) Lines 39-40 ("But this...unnecessary")

C) Lines 42-43 ("and degrade...classes")

D) Lines 48-51 ("Besides all...redress")

11

The phrase "agitatory movement" (line 18) contrasts most directly with which remark from Douglass in Passage 2?

A) "extraordinary meeting" (line 56)

B) "novel position" (line 58)

C) "dangerous heresy" (line 90)

D) "elective franchise" (line 110)

20

CONTINUE

Questions 1-10 are based on the following passage.

1.4

In 1877, Nez Perce tribal Chief Joseph surrendered after a brief war against U.S. government forces that had been sent to forcibly relocate the Nez Perce from their ancestral lands in Oregon to a reservation in Idaho. This passage is adapted from an 1879 speech he gave during a visit to Washington, D.C. In this speech, all the "chiefs" Joseph refers to are members of the U.S. government. "Great Father Chief" is President Hayes.

At last I was granted permission to come to Washington and bring my friend Yellow Bull and our interpreter with me. I am glad I came. I have shaken
Line hands with a good many friends, but there are some
5 things I want to know which no one seems able to explain.

I cannot understand how the Government sends a man out to fight us, as it did General Miles, and then breaks his word. Such a government has something
10 wrong about it. I cannot understand why so many chiefs are allowed to talk so many different ways, and promise so many different things. I have seen the Great Father Chief; the Next Great Chief; the Commissioner Chief; the Law Chief; and many other law chiefs and
15 they all say they are my friends, and that I shall have justice. But while all their mouths talk right, I do not understand why nothing is done for my people. I have heard talk and talk but nothing is done.

Good words do not last long unless they amount
20 to something. Words do not pay for my dead people. They do not pay for my country now overrun by white men. They do not protect my father's grave. They do not pay for my horses and cattle. Good words do not give me back my children. Good words will not give
25 my people a home where they can live in peace and take care of themselves. I am tired of talk that comes to nothing. It makes my heart sick when I remember all the good words and all the broken promises. There has been too much talking by men who had no right to
30 talk. Too many misinterpretations have been made; too many misunderstandings have come up between the white men and the Indians.

If the white man wants to live in peace with the Indian, he can live in peace. There need be no trouble.
35 Treat all men alike. Give them the same laws. Give them all an even chance to live and grow. All men were made by the same Great Spirit Chief. They are all brothers. The earth is the mother of all people, and all

people should have equal rights upon it. You might as
40 well expect all rivers to run backward as that any man who was born a free man should be contented penned up and denied liberty to go where he pleases. If you tie a horse to a stake, do you expect he will grow fat? If you pen an Indian up on a small spot of earth and
45 compel him to stay there, he will not be contented nor will he grow and prosper. I have asked some of the Great White Chiefs where they get their authority to say to the Indian that he shall stay in one place, while he sees white men going where they please. They
50 cannot tell me.

I only ask of the Government to be treated as all other men are treated. If I cannot go to my own home, let me have a home in a country where my people will not die so fast. I would like to go to Bitter Root Valley.
55 There my people would be happy; where they are now they are dying. Three have died since I left my camp to come to Washington. When I think of our condition, my heart is heavy.

I see men of my own race treated as outlaws and
60 driven from country to country, or shot down like animals. I know that my race must change. We cannot hold our own with the white men as we are. We only ask an even chance to live as other men live. We ask to be recognized as men. We ask that the same law
65 shall work alike on all men. If an Indian breaks the law, punish him by the law. If a white man breaks the law, punish him also. Let me be a free man, free to travel, free to stop, free to work, free to trade where I choose, free to choose my own teachers, free to follow
70 the religion of my fathers, free to talk, think and act for myself—and I will obey every law or submit to the penalty.

Whenever the white man treats the Indian as they treat each other then we shall have no more wars. We
75 shall be all alike—brothers of one father and mother, with one sky above us and one country around us and one government for all. Then the Great Spirit Chief who rules above will smile upon this land and send rain to wash out the bloody spots made by brothers'
80 hands upon the face of the earth. For this time the Indian race is waiting and praying. I hope no more groans of wounded men and women will ever go to the ear of the Great Spirit Chief above, and that all people may be one people.
85 Hin-mah-too-yah-lat-kekht has spoken for his people.

CONTINUE ➤

1

In writing this passage, Chief Joseph mainly seeks to

A) persuade the American government of the Nez Perce's peaceful nature.

B) present a compelling reason to end a war between two nations.

C) implore the American government to treat Indians as free men.

D) start a discussion about the wrongs committed against the Nez Perce.

2

In making his case for the freedom of his people, Chief Joseph uses language that

A) is notable for its use of anecdotes from life in the Nez Perce tribe.

B) evokes the philosophy and world view of the Indian race.

C) aims to impress the reader with unfamiliar titles of respect.

D) relates his people's grievances to those of the American public.

3

Chief Joseph makes which critique about the leaders of the American government?

A) They have continually depicted themselves as proponents of Indian rights but have ultimately proven to be insincere.

B) They are both unwilling and unable to explain or justify their cruel treatment toward the American Indians.

C) They have delegated the administration of Indian affairs to rogue officials who are unequal to the task.

D) They misconstrue the messages of Indian Chiefs due to their insensitivity to the complexities of Indian culture.

4

Which choice provides the best evidence for the answer to the previous question?

A) Lines 7-12 ("I cannot…things")

B) Lines 15-18 ("they all…done")

C) Lines 28-32 ("There has…Indians")

D) Lines 46-49 ("I have…please")

5

In lines 37-38, Chief Joseph calls upon the "Great Spirit Chief" and Earth as "mother of all people" primarily to

A) emphasize his argument that all men should be treated as equals.

B) give examples of the religious beliefs on which his claims are based.

C) characterize the conflict between white men and Indians as superficial.

D) question the jurisdiction of the American government to grant rights.

6

Chief Joseph would likely react to the widespread stereotyping of American Indians as barbaric by

A) pointing out the hypocrisy of such accusations from a race known for its brutality.

B) categorically rejecting the stereotype with an emphasis on their peaceful and diplomatic nature.

C) justifying these characteristics within the context of their suffering at the hands of white men.

D) acknowledging that some elements of the stereotype are true but can be overcome.

7

Which choice provides the best evidence for the answer to the previous question?

A) Lines 44-46 ("If you…prosper")

B) Lines 59-61 ("I see…animals")

C) Lines 61-62 ("I know…are")

D) Lines 73-74 ("Whenever the…wars")

8

As used in line 45, "compel" most nearly means

A) force.

B) persuade.

C) oblige.

D) order.

CONTINUE

9

Throughout the passage, Chief Joseph's repeated appeal to brotherhood serves most likely to

A) remind his audience of the past friendship between white men and Indians.

B) highlight the shared humanity of Americans regardless of heritage.

C) remind American leaders that some of them have Indian ancestry.

D) guilt the Great Father Chief into caring equally for all his children.

10

As used in line 64, "recognized" most nearly means

A) known.

B) perceived.

C) accepted.

D) acknowledged.

23

CONTINUE

Questions 1-10 are based on the following passage.

1.5

The following passage is adapted from Barbara Jordan's Statement on the Articles of Impeachment, delivered as part of the impeachment hearings against President Richard Nixon, who was accused of having covered up his administration's role in Watergate Scandal of 1972.

Today I am an inquisitor. An hyperbole would not be fictional and would not overstate the solemnness that I feel right now. My faith in the Constitution is
Line whole; it is complete; it is total. And I am not going to
5 sit here and be an idle spectator to the diminution, the subversion, the destruction, of the Constitution.

In the Federalist Papers, number 65, Hamilton said, "Who can so properly be the inquisitors for the nation as the representatives of the nation themselves?"
10 "The subjects of its jurisdiction are those offenses which proceed from the misconduct of public men." And that's what we're talking about. In other words, the jurisdiction comes from the abuse or violation of some public trust.
15 It is wrong, I suggest, it is a misreading of the Constitution for any member here to assert that for a member to vote for an article of impeachment means that that member must be convinced that the President should be removed from office. The Constitution
20 doesn't say that. The powers relating to impeachment are an essential check in the hands of the body of the Legislature against and upon the encroachments of the Executive. The division between the two branches of the Legislature, the House and the Senate, assigning
25 to the one the right to accuse and to the other the right to judge, the Framers of this Constitution were very astute. They did not make the accusers and the judges the same person.

We know the nature of impeachment. We've been
30 talking about it awhile now. It is chiefly designed for the President and his high ministers to somehow be called into account. It is designed to "bridle" the Executive if he engages in excesses. "It is designed as a method of national inquest into the conduct of public
35 men." The Framers confided in the Congress the power if need be, to remove the President in order to strike a delicate balance between a President swollen with power and grown tyrannical, and preservation of the independence of the Executive.
40 The Federal Convention of 1787 said that it limited impeachment to high crimes and

misdemeanors and discounted and opposed the term "maladministration." "It is to be used only for great misdemeanors," so it was said in the North Carolina
45 ratification convention. And in the Virginia ratification convention: "We do not trust our liberty to a particular branch. We need one branch to check the other."

"No one need be afraid" -- the North Carolina ratification convention stated-- "No one need be
50 afraid that officers who commit oppression will pass with immunity." "Prosecutions of impeachments will seldom fail to agitate the passions of the whole community," said Hamilton in the Federalist Papers, number 65. "We divide into parties more or less
55 friendly or inimical to the accused." I do not mean political parties in that sense.

The drawing of political lines goes to the motivation behind impeachment; but impeachment must proceed within the confines of the constitutional
60 term "high crimes and misdemeanors."

Of the impeachment process, it was Woodrow Wilson who said that "Nothing short of the grossest offenses against the plain law of the land will suffice to give them speed and effectiveness. Indignation so great
65 as to overgrow party interest may secure a conviction; but nothing else can."

Common sense would be revolted if we engaged upon this process for petty reasons. Congress has a lot to do: Appropriations, Tax Reform, Health Insurance,
70 Campaign Finance Reform, Housing, Environmental Protection, Energy Sufficiency, Mass Transportation. Pettiness cannot be allowed to stand in the face of such overwhelming problems. So today we are not being petty. We are trying to be big, because the task we have
75 before us is a big one.

James Madison again at the Convention: "A President is impeachable if he attempts to subvert the Constitution." The Constitution charges the President with the task of taking care that the laws be faithfully
80 executed, and yet the President has counseled his aides to commit perjury, willfully disregard the secrecy of grand jury proceedings, conceal surreptitious entry, attempt to compromise a federal judge, while publicly displaying his cooperation with the processes of
85 criminal justice. "A President is impeachable if he attempts to subvert the Constitution."

If the impeachment provision in the Constitution of the United States will not reach the offenses charged here, then perhaps that 18th-century Constitution
90 should be abandoned to a 20th-century paper shredder!

Has the President committed offenses, and planned, and directed, and acquiesced in a course of conduct which the Constitution will not tolerate?

CONTINUE

That's the question. We know that. We know the
95 question. We should now forthwith proceed to answer
the question. It is reason, and not passion, which must
guide our deliberations, guide our debate, and guide
our decision.

1

According to the author, the most significant allegation
against President Nixon is that his recent behavior can be
perceived as

A) posing a threat to the Constitution.

B) endangering the security of the nation.

C) abusing his office for personal gain.

D) destroying the integrity of the Presidency.

2

Which statement provides the best description of a
technique that Jordan uses throughout the passage to
advance her main point?

A) She cites passages from the Constitution and illustrates
   their relevance to the current impeachment hearings.

B) She makes references to the Framers' statements and
   demonstrates their application to the matter at hand.

C) She uses collective voice when describing the nation's
   grievance to emphasize the universality of her beliefs.

D) She alludes to the remarks of previous esteemed
   Presidents to evoke patriotic sentiment in her audience.

3

It can be reasonably inferred from the passage that the
Framers created the impeachment process as a means of

A) preventing the President from usurping the powers of
   the Legislative branch.

B) allowing the public to express their disapproval of a
   Presidential breach of trust.

C) protecting the nation from any potential overreach of the
   President's powers.

D) removing the President from office for enacting policies
   deemed to be egregious.

4

Which choice provides the best evidence for the answer
to the previous question?

A) Lines 10-14 ("The subjects...trust")

B) Lines 24-28 ("assigning to...person")

C) Lines 29-30 ("We know...now")

D) Lines 35-39 ("The Framers...Executive")

5

In the context of the passage as a whole, lines 15-19 ("It
is...office") primarily serve to

A) reassure those who might be hesitant about voting for
   an article of impeachment.

B) acknowledge a potential repercussion of voting for an
   article of impeachment.

C) give clarification on the significance of voting for an
   article of impeachment.

D) refute a potential assumption about the implications
   of voting for an article of impeachment.

6

Which choice provides the best evidence for Jordan's
claim that criteria for impeachment are independent of a
President's competence in office?

A) Lines 40-43 ("The Federal...maladministration")

B) Lines 48-51 ("No one...immunity")

C) Lines 57-60 ("The drawing...misdemeanors")

D) Lines 67-71 ("Common sense...Transportation")

7

As used in line 65, "interest" most nearly means

A) duty.

B) allegiance.

C) agenda.

D) policy.

8

As used in line 74, "big" most nearly means

A) moral.

B) rational.

C) responsible.

D) serious.

CONTINUE

9

Which choice provides the best evidence for Jordan's claim that President Nixon has subverted the Constitution?

A) Lines 76-78 ("James Madison...Constitution")

B) Lines 80-85 ("and yet...justice")

C) Lines 87-90 ("If the...shredder")

D) Lines 91-96 ("Has the...question")

10

Jordan evokes the image of the "18th-century Constitution...abandoned to a 20th-century paper shredder" (lines 89-90) most likely to

A) indicate that the crimes committed by the President are unambiguously impeachable.

B) promote amendments to what Jordan considers to be an outdated Constitution.

C) demonstrate the President's gross lack of regard for a sacred document.

D) express skepticism of the Constitution's ability to address the matter at hand.

STOP

Please turn to next page for answer keys and explanations.

Answer Key: CHAPTER ONE

1.1 | Sun Yat-Sen	1.2 | Garnet	1.3 | Seneca	1.4 | Chief Joseph	1.5 | Jordan
1: C	1: A	1: C	1: C	1: A
2: B	2: C	2: D	2: B	2: B
3: B	3: B	3: C	3: A	3: C
4: C	4: C	4: A	4: B	4: D
5: D	5: C	5: C	5: A	5: D
6: C	6: A	6: A	6: D	6: A
7: B	7: C	7: B	7: C	7: B
8: A	8: A	8: B	8: A	8: D
9: C	9: B	9: C	9: B	9: B
10: A	10: B	10: A	10: D	10: A
		11: A		

Answer Explanations

Chapter One

Chapter 1.1 | Sun Yat-Sen

Question 1: C
Choice C is the best answer because throughout the passage, Sun highlights the unique and unprecedented nature of the Chinese Revolution: he claims that "the aims of the Chinese Revolution are different from the aims in foreign revolutions" (lines 69-70) and that in their methods, the Chinese "are not merely imitating others" (line 59). Furthermore, he indicates that because the goal of the Chinese Revolution is liberty "within an organized group" (line 30) and not unbridled individual freedom, the proposed "Three Principles of the People...rather than a struggle for liberty, should be the basis for [their] revolution" (lines 50-54). Choice A is incorrect because Chinese methods of revolution have not yet been implemented and therefore cannot be proven more effective than Western methods; moreover, Sun does not deem one method as more valuable than the other, but merely indicates that each is needed in different contexts. Choice B is incorrect because Sun does not deflect criticism of the Chinese Revolution by highlighting its "formidable nature"; in fact, he admits that the revolution has been stunted because of the excessive freedom granted to Chinese citizens. Choice D is incorrect because Sun does not provide a timeline or "chronicle" of revolutionary ideas, nor does he identify the specific point in time at which the "advent of the notion of liberty" occurred.

Question 2: B
Choice B is the best answer because in lines 14-17, Sun describes foreigners' view of the Chinese as immature because they "have even have no idea of liberty" and therefore do not understand the concept of freedom. Moreover, he indicates that foreigners have compared Chinese revolutionaries to a "sheet of loose sand", thus highlighting their disunity and lack of organization. Choice A is incorrect because Chinese revolutionaries must have recognized some inherent benefit to attaining liberty; if not, they would not seek liberty in the first place. Choice C is incorrect because Sun indicates that Chinese revolutionaries have actually spent excessive time dedicating themselves to the study and implementation of Western ideals, which have proven inappropriate for a Chinese struggle: "earnest scholars...think that because European revolutions, like the French Revolution, were struggles for liberty, we, too, should fight for liberty. This is nothing but 'saying what others say'" (lines 42-46). Choice D is incorrect because while Sun agrees that the "common people" of China are unaware of the concepts of liberty or revolution (lines 2-7), he does not indicate that this view is shared by foreigners.

Question 3: B

Choice B is the best answer because lines 14-17 explain the reasons that foreigners perceive Chinese civilization as "inferior and their thinking [as] immature" (lines 13-14), before "criticizing the Chinese" for their disunity. Choice A is incorrect because lines 5-7 fail to address the topic; in these lines, Sun discusses the people of China, not the view of foreigners. Choice C is incorrect because lines 43-45 describe the view of Chinese "students" (line 41) and "ernest scholars" (line 42), not a foreign perspective. Choice D is incorrect because it is Sun himself who states that these proponents of a Chinese struggle for liberty have "no real insight into their meaning" (line 48) because "they have not applied their minds to the study" (lines 46-47); as he is Chinese himself, these lines do not express the viewpoints of foreigners.

Question 4: C

Choice C is the best answer because Sun claims that foreigners believe the Chinese people are "disunited as a sheet of loose sand" (line 17). He brings this metaphor up again in several other parts of his argument: "China is but a lot of separate sand particles" (line 23), "it is everybody's liberty which is making us a sheet of loose sand" (lines 36-37), and "the Powers...must break down individual liberty and become pressed together into an unyielding body like the firm rock which is formed by the addition of cement to sand" (lines 80-84). Choice A is incorrect because these "Chinese revolutionaries and intellectuals" are the same proponents of liberty whom he is criticizing; he does not want to further their agenda of emulating Western revolutions and their values. Choice B is incorrect because Sun does not create a clear contrast between past and future China; he mainly focuses on the present with his critiques of the misguided revolutionaries and the way in which China has been invaded and oppressed by imperial powers. Choice D is incorrect; Sun does not ground his argument in the past, or "historical anecdotes", because he is discussing the current state of China.

Question 5: D

Choice D is the best answer because Sun highlights that a key factor in rallying the masses is selecting an objective for revolution that seeks to relieve a common suffering of the people. Liberty does not achieve that goal, mainly because it is something that the Chinese already possess (in fact, in excess). Since liberty is not being denied to the people, they do not share this struggle and will not effectively organize under this value. Choice A is incorrect because Sun believes that liberty has actually run rampant throughout the population as a whole and not just among the intellectuals (although intellectuals are the only group that has a word to describe it): "Chinese today are enjoying so much freedom that they are showing the evils of freedom" (lines 84-86). Choice B is incorrect because Sun's grievance with liberty as a watchword is not rooted in its inadequate translation; even if the concept were perfectly encapsulated in a Chinese word, it would not change its effect on the outcome of the revolution. Choice C is incorrect because Chinese youth who have studied abroad are never mentioned in the passage and are thus irrelevant.

Question 6: C

Choice C is the best answer because lines 63-65 are the only lines which explain that Sun's belief that liberty does not fully encapsulate the needs of the Chinese Revolution. Choice A is incorrect because while Sun discusses the term liberty in those lines, he does not state the reason for it not being fitting for the Chinese Revolution. His only comment about liberty in those lines is that it has only been exposed to a select group of people, but that merely a fact and not an indict of liberty itself. Choice B is incorrect because Sun makes a point about appreciating the term liberty, but not about its aptness for the Chinese Revolution. Choice D is incorrect; while these lines indicate Sun's belief that liberty is problematic for the Chinese because they have had an excess of it, that is not the primary reason for liberty being not applicable to Chinese revolution.

Question 7: B

Choice B is the best answer because the term watchword refers to the overarching goal of the revolution, as Sun says later that "the aims of the Chinese Revolution are different from the aims in foreign revolutions" (lines 69-70). Sun compares it to "Liberty" in France and "Independence" in America, indicating that this is the battle cry, or the motto. Choice A is incorrect because "truism" has a negative connotation and these principles would be something the Chinese people are proud to say represents their revolution. Choice C is incorrect because the term "adage" implies an already known truth, whereas Sun is looking for an updated term that fits the current situation. Choice D is incorrect because an idiom is a phrase whose meaning cannot be accurately discerned from the denotation of its component words, such as "to clear the air," whereas these phrases are quite literal in encapsulating their respective revolutions' tenets.

Question 8: A

Choice A is the best answer because Sun indicates that the Chinese Revolution has disintegrated into a "sheet of loose sand" (line 78) and has become "invaded by foreign imperialism" (lines 78-79) because citizens have prioritized individual liberty over national unity. Therefore, national cohesion and greater organization would be necessary to ensure the revolution's success. Choice B is incorrect because disorganization is not synonymous with lack of autonomy: in fact, Sun criticizes Chinese citizens for overly exercising their autonomy, as they "are enjoying so much freedom that they are showing the evils of freedom" (lines 84-86). Choice C is incorrect because Sun primarily focuses on the misapplication of Western principles by "new students" and "earnest scholars" (lines 41-42), but does not suggest that the Chinese government has done the same. Choice D is incorrect because the increased prioritization of the self by Chinese citizens has actually proven detrimental to the revolution; thus, Sun is unlikely to characterize this perspective as sorely needed.

Question 9: C

Choice C is the best answer because Sun says earlier in the paragraph that the Chinese are suffering from "so much freedom that they are showing the evils of freedom" (lines 84-86). Therefore, when he later states that the problem is this "misuse of freedom" (lines 89-90), he means that they have too much of it, or an excess. Choice A is incorrect because while Sun does say that they are experiencing the evils of freedom, he does not indicate that this is wasteful; instead, he means that there is too much disunity as a result of its excess. Choice B is incorrect because we do not know for what the Chinese are using their excess of freedom; we only know that the result of the application is disunity, but do not know anything about the application itself. Choice D is incorrect because "exploitation" would mean that they are gaining some benefit from misusing their freedom, whereas Sun believes that the misuse of freedom is causing "evils" (lines 86), or negative results.

Question 10: A
Choice A is the best answer because Sun emphasizes the need to recognize different circumstances, or "local applicability", when enacting revolutions: "the aims of the Chinese Revolution are different from the aims in foreign revolutions, and the methods we use must also be different" (lines 69-71). Therefore, he characterizes attempts to mimic past revolutions conducted under different conditions foolish, as "this is nothing than 'saying what others say'" (lines 45-46). Choice B is incorrect because prioritization of a particular aim or goal does not necessarily lead to neglect of the revolution's other aspects. Choice C is incorrect because Sun does not prioritize the results of revolutions and therefore does not disparage revolutions that fail to achieve their goals and "eradicate the specific suffering of the country at issue"; instead, he criticizes revolutions that do not attempt to address a relevant or needed objective. Choice D is incorrect because Sun does not indicate that a misunderstanding of liberty is immoral, nor is morality a primary focus of the passage.

Chapter 1.2 | Garnet

Question 1: A
Choice A is the best answer because Garnet first proclaims his "consolation" to the slaves for their "unhappy condition" (lines 5-7) before indicating that the slave system has stunted the progression of even slaveowners: "the oppressors themselves have become involved in the ruin. They have become weak, sensual, and rapacious" (lines 77-79). Choice B is incorrect because the passage does not differentiate between the North and South in describing the way slavery is perceived in those areas. The only time at which Garnet refers to different geographical regions is when he addresses the places from which his audience may come from: "your brethren of the north, east, and west have been accustomed to meet together" (lines 2-3). Choice C is incorrect because Garnet does not discuss the economic benefits or harmful effects of slavery. At best, he refers to the "avarice" (line 50) which influenced the perpetuation of the institution, but he never actually indicates that this greed translated into profits or lack thereof. Choice D is incorrect because Garnet does not believe that slavery has done "irreparable damage"; on the other hand, he expresses his hope that progress will arise from "mankind [becoming] wiser and better": "the oppressor's power is fading, and you, every day, are becoming better informed and more numerous" (lines 29-32).

Question 2: C
Choice C is the best answer because Garnet specifies the relationship that some free and enslaved Americans have in lines 17-20: "many of you are bound to us...by the more tender relations of parents, wives, husbands, children, brothers, sisters, and friends". Choice A is incorrect, because the free and the enslaved share important bonds in the status quo, in which slavery still exists: the "ties of a common humanity" and the "tender relations of parents, wives, husbands, children, brothers, sisters, and friends" are two examples of this claim (lines 18-20). Thus, he would not agree that slavery has removed the possibility of meaningful bonds between the two demographics, as he is stating that such bonds live on in spite of the institution. Choice B is incorrect because the only time that Garnet mentions Christianity is in lines 44-45, where he indicates that the first slaves to arrive in America were treated in a manner that was antithetical to the tenets of Christianity, despite the fact that these propagators of slavery identified as Christians. This claim does not indicate that all Americans are presently bound by Christian values; it merely indicates that a subset of a former population self-identified as Christian. In fact, Garnet would likely state that the current propagators

of slavery similarly do not replicate Christian values in their actions. Choice D is incorrect because Garnet addresses free and enslaved Americans' past and present connections in lines 17-21: the past is represented by their familial ties, and the present is represented by the "ties of common humanity". Nowhere in the lines is a future relationship indicated.

Question 3: B

Choice B is the best answer because lines 17-21 refer to the "ties" of humanity and family that bind freed blacks to slaves, thus providing an answer relevant to the topic of "the bond between the free and the enslaved". Choice A is incorrect because lines 13-15 are relevant to the topic of the previous question, yet do not match with any choices from question 2. Choices C and D are incorrect because lines 39-41 and lines 44-50 do not mention freed blacks: Garnet indicates that "the first of our injured race" came to the New World "not with their own consent" (i.e. as slaves) and continues to describe the experiences of those slaves throughout the rest of the paragraph.

Question 4: C

Choice C is the best answer because Garnet refers to the "deep gulf" that was established, or "set", by slavery that has prevented slaves from recieving the "relief and consolation which [their] friends would willingly render". Choices A and D are incorrect because "solved" and "mended" are overly positive for Garnet's description of the harm that slavery has created. Choice B is incorrect because "solidified" implies that the "gulf" distancing free blacks from slaves had already been present, and was only exacerbated by slavery.

Question 5: C

Choice C is the best answer because Garnet acknowledges the harms of slavery in the topic sentence of the paragraph: "slavery has fixed a deep gulf between you and us, and while it shuts out from you the relief and consolation which your friends would willingly render, it afflicts and persecutes you with a fierceness which we might not expect to see in the fiends of hell". This sentence indicates that the condition of slavery has been worsened by the lack of communication between free blacks and slaves, which Garnet blames on the institution itself. However, he states that there is potential for a brighter future in lines 27-28, where he states that there is "a glimmering ray of hope". Choice A is incorrect because this paragraph is addressed to those in slavery, and there is no "appeal for global sympathy", which would imply a larger audience. Choice B is incorrect; although Garnet urges that "such a divide be closed", he does not suggest that there is "animosity between slaves and free African-Americans". He merely states that there is animosity among slaves due to the deep gulf, but he does not state that that animosity is directed toward their free counterparts. Choice D is incorrect because Garnet does not comment on the slaves' "ignorance of their plight"; he only suggests that there has been a gradual shift throughout all of society that has resulted in an increased awareness among all people about the damaging impacts of slavery.

Question 6: A

Choice A is the best answer because Garnet indicates in lines 55-58 that the slaves who arrived in America created "succeeding generations" who "inherited their chains", or became slaves themselves. Choice B is incorrect because Garnet directly states that Africans "were brought to the shores of America" as slaves (lines 39-41); therefore, the slaves could not have died on the way to the Americas. Choices C and D are incorrect because Garnet demonstrates that the slaves "were doomed to unrequited toil and deep degradation" until the day they died (lines 53-54), and thus could not have "escaped to the North" or "returned to Africa".

Question 7: C
Choice C is the best answer because lines 55-58 describe the "succeeding generations" that inherited the "chains" of their ancestors, thereby referring to the legacy of slaves who were brought to the New World from Africa. Choices A and B are relevant to the topic of the first slaves in America, but do not match with any of the choices in the previous question. Choice D is incorrect because lines 68-70 describe "the bleeding captive" as a symbolic figure of the enslaved and do not refer to the enslaved themselves.

Question 8: A
Choice A is the best answer because Garnet states that "avarice and lust" are the reasons for the propagation of slavery; thus, they are the motivating factors for slavery. Choices B and D are incorrect because the words "manipulated" and "tempted" imply that some greater force was tricking the slaveholders into perpetuating the institution of slavery, thereby removing the total responsibility that Garnet attributes to them. Choice C is incorrect because "inspired" is too positive for the somber tone of the passage.

Question 9: B
Choice B is the best answer because lines 62-65 describe the slaveholders' hypocrisy: they themselves came to America in order to pursue freedom that they subsequently denied others. Choice A is incorrect because there is no mention of the propagators of slavery deceiving slaves with the promise of being free in America in the indicated lines. Choice C is incorrect because it cannot be assumed that the slaveholders traveled to America for freedom from slavery; the passage only indicates that they were in pursuit of freedom. Choice D is incorrect because Garnet does not specify the origins of the slaves in lines 62-65; there is no discussion regarding whether they are American or African.

Question 10: B
Choice B is the best answer because Garnet claims in lines 77-79 that "the oppressors themselves have become involved in the ruin. They have become weak, sensual, and rapacious", thereby supporting "hedonistic" and "immoral". Choices A and D are incorrect because Garnet indicates that slaveholders are aware of the injustice of their actions and of the suffering they have inflicted upon slaves; however, they are so influenced by "avarice and lust" (lines 50) that they no longer care. Choice C is incorrect because Garnet does not discuss the economic results of slavery as an institution, merely the profit incentive.

Chapter 1.3 | Seneca

Question 1: C
Choice C is the best answer because the author of Passage 1 indicate that some of the "notices" (line 6) "praise the meetings highly; but the majority either deprecate or ridicule" them (lines 7-9); the authors of these notices are therefore writing opinion pieces, or "articles", about the Women's Rights Conventions at Seneca Falls. Choice A is incorrect because a minority of the articles "praise" the conventions instead of "warning" others about them. Choices B and D are incorrect because the articles are not written only to "proclaim" an announcement or to inform readers about the "news" of an event, but to voice the authors' opinions regarding a controversial issue; "proclamations" and "news" are thus too neutral for the tone of the passage and do not address the true intention of the writings described.

Question 2: D
Choice D is the best answer because the author of Passage 1 believes that women's suffrage would lead to a shift in the responsibilities of men and women, since men would have to make up for the "domestic duties" (line 30) that would likely be "neglected" (line 31) by women prioritizing their newfound political rights. This would then lead to a massive "breaking up" (line 38) of the "order of things established at the creation of mankind, and continued six thousand years" (lines 36-38), which the author of Passage 1 fears would only "prove a monstrous injury to all mankind" (line 44). Choices A and C are incorrect because while the author of Passage 1 voices his disapproval of women participating in activities other than their feminine duties and attempting to emulate the Declaration of Independence, he does not view them as the greatest threats that would arise from the suffrage movement. Choice B is incorrect because the author of Passage 1 suggests that the disruption of gender roles that had been present since "the creation of mankind" (lines 37) would not arise from the removal of men's rights, but from the transfer of women's responsibilities to men: "the males must...discharge an equal share of the domestic duties which now appertain to females, and which must be neglected, to a great extent, if women are allowed to exercise all the "rights" that are claimed by these Convention-holders" (lines 27-33).

Question 3: C
Choice C is the best answer because the author of Passage 1 uses quotations to indicate that the "rights" mentioned are "claimed by these Convention-holders" (lines 32-33), who he disparages throughout the passage. Because "rights" describe freedoms that are deserved by everyone, and the author of Passage 1 does not believe that the Convention holders are actually entitled to these rights, the quotation marks signify his disagreement, or "distance", from the idea. Choice A is incorrect because the author of Passage 1 describes his own perspective, not that of "true-hearted women", even if they would agree with him. Moreover, the discomfort that the author of Passage 1 has experienced is not upon the "granting" of the rights claimed by suffragists, but upon imagining the possibility of these rights. Choice B is incorrect because the author of Passage 1 does not depict women's rights activists as ignorant, but destructive to the overall order of society; therefore, he does not imply that they do not "understand" the rights they seek, but that such rights are indicative of a malicious agenda. Choice D is incorrect because it explains why the author of Passage 1 would use the word "rights", but does not account for the placement of the quotation marks.

Question 4: A
Choice A is the best answer because Douglass states that abolitionists must not "be deterred from an expression of our approbation of any movement, however humble, to "improve and elevate the character of any members of the human family" (lines 95-98) Since Douglass encourages the approbation, or support, of any movement that advocates for human rights, it can be inferred that he wholeheartedly supports women's rights. Moreover, Douglass characterizes this approbation as a duty of those who stand "upon the watch-tower of human freedom" (lines 93-94), or abolitionists, which highlights his belief that the two movements are parallel in intent and should therefore be treated similarly. Choice B is incorrect because Douglass does not predict the effect of women's rights on African-American rights and therefore cannot be describing the women's suffrage movement as a "catalyst". Choice C is incorrect because although Douglass depicts some African American activists as disagreeing with women's rights, he does not imply that such disagreement has negatively affected the success of the women's suffrage movement. Choice D is incorrect because Douglass does not critique any aspects of the women's suffrage movement; therefore, "lament' is too negative for the admiring tone of the passage.

Question 5: C

Choice C is the best answer because lines 95-98 address the women's rights movement as another "movement...to improve and elevate the character of any members of the human family" Choices A and B are incorrect because lines 83-86 and 86-91 describe the relationship between some members of the abolitionist movement and those of the women's rights movement, but does not indicate the relationship between the movements themselves; in addition, these lines do not reflect Douglass' opinion, as he believes that such statements are motivated by the "folly of prejudice" (lines 78-79). Choice D is incorrect because lines 99-102 express Douglass' support of the women's rights movement, but does not indicate the movement's relationship to abolitionism.

Question 6: A

Choice A is the best answer because the "objects" described are what the women in the convention "seek to attain" (line 74); these objects are thus their goals, or their "ends". Choice B is incorrect because "items" describes a physical object to be gained, while the women attending the convention aim to receive more conceptual political and social rights. Choice C is incorrect because "focus" describes the actions that women take to attain the goal of suffrage, but does not depict the goal itself. Choice D is incorrect because "privileges" are extended only to a select few, while women's rights activists are fighting for suffrage to become universalized.

Question 7: B

Choice B is the best answer because the author of Passage 1, being against the Women's Rights Convention, states that the Declaration of Sentiments is "a parody upon the Declaration of American Independence" (lines 4-5), while the author of Passage 2, being in support of the Convention, states that the women have set forth "several interesting documents...among these was a Declaration of Sentiments, to be regarded as the basis of a grand movement" (lines 64-67). Choice A is incorrect because, while the author of Passage 1 suggests that the women's Declaration is a parody, the author of Passage 2 openly praises the women's aims and never suggests that they need to be analyzed or discussed. Choice C is incorrect because it presents an extremely limited understanding of the beliefs of the author of Passage 2, suggesting that he only points out the call for civil and religious rights, when in reality he acknowledges the sweeping attempt of the Declaration to encompass the attainment of "the civil, social, political, and religious rights of women" (lines 68-69). Choice D is incorrect because the author of Passage 2 comes across as an avid supporter of the Declaration of Sentiments, arguing that "we cannot be deterred from an expression of our approbation of any movement, however humble, to improve and elevate the character of any members of the human family" (lines 95-98), which is far from regarding the movement with complacency.

Question 8: B

Choice B is the best answer because Douglass indicates that abolitionists, whom he describes as "standing as we do on the watch-tower of human freedom", "cannot be deterred from" the support of "any movement...to improve and elevate the character of any members of the human family" (lines 93-98). Douglass therefore claims that abolitionists have a duty to support any movement for the freedom of a group, matching with "guarding and praising the freedom of all". Choice A is incorrect because Douglass criticises some in the abolitionist movement for neglecting to be clear-sighted and morally upstanding: "Many who have made the discovery that the negros have some rights as well as some other members of the human family, have yet to be convinced that women are entitledd to any" (lines 83-86). Choice C is incorrect because Douglass depicts those standing on the "watch-tower of human freedom" as striving to attain equality, but does not imply that they have necessarily felt the "pains" of inequality. Choice D is incorrect because Douglass does not describe the women advocating for suffrage as "allies" of the abolitionist cause, but as leaders of a separate movement for equality that nonetheless deserve support and encouragement.

Question 9: C
Choice C is the best answer because the author of Passage 1's main argument against the women's rights movement is that it would drastically change the dynamic between men and women to the point that "society would have to radically remodelled" (lines 33-34). As a result, the author of Passage 1 would be less likely to criticise animal rights, since it is not as "incendiary" and therefore would not result in as great of an upheaval in society. Choice A is incorrect because, as explained above, the author of Passage 1 views the aim of the women's rights movement as potentially causing a "monstrous injury to all mankind" (line 44), which suggests that he would actually agree with the view that animal rights discussions would cause less of a problem than women's rights discussions. Choice B is incorrect because, while the author of Passage 1 would agree that women's rights are impractical and unnecessary, he would not be reluctant to believe that animal rights are less problematic, as has already been proven above. Choice D is incorrect because the wise and good cited in the lines are not questioned or doubted; Douglass just assumes what their position would be.

Question 10: A
Choice A is the best answer because the answer to the previous question states that the author of Passage 1 would agree with the viewpoint that animal rights are less incendiary than women's rights, which is supported by his belief, stated in lines 33-36, that women's advancement would mean that "society would have to be radically remodeled." Choice B is incorrect because it merely states that the advancement of women's rights is "impractical, uncalled for, and unnecessary" (lines 39-40), while neglecting to demonstrate that it is socially incendiary. Choice C is incorrect because it focuses on the degradation of women as a result of their attainment of rights, and not the degradation of society. Choice D is incorrect because it only implies that the attainment of rights would fail to solve women's real problems, and not that the attainment would necessarily cause more problems.

Question 11: A
Choice A is the best answer because the "agitory movement" alluded to in line 18 describes the women's rights "Conventions" (line 17), which the author of Passage 1 condemns. On the other hand, the author of Passage 2 praises the same meetings as being "characterized by marked ability and dignity" (lines 59-60) and voices his support for these "extraordinary meetings" (line 56); his positive tone thus directly contrasts with the author of Passage 1's disapproval. Choices B and D are incorrect because Douglass merely describes the "novel position" of women in leadership roles or the "elective franchise" they seek without commenting on these phrases with either a positive or negative tone. Choice C is incorrect because the phrase "dangerous heresy" depicts the views of those who dismiss women's rights and therefore does not represent Douglass' remarks on the issue.

Chapter 1.4 | Chief Joseph

Question 1: C
Choice C is the best answer because Joseph alludes to equal rights, liberty, and fair treatment under the same laws throughout the passage, which are all associated with "free men". For instance, Joseph asks the United States government in lines 35-36 for equality of treatment and opportunity. Joseph continues in his advocacy for the Nez Perce's freedom in lines 51-52: "I only ask of the Government to be treated as all other men are treated". Choice A is incorrect because Joseph does not explicitly indicate that the Indians' inherent nature is peaceful: he states that "[he] knows that [his] race must change" and that they "cannot hold [their] own with the white men as [they] are" (lines 61-62). In addition, he characterizes the peaceful nature of the Indians as contingent upon white men's recognition of their rights: "whenever the white man treats the Indian as they treat each other then we shall have no more wars" (lines 73-74). Choice B is incorrect because there is no war between the Nez Perce and U.S. government. Although there were previously conflicts, which have resulted in "dead people" (line 20), Joseph does not indicate that there is currently an extended violent confrontation between the Nez Perce and the U.S. government. Indeed, the description before the passage indicates that the war has already happened, thereby making it not current. Choice D is incorrect; while Joseph discusses "[his] country now overrun by white men" and the damage that white men have done to his horses, cattle, and children (lines 21-24), he mentions these wrongdoings to ultimately convince the U.S. government that this situation can be preventable if Indians have equal rights. Thus, Joseph only mentions the "wrongs committed against the Nez Perce as context for discussing the possibility of a peaceful future.

Question 2: B
Choice B is the best answer; Joseph cites the creation of all people by "Great Spirit Chief" and "the earth" as "the mother of all people" as the rationale for all people having equal rights (lines 37-39). Choice A is incorrect; Joseph primarily uses language from the Nez Perce, but he does not incorporate anecdotes, or short stories about the experience of the Nez Perce, to advocate for their right to freedom. Additionally, Joseph does not even describe what a typical life in the Nez Perce tribe is like; he only cites how their lives have been adversely affected from conflict with white men. Choice C is incorrect because Joseph's goal is not to "impress" his audience, but to implore them to extend equal rights to his people. Additionally, his audience here is the U.S. government, which is listening to his speech, which makes the word "reader" in the answer choice incorrect as well. Choice D is incorrect because Joseph does not draw a comparison between the wrongdoings committed against Indians and those committed against the American public. Instead, he cites these wrongdoings as examples of an unequal world in order to assert the necessity of equal rights for Indians and white men. He aims for unity centered around freedom and not hardship and "grievances".

Question 3: A
Choice A is the best answer because Joseph indicates in lines 15-18 that members of the government such as the "Great Father Chief" and "the Next Great Chief" (lines 12-13) have supposedly aligned themselves with Joseph and promised him and his people "justice". However, Joseph points out that he has "heard talk and talk but nothing is done", thus depicting leaders of the American government as unable to act when they are most needed. Choice B is incorrect because leaders of the American government are certainly unable to justify their hypocritical treatment of Indians

("They cannot tell me"), but are not necessarily unwilling, as Joseph never states the cause of their enablement of cruel behavior. Choice C is incorrect because Joseph's main grievance is that the administration of Indian affairs has not been delegated at all, and has therefore never been addressed in a productive way by the American government. Choice D is incorrect because Joseph cites "too many misunderstandings", but never specifies that those misunderstandings were of Indian culture in particular; moreover. These misunderstandings came up "between the white men and the Indians", suggesting that some Indians have also misinterpreted messages from leaders in American government.

Question 4: B
Choice B is the best answer because lines 15-18 refer to the "Great Father Chief; the Next Great Chief; the Commissioner Chief; the Law Chief; and many other law chiefs" (lines 12-14), which matches the topic of "leaders of the American government" in the previous question. Choice A is incorrect because lines 7-12 only refer to a generalized "Government", not specific members of that government. Choice C is incorrect because lines 28-32 allude to "men who had no right to talk", but does not indicate whether these men were members of the government or simply ordinary citizens. Choice D is incorrect because lines 46-49 refer to members of the government as "Great White Chiefs", but do not match with any of the choices in the previous question.

Question 5: A
Choice A is the best answer; Joseph calls upon the "Great Spirit Chief" who made all men (lines 36-37) and "the earth" who is the mother of all people (line 38) to suggest that all people ultimately come from the same source and are "all brothers" and equal. Thus, "all people should have equal rights upon [the earth]" (lines 38-39). Choice B is incorrect because Joseph does not base his argument for equality upon his religious belief. He bases it off of his belief that all people come from the same source, which is informed and expressed through spiritual language ("Great Spirit Chief"), but ultimately not representative of his religion as a whole. Choice C is incorrect because Joseph does not view conflict between white men and Indians as "superficial". It is, in fact, the reason for his presence in front of the U.S. government. The conflict has driven him to advocate for peace and equality. Choice D is incorrect; while Joseph states that the "Great White Chiefs" cannot explain where they derive the legitimacy to restrain Indians to a reservation (lines 46-50), he actually believes that they have the power to grant Indians equal rights. This belief is expressed in lines 51-52: "I only ask of the Government to be treated as all other men are treated". His perception of the U.S. government being able to grant equality is evident in line 67 as well: "let me be a free man". In asking for equality from the U.S. government, he inherently acknowledges that they have the "jurisdiction" to do so.

Question 6: D
Choice D is the best answer because lines 61-62 illustrate Joseph's reaction to white men's treatment of Indians as "outlaws...driven from country to country, or shot down like animals" (59-61). Joseph responds by admitting that "[his] race must change" because they cannot "hold their own with the white men" as they are. Yet Joseph also characterizes such barbarism as arising from white men's mistreatment of Indians: "If you pen an indian up on a small spot of earth and compel him to stay there, he will not be contented nor will he grow and prosper" (lines 44-46). Joseph thus recommends letting the Indian "be a free man" (line 67) in order to overcome these setbacks. Choice A is incorrect because Joseph acknowledges the privilege and power that white men have over Indians, but does

not imply that that white men as a whole have a propensity for brutality and therefore does not indicate that they are "known" for violence. Choice B is incorrect because Joseph does not reject the stereotype that white men have perpetuated; he actually acknowledges that some aspects of it are true and reveals that their "peaceful and diplomatic" nature is contingent upon their fair treatment by white men. Choice C is incorrect because Joseph does not allow Indians' "[suffering] at the hands of white men" to serve as an excuse for their brutishness, as he indicates that they "must change" (line 62).

Question 7: C
Choice C is the best answer because lines 61-62 reveal that Joseph believes in some portion of the stereotypes about Indians; as he states that Indians "cannot hold [their] own with the white men as [they] are", therefore recognizing that Indians are currently uncivilized. In addition, Joseph indicates later in the paragraph that Indians only ask to "be recognized as men" (lines 63-64), implying that white Americans currently do not view Indians as being at their level of humanity. Choices A and B are incorrect because lines 44-46 and lines 59-61 describe the treatment of Indians that arose as a consequence of the stereotype mentioned in the previous question, but does not describe the stereotype itself. Choice D is incorrect because lines 73-74 are off topic: Joseph addresses what must be done to overcome the "wars" between white men and Indians, but does not specify stereotypes about Indians' relationship to the conflict.

Question 8: A
Choice A is the best answer because Joseph compares Indians to "a horse [tied] to a stake" (line 43) and describes members of his race as having been "penned up and denied liberty to go as he pleases" (lines 41-42). Because Indians have been trapped or "penned up" in small plots of land by white men against their will, they have been "forced" to stay on that land. Choices B and C are incorrect because "persuade" and "oblige" describe a decision that, while influenced by pressure from an outside source, was made voluntarily by a willing subject. Choice D is incorrect because "ordering" someone to do something does not necessarily produce the desired results.

Question 9: B
Choice B is the best answer; in the fourth paragraph, Joseph states that "all men", including white men and Indians, are brothers because "[they] were made by the same Great Spirit Chief". He is grounding his argument for equality in their spiritual brotherhood and thus their common humanity. Choice A is incorrect because Joseph does not mention a "past friendship" with white men. In fact, he actually states that, although leaders in U.S. government "all say they are [his] friends" (line 15), they have not acted on their promise of friendship. Choice C is incorrect because Joseph's appeal to brotherhood is not literal: Indians and white men are spiritually "brothers" because they were all created by the "Great Spirit Chief" (lines 36-37). Choice D is incorrect because he does not see Indians as the children of the "Great Father Chief", or President Hayes, but of the "Great Spirit Chief". Furthermore, Joseph does not attempt to elicit an emotional response from President Hayes and therefore cannot be "guilting" him.

Question 10: D
Choice D is the best answer; Joseph takes issue with the fact that the U.S. government does not treat Indians as men. Thus, he wants an acknowledgement of their manhood through equal treatment and rights. Choices A and B are incorrect because they both allude to a literal understanding or view of manhood; the problem that Joseph has is that U.S. government objectively "knows" and "perceives" Indians to be men, but does not act in accordance with that understanding. Choice C is incorrect because the word "accept" refers to social equality. While Joseph might want social equality as well, the sixth paragraph is primarily concerned with legal equality, in which Indians are treated the same as white men under the law.

Chapter 1.5 | Jordan

Question 1: A
Choice A is the best answer because Jordan argues that the main question is whether or not "the President committed offenses, and planned, and directed, and acquiesced in a court of conduct which the Constitution will not tolerate" (lines 91-93), and she shows her opinion on the matter by openly stating that, if the hearing doesn't confirm his violation of the constitution, "then perhaps that 18th-century Constitution should be abandoned to a 20th-century paper shredder!" (lines 87-90). Choices B and D are incorrect for similar reasons as Jordan doesn't directly and repeatedly discuss the "security of the nation" or Nixon's "personal gain" as she does with the issue of constitutional violation. Choice C is incorrect because, while violating the Constitution could be seen as ruining the honor and strength of the Presidency, that is an effect of the initial violation, and not the first and primary allegation.

Question 2: B
Choice B is the best answer because Jordan frequently references the Federalist Papers (line 7), Alexander Hamilton (line 7, 53), and James Madison (line 76) throughout the passage and demonstrates how the laws they laid down apply to the present impeachment hearing. Choice A is incorrect because she only cites passages from the Federalist Papers and the "ratification convention" (line 45), never the Constitution itself. Choice C is incorrect because, while Jordan does call upon the collective voice at times, she does not suggest that her beliefs are held by all; in fact, the presence of this speech which attempts to explain her position and persuade people to impeach Nixon suggests that her belief isn't universal. Choice D is incorrect because Jordan only alludes to the remarks of one previous president, Woodrow Wilson (lines 61-62), and spends much more time citing and discussing the remarks of the Framers of the Constitution.

Question 3: C
Choice C is the best answer because, in the evidence for Question 4, Jordan states that the purpose of the impeachment process is to check "a President swollen with power and grown tyrannical" (lines 37-38). Choice A is incorrect because Jordan does not suggest that the Executive has taken power away from the Legislative branch completely, only that a balance of powers needs to remain in place. Choice B is incorrect because the impeachment process is undertaken by Congress and not the public, as stated in lines 35-36. Choice D is incorrect because Jordan actually argues that the impeachment worthy actions of the President should not refer to policy making, stating that "The Federal Convention of 1787 said that it limited impeachment to high crimes and misdemeanors and discounted and opposed the term 'maladministration'" (lines 40-43).

Question 4: D
Choice D is the best answer because the answer to the previous question states that the purpose of impeachment is to check the power of a President when necessary, which is supported by lines 35-40. Choice A is incorrect because it focuses on the "abuse of public trust" (line 14) and not the abuse of power, as stipulated in the answer to Question 3. Choice B is incorrect because it merely praises the power breakdown of the impeachment process as stipulated by the Framers. Choice C is incorrect because it simply states that Congress understands the character and essence of impeachment, but, as with the previous two options, fails to mention when exactly the impeachment process should be put into action.

Question 5: D
Choice D is the best answer because it emphasizes the potential misconception that voting for impeachment means voting for the removal of the President, since Jordan argues that the primary purpose is actually to check "the encroachments of the executive" (lines 22-23). Choice A is incorrect because Jordan does not frame the cited sentences as a reassurance, but as a response to a mistaken assumption. Choice B is incorrect because Jordan is actually acknowledging a misunderstanding of the "potential repercussions" and not any real consequences. Choice C is incorrect because, while she does give a clarification, it is framed as a response to those who believe that impeachment means the direct removal of the President, and thus Choice D is the better answer because it assumes that she is refuting the assumptions of others.

Question 6: A
Choice A is the best answer because it directly states that "maladministration" (line 43), or the President's competence in office, should not be used as grounds for impeachment. Choice B is incorrect because it only states that the President won't be able to get away with high crimes and misdemeanors, but neglects a discussion of what impeachment should not be based on. Choices C and D are incorrect for similar reasons because, while they both argue that an impeachment hearing should not be launched based on political affiliations or other "petty reasons" (line 68), they don't state that the President's competence in office falls under one of those categories and therefore don't adequately answer the question.

Question 7: B
Choice B is the best answer because Jordan is arguing that only an offense so terrible that it obliterates allegiance or loyalty to a certain political party may be used as grounds for impeachment. Choice A is incorrect because "duty" implies some sort of obligation, rather than an individual's free desire to act in accordance with a certain party, as is implied by the word "interest." Choices C and D are incorrect for similar reasons because agenda and policy refer to the interests of the political party as a whole rather than those of the people voting in accordance with the party.

Question 8: D

Choice D is the best answer because Jordan contrasts the idea of being "big" with the idea of being "petty" (line 74), thus suggesting that the task at hand needs to be taken seriously and should not be trivialized. Choice A is incorrect because Jordan, while acknowledging the seriousness of the matter, does not especially suggest that it is a matter of inherent right and wrong. Choices B and C are incorrect for similar reasons because, while thinking logically and responsibly are clear extensions of being serious, the dichotomy Jordan creates in the lines mentioned is between treating the matter as something petty or insignificant and treating it as important or consequential, thus making serious the best choice.

Question 9: B

Choice B is the best answer because it delineates President Nixon's precise actions that violated the Constitution by listing them in clear terms. Choice A is incorrect because, while it gives the definition of the basis for impeachment as prescribed by James Madison, it fails to state that President Nixon fits such a definition. Choice C is incorrect because, while is presents Jordan's strong opinion that Nixon should be impeached, it doesn't provide evidence or proof for why her opinion is correct. Choice D is incorrect because, while it raises the question of whether Nixon subverted the Constitution or not, it doesn't answer it, and thus does not provide evidence in support of such a claim.

Question 10: A

Choice A is the best answer because the image cited expresses the idea that, in the face of Nixon's flagrant disregard for the Constitution, a ruling acquitting him would be equivalent to destroying the Constitution. It shows, therefore, that Jordan believes the unconstitutional actions of the President are clear grounds for his impeachment, as the shredding of the Constitution, even metaphorically, is extremely improbable; it is one of America's most revered documents. Choice B is incorrect because the lines cited suggest the complete destruction of the Constitution, not mere revisions or modification as would result from new amendments. Choice C is incorrect because, while the lines indicate that he should be impeached unless Congress wants to completely throw out the Constitution, they don't directly show Nixon's transgressions. Choice D is incorrect because Jordan is not skeptical of the Constitution, as she states that her "faith in the Constitution is whole; it is complete; it is total" (lines 3-4).

Chapter Two

Questions 1-10 are based on the following passage.

2.1

This passage is adapted from Henry David Thoreau's 1849 essay "On the Duty of Civil Disobedience."

This American government,—what is it but a tradition, though a recent one, endeavoring to transmit itself unimpaired to posterity, but each instant losing some of its integrity? It has not the vitality and force
5 of a single living man; for a single man can bend it to his will. It is a sort of wooden gun to the people themselves; and, if ever they should use it in earnest as a real one against each other, it will surely split. But it is not the less necessary for this; for the people
10 must have some complicated machinery or other, and hear its din, to satisfy that idea of government which they have. Governments show thus how successfully men can be imposed on, even impose on themselves, for their own advantage. It is excellent, we must all
15 allow; yet this government never of itself furthered any enterprise, but by the alacrity with which it got out of its way. It does not keep the country free. It does not settle the West. It does not educate. The character inherent in the American people has done all that has
20 been accomplished; and it would have done somewhat more, if the government had not sometimes got in its way.

However, the government does not concern me much, and I shall bestow the fewest possible thoughts
25 on it. It is not many moments that I live under a government, even in this world. If a man is thought-free, fancy-free, imagination-free, that which is not never for a long time appearing to be to him, unwise rulers or reformers cannot fatally interrupt him.
30 I know that most men think differently from myself; but those whose lives are by profession devoted to the study of these or kindred subjects content me as little as any. Statesmen and legislators, standing so completely within the institution, never
35 distinctly and nakedly behold it. They speak of moving society, but have no resting-place without it. They may be men of a certain experience and discrimination, and have no doubt invented ingenious and even useful systems, for which we sincerely thank them; but all
40 their wit and usefulness lie within certain not very wide limits. They are wont to forget that the world is not governed by policy and expediency.

No man with a genius for legislation has appeared in America. They are rare in the history of the world.
45 There are orators, politicians, and eloquent men, by the thousand; but the speaker has not yet opened his mouth to speak who is capable of settling the much-vexed questions of the day. We love eloquence for its own sake, and not for any truth which it may utter, or
50 any heroism it may inspire. Our legislators have not yet learned the comparative value of free-trade and of freedom, of union, and of rectitude, to a nation. They have no genius or talent for comparatively humble questions of taxation and finance, commerce and
55 manufactures and agriculture. If we were left solely to the wordy wit of legislators in Congress for our guidance, uncorrected by the seasonable experience and the effectual complaints of the people, America would not long retain her rank among the nations.
60 The authority of government, even such as I am willing to submit to,—for I will cheerfully obey those who know and can do better than I, and in many things even those who neither know nor can do so well,—is still an impure one: to be strictly just, it must
65 have the sanction and consent of the governed. It can have no pure right over my person and property but what I concede to it. The progress from an absolute to a limited monarchy, from a limited monarchy to a democracy, is a progress toward a true respect for
70 the individual. Even the Chinese philosopher was wise enough to regard the individual as the basis of the empire. Is a democracy, such as we know it, the last improvement possible in government? Is it not possible to take a step further towards recognizing
75 and organizing the rights of man? There will never be a really free and enlightened State, until the State comes to recognize the individual as a higher and independent power, from which all its own power and authority are derived, and treats him accordingly. I
80 please myself with imagining a State at last which can afford to be just to all men, and to treat the individual with respect as a neighbor; which even would not think it inconsistent with its own repose, if a few were to live aloof from it, not meddling with it, nor embraced by
85 it, who fulfilled all the duties of neighbors and fellow-men. A State which bore this kind of fruit, and suffered it to drop off as fast as it ripened, would prepare the way for a still more perfect and glorious State, which also I have imagined, but not yet anywhere seen.

CONTINUE

1

The main purpose of the passage is to

A) discuss the quality of American government by emphasizing the foundational necessity of the individual.

B) criticize statesmen and legislators for their naive estrangement from the real concerns of the Nation.

C) argue that the current governmental structure lacks substance and must undergo specific reorganization.

D) compare the value of those who make up the government to that of those who are merely under its charge.

2

Over the course of the passage, Thoreau shifts from

A) An analysis of the deficiencies of the American government to an outline of the rectifying revisions that would further the perfection of the state.

B) A general discussion of governmental procedures to a perusal of the specified role that individuals play in navigating the nation.

C) A proclamation of the general impropriety of the government to an evaluation of the missteps that led America to this point.

D) A debate over the value of government officials to a suggestion of how they should proceed in the conduct of their rule.

3

Which choice provides the best evidence for Thoreau's claim that the government's power should only extend as far as the individual allows?

A) Lines 4-6 ("It has...will.")

B) Lines 17-18 ("It does...educate.")

C) Lines 65-67 ("It can...it.")

D) Lines 82-84 ("which even...it")

4

What does Thoreau suggest to be the ideal iteration of a government?

A) A passive institution that never initiates change and eagerly surrenders control.

B) A fostering presence that relinquishes power once society is securely established.

C) A self-imposed encumbrance that is nevertheless advantageous and practical.

D) A benevolent edifice that rarely requires the attention of the general public.

5

Which choice provides the best evidence for the answer to the previous question?

A) Lines 12-14 ("Governments show...advantage.")

B) Lines 15-17 ("yet this...way.")

C) Lines 23-25 ("However, the...it.")

D) Lines 86-88 ("A State...State")

6

The first paragraph is notable for the use of

A) rhetorical questions that highlight the absurdity of the government's overstated sense of worth.

B) figurative language that introduces Thoreau's understanding of the American government.

C) emphatic language that underscores the paradoxical nature of the government's intentions.

D) a facetious tone that juxtaposes the perceived severity of the issue with its actual triviality.

7

According to the passage, what is the primary shortcoming that is unique to statesmen and legislators?

A) They have never sought out the values and laws that actually govern the world.

B) The verbose nature of their discourse has cost America its international esteem.

C) They lack a crucial understanding of the nation's financial and agricultural affairs.

D) They have an inflated view of their own role in the effective governance of America.

CONTINUE

8

As used in line 65, "sanction" most nearly means

A) penalty.

B) approval.

C) concession.

D) acceptance.

9

In the final paragraph, Thoreau cites the development of political systems and the "Chinese philosopher" (line 70) in order to

A) present the monarchies and empires as the precursors to the enlightened state.

B) contextualize and support his claim that the individual is the most important political unit.

C) emphasize the necessity of the continued advancement and evolution of government.

D) further substantiate his belief that a truly free and perfect state has never existed.

10

As used in line 84, "aloof from" most nearly means

A) uninterested in.

B) detached from.

C) distant toward.

D) disdainful of.

CONTINUE

Questions 1-10 are based on the following passage.

2.2

The following passage is adapted from the speech "Vietnam Veterans Against the War Statement" by John Kerry, delivered on April 23, 1971 to the Senate Committee of Foreign Relations.

In our opinion and from our experience, there is nothing in South Vietnam which could happen that realistically threatens the United States of America.
Line And to attempt to justify the loss of one American life
5 in Vietnam, Cambodia or Laos by linking such loss to the preservation of freedom is to us the height of criminal hypocrisy, and it is that kind of hypocrisy which we feel has torn this country apart.

We found that not only was it a civil war, an effort
10 by a people who had for years been seeking their liberation from any colonial influence whatsoever, but also we found that the Vietnamese whom we had enthusiastically molded after our own image were hard put to take up the fight against the threat we were
15 supposedly saving them from.

We found most people didn't even know the difference between communism and democracy. They only wanted to work in rice paddies without helicopters strafing them and bombs with napalm
20 burning their villages and tearing their country apart. They wanted everything to do with the war, particularly with this foreign presence of the United States of America, to leave them alone in peace, and they practiced the art of survival by siding with
25 whichever military force was present at a particular time, be it Viet Cong, North Vietnamese or American.

We also found that all too often American men were dying in those rice paddies for want of support from their allies. We saw first hand how monies from
30 American taxes were used for a corrupt dictatorial regime. We saw that many people in this country had a one-sided idea of who was kept free by the flag, and blacks provided the highest percentage of casualties. We saw Vietnam ravaged equally by American bombs
35 and search and destroy missions, as well as by Viet Cong terrorism - and yet we listened while this country tried to blame all of the havoc on the Viet Cong.

We watched the United States falsification of body counts, in fact the glorification of body counts.
40 We listened while month after month we were told the back of the enemy was about to break. We fought using weapons against "oriental human beings." We fought using weapons against those people which I do not believe this country would dream of using

45 were we fighting in the European theater. We watched while men charged up hills because a general said that hill has to be taken, and after losing one platoon or two platoons they marched away to leave the hill for reoccupation by the North Vietnamese. We watched
50 pride allow the most unimportant battles to be blown into extravaganzas, because we couldn't lose, and we couldn't retreat, and because it didn't matter how many American bodies were lost to prove that point, and so there were Hamburger Hills and Khe Sanhs and Hill
55 81s and Fire Base 6s, and so many others.

Each day to facilitate the process by which the United States washes her hands of Vietnam someone has to give up his life so that the United States doesn't have to admit something that the entire world already
60 knows, so that we can't say that we have made a mistake. Someone has to die so that President Nixon won't be, and these are his words, "the first President to lose a war."

We are asking Americans to think about that
65 because how do you ask a man to be the last man to die in Vietnam? How do you ask a man to be the last man to die for a mistake? We are here to ask, and we are here to ask vehemently, where are the leaders of our country? Where is the leadership? We're here to
70 ask where are McNamara, Rostow, Bundy, Gilpatrick, and so many others? Where are they now that we, the men they sent off to war, have returned? These are the commanders who have deserted their troops. And there is no more serious crime in the laws of war. The Army
75 says they never leave their wounded. The marines say they never even leave their dead. These men have left all the casualties and retreated behind a pious shield of public rectitude. They've left the real stuff of their reputations bleaching behind them in the sun in this
80 country.

We wish that a merciful God could wipe away our own memories of that service as easily as this administration has wiped away their memories of us. But all that they have done and all that they can
85 do by this denial is to make more clear than ever our own determination to undertake one last mission - to search out and destroy the last vestige of this barbaric war, to pacify our own hearts, to conquer the hate and fear that have driven this country these last ten years
90 and more. And so when thirty years from now our brothers go down the street without a leg, without an arm, or a face, and small boys ask why, we will be able to say "Vietnam" and not mean a desert, not a filthy obscene memory, but mean instead where America
95 finally turned and where soldiers like us helped it in the turning.

CONTINUE

1

Throughout the passage, Kerry primarily takes the stance of

A) a former soldier trying to improve the public perception of his fellow fighters.

B) a conscientious objector choosing to explain the reasoning behind his disloyalty.

C) a war veteran seeking to provide perspective on and call for an end to a divisive war.

D) a politician looking for a diplomatic way to resolve a war that cannot be won.

2

Which choice provides the best evidence for the claim that the United States had projected an unrealistic idealization onto the South Vietnamese?

A) Lines 9-11 ("We found...whatsoever")

B) Lines 12-15 ("we found...from")

C) Lines 21-23 ("They wanted...peace")

D) Lines 31-33 ("We saw...casualties")

3

In context of the passage as a whole, Paragraph three (lines 16-26) serves mainly to characterize the Vietnamese people as

A) understandable, because their desperation explains their lack of allegiance.

B) ignorant, because they are unaware of the competing ideologies of the time.

C) untrustworthy, because they have fought alongside both the Viet Cong and the Americans.

D) pacifist, because they desire the combatants to arrive at a peace deal.

4

It can be reasonably inferred from the passage that the "glorification of body parts" (line 39) was used by the American military in order to

A) present a false image of a victorious military campaign to Americans at home.

B) encourage military conflict and prolong the war beyond its natural conclusion.

C) justify the pursuit of dubious military objectives that had cost many American lives.

D) prevent the potential loss of morale or obedience among American troops.

5

As used in line 45, "theater" most nearly means

A) warzone.

B) drama.

C) context.

D) stage.

6

Kerry references "Hamburger Hills and Khe Sanhs and Hill 81s and Fire Base 6s, and so many others" (lines 54-55) as examples of

A) defeats suffered due to ineffective military policy and insubordination.

B) defense objectives that were known to be doomed from the outset.

C) sites that should not have been allowed to fall into enemy hands.

D) battles that were unnecessarily escalated due to American military ego.

7

Kerry levies which primary critique against American leadership in the Vietnam war?

A) They have abandoned their soldiers and neglected responsibility for their part in the war.

B) They have denied the occurrence of war atrocities and enabled further military transgressions.

C) They have sacrificed American lives for the advancement of their own careers back home.

D) They have failed to provide adequate care and support for the American casualties of war.

CONTINUE

8

Which choice provides the best evidence for the answer to the previous question?

A) Lines 56-61 ("Each day...mistake")
B) Lines 61-63 ("Someone has...war")
C) Lines 69-73 ("Where is...troops")
D) Lines 84-86 ("But all...mission")

9

As used in line 77, "shield" most nearly means

A) defense.
B) denial.
C) facade.
D) sham.

10

In the final paragraph (lines 81-96), Kerry juxtaposes

A) the leadership's glorification of the war memory due to its safe degree of removal with the soldiers' suppression of it due to their firsthand experiences.
B) the bleak way the war will be remembered if the United States continues its current approach with the redeeming way it can be remembered if past errors are confronted.
C) the peace that will come from the sanitation of the public memory with the turmoil that will remain if the American soldier is asked to deny his experience.
D) the unrealistic desire for a positive collective memory of the Vietnam War with the pragmatic understanding that America's remorseless actions cannot truly be erased.

CONTINUE

Questions 1-10 are based on the following passage.

2.3
This passage is adapted from Shirley Chisholm's 1970 speech delivered in support of the Equal Rights Amendment.

Mr. Speaker, House Joint Resolution 264, before us today, which provides for equality under the law for both men and women, represents one of the most
Line clear-cut opportunities we are likely to have to declare
5 our faith in the principles that shaped our Constitution. It provides a legal basis for attack on the most subtle, most pervasive, and most institutionalized form of prejudice that exists. Discrimination against women, solely on the basis of their sex, is so widespread that is
10 seems to many persons normal, natural and right.

The argument that this amendment will not solve the problem of sex discrimination is not relevant. If the argument were used against a civil rights bill, as it has been used in the past, the prejudice that lies behind
15 it would be embarrassing. Of course laws will not eliminate prejudice from the hearts of human beings. But that is no reason to allow prejudice to continue to be enshrined in our laws, to perpetuate injustice through inaction.

20 The amendment is necessary to clarify countless ambiguities and inconsistencies in our legal system. For instance, the Constitution guarantees due process of law in the fifth and fourteenth amendments, but the applicability of due process to sex distinctions is not
25 clear. Women are excluded from some State colleges and universities. In some States, restrictions are placed on a married woman who engages in an independent business. Women may not be chosen for some juries. Women even receive heavier criminal penalties than
30 men who commit the same crime.

State labor laws applying only to women, such as those limiting hours of work and weights to be lifted, would become inoperative unless the legislature amended them to apply to men. There has for years
35 been great controversy as to the usefulness to women of these State labor laws. There has never been any doubt that they worked a hardship on women who need to work overtime and on women who need better paying jobs. If any labor laws applying only to women
40 still remained, their amendment or repeal would provide opportunity for women in better-paying jobs in manufacturing. More opportunities in public vocational and graduate schools for women would also tend to open up opportunities in better jobs for women.
45 There are objections raised to wiping out laws

protecting women workers. No one would condone exploitation. But what does sex have to do with it? Working conditions and hours that are harmful to women are harmful to men; wages that are unfair for
50 women are unfair for men.

Laws setting employment limitations on the basis of sex are irrational, and the proof of this is their inconsistency from State to State. The physical characteristics of men and women are not fixed,
55 but cover two wide spans that have a great deal of overlap. It is obvious, I think, that a robust woman could be more fit for physical labor than a weak man. The choice of occupation would be determined by individual capabilities, and the rewards for equal work
60 should be equal.

This is what it comes down to: artificial distinctions between persons must be wiped out of the law. Legal discrimination between the sexes is, in almost every instance, founded on outmoded views of
65 society and the pre-scientific beliefs about psychology and physiology. It is time to sweep away these relics of the past and set future generations free of them.

Federal agencies and institutions responsible for the enforcement of equal opportunity laws need the
70 authority of a Constitutional amendment. The 1964 Civil Rights Act and the 1963 Equal Pay Act are not enough; they are limited in their coverage–for instance, one excludes teachers, and the other leaves out administrative and professional women. The Equal
75 Employment Opportunity Commission has not proven to be an adequate device, with its power limited to investigation, conciliation, and recommendation to the Justice Department. In its cases involving sexual discrimination, it has failed in more than one-half. The
80 Justice Department has been even less effective. It has intervened in only one case involving discrimination on the basis of sex, and this was on a procedural point. In a second case, in which both sexual and racial discrimination were alleged, the racial bias charge was
85 given far greater weight.

Evidence of discrimination on the basis of sex should hardly have to be cited here. It is in the Labor Department's employment and salary figures for anyone who is still in doubt. Its elimination will
90 involve so many changes in our State and Federal laws that, without the authority and impetus of this proposed amendment, it will perhaps take another 194 years. We cannot be parties to continuing a delay. The time is clearly now to put this House on record for the fullest
95 expression of that equality of opportunity which our founding fathers professed.

CONTINUE

1

The main purpose of this passage is to

A) demonstrate the necessity of due process in gendered cases that are brought before a court.

B) argue that discrimination against working women needs to be addressed with legal action.

C) present and examine America's history of discrimination on the basis of sex.

D) discuss the merits of systematic legal reform in the eradication of discrimination nationwide.

2

Which choice best describes the author's perspective on the value of constitutional reform in

the fight against prejudice?

A) She finds it helpful, but not indispensable, in raising awareness on the issues of prejudice.

B) She believes that, although it may not eradicate prejudice, it will at least no longer enable it.

C) She deems it important, yet unable to fully address the most subtle and pervasive types of prejudice.

D) She thinks it will be useful only if backed by state legislations that criminalizes prejudice.

3

Which choice provides the best evidence for the answer to the previous question?

A) Lines 15-19 ("Of course…inaction")

B) Lines 22-25 ("For instance…clear")

C) Lines 70-74 ("The 1964…women")

D) Lines 78-85 ("In its…weight")

4

Lines 11-15 ("The argument…embarrassing") primarily serve which function in the passage?

A) They raise and refute a potential counterargument to the effectiveness of the proposed amendment.

B) They identify and concede a critical weakness in the validity of the author's argument.

C) They anticipate and correct a possible misinterpretation of the amendment's intentions.

D) They prove why sex discrimination deserves as much attention as any other civil rights bill.

5

In lines 56-57, the author refers to "a robust woman" and "a weak man" in order to

A) demonstrate that body type is irrelevant when it comes to occupational calling.

B) prove that it is irrational to think that, by virtue of gender, men are most fit for physical labor.

C) argue that states should not have stipulations regarding weight in their laws.

D) explain that men are equally entitled to protection under state labor laws.

6

As used in line 66, "relics" most nearly means

A) remnants.

B) artifacts.

C) notions.

D) opinions.

7

As used in line 76, "device" most nearly means

A) instrument.

B) organization.

C) gadget.

D) tactic.

8

Which choice provides the best evidence for the author's claim that discrimination is institutionalized?

A) Lines 25-30 ("Women are…crime")

B) Lines 39-42 (If any…manufacturing")

C) Lines 51-53 ("Laws setting…State")

D) Lines 86-89 ("It is…doubt")

9

According to the passage, institutionalized discrimination is most likely the result of which of the following?

A) Inconsistent state labor laws.

B) Subtle prejudice in people's hearts.

C) Antiquated notions about the human body and mind.

D) An ineffective justice department.

CONTINUE

10

Which choice best summarizes the final paragraph?

A) We must strive to live up to the values professed by the founding fathers and encourage equality for all.

B) Evidence from the labor department proves that there is a pertinent need for reform of our labor laws.

C) Constitutionally backed legal action is required to eradicate rampant discrimination throughout the nation.

D) We should no longer procrastinate in passing an urgently needed amendment that will guarantee equality for all.

CONTINUE

Questions 1-10 are based on the following passage.

2.4

Passage 1 is adapted from the 1896 Supreme Court ruling (Plessey V. Ferguson) that upheld "separate but equal" racial segregation laws. Passage 2 is adapted from the 1954 Supreme Court ruling (Brown V. Board of Ed.) that ended racial segregation in public schools.

Passage 1

The object of the Fourteenth Amendment was undoubtedly to enforce the absolute equality of the two races before the law, but, in the nature of things,
Line it could not have been intended to abolish distinctions
5 based upon color, or to enforce social, as distinguished from political, equality, or a commingling of the two races upon terms unsatisfactory to either. Laws permitting, and even requiring, their separation in places where they are liable to be brought into contact
10 do not necessarily imply the inferiority of either race to the other, and have been generally, if not universally, recognized as within the competency of the state legislatures in the exercise of their police power. The most common instance of this is connected with the
15 establishment of separate schools for white and colored children, which has been held to be a valid exercise of the legislative power even by courts of States where the political rights of the colored race have been longest and most earnestly enforced.
20 We think the enforced separation of the races, as applied to the internal commerce of the State, neither abridges the privileges or immunities of the colored man, deprives him of his property without due process of law, nor denies him the equal protection of the laws
25 within the meaning of the Fourteenth Amendment.
We consider the underlying fallacy of the plaintiff's argument to consist in the assumption that the enforced separation of the two races stamps the colored race with a badge of inferiority. If this be
30 so, it is not by reason of anything found in the act, but solely because the colored race chooses to put that construction upon it. The argument necessarily assumes that if, as has been more than once the case and is not unlikely to be so again, the colored
35 race should become the dominant power in the state legislature, and should enact a law in precisely similar terms, it would thereby relegate the white race to an inferior position. We imagine that the white race, at least, would not acquiesce in this assumption.
40 The argument also assumes that social prejudices may be overcome by legislation, and that equal

rights cannot be secured to the negro except by an enforced commingling of the two races. We cannot accept this proposition. If the two races are to meet
45 upon terms of social equality, it must be the result of natural affinities, a mutual appreciation of each other's merits, and a voluntary consent of individuals. When the government, therefore, has secured to each of its citizens equal rights before the law and equal
50 opportunities for improvement and progress, it has accomplished the end for which it was organized, and performed all of the functions respecting social advantages with which it is endowed.

Passage 2

Today, education is perhaps the most important
55 function of state and local governments. Compulsory school attendance laws and the great expenditures for education both demonstrate our recognition of the importance of education to our democratic society. It is required in the performance of our most basic public
60 responsibilities, even service in the armed forces. It is the very foundation of good citizenship. Today it is a principal instrument in awakening the child to cultural values, in preparing him for later professional training, and in helping him to adjust normally to his
65 environment. In these days, it is doubtful that any child may reasonably be expected to succeed in life if he is denied the opportunity of an education. Such an opportunity, where the state has undertaken to provide it, is a right which must be made available to all on
70 equal terms. We come then to the question presented: Does segregation of children in public schools solely on the basis of race, even though the physical facilities and other "tangible" factors may be equal, deprive the children of the minority group of equal educational
75 opportunities? We believe that it does. In finding that a segregated law school for Negroes could not provide them equal educational opportunities, this Court relied in large part on those qualities which are incapable of objective measurement but which make for greatness
80 in a law school. In requiring that a Negro admitted to a white graduate school be treated like all other students, this Court again resorted to intangible considerations: his ability to study, to engage in discussions and exchange views with other students, and, in general,
85 to learn his profession. Such considerations apply with added force to children in grade and high schools. To separate them from others of similar age and qualifications solely because of their race generates a feeling of inferiority as to their status in the community
90 that may affect their hearts and minds in a way unlikely ever to be undone. Segregation of white and colored

CONTINUE

children in public schools has a detrimental effect upon the colored children. The impact is greater when it has the sanction of the law, for the policy of separating the
95 races is usually interpreted as denoting the inferiority of the negro group. A sense of inferiority affects the motivation of a child to learn. Segregation with the sanction of law, therefore, has a tendency to retard the educational and mental development of negro children
100 and to deprive them of some of the benefits they would receive in a racially integrated school system. We conclude that, in the field of public education, the doctrine of "separate but equal" has no place. Separate educational facilities are inherently unequal. Therefore,
105 we hold that the plaintiffs and others similarly situated for whom the actions have been brought are, by reason of the segregation complained of, deprived of the equal protection of the laws guaranteed by the Fourteenth Amendment. This disposition makes unnecessary any
110 discussion whether such segregation also violates the Due Process Clause of the Fourteenth Amendment.

1

In Passage 1, The Supreme Court develops its argument that state laws upholding racial segregation do not violate the Fourteenth Amendment by

A) citing sections in the Fourteenth Amendment that make provisions for such separation.

B) highlighting flaws in the assumptions made by those who claim that such separation is unconstitutional.

C) pointing out that separation of the two races has been mutually enforced within each community regardless of the law.

D) arguing that it is not within the scope of the Fourteenth Amendment to address the issue of racial discrimination.

2

As used in line 29, "badge" most nearly means

A) emblem.

B) label.

C) blemish.

D) symbol.

3

The authors of Passage 1 would most likely respond to the statement by the authors of Passage 2 in lines 87-91 ("To separate...undone) by stating that such an interpretation is

A) only applicable when whites are the dominant political force.

B) based on feelings of inferiority that are pervasive across all races.

C) based on a misunderstanding of the spirit of the act.

D) itself a violation of the Fourteenth Amendment.

4

Which choice provides the best evidence for the answer to the previous question?

A) Lines 7-11 ("Laws permitting...other")

B) Lines 20-25 ("We think...Amendment")

C) Lines 29-32 ("If this...it")

D) Lines 48-51 (" When the...organized")

5

Which statement best expresses Passage 1 and Passage 2's respective views regarding the separation of the races?

A) Passage 1 sees it as a natural development arising from the inherent differences between the races, whereas Passage 2 sees it as a device that is only applicable in areas outside of education.

B) Passage 1 sees it as an inevitable consequence of multiple races living in close proximity, whereas Passage 2 sees it as a tactic that is psychologically detrimental to all children.

C) Passage 1 sees it as a means to preserve the tenuous equilibrium between the races, whereas Passage 2 sees it as a demonstration of the inadequate resources afforded to Black children.

D) Passage 1 sees it as a legitimate application of the legislative powers accorded to the state courts, whereas Passage 2 sees it as a violation of the intentions of the Fourteenth Amendment.

CONTINUE

6

Passage 2 differs from Passage 1 in that the authors develop an argument by focusing on

A) the constitutionality of segregation and similar legislation.

B) personal testimony of those affected by segregation.

C) the impact of segregation on a specific environment.

D) the flawed reasoning of the opposition to segregation.

7

The authors of Passage 2 would respond to Passage 1's claim that separate facilities can be equal by

A) pointing out that the schools designated for Black children had in fact been of inferior quality.

B) drawing attention to the elements of a well-rounded education that go beyond the physical setting.

C) claiming that isolation of Black children can foster resentment which will undermine their patriotism.

D) highlighting that early segregation in schools will negatively affect professional development.

8

What would be the response of Passage 2 to lines 40-41 ("The argument...legislation")?

A) Legislators have a moral obligation to at least attempt to correct an entrenched social ill.

B) Legislative action can have a positive impact if restricted in its application to schools.

C) The law legitimizes and enables the prejudices that are already present in society.

D) The ambiguity of the law makes it open to exploitation by bigoted politicians.

9

Which choice provides the best evidence for the answer to the previous question?

A) Lines 85-86 ("Such considerations...schools")

B) Lines 93-96 ("The impact...group")

C) Lines 97-99 ("Segregation with...children")

D) Lines 102-103 ("We conclude...place")

10

As used in line 105, "situated" most nearly means

A) positioned.

B) affected.

C) located.

D) placed.

CONTINUE

Questions 1-10 are based on the following passage.

2.5
This passage is adapted from a speech delivered by Chancellor of Germany Gerhard Schröder at the Auschwitz Memorial ceremony on January 25, 2005

Survivors of Auschwitz-Birkenau,
Ladies and gentlemen,
It would be fitting for us Germans to remain
Line silent in the face of what was the greatest crime
5 in the history of mankind. Words by government
leaders are inadequate when confronted with the
absolute immorality and senselessness of the murder
of millions. We look for rational understanding of
something that is beyond human comprehension. We
10 seek definitive answers, but in vain. What is left is
the testimony of those few who survived and their
descendants. What is left are the remains of the sites
of these murders and the historical record. What is left
also is the certainty that these extermination camps
15 were a manifestation of absolute evil.
Now, sixty years after the liberation of
Auschwitz by the Red Army, I stand before you as the
representative of a democratic Germany. I express my
shame for the deaths of those who were murdered and
20 for the fact that you, the survivors, were forced to go
through the hell of a concentration camp. Chelmno,
Belzec, Sobibor, Treblinka, Maidanek, and Auschwitz-
Birkenau are names that will forever be associated
with the history of the victims as well as with German
25 and European history. We know that. We bear this
burden with sadness, but also with a serious sense of
responsibility. Germany has faced this responsibility
for a long period of time now with its government
policies and court decisions, supported by a sense of
30 justice on the part of the people.
Today the Jewish community in Germany is the
third-largest in Europe. It is full of vitality and growing
rapidly. New synagogues are being built. The Jewish
community is and will remain an irreplaceable part of
35 our society and culture. Its brilliant as well as painful
history will continue to be both an obligation and
a promise for the future. We will use the powers of
government to protect it against the antisemitism of
those who refuse to learn the lessons of the past. There
40 is no denying that antisemitism continues to exist. It is
the task of society as a whole to fight it. It must never
again become possible for anti-Semites to attack and
cause injury to Jewish citizens in our country or any
other country and, in so doing, bring disgrace upon our

45 nation.
Right-wing extremists, with their spray-painted
slogans, have the special attention of our law
enforcement and justice authorities. But the process of
dealing politically with neo-Nazis and former Nazis is
50 something we all need to do together. It is the duty of
all democrats to provide a strong response to neo-Nazi
incitement and recurrent attempts on their part to play
down the importance of the crimes perpetrated by
the Nazi regime. For the enemies of democracy and
55 tolerance there can be no tolerance.
The survivors of Auschwitz have called upon us
to be vigilant, not to look away, and not to pretend
we don't hear things. They have called upon us
to acknowledge human rights violations and to
60 do something about them. They are being heard,
particularly by young people, for instance by those
who are looking at the Auschwitz memorial today
with their own eyes. They are speaking with former
prisoners. They are helping to maintain and preserve
65 the memorial. They will also help to inform future
generations of the crimes committed by the Nazi
regime.
The vast majority of the Germans living today
bear no guilt for the Holocaust. But they do bear a
70 special responsibility. Remembrance of the war and the
genocide perpetrated by the Nazi regime has become
part of our living constitution. For some, this is a
difficult burden to bear. Nonetheless, this remembrance
is part of our national identity. Remembrance of the
75 Nazi era and its crimes is a moral obligation. We owe
it to the victims, we owe it to the survivors and their
families, and we owe it to ourselves.
We know one thing for sure. There would be
no freedom, no human dignity, and no justice if we
80 were to forget what happened when freedom, justice,
and human dignity were desecrated by government
power. Exemplary efforts are being undertaken in
many German schools, in companies, in labor unions,
and in the churches. Germany is facing up to its past.
85 From the Shoa and Nazi terror a certainty has arisen
for us all that can best be expressed by the words
"never again." We want to preserve this certainty.
All Germans, but also all Europeans, and the entire
international community need to continue to learn to
90 live together with respect, humanity, and in peace.

CONTINUE

1

Over the course of the passage, Schröder's focus shifts from

A) enumerating the horrors of the Holocaust to describing the resurgence of antisemitism worldwide.

B) informing listeners about the basic facts of the Holocaust to listing all the steps that have been taken to prevent its recurrence.

C) recalling the horrors and painful realities of the Holocaust to outlining the obligations of German citizens.

D) depicting the current situations of Holocaust survivors to reminding the audience of their past suffering.

2

Which of the following roles is most analogous to that played by Schröder in the passage?

A) A politician running for office on an anti-racism platform.

B) A teacher admonishing his students for their previous misbehavior.

C) A community leader delivering an anti-bullying speech in a high school.

D) A judge issuing a ruling on a morally contentious issue.

3

Which of the following best describes the tone of the passage?

A) Cynical and angry

B) Somber but hopeful

C) Grieving but relieved

D) Disappointed and remorseful

4

According to Schröder, German guilt about the Holocaust is

A) outdated, since Germans have been redeemed through the eradication of Nazism.

B) dangerous, since it is so overwhelming that Germans have repressed their own history.

C) necessary, since it is instrumental to ensure that such atrocities never resurface.

D) justified, since antisemitism is still prevalent in contemporary Germany.

5

Which choice provides the best evidence for the answer to the previous question?

A) Lines 3-5 ("It would…mankind")

B) Lines 37-40 ("We will…exist")

C) Lines 68-69 ("The vast…Holocaust")

D) Lines 73-75 ("Nonetheless, this…obligation")

6

Which choice provides the best evidence for the claim that Germans feel responsible for acts of antisemitism on a global scale?

A) Lines 13-15 ("What is…evil")

B) Lines 21-25 ("Chelmno, Belzec…history")

C) Lines 41-45 ("It must…nation")

D) Lines 88-90 ("All Germans…peace")

7

As used in line 27, "faced" most nearly means

A) confronted.

B) met.

C) encountered.

D) endured.

8

The primary purpose of the fourth paragraph (lines 46-55) is to

A) inform readers that German authorities have recently caught a band of neo-Nazis.

B) link the prominence of right-wing political parties to the resurgence of neo-Nazism.

C) demonstrate the effectiveness of the government in combating neo-Nazism.

D) stress the importance of the role ordinary citizens play in fighting neo-Nazism.

9

As used in lines 63-65, the pronoun "they" most likely refers to

A) German youth.

B) Holocaust survivors.

C) reformed neo-Nazis.

D) German politicians.

CONTINUE

10

As used in line 73, "burden" most nearly means

A) setback.

B) pressure.

C) duty.

D) weight.

STOP

Please turn to next page for answer keys and explanations.

Answer Key: CHAPTER TWO

2.1 | Thoreau	2.2 | Kerry	2.3 | Chisholm	2.4 | SCOTUS	2.5 | Schröder
1: A	1: C	1: D	1: B	1: C
2: A	2: B	2: B	2: B	2: C
3: C	3: A	3: A	3: C	3: B
4: B	4: D	4: A	4: C	4: C
5: D	5: A	5: B	5: D	5: D
6: B	6: D	6: A	6: C	6: C
7: D	7: A	7: B	7: B	7: B
8: B	8: C	8: D	8: C	8: D
9: B	9: C	9: C	9: B	9: A
10: B	10: B	10: D	10: B	10: C

Answer Explanations

Chapter Two

Chapter 2.1 | Thoreau

Question 1: A
Choice A is the best answer because Thoreau primarily claims that a truly free and enlightened government can only be achieved when it "comes to recognize the individual as a higher and independent power" (lines 77-78), which supports the phrase "foundational necessity of the individual" in choice A. Choice B is incorrect because while Thoreau does state that legislators are removed from the daily concerns of the American people and thus require the experience of the independent citizen, the words "criticize" and "naïve" in choice B are too negative for what is ultimately a neutral observation on the effectiveness of an isolated legislature. Choice C is incorrect because Thoreau declares himself unconcerned by the government as a body in paragraph 2, and in paragraph 3, he admits that statesmen have "no doubt invented ingenious and even useful systems"; he does not present any criticism of the government's structure nor does he suggest any reform. Choice D is incorrect because the phrasing of the answer, particularly "those who are merely under [the government's] charge" implies the inferiority of the citizens to the state, when Thoreau emphatically argues the opposite.

Question 2: A
Choice A is the best answer because Thoreau opens the passage by claiming that the American government lacks the "vitality and force" of the individual, and by itself has never furthered the development of the nation. He develops this stance further in paragraphs 3 and 4, where he claims that the legislative body of this country operates within narrow limits and lacks the practical knowledge of taxation and commerce needed to maintain America's position in the world. He then declares that these abilities do lie in the hands of the individual citizenry, and the final paragraph is dedicated to defining the perfect state as one that recognizes the "individual as a higher and independent power". Choice B is incorrect because Thoreau never discusses any functions of the government, choosing instead to focus on the general inefficacy of a legislator in promoting the economic interests of the nation. Choice C is incorrect because at several points in the latter half of the passage, Thoreau does not detail any mistakes made in the history of America's governance; indeed, the only mention of that history speaks of progress from a monarchy to a democracy in the pursuit of a state that respects the individual. Choice D is incorrect because Thoreau is unilateral in his evaluation of legislators, which conflicts with the suggestion of a "debate".

Question 3: C
Choice C is the best answer because only lines 65-67 clearly state that the government should only be granted as much authority as an individual is willing to concede to it. Choice A is incorrect because lines 4-6 discuss the American government's lack of power. Choice B is incorrect because lines 17-18 are about the inability of the government to develop or strengthen the nation. Choice D is incorrect because lines 82-84 assert that some people are capable of living apart from society as a whole.

Question 4: B
Choice B is the best answer because lines 86-88 use the metaphorical image of a fruiting tree to define the ideal government as one that would drop the "fruit" as soon as it ripened. With the context of the previous sentence defining this fruit as the independent and dutiful individuals of a just society, this answer supports the idea of a fostering entity that releases its control once those under its governance are mature. Choices A and C are incorrect because in the first paragraph, we see Thoreau criticize this very form of government as one that inhibits the progress that could be made by its people. In addition, while the concept of a "self-imposed encumbrance" is mentioned in the first paragraph, and is even called excellent, it is also called one incapable of real and pragmatic advancement. Choice D is incorrect because in the final paragraph, Thoreau deliberates on the importance of allowing a few to live apart from the oversight of the state, and not necessarily the general public as a body.

Question 5: D
Choice D is the best answer because it is here where Thoreau explicitly refers to his concept of a "perfect and glorious State". Choices A and B are incorrect because lines 12-14 and 15-17detail his view of the governments that he has observed, rather than the ideal form that he advocates. Choice C is incorrect because Thoreau simply dismisses the relevance of the government to his argument in lines 23-25.

Question 6: B
Choice B is the best answer because Thoreau employs the metaphor of a "wooden gun" to illustrate his image of the government as functionally useless but effective in projecting a desired concept of authority. Choice A is incorrect because the only question that Thoreau poses in the paragraph simply discusses the government's lack of the creative energy present in the individual, not its complete absence of any worth. Choice C is incorrect because no contrast between the intentions and the actions of the government is discussed. Choice D is incorrect because at no point in the paragraph does Thoreau overexaggerate the flaws of the government, nor does he eventually dismiss them as insignificant.

Question 7: D
Choice D is the best answer because Thoreau claims that statesman tend "to forget that the world is not governed by policy and expediency", supporting the "inflated view of their own role". Choice A is incorrect because despite the legislators having "not yet learned the comparative value of free-trade and of freedom" (lines 50-52), "never sought out" implies a deliberate denial of these principles, rather than a simple ignorance as the text indicates. Choice B is incorrect because the eloquence of the legislators is described as pretty but ineffective, loved "for its own sake" (lines 48-49). However, Thoreau does not claim that this discourse has actually harmed America; it is

only mentioned as a theoretical if it was not tempered by the pragmatism of the American people. Choice C is incorrect because while Thoreau does claim that legislators have "no genius or talent for comparatively humble questions of taxation and finance", this is only a facet of the greater flaw of legislators as Thoreau defines it, which is a disconnect with the true elements needed to maintain America's status as a great nation.

Question 8: B
Choice B is the best answer because Thoreau asserts the authority of the government is derived from the active "consent" of its people, supporting "approval". Choice A is incorrect because the government is not being threatened for disobeying a rule, as is suggested by "penalty". Choices C and D are incorrect because "concession" and "acceptance" indicate a passive agreement in response to demands, thus placing the government in the position of strength instead of the individual.

Question 9: B
Choice B is the best answer because Thoreau describes the political shift from absolute monarchy to democracy indicates "true respect for the individual" (lines 69-70) and the ideology of the Chinese philosopher as regarding "the individual as the basis of the empire". Both of these claims are in agreement with Thoreau's main argument, as well as providing a global context for his beliefs that extend across history and cultures. Choice A is incorrect because Thoreau explicitly defines the eventual adaptation of democracy as "progress" from the monarchy. Choice C is incorrect because Thoreau focuses specifically on how both these examples emphasize the importance of the individual, not the form of governance itself. Choice D is incorrect because these examples do not make any comment on the existence of a free state, past or current.

Question 10: B
Choice B is the best answer because Thoreau describes people who neither meddle with nor embrace the rule of the State, but hold themselves separate from it, supporting "detached from". Choice A and D are incorrect because both "uninterested" and "disdainful" suggest that Thoreau is presenting an opinion about the State rather than discussing a lack of engagement. Choice C is incorrect because "distant toward" implies a personal relationship rather than a political model.

Chapter 2.2 | Kerry

Question 1: C
Choice C is the best answer because Kerry titles his speech "Vietnam Veterans Against the War Statement", implying he is speaking on behalf of veterans and therefore is one. He also repeatedly uses "we" when referring to armed forces throughout the speech. Several times, Kerry provides reasons the war should end; for example in the fifth paragraph in which he describes the United States' foolishness in extending battles that are clearly already lost or in the sixth and seventh paragraph when he calls the war a mistake. Choice A is incorrect because Kerry is speaking to the Senate, therefore he cannot be lobbying for improved public perception as he is not addressing the public. Choice B is incorrect because while Kerry is an objector, he's not disloyal to the war; in fact, he is a veteran himself. Furthermore, while Kerry is listing reasons in the speech, they're detailing why the war in Vietnam should end. Choice D is incorrect because Kerry does indicate that the war can be won when he says "how do you ask a man to be the last man to die in Vietnam" (lines 65-66), though he does indicate that he believes that the war has gone on far too long.

Question 2: B
Choice B is the best answer because by saying the United States has "enthusiastically molded [the Vietnamese] after [its] own image" (lines 12-13), Kerry indicates that the United States is projecting its own understanding of war and liberation onto the Vietnamese people. Choice A is incorrect because the statement in 9-11 details the truth about the Vietnamese civil war, not the image projected by Americans. Choice C is incorrect because the statement in lines 21-23 is a fact about the Vietnamese people, therefore it cannot be an idealization by the United States. Choice D is incorrect because lines 31-33 detail a fact about American men in the war, not about the Vietnamese people.

Question 3: A
Choice A is the best answer because Kerry primarily seeks to elicit sympathy for the Vietnamese people, saying "they only wanted to work in rice paddies without helicopters strafing them and bombs with napalm burning their villages" (lines 18-20), before revealing that they have had unreliable allegiance: "they practiced the art of survival by siding with whichever military force was present" (lines 24-25). Choice B is incorrect because their ignorance is only mentioned in the first line of paragraph three but he qualifies that statement with facts about their desires during wartime, all in support of the idea that these people only wanted the war to end so they could go on with their lives. Choice C is incorrect because while while Kerry does state that the Vietnamese people "sid[ed] with whichever military force was present" (lines 24-25), he does not say that they fought alongside them. Choice D is incorrect because Kerry merely claims that they want to be left alone, and not that it has to happen via a peace deal.

Question 4: D
Choice D is the best answer because Kerry qualifies his statement about the United States claims regarding the body count in Vietnam by saying, "[they] listened month after month while [they] were told the back of the enemy was about to break" (lines 40-41), indicating that he believes the claims were made to make Americans in the military believe that they were close to achieving their goal. It can therefore be reasonably inferred that American leadership believed that troops would keep pushing if their goal was in sight. Choice A is incorrect because the target audience was troops, not the people in America. This is clear because when Kerry uses "we," he's referring to those people who would "f[i]ght using weapons against 'oriental human beings'", or armed forces. Choice B is incorrect because the statement indicates the end is near and Kerry does not indicate anywhere in the paragraph that anyone wants the war to continue beyond its natural conclusion. Choice C is incorrect because while Kerry criticizes the weapons used against the people of Vietnam and the relentless pursuit of battle sites, he does not say the war has a dubious objective even though he seems to disagree with the method of carrying out that objective.

Question 5: A
Choice A is the best answer because in the sentence containing the word "theater", Kerry is comparing weapons that are being used by Americans in combat in Vietnam to weapons that would be used in combat in Europe, making the correct choice "warzone". Choice B is incorrect because while drama does mean a type of theatre, it doesn't fit in the context of a literal place where battles are fought. Choices C and D are incorrect because while Europe would be a different context or stage for war, Kerry is referring to the physical places where people would be fighting.

Question 6: D
Choice D is the best answer because Kerry introduces these examples by saying "[America] watched pride allow the most unimportant battles to be blown into extravaganzas" (lines 49-51), clearly indicating that these are instances of this issue. Choice A is incorrect because while Kerry does say the Vietnamese reoccupy the sites, he does not insinuate that insubordination has occurred; in fact, he's implying the opposite: troops attack these sites to follow orders even when defeat is inevitable. Choice B is incorrect because Kerry does not suggest that the outcome was known. His intention is to point out that America is escalating its efforts in "unimportant battles" because it simply does not want to lose. Choice C is incorrect because the sites were already in enemy hands prior to the start of the attack, as evidenced by Kerry saying the North Vietnamese reoccupied them in line 49.

Question 7: A
Choice A is the best answer because Kerry states that leadership is missing when veterans return from war in the correct evidence from question nine, going so far as to say they have "deserted their troops" (line 73). Choice B is incorrect because while Kerry does say in the passage that leadership has allowed more battles than were necessary, he does not mention it in lines 69-73, nor does he say they have denied that atrocities have happened, only that they deny their part in fighting a war with poor objectives. Choice C is incorrect because while Kerry does indicate that Nixon sacrificed American lives to protect his reputation in lines 61-63, he does not say that politicians in general did this, nor did he say that it was for advancement of Nixon's career, just to maintain his status. Choice D is incorrect because Kerry does not mention care of American soldiers in any of the reference lines and he is not only concerned about casualties of war-- he's concerned about living veterans as well.

Question 8: C
Choice C is the best answer because Kerry lobbies criticisms at several politicians who he calls out by name, saying "where are they now that we, the men they sent off to war, have returned?" (lines 71-72). Choices A, B, and D are all incorrect because they fail to address the topic of American leadership. Choice B does mention President Nixon, who is a leader, but not leadership in general.

Question 9: C
Choice C is the best answer because Kerry clearly does not believe that political leadership is actually pious, therefore their piety is only a facade, or a show they put on to act as if they have not "deserted their troops" (line 73). Choice A is incorrect because a defense implies a statement and it's clear that this isn't an actual instance-- it's a metaphor Kerry is using to describe the actions of cowardly politicians. Choices B and D are incorrect because while the whole situation is a grand denial or a sham, in context "denial/sham of public rectitude" is the opposite of what Kerry's saying; he means that they desire the appearance of rectitude.

Question 10: B
Choice B is the best answer because the juxtaposing word in the referenced lines is "but" and the two things Kerry are comparing there are the negative current situation/memories that exist of war and the pacification that can happen if Kerry's intended audience were to succeed in their mission "to search out and destroy the last vestige of this barbaric war" (lines 86-88). This indicates that the comparison is between a bleak reality and a more positive future regarding memories of the war. Choice A is incorrect because Kerry does not mention any leadership glorifying the war memory in lines 81-86; in fact, he says that the administration has taken part in denial of the war memory.

Choice C is incorrect because Kerry states that the administration has denied the war memory, not that American soldiers have been asked to deny it. Choice D is incorrect because if Kerry believes that he can "destroy the last vestige of this war", he clearly believes that it can be erased.

Chapter 2.3 | Chisholm

Question 1: D
Choice D is the best answer because Chisholm discusses the need for and benefits of reform that ensures discrimination against anyone cannot exist in the American legal system. She begins her speech by contending that the Equal Rights Amendment "provides for equality under the law for both men and women" (lines 2-3) and concludes it by stating that it is time for the government to exhibit the "fullest expression of the equality of opportunity which our founding fathers professed" (lines 94-96). Choice A is incorrect because the fairness of court cases, while important, is only one example of the many legal realms that need reform, and ultimately egregiously neglects the broad and systematic nature of the reform proposed by Chisholm. Choice B is incorrect because the Equal Rights Amendment, as Chisholm is careful to point out, is meant to protect the rights of all citizens, not just working women; female laborers and their disproportionate plight just serve as prime examples of why this amendment is especially necessary. Choice C is incorrect because, while Chisholm's speech aims to prove the need for this amendment by utilizing historical examples, it does not have as its main goal a presentation of the history of prejudice.

Question 2: B
Choice B is the best answer because in the evidence for question 10, Chisholm says "Of course, laws will not eliminate prejudice...but there is no reason...to perpetuate injustice through inaction" (lines 15-19), thus supporting the belief that, at the least, the amendment will ensure that prejudice is not expressed in our laws. Choice A is incorrect because Chisholm does, in fact, suggest that this amendment is necessary, or indispensable, since the other "federal agencies and institutions...need the authority of a Constitutional amendment" (lines 69-70) in order to make real change, as they are "not enough" (line 72) on their own. Choice C is incorrect because it is directly contradicted by Chisholm's statement in the first paragraph, which argues that the amendment "provides a legal basis for attack on the most subtle, most pervasive...form of prejudice that exists" (lines 6-8). Choice D is incorrect because Chisholm suggests that the inverse is true: state legislations must be backed by a constitutional amendment. The word "criminalizes" also makes this choice wrong, as the amendment is only working to ensure that discrimination is not preserved in law, not to make it illegal to be discriminatory.

Question 3: A
Choice A is the best answer because the previous question asks about the importance of constitutional reform. The answer, that it will make sure that prejudice cannot be legally manifested, is best supported by the argument that there is "no reason to allow prejudice to continue to be enshrined in our laws" (lines 17-18). The rest of the choices are incorrect because they fail to remain on the topic of constitutional reform, instead discussing inconsistencies in previous amendments (Choice B), examples of insufficient government acts (Choice C), and the failings of the justice department (Choice D).

Question 4: A

Choice A is the best answer because Chisholm acknowledges the argument that the amendment will not end discrimination in general, only to contend that such reasoning does not matter and would not be accepted as a counterargument in other, similar cases. The ultimate point of the amendment is not to "eliminate prejudice from the hearts of human beings" (lines 15-16) but to make sure that it cannot be exhibited and perpetrated by our legal system any longer. Choice B is incorrect because Chisholm negates the relevance of such a counterargument, and therefore does not concede anything in the lines cited. Choice C is incorrect because the lines do not reveal a misinterpretation, but rather a presumed limitation of the intentions of the amendment. Choice D is incorrect because Chisholm does not reference other civil rights bills in order to emphasize the importance of the Equal Rights Amendment, but only to suggest that a specific argument against the amendment at hand would not be accepted as valid if used in the context of other civil rights discussions.

Question 5: B

Choice B is the best answer because the two examples serve as proof that the presumed abilities of a person should be based on the individual, rather than on the gender as a whole. Chisholm states that "limitations on the basis of sex are irrational" (lines 51-52) due to the fact that "the physical characteristics of men and women are not fixed" (lines 53-54), hence the examples describing a man with the characteristics typically ascribed to women and vice versa. Choice A is incorrect because Chisholm is not concerned with what occupation a person believes they are meant or called to do, but only with what occupation they are legally allowed to do. Choice C is incorrect because, while some assume "weight" can differentiate between men and women, it is not what Chisholm suggests to be the ostracising factor at hand. Choice D is incorrect because, while Chisholm does believe that men require the same protection against labor exploitation as women do (lines 48-50), she does not bring up the "robust woman" and "weak man" in relation to that discussion or in support of that belief, and they are thus tangential to the discussion of equal protection for all.

Question 6: A

Choice A is the best answer because the "relics" Chisholm references are the "outmoded views of society" (lines 63-65), and "remnants" implies that something remains from "the past" (line 67) that is no longer considered applicable in the present. Choice B is incorrect because it suggests that Chisholm is referencing actual items from the past. Choice C and D are incorrect for similar reasons as they do not necessarily refer to ideas that are leftover from a previous time, but rather just to ideas in general.

Question 7: B

Choice B is the best answer because it refers to "the Equal Employment Opportunity Commision" (lines 74-75), which is an "organization". Choices A, C, and D are incorrect for similar reasons as they do not serve as adequate references to a commission. Choices A and D imply that the Commision is being used as an important or strategic plan, which is not stated. Choice C is incorrect because it is too literal (Choice C), suggesting that "device" refers to a physical object.

Question 8: D
Choice D is the best answer because Chisholm states that the "evidence of discrimination" (line 86) found in the figures from the "Labor Department" (line 88) should suffice for anyone "who is still in doubt" (line 89). It is the best evidence of institutionalization because it shows that descrimination exists within a specific organization. Choice A is incorrect because, while it refers to institutions that women are excluded from, it does not prove that such exclusions are an established part of an organization or of society. Choice B is incorrect because it merely suggests a way to improve the lot of working women, and neglects a discussion of the discrimination against them. Choice C is incorrect because the irrationality of a law does not prove its discriminatory nature.

Question 9: C
Choice C is the best answer because Chisholm suggests that past beliefs about the differing mental and physical abilities of the sexes were used as the basis for discriminating against women. She states that the legal, and thus institutionalized, prejudice against women is a result of "pre-scientific beliefs about psychology and physiology" (lines 65-66). Choices A, B and D are incorrect for similar reasons as they are all the discriminatory results of the initial ideas about the bodies and minds of women, rather than the impetus for the discrimination in the first place.

Question 10: D
Choice D is the best answer because it emphasizes the urgency of constitutional reform that will remedy the injustice discussed throughout the rest of the passage. Chisholm argues that "we cannot be parties to continuing a delay" (line 93) or else this important amendment could take "another 194 years" (line 92). Choice A is incorrect because it neglects Chisholm's emphasis throughout the entire passage on the need for action that sanctions equality for all, as opposed to just encouragement or awareness of the necessity for this change. Choice B is incorrect because, while she does make this point in the final paragraph, it is only in order to provide further and final support for her urgent call for the Equal Rights Amendment. Choice C is incorrect because, while it states the argument that Chisholm makes throughout the passage, it doesn't encompass the emphasis she adds in the final paragraph on the need for the constitutionally backed action to happen now.

Chapter 2.4 | SCOTUS

Question 1: B
Choice B is the best answer because the authors contend throughout the passage that the laws are only perceived as unconstitutional because "the colored race chooses to put that construction upon it" (line 31-32). Further, the authors directly dispute the beliefs that the Fourteenth Amendment could help "abolish distinctions based upon color" or "enforce social...equality" (lines 4-6). Choice A is incorrect because the authors never claim that there are sections of the amendment that specifically allow for the separation, only that there are no aspects of the amendment that denote such separation as demonstrating inferiority. Choice C is incorrect because the word "regardless" implies an overlooking of legality in favor of supposed mutual and common actions, while in fact the whole passage is an attempt to demonstrate the very legality of those actions. Choice D is incorrect because it states that the Fourteenth Amendment is not supposed to do exactly what it is written to do: grant former slaves equality under the law.

Question 2: B
Choice B is the best answer because to be labeled as something implies that one is being assigned to a specific categorization or classification, whether rightfully or not. Choices A and D are incorrect for similar reasons as they both suggest that a single thing serves as an embodying representation of some whole, and generally have a positive connotation. Choice C is incorrect because it implies an imperfection, generally of appearance, and therefore does not accurately describe the stamp of "inferiority" (line 29) being discussed.

Question 3: C
Choice C is the best answer because the authors of Passage 1 argue that any inferiority felt by African Americans based on segregation is "solely because the colored race chooses to put that construction upon it" (lines 31-32), thus suggesting that they are misinterpreting the "spirit" or intention of segregation. Choice A is incorrect because, while the authors "imagine" (line 38) the inverse scenario wouldn't breed inferiority in the minds of white people, they never suggest that they know it wouldn't, thus eliminating choice A for the phrase "only applicable." Choice B is incorrect because, while the authors of Passage 1 do think it's based on feelings of inferiority, they argue that "the white race, at least, would not acquiesce in this assumption" (lines 38-39), suggesting that they don't believe the interpretation would span "across all races." Choice D is incorrect because interpreting separate but equal laws as causing a sense of inferiority does nothing to transgress on the Fourteenth Amendment and its attempt to ensure equality under the law for all.

Question 4: C
Choice C is the best answer because the answer to the previous question suggests that the author of Passage 1 believe African Americans are "misinterpreting" segregation laws, which is supported by the statement in lines 29-32 that African Americans are choosing to read into the laws in a specific way and without "reason of anything found in the act" (line 30). Choice A is incorrect because, while it claims that such laws do not intend to "imply the inferiority of either race" (line 10), it does not mention the authors' belief that such an implication is only there because it is constructed by African Americans. Choice B and D are incorrect for similar reasons as they both merely state that there is no transgression of the Fourteenth Amendment, and fail to discuss anything about the African American "misinterpretation."

Question 5: D
Choice D is the best answer because it clarifies the central legal disagreement between the two passages which is that separate but equal segregation either violates the Constitution or it doesn't. The authors of Passage 1 claim that the "separation of the races, as applied to the internal commerce of the State, neither abridges the privileges or immunities of the colored man...nor denies him the equal protection of laws within the meaning of the Fourteenth Amendment" (lines 21-25), while the authors of Passage 2 claim that "the doctrine of 'separate but equal' has no place" as it deprives African Americans "of the equal protection of the laws guaranteed by the Fourteenth Amendment" (lines 103-109). Choice A is incorrect because the authors of Passage 1, while potentially implying it, never actually state that intrinsic differences are fueling segregation, and the authors of Passage 2, while discussing the iteration of segregations specifically in schools, never implies that the same problems of unconstitutionality are irrelevant "outside of education." Choice B is incorrect because, while Passage 1 does imply that people naturally segregate based on race (lines 6-7), Passage 2 is focused on the psychological detriment to African American children, not "all children." Choice C is

incorrect because the fragile balance of race relations is not cited as a reason for segregation by the authors of Passage 1, and "inadequate resources" are actually discusses as being an irrelevant factor (lines 77-80) by the authors of Passage 2.

Question 6: C
Choice C is the best answer because Passage 2, while dealing with the same question of separate but equal laws that is dealt with broadly in Passage 1, focuses in on their application in educational settings, arguing that "education is perhaps the most important function of state and local governments" (lines 54-55). Choice A is incorrect because Passage 2 is actually arguing for the unconstitutionality of segregation, as it violates the Fourteenth Amendment. Choice B is incorrect because a "personal testimony" or first hand account would have to come from a student who has experienced segregation, but the passage is from the perspective of the Supreme Court. Choice D is incorrect because Passage 2 is from the perspective of the "opposition to segregation" and therefore would not want to, and do not, point out the flaws in their own reasoning.

Question 7: B
Choice B is the best answer because the authors of Passage 2 contend that separate but equal schools for African American children are inferior even if their "physical facilities and other 'tangible' factors may be equal" (lines 72-73). They argue that "to separate them from others of similar age and qualifications solely because of their race generates a feeling of inferiority" (lines 87-89) that can cause extensive mental damage. Choice A is incorrect because, as mentioned above, the authors of Passage 2 allow that the physical design of a school might be equal, but such physical qualities alone do not account for the equality or excellence of a school. Choice C and D are incorrect for similar reasons since, while "good citizenship" (line 61) and "professional training" (lines 63-64) are mentioned in the first paragraph as eventual positive outcomes of a good education, they are only two specific examples of the way education can affect mentality in general, which is the ultimate point made by the authors of Passage 2.

Question 8: C
Choice C is the best answer because the authors of Passage 2 believe that, while, as the authors of Passage 1 contend, legal action won't immediately eliminate racial prejudice in the social sphere, it will ensure that such attitudes aren't promoted, or even merely overlooked, by the government. They argue that the impact of segregation is "greater when it has the sanction of the law" (lines 93-94). Choice A is incorrect because it goes beyond the argument that the court ruling is necessary because separate but equal segregation violates the Fourteenth Amendment and suggests instead that the ruling is necessary because it is right in its denouncement of behavior that we generally accept as wrong, which is not a moral claim that the authors of Passage 2 make. Choice B is incorrect because, even though they are concerned primarily with the issue of segregation in schools, that doesn't mean that the authors of Passage 2 do not or will not consider the problem of segregation in other environments. Choice D is incorrect because the authors of Passage 2 make a clear case for why and how segregation violates the law, therefore suggesting that there is no "ambiguity" in it; in this case, if the law is exploited, it isn't because it is vague.

72

Question 9: B
Choice B is the best answer because the answer to the previous question contends that the authors of Passage 2 would consider the belief that legislation won't change social prejudice limited in that it doesn't account for the ability of the law to send a message about what is right and wrong, and lines 93-96 state that the permission of the law can intensify the social and mental impact. Choice A and D are incorrect for similar reasons as neither discuss the role of legislature on the societal mindset. Choice C is incorrect because, while it mentions the "sanction of the law", it connects it to the detrimental impact it has on the education and minds of African American children, instead of to the impact it has on social prejudice, like choice B does.

Question 10: B
Choice B is the best answer because "similarly situated" refers to other African Americans who have also experienced the negative effects of segregation, and therefore also been similarly affected by it. The rest of the choices are incorrect for similar reasons as they suggest being set in a specific context (Choice A), locale (Choice C), or space (Choice D), thus referring primarily to the physical settings and not to the way one is influenced by a specific social practice.

Chapter 2.5 | Schröder

Question 1: C
Choice C is the best answer because Schröder first emphasizes the "absolute immorality and senselessness of the murder of millions" (lines 7-8) that occured during the Holocaust and indicates that what happened was "a manifestation of absolute evil", before claiming that Germans "bear a special responsibility" (lines 69-70) to "be vigilant and...to acknowledge human rights violations and to do something about them" (lines 56-60). Choice A is incorrect because Schröder addresses antisemitism that has "[continued] to exist" since the Holocaust (line 40) and does not imply that antisemitism ceased to be a threat for a period of time before reemerging. Choice B is incorrect because Schröder does not outline a comprehensive list, or "all", of the steps taken to curb antisemitism; furthermore, Schröder puts forth steps that must be implemented in the future, not steps that already "have been taken". Choice D is incorrect because throughout the second half of the passage, Schröder focuses on initiatives to address and mitigate Germans' past suffering, but does not focus on the suffering itself.

Question 2: C
Choice C is the best answer because Schröder identifies himself as "the representative of a democratic Germany" (line 17-18), positioning himself in a leadership position. He then characterizes neo-Nazis as 'the enemies of democracy and tolerance" (lines 54-55) before encouraging Germans to fight antisemitism as a "moral obligation": "We owe it to the victims, we owe it to the survivors and their families, and we owe it to ourselves" (lines 74-77). Choice A is incorrect because Schröder is not attempting to promote himself as a politician or out of any other self-interest, as he has already been elected to office. Choice B is incorrect because Schröder would most likely be "admonishing" neo-Nazis, while his audience is primarily comprised of survivors of the Holocaust and their descendants. Choice D is incorrect because Schröder does not consider two sides of a debate; moreover, the issue he addresses cannot be described as "morally contentious".

Question 3: B
Choice B is the best answer because Schröder soberly expresses his "shame for the deaths of those who were murdered" in the Holocaust (lines 18-19) and admits that remembrance of the violence committed by the Nazi regime is a "difficult burden to bear" (line 73). However, he expresses optimism that progress is underway: "exemplary efforts are being taken in many German schools, in companies, in labor unions, and in the churches. Germany is facing up to its past" (lines 82-84). Choice A is incorrect because Schröder indicates his belief that antisemitism can be mitigated; therefore, he cannot be "cynical". Choice C is incorrect because "relieved" wrongly implies that antisemitism has been abolished, while Schröder believes that Germany is making progress, but has not yet accomplished its goals. Choice D is incorrect because Schröder conveys disappointment and remorse, but does not exclusively express those sentiments throughout the passage.

Question 4: C
Choice C is the best answer because Schröder declares that Germans "owe it to the victims... survivors and their families...and [themselves]" (lines 75-77) to feel guilt about the Holocaust; if they did not feel any responsibility, "there would be no freedom, no human dignity, and no justice" (lines 78-80). Choice A is incorrect because Schröder expressly claims that Nazism has not been eradicated: "there is no denying that antisemitism continues to exist. It is the task of society as a whole to fight it" (lines 39-41). Choice B is incorrect because Schröder demonstrates that remembrance of the Holocaust has become "part of [Germany's] living constitution" (line 72); therefore, Germans cannot be said to have repressed their own history. Choice D is incorrect because Schröder does not describe the extent to which neo-Nazism is popular; in fact, he implies that neo-Nazism is the minority by stating "it must never again become possible for anti-Semites to attack and cause injury to Jewish citizens in our country or any other" (lines 41-44).

Question 5: D
Choice D is the best answer because lines 73-75 address the "burden" of "remembrance" that some Germans carry, thus matching with the topic of "guilt about the Holocaust" in the previous question. Choices A, B, and C are all off topic: lines 3-5 describe an action of Germans, not a feeling they might have, while lines 37-40 and 68-69 refer to those who do not feel guilt or remorse for the events of the Holocaust.

Question 6: C
Choice C is the best answer because lines 41-45 refer to "any other country" and "disgrace [brought] upon our nation", correctly identifying the topic of German responsibility for anti-Semitism worldwide. Choices A, B, and D are all off topic: lines 13-15 and lines 21-25 address extermination camps rather than a general sentiment of the German people, while lines 88-90 address "freedom, justice, and human dignity" but not the responsibility that Germans feel with regards to worldwide actions.

Question 7: B
Choice B is the best answer because Schröder indicates that the responsibility of mitigating antisemitism is being "faced" through "government policies and court decisions". "Faced" therefore refers to addressing responsibility with action, as one would "meet" a challenge. Choice A is incorrect because "confronting" a responsibility would entail hostility. Choice C is incorrect because "encountered" only encompasses recognizing a problem, and does not necessarily include addressing

it. Choice D is incorrect because "endured" is overly negative for the overall tone of the passage, while Schröder believes that the responsibility presented is one that is morally righteous.

Question 8: D
Choice D is the best answer because Schröder underscores the role that "all democrats" (line 51) can play in combating neo-Nazism: "the process of dealing politically with neo-Nazis and former Nazis is something we all need to do together" (lines 48-50). Choice A is incorrect because Schröder indicates that "right-wing extremists" (line 46) have caught "the special attention of our law enforcement and justice authorities" (lines 47-48), but neither refers to any specific "band" of neo-Nazis nor reveals that they have been apprehended by the police. Choice B is incorrect because the "right-wing extremists" alluded to throughout the paragraph are merely vandalizing citizens, not political figures. Choice C is incorrect because the government has not been explicitly shown to be effective in putting down right-wing activity; they are only depicted as paying "special attention" (line 47) to the perpetrators.

Question 9: A
Choice A is the best answer because those mentioned throughout lines 63-65 are described as "speaking with former prisoners" and "helping to maintain and preserve the memorial"; "they" then refers to the "young people" (line 61) who visited the Auschwitz memorial and will likely further awareness about the atrocities committed during the Holocaust. Choice B is incorrect because the people mentioned are "speaking with former prisoners" of Auschwitz and therefore cannot be the former prisoners of Auschwitz themselves. Choices C and D are incorrect because neither of those groups are mentioned throughout the fifth paragraph and thus cannot be the subjects of the pronoun "they".

Question 10: C
Choice C is the best answer because the "burden" refers to the "special responsibility" (line 70) that Germans have to "[remember] the Nazi era and its crimes". Furthermore, Schröder characterizes this as a "moral obligation" (lines 73-75), which corresponds to "duty". Choices A and B are incorrect because "setback" and "pressure" are overly negative for the tone of the passage, while Schröder calls the duty given to Germans a "special" one (line 70); in addition, the "burden" is portrayed as an imperative that will be the impetus for progress, which directly contradicts "setback". Choice D is incorrect because "weight" is overly literal: in describing the responsibility of facing neo-Nazism, Schröder refers to a moral and political "burden", not a physical one.

Chapter
Three

Questions 1-10 are based on the following passage.

3.1

The following passage is adapted from Mary Fisher's "A Whisper of AIDS" speech given at the 1992 Republican National Convention.

Less than three months ago at platform hearings in Salt Lake City, I asked the Republican Party to lift the shroud of silence which has been draped over
Line the issue of AIDS. I have come tonight to bring our
5 silence to an end. I bear a message of challenge, not self congratulation. I want your attention, not your applause.

The reality of AIDS is brutally clear. Two hundred thousand Americans are dead or dying. A million more
10 are infected. Worldwide, forty million, sixty million, or a hundred million infections will be counted in the coming few years. But despite science and research, White House meetings, and congressional hearings, despite good intentions and bold initiatives, campaign
15 slogans, and hopeful promises, it is, despite it all, the epidemic which is winning tonight.

In the context of an election year, I ask you to recognize that AIDS virus is not a political creature. It does not care whether you are Democrat or
20 Republican; it does not ask whether you are black or white, male or female, gay or straight, young or old. Though I am white and a mother, I am one with a black infant struggling with tubes in a Philadelphia hospital. Though I am female and contracted this disease in
25 marriage and enjoy the warm support of my family, I am one with the lonely gay man sheltering a flickering candle from the cold wind of his family's rejection.

We may take refuge in our stereotypes, but we cannot hide there long, because AIDS asks only one
30 thing of those it attacks. Are you human? And this is the right question because people with AIDS have not entered some alien state of being. They are human. They have not earned cruelty, and they do not deserve meanness. They don't benefit from being isolated or
35 treated as outcasts.

We cannot love justice and ignore prejudice, love our children and fear to teach them. Whatever our role as parent or policymaker, we must act as eloquently as we speak else we have no integrity. My call to the
40 nation is a plea for awareness. If you believe you are safe, you are in danger. Because I was not hemophiliac, I was not at risk. Because I was not gay, I was not at risk. Because I did not inject drugs, I was not at risk.

My father has devoted much of his lifetime
45 guarding against another holocaust. He is part of the generation who heard Pastor Nemoellor come out of the Nazi death camps to say:

They came after the Jews, and I was not a Jew, so, I did not protest. They came after the trade
50 unionists, and I was not a trade unionist, so, I did not protest. Then they came after the Roman Catholics, and I was not a Roman Catholic, so, I did not protest. Then they came after me, and there was no one left to protest.

55 The lesson history teaches is this: If you believe you are safe, you are at risk. If you do not see this killer stalking your children, look again. There is no family or community, no race or religion, no place left in America that is safe. Until we genuinely embrace
60 this message, we are a nation at risk.

My family has been a rock of support. But not all of you have been so blessed. You are HIV positive, but dare not say it. You have lost loved ones, but you dare not whisper the word AIDS. You weep silently. You
65 grieve alone. I have a message for you.

It is not you who should feel shame. It is we who tolerate ignorance and practice prejudice, we who have taught you to fear. We must lift our shroud of silence, making it safe for you to reach out for compassion. It
70 is our task to seek safety for our children, not in quiet denial, but in effective action.

Someday our children will be grown. I want my children to know that their mother was not a victim. She was a messenger. I do not want them to think, as
75 I once did, that courage is the absence of fear. I want them to know that courage is the strength to act wisely when most we are afraid. I ask no more of you than I ask of myself or of my children. To the millions of you who are grieving, who are frightened, who have
80 suffered the ravages of AIDS firsthand: Have courage, and you will find support. To the millions who are strong, I issue the plea: Set aside prejudice and politics to make room for compassion and sound policy.

To all within the sound of my voice, I appeal:
85 Learn with me the lessons of history and of grace, so my children will not be afraid to say the word "AIDS" when I am gone. Then, their children and yours may not need to whisper it at all.

CONTINUE →

1

The primary purpose of the passage is to

A) share the stories of diverse individuals struggling in the AIDs crisis.

B) prove that the AIDs crisis affects many Americans regardless of sexuality.

C) underscore the necessity of seeing the AIDs crisis out of political context.

D) condemn the current trend of political prejudice towards those with AIDs.

2

Fisher refers to the "shroud of silence" in lines 3 and 68 in order to refer to the

A) unjust actions of both the public and the government.

B) attempts by officials to downplay the extent of the crisis.

C) unwillingness of many to confront the crisis in a meaningful way.

D) fear and pain of those directly affected by the AIDs epidemic.

3

Which choice best reflects a technique that Fisher uses throughout her speech to advance her main point?

A) She draws attention to the effect of the stigma around AIDs by using individual examples.

B) She employs a collective voice when conveying central ideas in order to call her audience to action.

C) She quotes a moral authority who has spoken about a similar instance of injustice and inaction.

D) She uses juxtaposition in several ways at key points in order to appeal to the values of her audience.

4

It can most reasonably be inferred from the passage that Fisher believes she is advantaged over others affected by AIDS because she has

A) had access to the latest scientific and political initiatives to combat AIDS.

B) received less judgement due to her identity as a white married woman.

C) continually received loyalty and emotional support from her loved ones.

D) not been born with a condition or predilection that would put her at risk for AIDS.

5

Which choice provides the best evidence for the answer to the previous question?

A) Lines 12-15 ("But despite...promises")

B) Lines 24-27 ("Though I...rejection")

C) Lines 41-43 ("Because I...risk")

D) Lines 61-63 ("My family...it")

6

As used in line 30, "attacks" most nearly means

A) assaults.

B) targets.

C) bludgeons.

D) afflicts.

7

In context of the passage as a whole, the third paragraph (lines 17-27) serves primarily to

A) emphasize that Fisher faces the same struggles as others infected with AIDs.

B) refute the idea that Fisher has been fortunate while others have not.

C) highlight the fact that AIDs does more than physical harm to those it infects.

D) evoke sympathy for the families of those infected by AIDs.

8

Fisher most likely includes the quote from Pastor Nemoeller in order to

A) warn her audience that no crisis can be solved by ignoring it.

B) argue that legislative inaction is tantamount to committing genocide.

C) remind her audience of a particularly heinous event in modern history.

D) chastise politicians who have failed to act on the AIDs crisis.

CONTINUE

9

Which choice most strongly suggests that Fisher believes that the AIDs crisis has been worsened by prejudice?

A) Lines 28-30 ("We may … attacks")

B) Lines 33-35 ("They have … outcasts")

C) Lines 37-39 ("Whatever our … integrity")

D) Lines 55-57 ("If you...again")

10

The main purpose of the tenth paragraph (lines 72-83) is most likely to

A) convey Fisher's personal vision for the future of politics.

B) implore diverse audience members to convene action committees.

C) propose a definitive solution to the AIDs epidemic worldwide.

D) suggest that the best action on the crisis requires unity and courage.

CONTINUE

topic: women's suffrage

Questions 1-10 are based on the following passage.

3.2

The following passage is adapted from French suffragettes Jeanne Deroin and Pauline Roland's 1851 letter to the Convention of the Women of America, which they wrote while in prison for their efforts to organize associations of male and female workers.

Dear Sisters: —Your courageous declaration of Woman's Rights has resounded even to our prison, and has filled our souls with inexpressible joy. In
Line France though, the reaction has suppressed the cry of
5 liberty of the women of the future. The darkness of this reaction has obscured the sun of 1848, which seemed to rise so radiantly. Why? Because the revolutionary tempest, in overturning at the same time the throne and the scaffold, forgot to break the chain of the most
10 oppressed of all the pariahs of humanity.

"There shall be no more slaves," said our brethren. "We proclaim universal suffrage. All shall have the right to elect the agents who shall carry out the Constitution which should be based on the principles of
15 liberty, equality, and fraternity. Let each one come and deposit his vote; the barrier of privilege is overturned; before the electoral urn there are no more oppressed, no more masters and slaves." Woman, in listening to this appeal, rises and approaches the liberating urn to
20 exercise her right of suffrage as a member of society. But the barrier of privilege rises also before her. "You must wait," they say. But by this claim alone woman affirms the right, not yet recognized, of the half of humanity—the right of woman of liberty, equality, and
25 fraternity. She obliges man to verify the fatal attack which he makes on the integrity of his principles. It is in the name of these principles that woman comes to claim her right to take part in the Legislative Assembly, and to help form the laws which must govern society,
30 of which she is a member. She comes to demand of the electors the consecration of the principle of equality by the election of a woman, and by this act she obliges man to prove that the fundamental law is still based upon privilege, and soon privilege triumphs over this
35 phantom of universal suffrage.

But while those selected by the half of the people—by men alone—evoke force to stifle liberty, and forge restrictive laws to establish order by compression, woman, guided by fraternity, foreseeing
40 incessant struggles, and in the hope of putting an end to them, makes an appeal to the laborer to found liberty and equality on fraternal solidarity. The participation of woman gave to this work of enfranchisement an eminently pacific character, and the laborer recognizes
45 the right of woman, his companion in labor. In this organization all the workers, without distinction of sex or profession, having an equal right to election, and being eligible for all functions, and all having equally the initiative and the sovereign decision in the acts of
50 common interests, they laid the foundation of a new society based on liberty, equality, and fraternity.

Fraternal associations were formed with the object of enfranchising the laborer from the yoke of spoilage and patronage, but, isolated in the midst
55 of the Old World, their efforts could only produce feeble amelioration for themselves. It is in the name of the law framed by man only—by those elected by privilege—that the Old World, wishing to stifle in the germ the holy work of enfranchisement, has shut
60 up within the walls of prison those who had founded it. But the impulse has been given, a grand act has been accomplished. The right of woman has been recognized by the laborers, and they have consecrated that right by the election of those who claimed it in
65 vain for both sexes. They have received the true civil baptism, were elected by the laborers to accomplish the mission of enfranchisement, and after having shared their rights and their duties, they share today their captivity.
70 It is from the depths of their prison that they address to you the relation of these facts, which contain in themselves high instruction. It is by labor, it is by entering resolutely into the ranks of the working people, that women will conquer the civil and political
75 equality on which depends the happiness of the world. As to moral equality, has she not conquered it by the power of sentiment? It is, therefore, by the sentiment of the love of humanity that the mother of humanity will find power to accomplish her high mission. It is
80 when she shall have well comprehended the holy law of solidarity—which is not an obscure and mysterious dogma, but a living providential fact—that the kingdom of equality and justice shall be realized on earth.
85 Sisters of America! Your socialist sisters of France are united with you in the vindication of the right of woman to civil and political equality. We have, moreover, the profound conviction that only by the power of association based on solidarity—by the
90 union of the working-classes of both sexes to organize labor—can be acquired the civil and political equality of woman, and the social right for all. It is in this confidence that, from the depths of the jail which still imprisons our bodies without reaching our hearts, we
95 cry to you and send you our sisterly salutations.

CONTINUE

1

The central claim of this passage is that

A) the integrity of a revolution is undermined if it fails to free and uplift all members of society.

B) male privilege is the final inhibitor blocking women's continued education and advancement.

C) it is through entering and organizing the workforce that women will achieve true equality.

D) women across the world must unite and support their sisters in the struggle for suffrage.

2

How do the authors use rhetoric to elevate the value of their cause?

A) They position their problems as a plea to the women of America.

B) They use religious allusions and diction to suggest that their fight is virtuous.

C) They emphasize their subjugation by foregrounding their imprisonment.

D) They juxtapose the entitlement of men with the disenfranchisement of women.

3

Which choice provides the best evidence for the answer to the previous question?

A) Lines 32-34 ("by this...privilege")

B) Lines 65-67 ("They have...enfranchisement")

C) Lines 85-87 ("Sisters of...equality")

D) Lines 92-94 ("It is...hearts")

4

Over the course of the passage, the main focus shifts from

A) a dramatization of the rights that women are denied to a declaration of the ways that they are denied them.

B) a critique of the decency of men to a novel proposal for the achievement of inclusive happiness.

C) an illustration of women's struggle for suffrage to an explanation of a strategy for achieving equality.

D) an appeal to foreign women's rights advocates to an analysis of the reform tactics in France.

5

It can be most reasonably inferred from the passage that the suffragettes and laborers unite because

A) they have a common plight that they are too weak to achieve on their own.

B) they both wish to rid themselves of the binding chains of male oppression.

C) they were similarly overlooked by the revolution's revisions to society.

D) they realize the laborer's need for a competent ally to accomplish their goals.

6

As used in line 38, "forge" most nearly means

A) manufacture.

B) fake.

C) replicate.

D) create.

7

Which quality do the authors instruct women to exploit in order to achieve universal suffrage?

A) Their compassionate disposition.

B) Their brave resilience.

C) Their peaceful dedication.

D) Their frank initiative.

8

Which choice provides the best evidence for the answer to the previous question?

A) Lines 1-3 ("Your courageous...joy")

B) Lines 18-21 ("Woman, in...her")

C) Lines 42-45 ("The participation...labor")

D) Lines 76-79 ("As to...mission")

9

As used in line 58, "stifle" most nearly means

A) silence.

B) subdue.

C) withhold.

D) constrain.

82

CONTINUE

10

Throughout the passage, the recurring reference to "liberty, equality, and fraternity" (line 15) most likely serves to

A) reference the diminished significance of such values due to the privilege barrier.

B) underscore France's insufficient adherence to its own guiding principles.

C) allude to lofty notions that deserve further discussion and feminist interpretation.

D) compare the ideals of France to those of the fraternal workers' association.

CONTINUE

Questions 1-10 are based on the following passage.

3.3

The following passage is adapted from Thomas Paine's Common Sense, published in 1776.

The authority of Great-Britain over this continent, is a form of government, which sooner or later must have an end: And a serious mind can draw no true
Line pleasure by looking forward, under the painful and
5 positive conviction, that what he calls "the present constitution" is merely temporary.

Though I would carefully avoid giving unnecessary offence, yet I am inclined to believe, that all those who espouse the doctrine of reconciliation,
10 may be included within the following descriptions: Interested men, who are not to be trusted; weak men, who cannot see; prejudiced men, who will not see; and a certain set of moderate men, who think better of the European world than it deserves; and this last class, by
15 an ill-judged deliberation, will be the cause of more calamities to this continent, than all the other three.

Men of passive tempers look somewhat lightly over the offences of Britain, and, still hoping for the best, are apt to call out, "Come, come, we shall be
20 friends again, for all this." But examine the passions and feelings of mankind, Bring the doctrine of reconciliation to the touchstone of nature, and then tell me, whether you can hereafter love, honour, and faithfully serve the power that hath carried fire and
25 sword into your land? If you cannot do all these, then are you only deceiving yourselves, and by your delay bringing ruin upon posterity. Your future connection with Britain, whom you can neither love nor honour, will be forced and unnatural, and being formed only on
30 the plan of present convenience, will in a little time fall into a relapse more wretched than the first. But if you say, you can still pass the violations over, then I ask, Hath your house been burnt? Hath your property been destroyed before your face? Are your wife and children
35 destitute of a bed to lie on, or bread to live on? Have you lost a parent or a child by their hands, and yourself the ruined and wretched survivor? If you have not, then are you not a judge of those who have.

I mean not to exhibit horror for the purpose of
40 provoking revenge, but to awaken us from fatal and unmanly slumbers, that we may pursue determinately some fixed object. It is not in the power of Britain, or of Europe, to conquer America, if she, by delay and timidity, do not conquer herself. The present
45 winter is worth an age if rightly employed, but if lost or neglected, the whole continent will partake of the misfortune; and there is no punishment which that

man will not deserve, be he who, or what, or where he will, that may be the means of sacrificing a season so
50 precious and useful.

It is repugnant to reason, to the universal order of things to all examples from former ages, to suppose, that this continent can longer remain subject to any external power. The utmost stretch of human wisdom
55 cannot, at this time, compass a plan short of separation, which can promise the continent even a year's security. Reconciliation is now a fallacious dream. For, as Milton wisely expresses, "never can true reconcilement grow where wounds of deadly hate have pierced so
60 deep."

Every quiet method for peace hath been ineffectual. Our prayers have been rejected with disdain; and only tended to convince us, that nothing flatters vanity, or confirms obstinacy in Kings
65 more than repeated petitioning—and nothing hath contributed more than that very measure to make the Kings of Europe absolute. Wherefore, since nothing but blows will do, for God's sake, let us come to a final separation, and not leave the next generation to be
70 cutting throats, under the violated unmeaning names of parent and child.

As to government matters, it is not in the power of Britain to do this continent justice: The business of it will soon be too weighty, and intricate, to be managed
75 with any tolerable degree of convenience, by a power, so distant from us, and so very ignorant of us; for if they cannot conquer us, they cannot govern us. To be always running three or four thousand miles with a tale or a petition, waiting four or five months for an
80 answer, which when obtained requires five or six more to explain it in, will in a few years be looked upon as folly and childishness—There was a time when it was proper, and there is a proper time for it to cease. Small islands not capable of protecting themselves, are the
85 proper objects for kingdoms to take under their care; but there is something very absurd, in supposing a continent to be perpetually governed by an island. In no instance hath nature made the satellite larger than its primary planet, and as England and America, with
90 respect to each other, reverses the common order of nature, it is evident they belong to different systems: England to Europe, America to itself.

CONTINUE

1

Which of the following choices best describes Paine's primary grievance with Britain?

A) The British government is violating the sovereign rights to which all territories are inherently entitled.

B) The British government is neither equipped for nor justified in exercising control over the American continent.

C) The British government has imposed a state of rule that will devolve into chaos if it is not resolved.

D) The British government has created a political uprising which will only result in unnecessary bloodshed.

2

Which choice best describes Paine's perspective of those who continue to downplay British transgressions toward the American colonies?

A) He accuses them of hypocrisy that has furthered the conflict.

B) He deems them traitors for enabling the tyranny of Britain.

C) He condemns their apathy towards a clearly immoral issue.

D) He denounces their willful ignorance and lack of empathy.

3

Based on the passage, Paine foresees which consequences as arising from a policy of reconciliation?

A) A period of misfortune caused by the misguided judgments of those who seek to emulate the policies of Britain.

B) A growing divide among the citizenry of the colonies caused by the insensitivity of those who seek compromise.

C) A resurgence of hostility resulting from a fragile and meaningless alliance contrived for short-term benefit.

D) A descent into chaos resulting from the escalation of violence perpetrated by an emboldened British government.

4

Which choice provides the best evidence for the answer to the previous question?

A) Lines 12-16 ("and a...three")

B) Lines 21-25 ("Bring the...land")

C) Lines 27-31 ("Your future...first")

D) Lines 31-35 ("But if...on")

5

In context of the passage as a whole, lines 44-47 ("The present...misfortune") primarily serve to emphasize the

A) inevitable hardship awaiting Americans if they lose the conflict against Britain.

B) improbability of conducting a successful military campaign in wintertime.

C) unlikelihood that military conflict against Britain will lead to American victory.

D) urgency of confronting an issue that would otherwise result in widespread ruin.

6

As used in line 55, "compass" most nearly means

A) navigate.

B) direct.

C) envision.

D) predict.

7

Paine cites Milton in lines 58-60 ("never can...deep") mainly to indicate that

A) Britain's animosity towards the colonies has already caused irreparable damage.

B) ongoing efforts to make peace with Britain have been superficial and insincere.

C) continued attempts at compromise will only result in unnecessary bloodshed.

D) the tension between Britain and the colonies has reached a point of no return.

CONTINUE

8

In context of the passage as a whole, the sixth paragraph (lines 61-71) primarily serves which purpose?

A) It characterizes kings as narcissistic and susceptible to excessive praise.

B) It provides an explanation for the colonies' previous campaigns against Britain.

C) It questions the traditional relationship between kings and their subjects.

D) It anticipates and addresses a potential argument in favor of appeasement.

9

Paine would most likely describe British governance of the colonies as

A) Obsolete, because societal expectations have evolved to include individual representation.

B) Preposterous, because Britain is far too small to govern the expansive American territory.

C) Unnatural, because it distorts the relationship between the colonizer and the colonized.

D) Ineffective, because communication is hampered by Britain's distance from the colonies.

10

Which choice provides the best evidence for the answer to the previous question?

A) Lines 73-74 ("The business...managed")

B) Lines 82-83 ("There was...cease")

C) Lines 86-87 ("but there...island")

D) Lines 91-92 ("it is...itself")

CONTINUE

Questions 1-10 are based on the following passage.

3.4

The Eighteenth Amendment, which prohibited the manufacture and sale of liquor, was the only amendment to be repealed by a subsequent amendment. Prohibition was highly controversial, giving rise to heated debates. Passage 1 is adapted from a speech given by Congressman Richard Bartholdt. Passage 2 is adapted from Rev. Walter A. Morgan's essay: "A Moral and Ethical Argument for Prohibition."

Passage 1

Neither a monarchical nor even a despotic government has ever attempted to prohibit what in itself is not morally wrong. In all countries and at
Line all times it has been held to be wrong to deny an
5 individual a natural right where its exercise does not conflict with the equal rights of his fellow-man. Especially is this true as relating to mere personal habits. Deviations from this wise rule have invariably caused social disturbances, bloodshed, and revolution.
10 Lawful liberty is nothing more and nothing less than a guarantee of the natural rights of man, as I have just circumscribed them, and constitutions are made to protect these rights.

The right to eat and to drink can never be
15 interfered with by any majority, and a law prohibiting it, namely, the act of eating and drinking itself, if put upon the statute books by the 51 outvoting the 49, would immediately be declared unconstitutional. That is the reason why our friends on the other side seek
20 to accomplish their purpose by indirection. They shrewdly do not prohibit the use of spirituous and malt liquors and wines, but only their manufacture and sale. But what will the American people do when they awaken to a full realization of the fact that the exercise
25 of a personal right, dear even to the serf of Russia and cherished by all as a right, whether really exercised or not, has been or is to be denied them by a trick? Or do you believe for one moment that the present generation of Americans places a less valuation on their priceless
30 heritage than do other nations on whatever liberty they may enjoy, merely because they have inherited it and hence lack a true appreciation of its value? Wait and see.

A man eats and drinks in obedience to a natural
35 law and the only power between heaven and earth which can stop him from eating and drinking when and what he wants is his own intellect and his instinctive regard for the preservation of health and life. Attempt to stop him, and he will violate law and overthrow

40 even constitutions…Our friends on the other side foolishly believe that by removing the temptation they will kill the desire. How childish! You might as well abolish money, for there is no gainsaying the fact that the existence of money has caused more crimes in the
45 world than all other temptations put together. And by the time you would get through removing temptations the earth would be desolate, the human race extinct, and there would be nothing left but the stones to cry to heaven and bewail the idiocy of those who had once
50 been made in the image of the Creator…

The only logical conclusion is that temptation can successfully be resisted only from within. The fact is sobriety, the same as charity, begins at home. Hence we had better turn our faces homeward. And if it
55 were not presumptuous to undertake the teaching of teachers, I would say to my reverend friends: Retrace your steps, because you are on the wrong track. You do not need the Government to make the world better. You are already in possession of the only means
60 by which the evils you complain of can be cured— namely, by good example and precept.

Passage 2

The first moral significance of the particular Eighteenth Amendment, it needs to be repeated, lies in the fact that it registers the will of the great majority
65 of the American people. It sets the standard of a dry nation. To permit one's thinking to become befogged over the matter of enforcement is to refuse to think straight or hard. All men admit that the Eighteenth Amendment is not enforced always and everywhere.
70 Where on American soil is any law always enforced? How many uncaught and unpunished murderers are there today living in Chicago and New York?

The moral quality of the will that voted the nation dry had its origin in a moral and social source. It was
75 an honest desire to protect human life. This wish was made concrete and appealing through the lives of women and children. The moral tone of any people rises or falls in accordance with its attitude towards mothers and their young. As the race has evolved,
80 womanhood and childhood have come to occupy more commanding positions. Today, in the United States, the moral sense of the people puts them first. What is good for them should become a law. So the voters were led to believe and so they acted. Men and women merely
85 said, "The liquor business is a menace to our women and children. Let us get rid of it."

Salvation Army leaders, social workers, district nurses, Prohibition officers, child welfare organizations, and others who are in close observance
90 of social conditions, have repeatedly declared that no

CONTINUE ➡

other law has worked so great a revolution in social welfare as has Prohibition. Nearly one hundred million dollars of funds once spent to cure the harm done by the saloon is now expended in fresh air work,
95 free dental clinics, pre-maternity care, district nursing, hospitalization, and other forms of work.

1

According to Passage 1, prohibitionists in pursuit of their aims are resorting to

A) outright coercion.
B) deceptive practices.
C) legal argumentation.
D) moral suasion.

2

Which choice provides the best evidence for the answer to the previous question?

A) Lines 18-20 ("That is...indirection")
B) Lines 27-32 ("Or do...value")
C) Lines 40-42 ("Our friends...desire")
D) Lines 59-61 ("You are...precept")

3

As used in line 27, "trick" most nearly means

A) illusion.
B) stunt.
C) joke.
D) ruse.

4

Which choice best captures the views of Passages 1 and 2 regarding the morality of prohibition?

A) Passage 1 claims that prohibition is immoral as it infringes on personal liberties, while passage 2 says that it is moral as it protects the welfare of women and children.
B) Passage 1 claims that prohibition is immoral because it does not reflect the majority opinion, while passage 2 says that it is moral because it reflects the will of the majority.
C) Passage 1 claims that prohibition is immoral because it only restricts the trade of liquor, while passage 2 says that it is moral because it has redirected funds to social programs.
D) Passage 1 claims that prohibition is immoral because even despots don't forbid liquor, while Passage 2 says that it is moral because it not enforced more than any other law.

5

How would Passage 1 most likely respond to the statement made in Passage 2 in lines 74-75 ("It was... life")?

A) The preservation of life is so instinctive that any law to ensure it would be counterproductive.
B) Laws cannot successfully influence a man's behavior if he is not willing to change his habits.
C) No law can force a man to take care of his health more so than he can by his own volition.
D) Laws that enforce actions that people naturally and willingly do on their own are unnecessary.

6

Which choice provides the best evidence for the answer to the previous question?

A) Lines 3-6 ("In all...fellow-man")
B) Lines 35-38 ("the only...life")
C) Lines 42-45 ("You might...together")
D) Lines 51-52 ("The only...within")

CONTINUE

7

Passage 1 would most likely characterize the claim made in the opening sentence of Passage 2 (lines 62-65") as

A) irrelevant.

B) false.

C) illegal.

D) ambiguous.

8

Which choice provides the best evidence for the answer to the previous question?

A) Lines 8-9 ("Deviations from...revolution")

B) Lines 10-13 ("Lawful liberty...rights")

C) Lines 14-18 ("The right...unconstitutional")

D) Lines 20-23 ("They shrewdly...sale")

9

According to Passage 2, the enforcement of Prohibition

A) is a topic that is of no concern to the advocates of prohibition.

B) has caused the debate over prohibition to drift from its primary concern.

C) needs to be more consistently and fairly applied across the nation.

D) is superseded by a pressing need to enforce more serious crimes.

10

As used in line 78, "attitude" most nearly means

A) stance.

B) reaction.

C) bias.

D) indifference.

89

CONTINUE

Questions 1-10 are based on the following passage.

3.5

This passage is adapted from a speech by Senate Minority Leader Everett Dirksen in which he sought to invoke a senate rule known as "cloture" to bring the debate to a close, thereby allowing a long-overdue vote on the 1964 Civil Rights Bill.

Since the act of 1875 on public accommodations and the Supreme Court decision of 1883 which struck it down, America has changed. The population then
Line was 45 million. Today it is 190 million. In the Pledge
5 of Allegiance to the Flag we intone, "One nation, under God." And so it is. It is an integrated nation. Air, rail, and highway transportation make it so. A common language makes it so. A tax pattern which applies equally to white and nonwhite makes it so.
10 The mobility provided by eighty million autos makes it so. The fair employment practice laws in thirty states make it so. Yes, our land has changed since the Supreme Court decision of 1883. America grows. America changes. And on the civil rights issue we must
15 rise with the occasion. That calls for cloture and for the enactment of a civil rights bill.

There is another reason why we dare not temporize with the issue which is before us. It is essentially moral in character. It must be resolved. Its
20 time has come. Nor is it the first time in our history that an issue with moral implications has swept away the resistance, lamentations and thought patterns of an earlier generation and pushed forward to fruition.

More than sixty years ago came the first efforts
25 to secure federal pure food and drug legislation. The speeches made on this floor against this intrusion of federal power sound fantastically incredible today. But it would not be stayed. Its time had come and since its enactment, it has been expanded and strengthened in
30 nearly every Congress.

When the first efforts were made to ban the shipment of goods in interstate commerce made with child labor, it was regarded as quite absurd. But all the trenchant editorials, the bitter speeches, the noisy
35 onslaughts were swept aside as this limitation on the shipment of goods made with sweated child labor moved on to fulfillment. Its time had come.

More than sixty years ago, the elder La Follette thundered against the election of U.S. senators by the
40 state legislatures. The cry was to get back to the people and to first principles. On this Senate floor, senators sneered at his efforts and even left the chamber to show their contempt. But fifty years ago, the Constitution was amended to provide for the direct election of
45 senators. Its time had come.

Ninety-five years ago came the first endeavor to remove the limitation on sex in the exercise of the franchise. The comments made in those early days sound unbelievably ludicrous. But on and on went the
50 effort and became the Nineteenth Amendment to the Constitution. Its time had come.

These are but some of the things touching closely the affairs of the people which were met with stout resistance, with shrill and strident cries of radicalism,
55 with strained legalisms, with anguished entreaties that the foundations of the Republic were being rocked. But a moral force which operates in the domain of human affairs swept these efforts aside and today they are accepted as parts of the social, economic and political
60 fabric of America.

Pending before us is another moral issue.

The problem began when the Constitution makers permitted the importation of slaves to continue for another twenty years. That problem was to generate
65 the fury of civil strife seventy-five years later. Out of it was to come the Thirteenth Amendment ending servitude, the Fourteenth Amendment to provide equal protection of the laws and dual citizenship, the Fifteenth Amendment to prohibit government from
70 abridging the right to vote.

Other factors had an impact. Two and three-quarter million young Negroes served in World Wars I, II, and Korea. Some won the Congressional Medal of Honor and the Distinguished Service Cross. Today
75 they are fathers and grandfathers. They brought back impressions from countries where no discrimination existed. These impressions have been transmitted to children and grandchildren. Meanwhile, hundreds of thousands of colored have become teachers
80 and professors, doctors and dentists, engineers and architects, artists and actors, musicians and technicians. They have become status minded. They have sensed inequality. They are prepared to make the issue. They feel that the time has come for the
85 idea of equal opportunity in sharing in government, in education, and in employment. It will not be stayed or denied. It is here.

There is no substitute for a basic ideal. We have a firm duty to use the instrument at hand; namely, the
90 cloture rule, to bring about the enactment of a good civil rights bill.

I appeal to all senators. We are confronted with a moral issue. Today let us not be found wanting in whatever it takes by way of moral and spiritual
95 substance to face up to the issue and to vote cloture.

CONTINUE

1

The primary purpose of the speech is to

A) argue that there is no reason for further debate over the Civil Rights Bill.

B) persuade Americans that they must immediately enact the Civil Rights Bill.

C) explain how the Civil Rights Bill follows a historical pattern of increasing rights.

D) contend that the United States has not always closely adhered to its founding principles.

2

Over the course of the speech, Dirksen's focus shifts from

A) an analysis of the relations between citizens and immigrants in the past to an examination of the condition of present racial interactions.

B) an overview of the history of human rights legislation to a discussion of a current issue and the pressing bill that affects it.

C) an exploration of America's reaction to cultural shifts in the past to a prediction of it's reception of important changes going forward.

D) an enumeration of civil rights enactments in the nineteenth century to a conversation of their enforcement at the time the speech was given.

3

As used in line 18, "temporize with" most nearly means

A) procrastinate on.

B) tamper with.

C) mitigate.

D) trivialize.

4

One central idea of the passage is that traditional values

A) should not be used to measure the morality of civil rights legislation except in dire circumstances.

B) may be inherently flawed in their moral foundations, but are necessary for examining the implications of legislation.

C) often appear to be correct before legal and cultural change comes to pass, but will seem immoral after the fact.

D) have played major roles in protecting citizens' rights in the past, but must be receptive to change to remain relevant.

5

Dirksen's discussion of human rights' milestones throughout history is notable for which of the following?

A) Vivid diction that characterizes opposition to the expansion of rights as deeply negative.

B) Slightly humorous anecdotes from the previous debates about the legislation.

C) Dramatic rhetorical questions that imply that legal action has not been timely enough.

D) A controlled tone throughout the dry summary of the opposition's reasoning.

6

As used in line 52, "touching closely" most nearly means

A) enveloping.

B) referencing.

C) adjoining.

D) concerning.

7

Based on the passage, how does Dirksen respond to those who claim that "the foundations of the Republic were being rocked" (line 56) by the Civil Rights Bill?

A) By acknowledging that most Americans already believe it should be included in the Constitution.

B) By arguing that the growing population of immigrants calls for greater rights at the federal level.

C) By citing the fact that American law and culture are neither fixed nor unchanging.

D) By countering with the idea that it is immoral to deny rights to the American majority.

8

Which choice provides the best evidence for the answer to the previous question?

A) Lines 3-4 ("The population … million")

B) Lines 4-6 ("In the … God")

C) Lines 12-15 ("Yes our … occasion")

D) Lines 18-20 ("It is … come")

91

CONTINUE

9

In addition to historical precedents, Dirksen points to which of the following as contributing to the urgency of the Civil Rights Bill?

A) African-Americans becoming the majority in several notable professions.

B) The military granting greater civil rights than the American government.

C) Most Americans becoming frustrated with the lack of progress in civil rights.

D) The African American community demanding an end to its disenfranchisement.

10

Which choice provides the best evidence for the answer to the previous question?

A) Lines 73-75 ("Some won…grandfathers")

B) Lines 78-82 ("Meanwhile, hundreds…technicians")

C) Lines 82-86 ("They have become…employment")

D) Lines 88-91 ("We have...bill.")

STOP

Please turn to next page for answer keys and explanations.

Answer Key: CHAPTER THREE

3.1 | Fisher	3.2 | Deroin	3.3 | Paine	3.4 | Prohibition	3.5 | Dirksen
1: C	1: C	1: B	1: B	1: A
2: C	2: B	2: D	2: A	2: B
3: B	3: B	3: C	3: D	3: A
4: C	4: C	4: C	4: A	4: C
5: D	5: A	5: D	5: B	5: A
6: D	6: D	6: C	6: B	6: D
7: A	7: A	7: D	7: A	7: C
8: A	8: D	8: D	8: C	8: C
9: B	9: D	9: B	9: B	9: D
10: D	10: B	10: C	10: A	10: C

Answer Explanations

Chapter Three

Chapter 3.1 | Fisher

Question 1: C
Choice C is the best answer because Fisher develops her argument by asserting that she wants to "life the shroud of silence which has been draped over the issue of AIDS" (lines 3-4) and that the issue is "not a political creature" (line 18), supporting her claim that AIDS should be seen for what it is: a human issue. Choice A is incorrect because Fisher's examples of demographics afflicted with AIDS are only hypothetical and do not refer to any individual in particular; in fact, the individual stories she shares are those of people who are not struggling with AIDS, such as that of her father (line 44). Choice B is incorrect because Fisher does not merely focus on looking beyond "sexuality": she also calls upon her audience to realize that AIDS "does not care whether you are Democrat or Republican; it does not ask whether you are black or white, male or female, gay or straight, young or old" (lines 19-21). Choice D is incorrect because "condemn" is overly negative for the overall tone of the passage; while Fisher does criticize those who harbor prejudice towards victims of AIDS, she also expresses hope that such prejudice will subside with increased awareness.

Question 2: C
Choice C is the best answer because Fisher argues that the "shroud of silence" has made it unsafe for those with AIDS to "reach out for compassion" (lines 68-69). She further characterizes the shroud as creating "quiet denial" instead of "effective action" (lines 70-71), supporting "unwillingness to confront the crisis". Choices A and B are incorrect because Fisher calls upon members of the Republican party to "lift the shroud of silence" (lines 2-3), but does not imply that they were the "officials" who evoked it to "downplay the extent of the AIDS crisis"; the shroud of silence thus cannot be considered an "unjust action" that was enacted by the government. Choice D is incorrect because the "shroud" is a consequence of the fear and pain felt by those affected by the AIDS crisis and does not describe fear and pain themselves.

Question 3: B
Choice B is the best answer because Fisher continually uses the words "we" "our" and "us" to underscore the responsibility those in her audience share for the suppression of AIDS awareness and the necessity for more proactive tolerance: "we cannot love justice and ignore prejudice, love our children and fear to teach them" (lines 36-37). Moreover, she uses the collective voice again to urge her audience "lift our shroud of silence": "it is our task to seek safety for our children...in

effective action" (lines 68-71), thus "calling her audience to action". Choice A is incorrect because the individual examples such as the "black infant" (lines 22-23) and the "lonely gay man" (line 26) listed by Fisher are not meant to draw attention to effects of the stigma surrounding AIDS, as the reader is not made aware of those effects until the next paragraph, but to the presence of the undeserved stigma itself. Choice C is incorrect because Fisher only quotes Pastor Nemoellor on one occasion. Though she uses an excerpt from his speech to highlight the parallels between the AIDS crisis and another instance of injustice and inaction, these quotes do not appear "throughout" her speech. Choice D is incorrect because "juxtaposition" entails the strategic position of two contrasting examples to highlight their differences, while Fisher places two examples of demographics afflicted with AIDS in order to reveal their underlying similarities: "though I am white and a mother, I am one with a black infant struggling with tubes in a Philadelphia hospital" (lines 22-23).

Question 4: C
Choice C is the best answer because Fisher indicates in lines 61-63 that "not all [other affected by AIDS] have been so blessed" as to have a family like Fisher's which "has been a rock of support"; this matches with "emotional support" and "loyalty". Choice A is incorrect because Fisher never states that she is undergoing treatment, much less that she has had "access to the latest scientific and political initiatives to combat AIDS". Choice B is incorrect because Fisher indicates that she is supported by a loving family, but does not mention how she has been perceived by others in the line references. Choice D is incorrect because although Fisher was not born with a condition or prediction that would increase her likelihood of AIDS, she became afflicted with the disease regardless; she can thus be considered especially unlucky and "disadvantaged" given her circumstances.

Question 5: D
Choice D is the best answer because lines 61-63 are the only line references in which Fisher explicitly admits her position of privilege and that "not all [others affected by AIDS] have been so blessed". Choice A is incorrect because lines 12-15 are off topic; Fisher indicates that there have been "science and research...good intentions and bold initiatives", but does not suggest that she herself was the recipient of such initiatives. Choices B and C are incorrect because Fisher attempts to emphasize her unity with those who might appear to be disadvantaged and her eventual lack of advantage, as she still became afflicted with the same disease as they did in the end: lines 24-27 claims that Fisher "is one" with a marginalized gay man, while lines 41-43 reveal that Fisher's "lack of risk" ultimately proved to be meaningless.

Question 6: D
Choice D is the best answer because Fisher describes those who are affected and suffer from AIDS, or those who are "afflicted" with the disease. Choices A and C are incorrect because "assaults" and "bludgeons" are too literal for the context of the passage, as AIDS does not physically hit or strike its victims. Choice B is incorrect because "targets" entails conscious thought or decision-making, of which AIDS, a disease, is not capable.

Question 7: A
Choice A is the best answer because Fisher begins the third paragraph by emphasizing that "the AIDS virus is not a political creature" (line 18) and is destructive regardless of its victim's identity. She then indicates that despite her differences in circumstances, she "is one" with and thus "faces

the same struggles" as those who are marginalized for their AIDS diagnosis. Choice B is incorrect because Fisher does not "refute the idea" or deny that she has been fortunate: she is "white and a mother" (line 22), and "contracted this disease in marriage and enjoy the warm support of [her] family" (lines 24-25). Choice C is incorrect because Fisher clarifies the analogy with the explanation that "[AIDS] does not care whether you are Democrat or Republican" (lines (19-20); the comparison she's making, then, is between different types of people who may contract the virus, not the harm inflicted. Choice D is incorrect because Fisher only describes the experiences of the victims afflicted with AIDS, not their families; thus, she cannot be "evoking sympathy for the families of those infected by AIDS".

Question 8: A
Choice A is the best answer because Fisher summarizes the "history lesson" embodied by Pastor Nemoeller's quote as "if you believe you are safe, you are at risk" (line 56); the quote thus serves as a warning that ignorance of the AIDS crisis will only put more people at risk and in turn will fail to "solve the crisis". Choice B is incorrect because Fisher parallels the inaction of governments and the public towards the AIDS crisis to the inaction of governments and the public to the Holocaust, not inaction to the Holocaust itself. Choice C is incorrect because Fisher aims to connect the "heinous event" to another catastrophe in modern history and thus does not present Pastor Nemoeller's quote in isolation. Choice D is incorrect because Fisher does not specifically blame "politicians" for furthering the AIDS crisis and thus cannot be "criticizing" them; instead, she calls attention to the need for every American to forgo inaction: "until we genuinely embrace this message, we are a nation of risk" (lines 59-60).

Question 9: B
Choice B is the best answer because lines 33-35 indicate that those who face stigma for their AIDS diagnosis "don't benefit from being isolated or treated as outcasts", implying that such isolation or treatment has actually prevented those infected with AIDS from seeking help. Choices A, C, and D are off topic: lines 28-30 indicate that stereotypes exist, but do not state their effects on those afflicted with AIDS; lines 37-39 encourage the audience to mitigate the damage done by prejudice, but does not describe the damage itself; lines 55-57 warn the audience of future devastation caused by AIDS, but does not address the devastation that has already happened.

Question 10: D
Choice D is the best answer because Fisher asks her audience to have the "strength to act wisely when most we are afraid" (lines 76-77), and to "have courage, and you will find support" (lines 80-81), indicating that she wants both support and courage. Choice A is incorrect because Fisher refers to her children in the passage, but states her vision for the future of all people with regards to their relationship with the AIDS epidemic, not with regards to the future of politics. Choice B is incorrect because Fisher urges her audience to "set aside prejudice and politics to make room for compassion and sound policy" (lines 83-84), which is a personal commitment, not a group commitment such as one held by a "committee". Choice C is incorrect because there is no solution to the "AIDS epidemic worldwide", only a solution to the fear felt about confronting the AIDS epidemic.

Chapter 3.2 | Deroin

Question 1: C
Choice C is the best answer because in lines 87-92 the authors emphasize their overall message about "the power of association based on solidarity" between women and laborers for greater social rights. Choice A is incorrect because, although the authors do make the point that the 1848 revolution failed its principles, the larger claim of the passage is not an analysis of the integrity of the revolution itself. Choice B is incorrect because the authors do not discuss education in any meaningful way. Choice D is incorrect because the unity urged by the authors is that between women and laborers, not that among women of the world.

Question 2: B
Choice B is the best answer because the cause and its principles are described with religious words throughout the passage such as "consecration" (line 31) and "holy" (line 59); moreover, in lines 65-67 the authors state that the unification of laborers and women has "received the true civil baptism" in order to "accomplish the mission of enfranchisement," which means that the only legitimate path forward is through this partnership. Choice A is incorrect because the authors are not pleading their own case to American women. Choice C is incorrect because the authors mention their imprisonment more as an aside than as a grave injustice on which to focus. Choice D is incorrect because they do not suggest that all men are necessarily more entitled than all women.

Question 3: B
See above for further clarification of the best answer. Choice B is correct because the phrase "true civil baptism" indicates that theirs is the only cause with legitimate or elevated value. Choice A is incorrect because the focus of lines 32-34 is on a "fundamental law" rather than the author's cause. Choice C is incorrect because the lines are made up of call for unity under a cause, but do not elevate the value of their cause above other causes. Choice D is incorrect because the lines are a statement of solidarity.

Question 4: C
Choice C is the best answer because the opening of the letter is the summary of a revolution and its failure of women; from there, the authors put forward the idea that an alliance between laborers and suffragettes will rectify the failure. Choice A is incorrect because only one right is discussed in the passage. Choice B is incorrect because the authors do not discuss happiness or the decency of men. Choice D is incorrect because the authors do not have a strong focus on reform tactics in France in the second half of their letter.

Question 5: A
Choice A is the best answer because the authors state that "woman, guided by fraternity, foreseeing incessant struggles, and in hope of putting an end to them, makes an appeal to the laborer to found liberty and equality on fraternal solidarity" (lines 39-42). This action is a response to the stifled liberty, "restrictive laws," and "compression" in lines 37-39. Choice B is incorrect because the laborers' specific interest in equality does not necessarily have to do with male oppression. Choice C is incorrect because the problems for laborers and suffragettes after the revolution were not similar. Choice D is incorrect because the unification of suffragettes and laborers is not centered solely on the needs of the laborers, but rather on the needs of both groups.

Question 6: D

Choice D is the best answer because the authors state that "those selected by the half of the people — by men alone" are responsible for the "restrictive laws." This means that those who were elected were creating the laws. Choice A is incorrect because when "manufacture" is a synonym of "forge" it is in the context of industry rather than legislation. Choice B is incorrect because the authors do not suggest that the laws were not real. Choice C is incorrect because the authors do not imply that anyone other than the elected legislators was responsible for the concepts behind and enactment of the laws; therefore, the laws were not copied.

Question 7: A

Choice A is the best answer because the authors state that the quality in lines 76-79 — the "love of humanity" — is crucial to the "high mission" of enfranchisement. Choices B and D are incorrect because neither resilience nor initiative is suggested as an important quality for universal suffrage. Choice C is incorrect because, although they draw attention to the "pacific character" of the cause in line 44, the authors do not say that peaceful dedication is a quality to use to achieve universal suffrage.

Question 8: D

See above for further clarification of the best answer. Choice D is correct because the authors state that "by the sentiment of the love of humanity" woman will "accomplish her high mission." This is the only choice that shows that the authors identified a quality that can be used to achieve universal suffrage. Choices A and B are incorrect because neither choice shows how to achieve universal suffrage. Choice C is incorrect because it focuses more on the nature of the unity between suffragettes and laborers rather than how to achieve universal suffrage.

Question 9: D

Choice D is the best answer because the authors say that the "Old World" has stopped, or constrained, progress toward equality "in the germ," which means "in its very beginning." Choices A and B are incorrect because "silence" and "subdue" are actions taken against a cause that has had time to grow, but not the cause that the authors discuss here. Choice C is incorrect because the "Old World" is not keeping, or withholding, the "holy work of enfranchisement" from people as much as it is stopping people from taking that work on themselves.

Question 10: B

Choice B is the best answer because the authors devote the second paragraph (lines 11-35) to elaborating on the fact that during and after the 1848 Revolution in France, leaders "forgot to break the chain of the most oppressed of all the pariahs of humanity" (lines 9-10). Throughout the passage, the authors refer to the principles underpinning the revolution in order to show that they are putting forward a cause that follows those principles better than the revolution did. Choice A is incorrect because the authors never state that the values themselves were tarnished by the revolution. Choice C is incorrect because do not emphasize discussion but action on those principles in order to forward their cause. Choice D is incorrect because the authors do not claim that there is a difference between the principles of France and those of the fraternal workers' association (only adherence to those principles), and therefore do not compare the principles themselves.

Chapter 3.3 | Paine

Question 1: B
Choice B is the best answer because Paine argues that "it is not in the power of Britain, or of Europe, to conquer America" (lines 42-43) and that because of its distance and size, the "business of" (line 73) adminsitrating governance in America has proven "too weighty, and intricate" (line 74) for Britain to manage "with any tolerable degree of convenience" (line 75). Paine therefore primarily characterizes Britain as being incapable, or "unequipped", for rule of the colonies. Choice A is incorrect because Paine declares that the American colonies are entitled to self-governance, due to the conditions that disqualify Britain from conducting effective rule, but does not imply that these conditions hold true for "all" territories or that all colonies would be justified in seeking sovereignty. Choice C is incorrect because Paine does not consider the potential "chaos" that might result from continued hostility as a "grievance"; in fact, he sees it as the only way to free the colonies from British rule. Choice D is incorrect because Paine does not indicate that a political uprising has occurred yet; in addition, Paine indicates that "nothing but blows will do" (lines 67-68) in stopping British oppression and thus would not consider such bloodshed "unnecessary".

Question 2: D
Choice D is the best answer because Paine suggests that supporters of British rule "are...only deceiving [themselves]" (line 26); moreover, he implores them to understand the "passions and feelings of mankind" (lines 20-21) and imagine the pain that has been inflicted on families under British control, before stating that since they have neither experienced nor considered such pain, they cannot be the judges "of those who have" (line 38). In urging British sympathizers to reflect on the violence committed against colonial families, Paine is thus pleading for their increased empathy and compassion. Choice A is incorrect because Paine does not accuse supporters of Britain of hypocrisy, since he does not indicate that these supporters have ever claimed allegiance to or love for the colonies. Choice B is incorrect because "traitors" suggests that supporters of British rule have acted against the colonies' interests to actively aid Britain, while Paine argues that they have caused harm by doing nothing and allowing themselves to be guided by their "passive tempers" (line 17). Choice C is incorrect because Paine does not directly label British transgressions against the colonists as "immoral", although he does characterize them as violent and disastrous.

Question 3: C
Choice C is the best answer because Paine states in lines 27-31 that any alliance formed with Britain "will be forced and unnatural, and...formed only on the plan of present convenience", therefore characterizing the reconciliation as insincere and founded only on a short-term basis. He then indicates that such an alliance, unable to be sustained by the colonists, would collapse and lead to "a relapse more wretched than the first", supporting "a resurgence of hostility". Choice A is incorrect because Paine characterizes the policy of reconciliation as entailing the colonists' endurance of oppressive policies conducted by the British, not the adoption of those policies by the colonists themselves. Choice B is incorrect because Paine does not take into consideration the thoughts or opinions of the colonists, only the actions inflicted upon them by the British. Choice D is incorrect because Paine implies that the violence perpetrated by the British would continue in the event of reconciliation, but does not claim that it would get worse, or "escalate".

Question 4: C
Choice C is the best answer because lines 27-31 discuss Paine's prediction of the colonists' "future connection with Britain", which matches with the topic of a "policy of reconciliation" in the previous question. Choice A is incorrect because lines 12-16 refer to men who "think better of the European world than it deserves", but does not specify that these are the same men who would propose a policy of reconciliation. Choices B and D are incorrect because lines 21-25 and lines 31-35 describe the consequences that are occuring now as a result of the colonists' passivity, not the consequences that Paine sees arising in the future.

Question 5: D
Choice D is the best answer because Paine highlights the potential benefits of America "[conquering] herself" (line 44), before explaining that if such a cause were neglected, "the whole continent will partake of the misfortune" (lines 45-47). By emphasizing the potential "misfortune" of the colonists, Paine attempts to make them realize the necessity of the "so precious and useful" (lines 49-50) time they have and reminds them of the "urgency" of the situation. Choice A is incorrect because Paine describes the hardship as occurring not because of America losing the conflict against Britain, but because of America neglecting to pursue a separation in the first place. Choices B and C are incorrect because Paine does not imply that the conflict for the colonies' independence from Britain will be military in nature and therefore does not comment on the likelihood of the colonies succeeding or failing in such a campaign.

Question 6: C
Choice C is the best answer because Paine discusses the inability for the colonists to "dream" (line 57) of reconciliation or "reason" (line 51) a solution for the problem which does not involve separation from Britain; the colonists are thus unable to think of, or "envision" a plan to resolve the current conflict. Choices A and B are incorrect because "navigate" and "direct" both suggest action, while Paine is only concerned with imagining a situation. Choice D is incorrect because "predict" indicates that a plan might be formed in the future, while Paine strongly implies that a plan of reconciliation will never be constructed.

Question 7: D
Choice D is the best answer because Paine suggests that "reconciliation is now a fallacious dream" (line 57) and that, because "wounds of deadly hate have pierced so deep", the colonies have reached a point at which they "can no longer remain subject to any external power" (lines 53-54). Choice A is incorrect because Paine implies that the "wounds of deadly hate" refer to the resentment that the colonists now feel towards Britain, not the animosity that Britain feels towards the colonies. Choice B is incorrect because the lines referenced describe the consequences of oppressive British policies, not those of ongoing efforts to repair relationships with Britain. Choice C is incorrect because Paine does not consider "bloodshed" to be unnecessary; in fact, he states that British rule has forced the colonists to resort to violence, "since nothing but blows will do" (lines 67-68).

Question 8: D
Choice D is the best answer because the sixth paragraph reveals that "every quiet method for peace" (line 61) has already been tried and has proved "ineffectual" (line 62), thus rebutting the argument that appeasement would be the most practical solution to the hostility between Britain and the colonies. Choice A is incorrect because Paine only uses the narcissistic temperment of kings to

support his point about the necessity for a "final separation"; thus, discussion of the kings themselves is not a primary focus of the sixth paragraph. Choice B is incorrect because the sixth paragraph provides an explanation for the colonists' current campaign against Britain (the previous ones did not work), not their previous attempts to reconcile. Choice C is incorrect because Paine does not describe the relationship between the British king and his subjects as "traditional".

Question 9: B
Choice B is the best answer because Paine argues that the "proper objects for kingdoms to take under their care" (line 85) were "small islands not capable of protecting themselves" (lines 83-84). Paine then cites the preposterous nature of the opposite—a small island governing a large expanse of land: "there is something very absurd, in supposing a continent to be perpetually governed by an island" (lines 86-87). Choice A is incorrect because Paine claims that nations should have sovereignty over themselves in lines 91-92 ("it is evident that they belong to different systems: England to Europe, America to itself"), but neglects to extend that same right of representation to "individual" people. Choice C is incorrect because Paine does not discuss the "proper" relationship between the colonizer and the colonized and therefore cannot explain how it has been "distorted". Choice D is incorrect because, although Paine does cite the difficulty of communication as a reason to separate from Britain, it is not supported by any of the line references in the next question.

Question 10: C
Choice C is the best answer because lines 86-87 indicate one of Britain's qualities that make it incapable of governing the American colonies and therefore matches with the topic of the previous question. Choice A is incorrect because lines 73-74 are on topic but do not correspond with any of the choices in the previous question. Choice B is incorrect because lines 82-83 indicate that British rule of the colonies is no longer suitable, but does not specify why. Choice D is incorrect because lines 91-92 state a conclusion that Paine makes after consideration of British governance over the American colonies, but does not comment on the effectiveness of the governance itself.

Chapter 3.4 | Prohibition

Question 1: B
Choice B is the best answer because the author of Passage 1 believes that the Eighteenth Amendment has deceived people by prohibiting the trade and manufacture of alcohol, but not outright explaining that that would in turn restrict the consumption of it. He writes, "what will the American people do when they awaken to a full realization of the fact that the exercise of a personal right...has been or is to be denied them by a trick" (lines 23-27). Choice A is incorrect because technically the American people are not being forced or coerced into to following Prohibition as it was voted on and passed legally. Choice C is incorrect because "legal argumentation" would be the initial and accepted way of attempting to pass an amendment and therefore wouldn't be something they would have to resort to. Choice D is incorrect because the moral argument for Prohibition is the primary and honest argument, whereas "resorting to" something implies turning to a less honorable or desirable strategy to achieve your end; the author of Passage 2 openly admits his attempt at "moral suasion," but never admits, or presumably would admit, an attempt at deceiving people into supporting Prohibition.

Question 2: A
Choice A is the best answer because the answer to the previous question states that the attempt to get Prohibition passed has devolved into a reliance on misleading people, and that is supported by lines 18-20 which state that "the other side seek[s] to accomplish their purpose by indirection." The rest of the choices are incorrect because, while all are directed at proponents of Prohibition, the lines discuss the belief that american's value liberty less because it is something they inherited (Choice B), temptation is the catalyst of desire (Choice C), and the negative effects of drinking can't be cured by the government (Choice D), therefore neglecting the crucial discussion of "indirection" or deception.

Question 3: D
Choice D is the best answer because the "trick" mentioned refers to the way proponents of the Eighteenth Amendment have attempted to get it passed by misleading people about what the amendment is actually restricting, therefore intentionally deceiving or creating a ruse. Choice A is incorrect because, while it does imply a false belief or impression of something, it doesn't imply intentional deception and generally refers to something that is incorrectly perceived and therefore understood through the senses. Choice B is incorrect because it implies something done in order to attract attention or show daring, while the "trick" of Prohibition is supposed to deceive people and is therefore not trying to be noticed. Choice C is incorrect because it implies something done in order to cause amusement, not deceit.

Question 4: A
Choice A is the best answer because Passage 1 cites the fact that no ruler or government has attempted "to prohibit what in itself is not morally wrong" (lines 2-3), suggesting that drinking is not wrong in itself and, therefore, prohibiting it is; he states that "it has been held to be wrong to deny an individual a natural right where its exercise does not conflict with the equal rights of his fellow-man" (lines 4-6). It is additionally correct because Passage 2 states that the protection and well-being of women and children was the main intent of Prohibition, arguing that "the moral quality of the will that voted the nation dry had its origin in a moral and social source. It was an honest desire to protect human life" (lines 73-75). Choice B is incorrect because, while Passage 2 does believe that "the moral significance of the particular Eighteenth Amendment..lies in the fact that it registers the will of the great majority" (lines 62-64), Passage 1 never connect the lack of majority opinion to morality, only to unconstitutionality (lines 16-18). Choice C is incorrect because Passage 1 believes that even the mere restriction of trade in effect restricts "individual[s] natural right[s]" (line 5) and is thus immoral, and Passage 2 believes that Prohibition has actually helped social programs, states that "no other law has worked so great a revolution in social welfare as has Prohibition" (lines 90-92). Choice D is incorrect because Passage 1 never implies that morality is based on the actions of despots, and Passage 2, while discussing the fact of enforcement, does not suggest that that is a measure of the morality or immorality of a law.

Question 5: B
Choice B is the best answer because the main crux of the argument in Passage 1 is that the Eighteenth Amendment is essentially useless because the only way man is going to stop "eating and drinking when and what he wants is his own intellect and his instinctive regard for the preservation of health and life" (lines 37-38), thus supporting the idea that laws are ineffective unless man, in his own right, is willing to adhere to them. Choice A is incorrect because, while the author of Passage 1 does suggest that the preservation of life is instinctive and the law is inadequate, he doesn't go so

far as to claim that Prohibition is working against its own aims or counterproductive. Choice C is incorrect because, in the context of Passage 2 as a whole, the "health" that the author is concerned with is specifically the health of women and children, not the health of the men themselves, therefore making this choice incorrect for its emphasis on the health of men. Choice D is incorrect because it suggests that people will "naturally and willingly" stop drinking on their own, when the author of Passage 1 only suggests that they won't stop drinking just because a law tells them to; the author actually seems to think that man won't stop drinking as he does so "in obedience to a natural law" (lines 34-35).

Question 6: B
Choice B is the best answer because the answer to the previous question states that only man himself can decide to change his habits, which is supported by lines 35-38 as they emphasize that man's own intellect and instinct are "the only power[s] between heaven and earth" (line 35) that are capable of this end. Choice A is incorrect because it only states that no country has attempted to pass or enforce a law like this before, but doesn't discuss any reason as to why. Choice C is incorrect because it just serves to highlight the absurdity of abolishing drinking by comparing it to the abolition of money, which does nothing to show the ineffectual nature of the Prohibition. Choice D is incorrect because, while it mentions that resistance can only come from within, it doesn't account for human life and its preservation.

Question 7: A
Choice A is the best answer because the claim in Passage 2 that Prohibition is moral because the majority is in favor of it would be beside the point for the author of Passage 1 who is more concerned with the constitutionality of the amendment. The author of Passage 1 takes care to point out that "a law prohibiting...the act of eating and drinking itself...would immediately be declared unconstitutional" (lines 15-18) and would never be passed in the first place if it was honestly put to a vote under those terms, which it wasn't. Choice B is incorrect because the author of Passage 1 wouldn't claim that the statement made by Passage 2 is false per se, only that it is true due to "a trick" (line 27). Choice C is incorrect because the claim itself is clearly not illegal. Choice D is incorrect because what the author of Passage 2 is saying in that statement is clear, and therefore not vague or ambiguous, even if they achieved that majority through ambiguous language in the amendment.

Question 8: C
Choice C is the best answer because the answer to the previous question states that the morality of the amendment due to its majority ruling is inconsequential, which is supported by lines 14-18 as they state that, had the amendment been put to a vote as a law prohibiting eating and drinking, it would have been "declared unconstitutional" (line 18). Choices A and B are incorrect for similar reasons because, while they suggest that a law such as Prohibition is wrong (Choice A) and that the protection of the right it is restricting is the reason the constitution exists in the first place (Choice B), they don't encompass the idea that the majority is irrelevant in the case at hand due to the fact that the majority was not actually asked to vote on the real issue. Choice D is incorrect because, while it suggests the deceptive nature of the amendment, it doesn't discuss the issue of a majority decision.

Question 9: B

Choice B is the best answer because the author of Passage 2 argues that whether or not the law is followed has never stopped a law from existing before, going so far as to question "Where on American soil is any law always enforced?" (line 70). He further suggests that to worry over the issue of enforcement is "to permit one's thinking to become befogged" (line 66), thus straying from the primary concern that the author of Passage 2 thinks Prohibition is trying to deal with: the protection of women and children. Choice A is incorrect because, if the topic were of no concern whatsoever, then it would not need to be addressed as minor concern, let alone a concern at all. Choice C is incorrect because it states the opposite of the author's belief that it does not need to be enforced consistently everywhere; he states that "all men admit that the Eighteenth Amendment is not enforced always and everywhere" (lines 68-69). Choice D is incorrect because, while he mentions the more pressing crime of murder, it is to suggest that laws prohibiting more serious crimes are also unable to be enforced consistently everywhere.

Question 10: A

Choice A is the best answer because it refers to the way a person or society views something or someone, thus encompassing the overarching standpoint of a people "towards mothers and their young" (lines 78-79). Choice B is incorrect because it implies a response to a specific event, and thus does allow for a more pervasive understanding of the attitude a society as a whole has toward women and children. Choice C is incorrect because it suggests a preference for women and children, or partiality toward them, while in context the "attitude" referred to could be positive or negative. Choice D is incorrect for a similar reason because it suggests a lack of interest in women and children, which is a specific type of attitude, and doesn't account for the potentially overarching aspect of the word attitude.

Chapter 3.5 | Dirksen

Question 1: A

Choice A is the best answer because throughout the passage, Dirksen references former issues in which the Senate debated and eventually passed controversial issues. Furthermore, he asserts that "on the civil rights issue [the Senate] must rise with the occasion. That calls for cloture and the enactment of a civil rights bill." (lines 14-16). Choice B is incorrect because Dirksen is addressing the Senate (as he says "I appeal to all senators"in line 92), not the American people. Choice C is incorrect because while Dirksen does show throughout the passage that the Civil Rights Bill follows a historical pattern of increasing rights, his purpose is not to show how that happened; in fact, the only explanation of the way each other right was granted that Dirksen offers is "its time had come" (line 28). Choice D is incorrect because although Dirksen does state that "America has changed" (line 3) in the first paragraph, he does not claim that these changes have caused Americans to stray from their founding principles. He actually states that Americans do adhere to the important principle of unity, or, as he cites, "one nation, under God" (lines 5-6).

Question 2: B

Choice B is the best answer because the passage begins with Dirksen citing relevant history of the United States including the ways in which it has changed in order to show how the current bill is important; in the following paragraphs, he enumerates several bills that seemed unpopular at first but were passed because the attitudes of former generations passed; finally, he pivots back to the current bill, saying "pending before us is another moral issue" (line 61) before listing recent events that make the civil rights bill urgent at this point in time, including that "two and three-quarter million young Negroes served in World Wars I, II, and Korea." (lines 71-73) and "hundreds of thousands of colored have become teachers and professors, doctors and dentists, engineers and architects, artists and actors, musicians and technicians. They have become status minded" (lines 78-82). Choice A is incorrect because Dirksen does not analyze relations between citizens and immigrants in the past; rather, he discusses past issues and the legislation that was passed to resolve them. Choice C is incorrect because Dirksen does not predict how America will receive future cultural shifts; he addresses the way that Americans should receive the current civil rights issue. Choice D is incorrect because no laws were enforced at the time of Dirksen's speech.

Question 3: A
Choice A is the best answer because the point Dirksen is making is that the bill's "time has come" (line 20), indicating that "temporize with the issue" (line 18) means wait too long to pass the bill. Choice B is incorrect because tampering with the bill would mean changing it but Dirksen doesn't indicate at any time in the speech that anyone is attempting to change the bill; he only wants Senators to change their minds and pass the bill. Choices C and D are incorrect because while mitigating or trivializing the bill are actions that Dirksen would not want to happen, they are not supported by the context of the paragraph. Specifically, the evidence in the next two sentences supporting why "we should not temporize with the issue": the bill is moral and its time has come.

Question 4: C
Choice C is the best answer because Dirksen argues that there is a pattern in the United States of changing past beliefs about certain issues of moral character and moving toward more inclusive ideas. He contends that, "Nor is this the first time in our history that an issue with moral implications has swept away the resistance, lamentations and thought patterns of an earlier generation" (lines 20-23). He goes on to describe a series of issues of which this has been the case, emphasizing the turning point by repetition of the phrase, "Its time had come." Choice A is incorrect because Dirksen doesn't suggest that it is acceptable to measure morality on traditional values in any circumstances, as his entire point is that the morality of the past is continually being revised and made more inclusive. Choice B is incorrect because as the word "necessary" implies that Dirksen is in support of the existence of our past beliefs, when in reality he seems to suggest that the only necessary aspect of them is that they be "swept away" so as to make way for new and more morally aligned legislation. Choice D is incorrect because, while he does believe that traditional values must be receptive to change, he doesn't suggest that they have ever protected the rights of citizens, but instead suggests that they have played a role in prolonging the curtailment of such rights.

Question 5: A
Choice A is the best answer because Dirksen uses phrases such as "fantastically incredible" (line 27), "sneered" (lines 41-42), "unbelievably ludicrous" (line 49), and "stout resistance" (lines 53-54) to describe the way that members of the Senate responded to previous legislation, indicating that the reactions were negative prior to the passing of each bill. Choice B is incorrect because throughout the passage Dirksen uses an urgent and serious tone and he does not ever shift to humor. Choice C is incorrect because there are no questions in the speech. Choice D is incorrect because while Dirksen does use a controlled tone, his characterizations of the opposition's reactions is not dry; in fact, the diction used by Dirksen colors his argument to make it clear that

Question 6: D
Choice D is the best answer because refers to the list of legislation that has been passed in order to correct morally corrupt beliefs, and suggests that that is a list of the things that concern "the affairs of the people" (line 53). Choice A and C are incorrect for similar reasons as they both imply the physical engulfing (Choice A) or nearness (Choice C) rather than the conceptual notion of being on the topic of or about something. Choice B is incorrect because it isn't only alluding to or mentioning the issues at hand but directly explaining them and how they are connected to the greater problem of morality and progress.

Question 7: C
Choice C is the best answer because the majority of the passage is focused on establishing a historical precedent of change and progress, of revision to societal mindset and laws; Dirksen argues that "America grows. America changes. And on the civil rights issue we must rise with the occasion" (lines 13-15), therefore supporting the idea that our foundations are not being "rocked" as they were not fixed in the first place. Choice A is incorrect because the word "already" suggests that Dirksen's speech is redundant due to the fact that people already agree with him, when in fact they don't and this speech is an attempt to force the Senate into a vote on a topic they want to avoid. Choice B is incorrect because it assumes that immigrants are the ones calling for change when in reality it is the former slaves who have already achieved their rights as citizens and now want equal civil rights enshrined in law as well. Choice D is incorrect because it implies that the Civil Rights Bill will only ensure the rights of the majority, when its goal is to ensure rights for all.

Question 8: C
Choice C is the best answer because the answer to the previous question states that America is constantly changing and progressing and that therefore the "foundations of the Republic" are not being rocked, which is supported by lines 12-15 as they directly state that America "grows" and "changes." Choice A is incorrect because, while it highlights a change in America, it focuses on a population change which does not relate to the issue of increasing rights and morality in our laws and culture. Choice B is incorrect because it merely states that we are one nation, and neglects any discussion of our progress and change. Choice D is incorrect because, while it states the morality of the Civil Rights Bill, it also fails to emphasize the history of change in America.

Question 9: D
Choice D is the best answer because, in the final paragraph, Dirksen makes the additional point that, not only has the time come in the general sense, but African Americans themselves "feel that time has come...It will not be stayed or denied. It is here" (lines 84-87), which highlights the urgency of the issue as felt by African Americans as well. Choice A is incorrect because, while Dirksen does state that African Americans have attained many notable professions (lines 78-82), he doesn't suggest that they have become the majority in those fields. Choice B is incorrect because being allowed to serve in war and win medals of honor doesn't necessarily mean that they are afforded greater civil rights in the army and is never stated in the passage. Choice C is incorrect because, in the context of the passage as a whole, the suggestion that most americans want this bill is absurd, as if they did it would be an easy and clear vote and his speech would be unnecessary.

Question 10: C
Choice C is the best answer because the answer to the previous question states that African Americans themselves are now using their voices to demand an end to inequality against them, which is supported by lines 82-86 that state, "They have sensed inequality. They are prepared to make the issue." The rest of the choices are incorrect because, while they discuss the military (Choice A), good professions (Choice B), and the morality of the Civil Rights Bill (Choice D), they all fail to suggest any sense of urgency in the resolution of the issue.

Chapter Four

Questions 1-10 are based on the following passage.

4.1

This passage is adapted from Carrie Chapman Catt, "The Crisis." Originally delivered in 1916.

Behind us, in front of us, everywhere about us are suffragists - millions of them, but inactive and silent. They have been "agitated and educated" and are with us in belief. There are thousands of women
5 who have at one time or another been members of our organization but who have dropped out because, to them, the movement seemed negative and pointless. Many have taken up other work whose results were more immediate. Philanthropy, charity, work for
10 corrective laws of various kinds, temperance, relief for working women and numberless similar public services have called them. Others have turned to the pleasanter avenues of clubwork, art or literature.

There are thousands of other women who have
15 never learned of the earlier struggles of our movement. They found doors of opportunity open to them on every side. They found well-paid posts awaiting the qualified woman and they have availed themselves of all these blessings; almost without exception they
20 believe in the vote but they feel neither gratitude to those who opened the doors through which they have entered to economic liberty nor any sense of obligation to open other doors for those who come after.

There are still others who, timorously looking over
25 their shoulders to see if any listeners be near, will tell us they hope we will win and win soon but they are too frightened of Mother Grundy to help. There are others too occupied with the small things of life to help. They say they could find time to vote but not to work for
30 the vote. There are men, too, millions of them, waiting to be called. These men and women are our reserves. They are largely unorganized and untrained soldiers with little responsibility toward our movement. Yet these reserves must be mobilized. The final struggle
35 needs their numbers and the momentum those numbers will bring. Were never another convert made, there are suffragists enough in this country, if combined, to make so irresistible a driving force that victory might be seized at once.
40 How can it be done? By a simple change of mental attitude. If we are to seize the victory, that change must take place in this hall, here and now!

The old belief, which has sustained suffragists in many an hour of discouragement, "woman suffrage
45 is bound to come," must give way to the new, "The Woman's Hour has struck." The long drawn out

struggle, the cruel hostility which, for years was arrayed against our cause, have accustomed suffragists to the idea of indefinite postponement but eventual
50 victory. The slogan of a movements sets its pace. The old one counseled patience; it said there is plenty of time; it pardoned sloth and half-hearted effort. It set the pace of an educational campaign. The "Woman's Hour has struck" sets the pace of a crusade which will have
55 its way. It says: "Awake, arise, my sisters, let your hearts be filled with joy. The time of victory is here. Onward March."

If you believe with me that a crisis has come to our movement, if you believe that the time for final
60 action is now, if you catch the rosy tints of the coming day, what does it mean to you? Does it not give you a thrill of exaltation; does the blood not course more quickly through your veins; does it not bring a new sense of freedom, of joy and of determination? Is it
65 not true that you who wanted a little time ago to lay down the work because you were weary with long service, now, under the compelling influence of a changed mental attitude, are ready to go on until the vote is won. The change is one of spirit! Aye, and the
70 spiritual effect upon you will come to others. Let me borrow an expression from Hon. John Finlay: "What our great movement needs now is a mobilization of spirit, - the jubilant, glad spirit of victory." Then let us sound a bugle call here and now to the women of
75 the Nation: "The Woman's Hour has struck." Let the bugle sound from the suffrage headquarters of every State at the inauguration of a State campaign. Let the call go forth again and, again and yet again. Let it be repeated in every article written, in every speech made,
80 in every conversation held. Let the bugle blow again and yet again. The Political emancipation of our sex calls you, women of America, arise! Are you content that others shall pay the price of your liberty? Women in schools and counting house, in shops and on the
85 farm, women in the home with babes at their breasts and women engaged in public careers will hear. The veins of American women are not filled with milk and water. They are neither cowards nor slackers. They will come. They only await the bugle call to learn that the
90 final battle is on.

CONTINUE

1

Catt's main purpose in this passage is to

A) highlight the milestones of a national movement.

B) stress the momentous and pressing nature of a matter at hand.

C) criticize the former members of her organization.

D) enlist the support of men in a cause that benefits women.

2

Which choice best summarizes the third paragraph (lines 24-39)?

A) A discussion of the suffrage movement in the armed forces

B) A plea to win over the opponents of women's suffrage

C) An appeal to the collective conscience of passive supporters

D) An optimistic prediction for the outcome of the suffrage movement.

3

Which statement provides the best description of a technique Catt uses throughout the passage to advance her main point?

A) She presents claims in the form of rhetorical questions that mostly have implicit negative answers.

B) She compares the suffrage movement to a battle that can only be won by stimulating the nation's morale.

C) She illustrates the importance of her central ideas by ending each with an emotionally powerful anecdote.

D) She emphasizes the logic behind her arguments by supporting them with universally accepted facts.

4

In context, what is the main effect of the author's repeated reference to the "bugle call" in the final paragraph?

A) It engenders a feeling of sympathy.

B) It creates a sense of urgency.

C) It instills a spirit of honor.

D) It provokes a state of intimidation.

5

Over the passage, author's main focus shifts from

A) drawing attention to the large number of inactive suffragists to a call for their active involvement in the cause.

B) detailing the reasons behind the dwindling membership of the suffrage movement to a rebuke of those reasons.

C) describing the various forms of opposition faced by the suffrage movement to a discussion of how to overcome such resistance.

D) celebrating the recent achievements of the suffrage movement to a warning against becoming complacent in its final hour of victory.

6

As used in line 48, "arrayed" most nearly means

A) aligned.

B) displayed.

C) marshalled.

D) presented.

7

As used in line 43, "sustained" most nearly means

A) comforted.

B) reinforced.

C) maintained.

D) endured.

8

Which choice provides the best evidence for Catt's claim that some women have become impatient with the suffrage movement?

A) Lines 4-9, ("There are...immediate")

B) Lines 14-14 ("There are … movement")

C) Lines 27-28, ("There are … help")

D) Lines 50-52, ("The old … effort")

CONTINUE

9

The passage states that one consequence of the current success of the suffrage movement is that

A) it has opened the way for the enactment of laws that will protect women's rights, including the right to vote.

B) it has afforded greater participation to women throughout the country in the affairs of government and business.

C) it has alienated a number of supporters who have become intimidated by its opponents and who fear a negative backlash.

D) it has created a class of women who have been empowered by the movement's efforts but who do not contribute to it in any way.

10

Which choice provides the best evidence for the answer to the previous question?

A) Lines 17-23, ("They found…after")

B) Lines 24-27 ("There are … help")

C) Lines 36-39, ("Were never … once")

D) Lines 83-86, ("Women in … hear")

CONTINUE

Questions 1-10 are based on the following passage.

4.2

This passage is adapted from Stephen A. Douglas' speech delivered in Chicago on May 1st, 1861.

That the present danger is imminent, no man can conceal. If war must come—if the bayonet must be used to maintain the Constitution—I can say, before
Line God, my conscience is clean. I have struggled long for
5 a peaceful solution to the difficulty. I have not only tendered those States what was theirs of right, but I have gone to the very extreme of magnanimity.

The return we receive is war, armies marched upon our capital, obstructions and dangers to our
10 navigation, letters of marque to invite pirates to prey upon our commerce, a concerted movement to blot out the United States of America from the map of the globe. The question is, are we to maintain the country of our fathers, or allow it to be stricken down by those
15 who, when they can no longer govern, threaten to destroy?

What cause, what excuse do disunionists give us for breaking up the best Government on which the Sun of heaven ever shed its rays? They are dissatisfied with
20 the result of a Presidential election. Did they never get beaten before? Are we to resort to the sword when we get defeated at the ballot box? I understand it that the voice of the people expressed in the mode appointed by the Constitution must command the obedience
25 of every citizen. They assume, on the election of a particular candidate, that their rights are not safe in the Union. What evidence do they present of this? I defy any man to show any act on which it is based. What act has been omitted? I appeal to these assembled
30 thousands that, so far as the constitutional rights of the Southern States - the constitutional rights of slaveholders - are concerned, nothing has been done, and nothing omitted, of which they can complain.

If they say the Territorial question, there is no act
35 of Congress prohibiting slavery anywhere. If it be the non-enforcement of the laws, the only complaints that I have heard have been of the too vigorous and faithful fulfillment of the Fugitive Slave Law. Then what reason have they?
40 The Slavery question is a mere excuse. The election of Lincoln is a mere pretext. The present secession movement is the result of an enormous conspiracy formed, more than a year since, by leaders in the Southern Confederacy. They use the Slavery
45 question as a means to aid the accomplishment of

their ends. They desired the election of a Northern candidate, by a sectional vote, in order to show that the two sections cannot live together.

But this is no time for a detail of causes. The
50 conspiracy is now known. Armies have been raised, war is levied to accomplish it. There are only two sides to the question: every man must be for the United States, or against it. There can be no neutrals in this war, only patriots or traitors.
55 We cannot close our eyes to the sad and solemn fact that war does exist. The Government must be maintained, its enemies overthrown, and the more stupendous our preparations the less the bloodshed, and the shorter the struggle.
60 The Constitution and its guarantees are our birthright, and I am ready to enforce that inalienable right to the last extent. We cannot recognize secession. Recognize it once, and you have not only dissolved government, but you have destroyed social order—
65 upturned the foundations of society. You have inaugurated anarchy in its worst form, and will shortly experience all the horrors of the French Revolution.

Then we have a solemn duty to maintain the Government. The greater our unanimity, the speedier
70 the day of peace. We have prejudices to overcome from the few short months since of a fierce party contest. Yet these must be allayed. Let us lay aside all criminations and recriminations as to the origin of these difficulties. When we shall have again a country with the United
75 States flag floating over it, and respected on every inch of American soil, it will then be time enough to ask who and what brought all this upon us.

I have said more than I intended to say. It is a sad task to discuss questions so fearful as civil war; but
80 sad as it is, bloody and disastrous as I expect it will be, I express it as my conviction before God that it is the duty of every American citizen to rally around the flag of his country.

CONTINUE

1

The main purpose of the passage is to

A) explain that the Constitution protects the rights of all citizens regardless of the party in power.

B) frame the attempt by the Confederate States to secede from the Union as a violation of the Constitution.

C) remind Americans that neutrality is not an option at a time when the nation is threatened.

D) rally the support of Northern States for a righteous war that will end slavery in the Southern States.

2

Which best describes Douglas' attitude towards the Southern States?

A) Universal anger toward Southerners as participants in the conspiracy of secession.

B) Disapproval of their unjustified and hostile stance following the presidential election.

C) Sympathy for those who fear the government of the United States after the presidential election.

D) Grudging respect for the right of Southerners to engage in the immorality of slavery.

3

Which choice provides the best evidence for the answer to the previous question?

A) Lines 4-7 ("I have…magnanimity")

B) Lines 17-20 ("What cause…election")

C) Lines 41-44 ("The present…Confederacy")

D) Lines 70-72 ("We have…allayed")

4

As used in line 8, the word "return" most nearly means

A) retaliation.

B) response.

C) report.

D) resurgence.

5

The second paragraph (lines 8-16) primarily serves to

A) discount the arguments made by Southern States for secession.

B) challenge potential arguments made in favor of a peaceful resolution.

C) demonstrate the severity of the current crisis faced by the United States.

D) outline the progression of events that marked the outbreak of the Civil War.

6

Which choice provides the best evidence for Douglas' claim that disunionists have overreacted to the results of a recent election?

A) Lines 20-22 ("Did they never…ballot box")

B) Lines 25-27 ("They assume…Union")

C) Lines 34-35 ("If they say…anywhere")

D) Lines 40-41 ("The Slavery question…pretext")

7

As used in line 27, the word "defy" most nearly means

A) resist.

B) disobey.

C) confront.

D) challenge.

8

Over the course of the passage, Douglas shifts his focus from a discussion of divisive issues to

A) a comparison of secession to the outcome of the French Revolution.

B) a description of American politics in cautionary yet favorable terms.

C) a romanticized depiction of war as the greatest expression of patriotic duty.

D) a rallying call for a strong military response as a way to hasten peace.

CONTINUE

9

In describing his efforts to reach a peaceful resolution with the Southern States, Douglas presents himself as having

A) exhausted all diplomatic options.

B) given a reasonable ultimatum.

C) transgressed Constitutional boundaries.

D) dismissed all offers made in bad faith.

10

Throughout lines 68-77 ("Then we…us") Douglas asserts that

A) the transgressions of the Southern States will forever be irredeemable.

B) both sides have equal responsibility in the events that led to the war.

C) assigning blame should be postponed until after the war is resolved.

D) national self-reflection will be necessary to prevent any future conflicts.

CONTINUE

Questions 1-10 are based on the following passage.

4.3

The following passage is adapted from a speech delivered on May 18, 1941, during an "I am an American Day" gathering in Central Park, N.Y., by U.S. Secretary of the Interior Harold L. Ickes. At that time, the U.S. had not yet joined Great Britain in its fight against Nazi world domination.

For years it has been dinned into us that we are a weak nation; that we are an inefficient people; that we are simple-minded. For years we have been told
Line that we are beaten, decayed, and that no part of the
5 world belongs to us any longer. Some amongst us have fallen for this carefully pickled tripe. Some amongst us have begun to preach that the "wave of the future" has passed over us and left us a wet, dead fish. They shout from public platforms, in printed pages, through
10 the microphones, that it is futile to oppose the "wave of the future." They cry that we Americans -- we free Americans nourished on Magna Carta and the Declaration of Independence -- hold moth-eaten ideas. They exclaim that there is no room for free men in the
15 world anymore and that only the slaves will inherit the earth. America -- the America of Washington and Jefferson and Lincoln and Walt Whitman -- they say, is waiting for the undertaker and all the hopes and aspirations that have gone into the making of America
20 are dead too.

I say that it is time for the great American people to raise their voices and cry out in mighty triumph what it is to be an American. What constitutes an American? Not color nor race nor religion. Not the
25 pedigree of his family nor the place of his birth. Not the coincidence of his citizenship. Not his social status nor his bank account. Not his trade nor his profession. An American is one who loves justice and believes in the dignity of man. An American is one who will fight
30 for his freedom and that of his neighbor. An American is one who will sacrifice his property, ease, and security in order that he and his children may retain the rights of free men. An American is one in whose heart is engraved the immortal second sentence of the
35 Declaration of Independence.

We Americans know that freedom, like peace, is indivisible. We cannot retain our liberty if three-fourths of the world is enslaved. If we are to retain our own freedom, we must do everything within our power to
40 aid Britain. We must also do everything to restore to the conquered peoples their freedom. This means the Germans too. We should be clear on this point. What

is convulsing the world today is not merely another old-fashioned war. It is a counter-revolution against
45 our ideals, against our sense of justice and our human values.

Three systems today compete for world domination: communism, fascism, and democracy. As the conflict sharpens, it becomes clear that the
50 other two -- fascism and communism -- are merging into one. They have one common enemy, democracy. This is why this war is not an ordinary war. It is not a conflict for markets or territories. It is a desperate struggle for the possession of the souls of men.
55 Today in Europe, the Nazi Attila may gloat that he has destroyed democracy. He is wrong. In small farmhouses all over Central Europe, in the shops of Germany and Italy, on the docks of Holland and Belgium, freedom still lives in the hearts of men. It
60 will endure like a hardy tree gone into the wintertime, awaiting the spring.

We, free, democratic Americans are in a position to help. We know that the spirit of freedom never dies. We know that men have fought and bled for freedom
65 since time immemorial. We realize that the liberty-loving German people are only temporarily enslaved. We do not doubt that the Italian people are looking forward to the appearance of another Garibaldi. We know how the Poles have for centuries maintained a
70 heroic resistance against tyranny. We remember the brave struggle of the Hungarians under Kossuth and other leaders. We recall the heroic figure of Masaryk and the gallant fight for freedom of the Czech people. The story of the Yugoslavs', especially the Serbs'
75 blows for liberty and independence, is a saga of extraordinary heroism. The Greeks will stand again at Thermopylae, as they have in the past.

Here in America, we have something so worth living for that it is worth dying for! The so-called
80 "wave of the future" is but the slimy backwash of the past. We have not heaved from our necks the tyrant's crushing heel only to stretch our necks out again for its weight. Not only will we fight for democracy, we will make it more worth fighting for. Under our free
85 institutions, we will work for the good of mankind, including Hitler's victims in Germany, so that all may have plenty and security.

116

CONTINUE

This passage can best be described as

A) a dramatic exultation.

B) a formal request.

C) a fervent call to action.

D) a stern reproach.

2

Over the course of this passage, the main focus shifts from

A) a forthright depiction of a mindset to an explanation of its inaccuracy.

B) a detailing of America's faults to a proposal on how they can be overcome.

C) a condemnation of a weak America to an approval of a strong Europe.

D) an analysis of a viewpoint to an objective rejection of its premise.

3

The passage suggests that the Americans who believe in the "wave of the future"(line 7) have claimed that other Americans

A) have become downtrodden and disillusioned with their country.

B) are easily manipulated with the false promises of democracy.

C) compromise the safety of their country through their ignorance.

D) cling stubbornly to their ideals even in the face of progress.

4

In context of the first paragraph, the phrases in lines 11-13 ("we free…Independence") and lines 16-17 ("the America…Whitman") primarily serve which purpose?

A) They reveal the author's true sentiments about a previous statement.

B) They highlight the absurdity of a viewpoint with which the author disagrees.

C) They juxtapose the author's opinions with those held by his critics.

D) They provide examples that the author considers useful in defining a group.

5

What point does Ickes seek to convey in the second paragraph (lines 21-35)?

A) Americans have always understood that personal sacrifice is instrumental to the wellbeing of their nation.

B) Americans are proud of their prosperous nation because its success results from the rich diversity of its citizens.

C) Americans are united in their unwavering devotion to the pursuit of justice and freedom.

D) Americans gain fulfillment through the achievement of their ideals rather than through the accumulation of wealth.

6

As used in line 37, "indivisible" most nearly means

A) absolute.

B) uncompromising.

C) integral.

D) indestructible.

7

Ickes would most likely agree with which statement about freedom?

A) Those who fight for freedom have the advantage over those who fight for pay.

B) Although freedom can be pushed into dormancy, it will inevitably resurface.

C) No cause can raise an army of volunteers as effectively as can a struggle for freedom.

D) Most rebellions throughout history have been reactions against threats to freedom.

8

Which choice provides the best evidence for the answer to the previous question?

A) Lines 29-30 ("An American…neighbor")

B) Lines 44-46 ("It is…values")

C) Lines 56-59 ("In small…men")

D) Lines 59-61 ("It will…spring")

CONTINUE

9

Throughout the passage, Ickes makes use of which rhetorical device?

A) Personal Anecdotes

B) Understatement

C) Sarcasm

D) Metaphor

10

Which choice provides the best evidence for Ickes' claim that Nazi Germany will not win the "struggle for the possession for the souls of men" (line 54)?

A) Lines 55-56 ("Today in…wrong")

B) Lines 64-66 ("We know…enslaved")

C) Lines 79-81 ("The so-called…past")

D) Lines 85-87 ("we will..security")

CONTINUE

Questions 1-10 are based on the following passage.

4.4

This passage is adapted from "Progress and Poverty," written by Henry George, and published in 1898.

The present century has been marked by a prodigious increase in wealth-producing power. The utilization of steam and electricity, the introduction of
Line improved processes and labor-saving machinery, the
5 greater subdivision and grander scale of production, the wonderful facilitation of exchanges, have multiplied enormously the effectiveness of labor. At the beginning of this marvelous era it was natural to expect that labor-saving inventions would lighten the toil and
10 improve the condition of the laborer; that the enormous increase in the power of producing wealth would make real poverty a thing of the past.

It is true that wealth has been greatly increased, and that the average of comfort, leisure, and refinement
15 has been raised; but these gains are not general. In them the lowest class do not share. I do not mean that the condition of the lowest class has nowhere nor in anything been improved; but that there is nowhere any improvement which can be credited to increased
20 productive power. I mean that the tendency of what we call material progress is in no way to improve the condition of the lowest class in the essentials of healthy, happy human life. Nay, more, that it is still further to depress the condition of the lowest class.
25 The new forces, elevating in their nature though they be, do not act upon the social fabric from underneath, as was for a long time hoped and believed, but strike it at a point intermediate between top and bottom. It is as though an immense wedge were being forced, not
30 underneath society, but through society. Those who are above the point of separation are elevated, but those who are below are crushed down.

From all parts of the civilized world come complaints of industrial depression; of labor
35 condemned to involuntary idleness; of capital massed and wasting; of pecuniary distress among business men; of want and suffering and anxiety among the working classes. All the dull, deadening pain, all the keen, maddening anguish, that to great masses of men
40 are involved in the words "hard times," afflict the world to-day.

This association of poverty with progress is the great enigma of our times. It is the central fact from which spring industrial, social, and political difficulties
45 that perplex the world, and with which statesmanship and philanthropy and education grapple in vain. All-important as this question is, pressing itself from every quarter painfully upon attention, it has not yet received a solution which accounts for all the facts and points
50 to any clear and simple remedy. This is shown by the widely varying attempts to account for the prevailing depression. Upon high economic authority, we have been told that it is due to overconsumption; upon equally high authority, that it is due to overproduction;
55 while the wastes of war, the extension of railroads, the attempts of workmen to keep up wages, the demonetization of silver, the issues of paper money, the increase of laborsaving machinery, the opening of shorter avenues to trade, etc., are separately pointed
60 out as the cause by writers of reputation.

And while professors thus disagree, the ideas that there is a necessary conflict between capital and labor, that machinery is an evil, that competition must be restrained and interest abolished, that wealth
65 may be created by the issue of money, that it is the duty of government to furnish capital or to furnish work, are rapidly making way among the great body of the people, who keenly feel a hurt and are sharply conscious of a wrong. Such ideas, which bring great
70 masses of men, the repositories of ultimate political power, under the leadership of charlatans and demagogues, are fraught with danger.

The poverty which in the midst of abundance pinches and imbrutes men, and all the manifold evils
75 which flow from it, spring from a denial of justice. In permitting the monopolization of the opportunities which nature freely offers to all, we have ignored the fundamental law of justice. These rights are denied when the equal right to land—on which and by which
80 men alone can live—is denied. Political liberty, when the equal right to land is denied, becomes, as population increases and invention goes on, merely the liberty to compete for employment at starvation wages. And so there come beggars in our streets and tramps on
85 our roads; and poverty enslaves men whom we boast are political sovereigns.

But by sweeping away this injustice and asserting the rights of all men to natural opportunities, we shall conform ourselves to the law—we shall remove the
90 great cause of unnatural inequality in the distribution of wealth and power; we shall abolish poverty; tame the ruthless passions of greed; dry up the springs of vice and misery; light in dark places the lamp of knowledge; give new vigor to invention and a fresh
95 impulse to discovery; substitute political strength for political weakness; and make tyranny and anarchy impossible.

CONTINUE ➡

1

Which choice best describes the developmental pattern of the passage?

A) He begins by listing the technological and business changes of the 19th century, goes on to describe how they have changed the lives of poor Americans, and ends by pushing for future technological changes to end poverty.

B) He begins by discussing recent business innovations and their potential benefits for society, goes on to discuss societal problems caused by immoral use of these innovations, and finally calls for sweeping societal change.

C) He begins with a discussion of recent social upheaval in the United States, goes on to discuss its causes, then pushes for governmental reform to prevent future instability.

D) He begins by comparing and contrasting life before and after the industrial revolution, then describes the benefits and drawbacks of both pre-industrial and industrial living for lower-class Americans, and finally comes to the conclusion that such individuals were better off before industrialization.

2

As used in line 15, "general" most nearly means

A) widespread.

B) traditional.

C) usual.

D) popular.

3

In context of the second paragraph, lines 16-20 ("I do… power") serve which purpose?

A) They anticipate and correct a potential misinterpretation of the author's argument.

B) They acknowledge a valid counterargument and admit a limitation to the author's claim.

C) They illustrate the unprecedented nature of the situation described by the author.

D) They address and refute a popular misconception about the current state of affairs.

4

To what does George state that all men are entitled but are currently being denied?

A) Money

B) Land

C) Political representation

D) Safe working conditions

5

Which choice provides the best evidence for the answer to the previous question?

A) Lines 7-10 ("At the beginning...laborer")

B) Lines 13-15 ("It is...general")

C) Lines 33-38 ("From all...classes")

D) Lines 78-80 ("These rights...denied")

6

The author believes that the relationship between the mechanical and business innovations of the 19th century and the average person's economic situation is

A) paradoxical and indefensible.

B) understandable and expected.

C) upsetting but necessary.

D) unsurprising but inexplicable.

7

Which of the following does George NOT mention as a theorized cause of increased poverty after industrialization?

A) The conversions made in the issue and type of currency

B) The overspending by the government on war and infrastructure

C) The absence of a federal minimum wage for industrial workers

D) The automatization of work formerly done by humans

CONTINUE

8

Which choice provides the best evidence for George's claim that movements against the circumstances caused by industrial progress are equally destructive?

A) Lines 46-50 ("All-important as…remedy")

B) Lines 69-72 ("Such ideas…danger")

C) Lines 73-75 ("The poverty…justice")

D) Lines 84-86 ("And so…sovereigns")

9

With which of the following statements would the author most likely agree?

A) The government has failed in its duty to ensure that citizens do not fall into poverty.

B) Political liberty is rendered meaningless in an environment of widespread poverty.

C) Industrialization must be reversed to a degree in order to increase employment and thus decrease poverty.

D) Destitute individuals could better their circumstances by embracing technological advancements.

10

As used in line 88, "natural" most nearly means

A) organic.

B) valid.

C) inherent.

D) fair.

CONTINUE

Questions 1-10 are based on the following passage.

4.5

In the years immediately following the Civil War, Congress began efforts to secure rights for former slaves. Their first attempt—the Civil Rights Act of 1866—met with considerable resistance from President Andrew Johnson. Passage 1 is adapted from President Johnson's Veto Message. Passage 2 is adapted from U.S. Congressman William Lawrence's 1866 Speech in support of the Act.

Passage 1

I do not propose to consider the policy of this bill. To me the details of the bill seem fraught with evil. The white race and the black race of the South have
Line hitherto lived together under the relation of master and
5 slave capital owning labor. Now, suddenly, that relation is changed, and as to ownership capital and labor are divorced. They stand now each master of itself. In this new relation, one being necessary to the other, there will be a new adjustment, which both are deeply
10 interested in making harmonious. Each has equal power in settling the terms, and if left to the laws that regulate capital and labor it is confidently believed that they will satisfactorily work out the problem. Capital, it is true, has more intelligence, but labor is never so
15 ignorant as not to understand its own interests, not to know its own value, and not to see that capital must pay that value.

This bill frustrates this adjustment. It intervenes between capital and labor and attempts to settle
20 questions of political economy through the agency of numerous officials whose interest it will be to foment discord between the two races, for as the breach widens their employment will continue, and when it is closed their occupation will terminate.
25 In all our history, in all our experience as a people living under Federal and State law, no such system as that contemplated by the details of this bill has ever before been proposed or adopted. They establish for the security of the colored race safeguards which go
30 infinitely beyond any that the General Government has ever provided for the white race. In fact, the distinction of race and color is by the bill made to operate in favor of the colored and against the white race. They interfere with the municipal legislation of the States,
35 with the relations existing exclusively between a State and its citizens, or between inhabitants of the same State-an absorption and assumption of power by the General Government which, if acquiesced in, must sap and destroy our federative system of limited powers
40 and break down the barriers which preserve the rights of the States. It is another step, or rather stride, toward centralization and the concentration of all legislative powers in the National Government. The tendency of the bill must be to resuscitate the spirit of rebellion
45 and to arrest the progress of those influences which are more closely drawing around the States the bonds of union and peace.

Passage 2

It is idle to say that a citizen shall have the right to life, yet to deny him the right to labor, whereby alone
50 he can live. It is a mockery to say that a citizen may have a right to live, and yet deny him the right to make a contract to secure the privilege and the rewards of labor. It is worse than mockery to say that men may be clothed by the national authority with the character of
55 citizens, yet may be stripped by State authority of the means by which citizens may exist.

Every citizen, therefore, has the absolute right to live, the right of personal security, personal liberty, and the right to acquire and enjoy property. These
60 are rights of citizenship. As necessary incidents of these absolute rights, there are others, as the right to make and enforce contracts, to purchase, hold, and enjoy property, and to share the benefit of laws for the security of person and property.
65 Now, there are two ways in which a State may undertake to deprive citizens of these absolute, inherent, and inalienable rights: either by prohibitory laws, or by a failure to protect any one of them.

If the people of a State should become hostile to
70 a large class of naturalized citizens and should enact laws to prohibit them and no other citizens from making contracts, from suing, from giving evidence, from inheriting, buying, holding, or selling property, or even from coming into the State, that would be
75 prohibitory legislation. If the State should simply enact laws for native-born citizens and provide no law under which naturalized citizens could enjoy any one of these rights, and should deny them all protection by civil process or penal enactments, that would be a denial of
80 justice.

This bill, in that broad and comprehensive philanthropy which regards all men in their civil rights as equal before the law, is not made for any class or creed, or race or color, but in the great future that
85 awaits us will, if it become a law, protect every citizen, including the millions of people of foreign birth who will flock to our shores to become citizens and to find here a land of liberty and law.

CONTINUE

It is barbarous, inhuman, infamous, to turn over
90 four million liberated slaves, always loyal to the
Government, to the fury of their rebel masters, who
deny them the benefit of all laws for the protection of
their civil rights. The Constitution does not define what
these privileges and immunities are; but all privileges
95 and immunities are of two kinds, to wit, those which
I have shown to be inherent in every citizen of the
United States, and such others as may be conferred by
local law and pertain only to the citizen of the State.

1

Which choice best identifies a distinction in how Johnson
and Lawrence characterize the Civil Rights Act?

A) Johnson views it as an offensive act that detracts from
state progress, while Lawrence views it as a positive act
because states are otherwise incapable of change.

B) Johnson characterizes it as a threat to the natural
relationship between whites and blacks, while
Lawrence characterizes it as a delayed but appreciated
solution to racial inequality.

C) Johnson regards it as an unfair policy that grants blacks
unnecessary leverage over whites, while Lawrence
regards it as an essential policy that will be beneficial to
citizens of all races.

D) Johnson sees it as an obsolete act because reconciliation
between whites and blacks is already underway, while
Lawrence sees it as a vindicating act because of the
historic oppression of blacks.

2

Which statement, if correct, would undermine Johnson's
claim in the first paragraph of Passage 1?

A) The longstanding tradition of slavery has given whites
an advantageous position that continues to play a role in
the current economic system.

B) New adjustments to the market will eventually reach
equilibrium because both capital and labor have a
vested interest in their own prosperity.

C) All laborers recognize and act in their own-interest in a
self-regulating system of capital and labor.

D) Newly emancipated slaves will have the resources and
intelligence to demand fair compensation.

3

According to Johnson, the primary negative outcome of
the Civil Rights Bill would be to

A) overhaul the status quo by proposing a radically new
piece of legislation.

B) prolong the employment of those who depend on
continued racial tensions.

C) elevate the political power of black Americans to
above that of white Americans.

D) encroach upon local governments by expanding the
federal system of limited powers.

4

Which choice provides the best evidence for Johnson's
assertion that the Civil Rights Act has potentially
disastrous consequences for local governments?

A) Lines 25-28 ("In all...adopted")
B) Lines 37-41 ("an absorption...States")
C) Lines 41-43 ("It is...Government")
D) Lines 43-47 ("The tendency...peace")

5

As used in line 43, "tendency" most nearly means
A) objective
B) moral
C) trajectory
D) method

6

Based on the passages, Lawrence would most likely
describe Johnson's belief that white and black
Americans will be harmonious without the bill's
passage as

A) misguided, because state intervention would overturn
racial progress.

B) hypocritical, because Johnson himself did not support
civil rights.

C) idealist, because the system inherently places blacks
at a disadvantage.

D) unlikely, because there is no law to protect blacks
from discrimination.

123

CONTINUE

7

Which choice provides the best evidence for the answer to the previous question?

A) Lines 48-53 ("It is...labor")

B) Lines 53-56 ("It is...exist")

C) Lines 69-75 ("If the...legislation")

D) Lines 89-93 ("It is...rights")

8

As used in line 54, "character" most nearly means

A) identity

B) status

C) privileges

D) responsibilities

9

One aspect of the Civil Rights Act which is considered by Lawrence but not Johnson is

A) its intent to safeguard the rights of black citizens.

B) its effects on the jurisdiction of local governments.

C) its relevance to both native-born and naturalized citizens.

D) its interference in a free-market economy.

10

What is the purpose of the last paragraph of Passage 2 (lines 89-98)?

A) To underscore the importance of the federal government protecting the inherent rights of citizens.

B) To stress the unprecedented nature of the present debate by referring to the ambiguity of the Constitution.

C) To reaffirm former slaves' loyalty to their government as justification for federal intervention.

D) To differentiate between rights protected by the federal government and those of the states.

STOP

Please turn to next page for answer keys and explanations.

Answer Key: CHAPTER FOUR

4.1 | Catt	4.2 | Douglas	4.3 | Ickes	4.4 | Henry George	4.5 | CVA 1866
1: B	1: C	1: C	1: B	1: C
2: C	2: B	2: A	2: A	2: A
3: B	3: B	3: D	3: A	3: D
4: B	4: B	4: C	4: B	4: B
5: A	5: C	5: C	5: D	5: A
6: A	6: A	6: A	6: A	6: A
7: A	7: D	7: B	7: C	7: B
8: A	8: D	8: D	8: B	8: B
9: D	9: A	9: D	9: B	9: C
10: A	10: C	10: B	10: D	10: A

Answer Explanations

Chapter Four

Chapter 4.1 | Catt

Question 1: B
Choice B is the best answer because Catt primarily claims that the struggle for women's suffrage has come to a head and that "the time for final action is now" (lines 59-60), which supports "momentous" and "pressing" in choice B. Choice A is incorrect because Catt indicates that the most significant "milestones" of the women's suffrage movement have yet to come; in addition, any other achievements of the movement are restricted to the second paragraph (lines 14-23), and therefore cannot be Catt's primary focus throughout the passage. Choice C is incorrect because Catt only describes the motives which compelled some former suffragists to abandon the cause, without using negative language or disparaging them for their choice; the passage thus cannot be described as a "critique". Choice D is incorrect because Catt mainly aims to enlist the support of all passive sympathizers of the suffrage movement, while her appeal to men is limited to lines 30-31 ("There are...reserves").

Question 2: C
Choice C is the best answer because Catt gives several examples of people who are generally aligned with the movement but are not proactively contributing to it, such as people who are too afraid to help or those who do not have the time to do so. Catt states that these people are their reserves and "must be mobilized" so that "victory might be seized", which is a call to action meant to rally those who have been passive up to this point in time. Choice A is incorrect because Catt's allusions to "reserves", "soldiers", and "struggle" are part of her comparison of the suffrage movement to a battle, but do not literally refer to the armed forces. Choice B is incorrect because the "reserves" whom Catt cites are not opponents of women's suffrage: they actually "tell [Catt and other suffragists] that they hope [the movement] will win and win soon". Choice D is incorrect because Catt does not specify a certain result for the movement, positive or negative, within the paragraph. Catt merely calls the supporters to action in hopes that they will win, but there is no aspect of certainty within that rallying cry.

Question 3: B
Choice B is the best answer because Catt repeatedly uses military terminology such as "soldiers" (line 33) and "crusade" (line 54) to compare the struggle for women's suffrage to a war. Moreover, she uses the motif of the "bugle call" to indicate to her audience that the "final battle is on" (line 90), thus highlighting the importance of raising suffragists' morale. Choice A is incorrect; although Catt uses rhetorical questions to further her argument, they mainly have positive answers. For instance, the questions "does it not give you a thrill of exaltation?" and "does the blood not course more quickly through your veins?" are being posed to suffragists and are therefore meant to be answered with "it does", which is a positive answer. Choice C is incorrect because Catt never cites her own experiences and thus never includes "anecdotes" in her speech. Choice D is incorrect because Catt's support for the inherent nature of women's rights would not have been "universally accepted" at the time her speech was delivered.

Question 4: B
Choice B is the best answer because the bugle call signifies the beginning of "the final battle" for women's suffrage (line 90). Thus, the sound of the bugle serves to rouse the supporters of the movement and call them to action, supporting "urgency". Choices A and C are incorrect because "sympathy" and "honor" are feelings that, while important in providing a sense of purpose for the suffrage movement, are not enough for the realization of the movement's ultimate goal. Choice D is incorrect because "intimidation" suggests wrongly that Catt aims to prevent women's suffrage by instilling fear in its supporters.

Question 5: A
Choice A is the best answer because Catt begins with an extended description of the "millions" of "inactive and silent" (lines 2-3) people who are not actively contributing to the suffrage movement, before stating that "these reserves must be mobilized" (line 34). Choice B is incorrect because the passive supporters' lack of active participation in the movement does not mean that the current membership of the suffrage movement is dwindling; it merely means that there are more potential members. Choice C is incorrect because the lack of membership does not constitute a form of oppression; nor is the oppression faced by the suffragists the main idea of the first part of the passage. Choice D is incorrect because Catt does not specify any achievements of the women's suffrage movement; at best, Catt states that the women's suffrage movement has enacted some positive change when she discusses the women who do not feel grateful for the movement (line 20), but she never explicitly mentions what these achievements are or when they happened, which makes it impossible to verify that they are "recent" as well.

Question 6: A
Choice A is the best answer because Catt refers to the "cruel hostility" that was ideologically opposed to the suffrage movement, supporting "aligned". Choices B and D are incorrect because "displayed" and "presented" both indicate a literal showing of dissent, and moreover suggest that such a showing is a facade. Choice C is incorrect because people must be "marshalled" by an authority, implying a hidden force behind the opposition to women's suffrage that Catt never mentions.

Question 7: A

Choice A is best because Catt describes the "old belief" that gave suffragists faith "in many an hour of discouragement"; this belief thus "sustained" the suffragists in times of difficulty. Choices B and C are incorrect because the suffragists' beliefs or opinions would be "reinforced" or "maintained", not the suffragists themselves, while the use of passive voice in choice D implies that the suffragists are the ones being "endured", which would depict them in an overly negative light.

Question 8: A

Choice A is the best answer because Catt illustrates that some women are no longer members because the movement seemed "pointless". Catt implies that these women viewed the movement as pointless because there were no immediate results, which is indicated in the comparison she presents in lines 8-9: "many have taken up other work whose results were more immediate". Thus, these women were impatient. Choice B is incorrect because it merely states some women are not aware that some of the benefits in their lives are because of the suffrage movement. This statement does not indicate that they're impatient with the movement; it only indicates that they don't credit it appropriately. Choice C is incorrect because Catt states in these lines that there are some women who have other concerns besides suffrage, hence their lack of participation. But she does not state that the reason behind their lack of participation is that the movement takes too long; thus, Catt does not claim that women are impatient within these lines. Choice D is incorrect because stating that the old movement endorsed patience does not necessarily mean that some women grew impatient with the movement as a whole.

Question 9: D

Choice D is the best answer because lines 17-23 describe how the suffrage movement has produced opportunities that did not exist for women before, such as "well-paid posts", which means that they have been empowered by the movement. Within the same lines, Catt indicates that they feel no "sense of obligation to open other doors", which implies that they are not contributing to the movement. Choice A is incorrect because Catt does not specify any legislation that has been proposed or enacted in favor of women's rights. Choice B is incorrect because Catt does not illustrate instances in which women now have increased access to business and government affairs, which is what the phrase "greater participation" implies. Choice C is incorrect because Catt never mentions any formerly active supporters of the movement who distanced themselves from it because of their intimidation. She only states that there are some women who passively support the movement but have not become active members because they are afraid.

Question 10: A

Choice A is the best answer because only lines 17-23 directly refer to the empowering effects of women's suffrage movement. Choice B is incorrect because lines 24-27 discuss those who have never actively participated in the suffragist movement, but never implies that they have reaped the benefits of the movement's success themselves. Choices C and D are incorrect because lines 36-39 and 83-86 describe the potential success of the suffrage movement, not the progress that has already been made.

Chapter 4.2 | Douglas

Question 1: C
Choice C is the best answer because Douglas asserts that "there can be no neutrals in this war, only patriots or traitors" (lines 53-54), "we have a solemn duty to maintain the Government" (lines 68-69), and lastly that "it is the duty of every American citizen to rally around the flag of his country" (lines 81-83). Choice A is incorrect because while Douglas does make a point of discussing the issue some people have with the party in power, his main point is about protecting the country, not about the constitution. Choice B is incorrect because Douglas is not only pointing out that what the Confederate States are doing is unconstitutional; more than that, he is stating that Americans must go to war to stop the "armies marched upon our capital" (lines 8-9) by the South. Choice D is incorrect because Douglas, while he does mention slavery, characterizes the reasons for needing to go to war as imminent because of the South's "[threat] to destroy" (lines 15-16) the country.

Question 2: B
Choice B is the best answer because Douglas presents several examples in paragraphs two, three, and four explaining why claims made by "disunionists" (line 17) are not justified in their stance. Choice A is incorrect because although lines 41-44 mention the conspiracy of the south, Douglas does not depict anger; moreso, he is being diplomatic in ruling out the reasons the South could claim regarding the reasons for their hostility. Choice C is incorrect because Douglas is hostile throughout the passage and shows no sympathy or positive emotions towards secessionists. Choice D is incorrect because Douglas is unconcerned with the claim Southerners make about slavery; his issue is that they are using false claims to support waging war.

Question 3: B
Choice B is the best answer because by characterizing the US Government as "the best Government on which the Sun of heaven ever shed its rays" (lines 18-19) and asking a rhetorical question implying there is no cause to break this government up, Douglas frames the Southern States as hostile and unjustified. Choice A is incorrect because lines 4-7 show what Douglas has done up to this point but not his attitude. Choice C is incorrect because although lines 41-44 do mention the conspiracy by leaders in the Southern Confederacy, it does not align with the only answer in question two that mentions conspiracy as it does not show Douglas' anger. Choice D is incorrect because it is not on topic of Douglas' attitude towards the Southern States.

Question 4: B
Choice B is the best answer because in line 8, Douglas is referring to the actions of the South in response to him having "gone to the very extreme of magnanimity" (line 7). Choice A is incorrect because "retaliation" would happen in response to an attack, not to kindness. Choice C is incorrect because the South's response is neither a formal written or spoken reply nor someone officially arriving for duty. Choice D is incorrect because "resurgence" indicates something happening again, but this action by the South is the first of its kind.

Question 5: C

Choice C is the best answer because by detailing dangerous issues regarding the current situation, Douglas makes it apparent that the future of the United States is at risk. Choice A is incorrect because Douglas discounts the arguments made by the South in paragraphs three through five, not in paragraph two. Choice B is incorrect because in the second paragraph, Douglas is not challenging arguments but revealing his argument that "the present danger is imminent" (line 1). Choice D is incorrect because "progression" implies an ordered structure to the events, but Douglas is simply stating that certain things have happened, not the particular order in which they may have occurred.

Question 6: A

Choice A is the best answer because by using hyperbolic rhetorical questions, Douglas highlights the absurdity of the response from Southern States to the result of the election. Choices B, C, and D are incorrect because lines 25-27, lines 34-35 and 40-41 describe Southern states' reactions to the results of the presidential election and their rationales for leaving the Union, but do not express present those views as excessively absurd.

Question 7: D

Choice D is the best answer because Douglas first asks "What evidence do they present of this?" (line 27) then invites any man to provide him with said evidence, thereby challenging those who believe something has been done to provoke war. Choices A and B are incorrect because Douglas himself is not resisting nor disobedient; instead, he implies that the South is being resistant disobedient unless they can provide confirmation that they have been constitutionally wronged. Choice C is incorrect because Douglas is neither hostile in his stance nor attacking a problem head-on; rather, he wants to give the South the opportunity to prove that he is mistaken.

Question 8: D

Choice D is the best answer because the focus shift, which occurs in paragraph 5, pivots from detailing Douglas' rebuttals to claims the Southern States have made regarding why war is necessary to an urgent call to action to hasten peaceful relations between the two sides. Douglas makes several direct assertions in paragraph five and beyond, including "there can be no neutrals" (line 53), "we cannot close our eyes to the...face that war does exist" (lines 55-56), and "we cannot recognize secession" (line 62), all supporting the idea that a strong, unified response is necessary. Choice A is incorrect because while Douglas does make an analogy between the current situation in the United States and the French Revolution in line 67, it is only one minor point supporting that something must be done to fix relations. Choice B is incorrect because Douglas does not describe politics in favorable terms. He is terse and clearly not pleased with what must happen: "I have struggled" (line 4) and "It is a sad task to discuss questions as fearful as civil war" (lines 78-79). Choice C is incorrect because Douglas is not romantic in his characterization of the impending war; in fact, he is quite the opposite: he describes it as "sad and solemn" (line 55).

Question 9: A

Choice A is the best answer because Douglas asserts that "[his] conscious is clean. [he has] struggled long for a peaceful solution to the difficulty [and]...gone to the very extreme of magnanimity" (lines 3-7) with regards to relations with the South, indicating that the only option left is war. Choice B is incorrect because there is no ultimatum in the passage; Douglas discusses the present situation, possible causes, and urgency for the tasks ahead. Choice C is incorrect because Douglas insists that "so far as the constitutional rights of the Southern States...nothing has been done...of which they can complain" (lines 30-33). Choice D is incorrect because while he does dismiss all possible reasons the South has for their behavior, there have been no offers made to Douglas; he simply states that "armies marched upon our capital" (lines 8-9).

Question 10: C
Choice C is the best answer because Douglas insists that the most important consideration is that "the Government must be maintained [and] its enemies overthrown" (lines 56-57), and that until that is done they need to "lay aside all criminations and recriminations as to the origin of these difficulties (lines 72-73). Choice A is incorrect because Douglas does not think that the offenses that have transpired are irredeemable; in fact, he maintains that he wants the country back together as one united entity: "we shall have again a country with the United States flag floating over it" (lines 74-75). Choice B is incorrect because when Douglas said "lay aside all criminations" (line 72), he made it clear that blame is not of concern at this time. Choice D is incorrect because Douglas does not mention future conflicts, only that in the future, the people of the United States will have the opportunity to understand what got them to this point.

Chapter 4.3 | Ickes

Question 1: C
Choice C is the best answer because Ickes begins by addressing unflattering statements made about the American people such as "we are a weak nation" (lines 1-2) and "we...hold moth-eaten ideas" (lines 11-13) with the intention of galvanizing Americans. He then asserts that "we cannot retain our liberty if three-fourths of the world is enslaved" (lines 36-38), "we know that the spirit of freedom never dies" (line 63) and, lastly, that "not only will we fight for democracy, we will make it more worth fighting for" (lines 83-84). Choice A is incorrect because Ickes is not exultant about the current state of affairs, but he is hopeful that things will change, as indicated with "[freedom] will endure like a hardy tree gone into the wintertime, awaiting the spring" (lines 59-61), and "liberty-loving German people are only temporarily enslaved" (lines 65-66). Choice B is incorrect because while Ickes uses collective voice throughout the passage to address his audience, there is no direct formal address in this speech, just a general appeal for "the great American people to raise their voices and cry out in a mighty triumph" (lines 21-22). Choice D is incorrect because although Ickes does mention parties which he may want to address with reproach, he does so with hope and urgency, not by admonishing any person or group of people.

Question 2: A
Choice A is the best answer because while in the first paragraph Ickes presents evidence that foreigners believe Americans are "a weak nation" (line 1) and that it is infiltrating the minds of some Americans. He later undermines that idea, stating that "Americans are in a position to help. [They] know that freedom never dies" and that "here in America, we have something so worth living for that it is worth dying for!" (lines 78-79). Choice B is incorrect because although the claims stated in the first paragraph could be seen as America's faults in the eyes of foreign influencers and the Americans who have allowed these ideas to infiltrate their minds, Ickes himself corrects the assertion in the second paragraph with a list of things that "the great American people" (line 21) stand for. Choice C is incorrect because the statements Ickes makes about European nations are in reference to the possibility of future greatness, not present strength. Choice D is incorrect because Ickes is not rejecting a premise of the viewpoint, he wholly rejects the viewpoint.

Question 3: D

Choice D is the best answer because Ickes indicates that those who believe in the "wave of the future" characterize other Americans as "[holding] moth-eaten ideas" (line 13), even though the "'wave of the future' has passed over [them] and left [them] a wet, dead fish" (lines 7-8). The word "moth-eaten" suggests that those who believe in the wave of the future perceive American ideals as outdated; therefore, holding onto such outdated ideas despite it being "futile to oppose 'the wave of the future'" (lines 10-11) would be perceived as "stubborn". Choice A is incorrect because Ickes does not specify the circumstances that have made Americans downtrodden, nor does he indicate that they are undergoing times of difficulty at all. Moreover, some Americans have indeed become disillusioned and have "fallen for this carefully pickled tripe" (lines 5-6), but do not constitute the majority of the population; when "Americans" in general are described, they are characterized as being "nourished on the magna Carta and the Declaration of Independence" (lines 12-13) and "[holding] moth-eaten ideas" of democracy and independence (line 13). Choice B is incorrect because Ickes does not indicate that those who believe in the "wave of the future" dismiss the promises of democracy as "false"; after all, in the past, such promises led to "the making of America" (line 19). Such ideals might not be relevant or needed for the events of the "wave of the future", but that does not invalidate the progress that they furthered before. Choice C is incorrect because those who believe in the wave of the future have depicted Americans as "simple-minded" (line 3), but do not indicate the results of that simplemindedness.

Question 4: C

Choice C is the best answer because at the beginning of both sentences, Ickes refers to the viewpoints of some other entity, referring to the holders as "they" (line 11 & line 17). This is in direct contrast to his opinions, which he characterizes using the pronoun "we" (line 11). Furthermore, Ickes main point is to show that "[Americans] know that the spirit of freedom never dies" (line 63), again contrasting the lines referenced, in which he says "they say [America] is waiting for the undertaker and all the hopes and aspirations...are dead too" (lines 17-20). Choice A is incorrect because the author makes it clear that his true sentiments are pro-America, and not anti-America. Choice B is incorrect because although the idea could be seen as absurd, Ickes never makes that claim, rather he admits that "some amongst us have fallen for this carefully pickled tripe" (lines 6-7). It would not serve his argument to alienate Americans whom he's aiming to inspire with this speech. Choice D is incorrect because these are general statements, not specific examples.

Question 5: C

Choice C is the best answer because in the topic sentence of paragraph two, Ickes asserts that "it is time for the great American people to raise their voices and cry out in mighty triumph what it is to be an American." (lines 21-23). Following this main claim, Ickes elaborates on many important qualities held by americans, all relating to "justice" (line 28) and "[fighting] for freedom" (lines 29-30). Choice A is incorrect because personal sacrifice is only part of what it means to be an American. Choice B is incorrect because while Ickes does denote many different qualities that "constitute an American" (lines 23-24), he is using these descriptions to show that they all share a common goal. Choice D is incorrect because Ickes never mentions accumulation of wealth in this paragraph, only "profession" (line 27) but not whether professions yield a lot of wealth, and "property" (line 31) but again not the monetary value of this property.

Question 6: A

Choice A is the best answer because Ickes elaborates on the idea that freedom is indivisible with the assertion "we cannot retain our liberty if three-fourths of the world is enslaved." (lines 37-38), implying that liberty is "all-or-nothing", or cannot be divided up and distributed to certain areas yet not to others. Choice B is incorrect because the claim isn't about arguing whether the qualities of freedom can be changed, just whether it can exist in one place and not in another. Choice C is incorrect because to describe something as integral, it needs to be clarified to what it is integral, but the sentence merely states that it is indivisible and not to what. Choice D is incorrect because although the entity of freedom may be indestructible, that does not fit with Ickes main point in this paragraph, which is that freedom is essentially worthless when it is broken apart.

Question 7: B

Choice B is the best answer because the term dormancy refers to freedom, or the tree, not being expressed to its fullest expectations, but if it will "endure like a hardy tree" (line 60) then freedom's resurfacing is bound to happen. Choice A is incorrect because Ickes doesn't mention pay in any of the reference lines. Choice C is incorrect because although lines 29-30 do mention Americans fighting for freedom, Ickes does not say that nothing else arouses as much support. Choice D is incorrect because in the lines referenced in question eight, Ickes does not mention rebellions throughout history, just the one ongoing at the time of the speech.

Question 8: D

Choice D is the best answer because the simile Ickes uses, comparing freedom's endurance to a "hardy tree gone into the wintertime" (line 60), conjures the image of freedom being put into a compromised position, yet the tree is simply "awaiting the spring" (line 61), implying that once this period of oppression is over, freedom will return to its earlier state. Choice A is incorrect because although it is on the correct topic of freedom, there is no match in question seven that makes a claim about the readiness of Americans to fight for freedom. Choice B and C are incorrect because there is no match in question seven that makes the claim that freedom is weakened in certain places in the world.

Question 9: D

Choice D is the best answer because Ickes continually uses metaphorical language like "carefully pickled tripe" (line 6), "wet, dead fish" (line 8), and "moth-eaten ideas" (line 13) to describe the ways in which democrats and communists perceive each other. Choice A is incorrect because Ickes does not call upon his personal history to prove his point. Choice B is incorrect because Ickes does not understate, or minimize, the threat of the "wave of the future"—in fact, he calls the imminent war "a counter-revolution against...our sense of justice and our human values" (lines 44-46) and "a desperate struggle for the possession of the souls of men" (lines 53-54). Choice C is incorrect because Ickes' enthusiasm for American values is genuine; sarcasm would thus align him with those who believe that the future lies in communism and facism, which is evidently false from the context of the passage.

Question 10: B

Choice B is the best answer because by calling the people of Germany "only temporarily enslaved" (line 66), Ickes implies that it is only a matter of time until their freedom is restored. Choice A is incorrect because in it, Ickes only states that Atilla thinks he has "destroyed democracy" but it is not until the next sentence, outside of the evidence lines referenced, that he says Atilla is wrong. Choice C is incorrect because Ickes is referencing the "wave of the future" first mentioned in the first paragraph, which concerns Americans, not Germans. Choice D is incorrect because although Ickes does say Americans will "work for the good of mankind, including Hitler's victims in Germany" (lines 85-86), he does not say in these lines that it is inevitable that Germany will be defeated.

Chapter 4.4 | Henry George

Question 1: B
Choice B is the best answer because George introduces the passage with the statement that "the present century has been marked by a prodigious increase in wealth-producing power" (lines 1-2) and that society has been improved by the introduction of "labor-saving machinery" (line 4), which he says has caused "the average of comfort, leisure, and refinement [to be] raised" (lines 14-15), supporting the idea that recent innovations have benefited society. He then characterizes these developments as having disproportionate effects on different classes, stating that they are forcing an "immense wedge...not underneath society, but through society" (lines 29-30), which George implies is causing societal problems. He later calls for "sweeping away this injustice and asserting the rights of all men to natural opportunities" (lines 87-88), an assertion of desired societal change. Choice A is incorrect because the phrase "changed the lives of the poor" is too narrow, since recent changes have also elevated 'those above the point of separation" (lines 30-31). Choice C is incorrect because George does not push for "governmental reform"; rather, he asserts that "we shall remove the great cause of unnatural inequality in the distribution of wealth and power; we shall abolish poverty" (lines 89-91), implying that it is the job of the collective people and not the government, as he is not a politician. Choice D is incorrect because although George acknowledges that some people believe "machinery is an evil" (line 63), he does not present the view as his own, nor does he agree with it: George later contends that "such ideas...are fraught with danger" (lines 69-73).

Question 2: A
Choice A is the best answer because the word "general" refers to the societal gains afforded by technology including "comfort, leisure, and refinement" (lines 14-15), in which "the lowest class does not share". This means that the gains are not common or applicable to all, or "widespread" throughout the population. Choices B and C are incorrect because the descriptions "traditional" and "usual" refer to either duration or frequency of occurrence, failing to touch on their societal reach. Choice D is incorrect because to describe something as "popular" is to imply that it is liked or preferred by the majority, but does not necessarily indicate that it is possessed by the majority.

Question 3: A
Choice A is the best answer because George makes the claim that "in [these gains] the lowest class does not share" (lines 15-16), which he follows up with a clarification, stating "I do not mean that the condition of the lowest class has nowhere...been improved" (lines 16-18). George then clears up ambiguity in his original statement, asserting that "there is nowhere any improvement which can be credited to increased productive power" (lines 18-20). Choice B is incorrect because George is able to refute the counter argument by saying that "the [material progress]... do not act upon the social fabric from underneath, as was for a long time hoped and believed" (lines 25-27), showing that the argument against the idea that the lowest class does not share in the gains of technological progress cannot be refuted. Choice C is incorrect because" unprecedented" refers to something that

is the first of its kind, and nowhere in the passage does George address whether this has or has not happened prior to the current situation. Choice D is incorrect because although George refutes a misconception about his argument, he does not explain how many people have this belief; therefore, the misconception cannot be "popular".

Question 4: B
Choice B is the best answer because George states in lines 78-80 that the fundamental law of justice is denied "when the equal right to land—on which and by which men alone can live—is denied". As George then demonstrates that injustice is prevalent throughout the nation—"and so there come beggars in our streets and tramps on our roads; and poverty enslaves men whom we boast are political sovereigns" (lines 84-86)—it can then be inferred that the right to land is also being denied. Choices A and D are incorrect because George never describes money or safe working conditions as "rights", though he recognizes that their disproportionate distribution is unjust. Choice C is incorrect because "political representation", though listed as a right by George in lines 80-83, is not supported by any line references in the following question.

Question 5: D
Choice D is the best answer because lines 78-80 describe a situation that would occur when "the equal right to land...is denied", which matches with the topic of the previous question. Choices A and C are off topic: lines 7-10 recount the predictions that were made at the dawn of the industrial revolution, and lines 33-38 outline the unfortunate consequences of industrialization. Choice B is incorrect because lines 13-15 claim that wealth and adequate standards of living have been denied to the poor, but does not indicate that wealth or improved standards of living are "rights".

Question 6: A
Choice A is the best answer because George describes the current situation as "poverty...in the midst of abundance" (lines 73-74), which is a contradiction, matching with "paradoxical". He then says that "we have ignored a fundamental law of justice" (lines 77-78) and that "rights are denied" (line 78), both of which are unjust and immoral, matching with "indefensible". Choice B is incorrect because although it is possible to make the argument that unequal division of wealth and material gains is expected, George describes the situation as one which "pinches and imbrutes men" (line 74), implying that it is not expected or natural. Choice C is incorrect because George emphasizes the possibility that economic progress could exist alongside "the rights of all men to natural opportunities" (line 88) in the last paragraph; therefore, the divide between innovation and workers' rights is not "necessary". Choice D is incorrect because the phenomenon that George describes is not "unsurprising": he reveals that in the beginning of the industrial revolution, "it was natural to expect" that machinery would "make real poverty a thing of the past" (lines 7-12) and calls the accompaniment of poverty with progress "the great enigma of our times" (lines 42-43).

Question 7: C
Choice C is the best answer because George does not list the lack of a minimum wage as contributing to poverty; in fact, as indicated in the theories proposed by some writers, people believe that poverty was caused by "the attempts of workmen to keep up wages" (line 56). Choices A, B, and D are incorrect, as "the demonetization of silver [and] the issues of paper money" (line 57), "the wastes of war [and] the extension of railroads" (line 55), and "the increase of laborsaving machinery" (line 58) are all mentioned throughout the fourth paragraph as proposed causes for wealth inequality.

Question 8: B

Choice B is the best answer because lines 69-72 reveal George's opinion on the idea that "there is a necessary conflict between capital and labor, that machinery is an evil, that competition must be restrained and interest abolished, that wealth may be created by the issue of money, that it is the duty of government to furnish capital or to furnish work" (lines 61-67); those ideas are clearly against the circumstances caused by industrial progress and are thus on topic. George then indicates that "such ideas...are fraught with danger" (lines 69-72), matching with "equally destructive" in the topic of the question. Choices A, C, and D are incorrect because lines 46-50, lines 73-75, and lines 84-86 all describe the destruction and injustice caused not by movements against industrialization and the growth of capital, but by industrialization itself.

Question 9: B

Choice B is the best answer because George claims that in "political liberty...becomes, as population increases and invention goes on, merely the liberty to compete for employment at starvation wages" (lines 80-83); as economic deprivation has degraded men despite the theoretical presence of political rights, such political "liberty" can be characterized as "meaningless". Choice A is incorrect because George does not believe that it is the government's "duty" to prevent poverty; in fact, he calls the idea that "it is the duty of government to furnish capital or to furnish work" (lines 65-67) "fraught with danger" (line 72). Similarly, choice C is incorrect, as George includes the idea that "machinery is an evil" (line 63) in his list of those that are "fraught with danger". Choice D is incorrect because George states that only "sweeping away this injustice" (line 87) could better the circumstances of destitute individuals; as such, it is unlikely that he would recommend "embracing technological developments".

Question 10: D

Choice D is the best answer because once society is through "sweeping away this injustice" (line 87), the same opportunities will be afforded to all men, thus making the opportunities just, or "fair". Choice A is incorrect because "organic" describes the source of the opportunities listed, while George describes the quality of the opportunities themselves. Choice B is incorrect because "valid" opportunities are logical or rooted in sound reasoning, whereas George refers to circumstances that are not subject to "unnatural inequality" (line 90) and are accessible to every man. Choice C is incorrect because George indicates that rights are "inherent", not opportunities; if opportunities were inherent, they would be available to all workers and wealth inequality as described in the passage would not exist.

Chapter 4.5 | CVA 1866

Question 1: C

Choice C is the best answer because Johnson asserts that "[the bill] establish[es] for the security of the colored race safeguards which go infinitely beyond any that the General Government has ever provided for the white race" (lines 28-31) and that the bill is "in favor of the colored and against the white race" (lines 32-33). On the other hand, Lawrence claims that the bill is "not made for any class or creed, or race or color, but in the great future that awaits us [to]...protect every citizen" (lines 83-86). Choice A is incorrect because Johnson does not indicate that the bill takes away form state progress; instead, his concern is that it might take away from progress made between "capital and labor" (line 6) which he describes as distinct from the government. Choice B is incorrect because

Lawrence does not characterize the bill as a delayed solution to inequality. His primary points about the bill are that it prohibits states from "becom[ing] hostile to a large class of naturalized citizens" (lines 69-70) and it "will...protect every citizen, including the millions of people of foreign birth who will flock to our shores to become citizens" (lines 85-88). Choice D is incorrect because Lawrence's primary concern is current oppression and inequality, not what has happened historically.

Question 2: A
Choice A is the best answer because Johnson's main claim in the first paragraph is that "the details of the bill seem fraught with evil" (line 2) and is unnecessary: both races "deeply interested in making [the new relation between them] harmonious" (lines 9-10) and "each has equal power in settling the terms" (lines 10-11). Therefore, if one race had leverage over the other, his claim would be undermined. Choices B, C, and C are incorrect because they all address claims in agreement with Johnson's argument in the first paragraph: "if left to the laws that regulate capital and labor it is confidently believed that they will satisfactorily work out the problem" (lines 10-12) (choice B); and "labor is never so ignorant as not to understand its own interests, not to know its own value, and not to see that capital must pay that value" (lines 14-17) (choices C & D).

Question 3: D
Choice D is the best answer because Johnson claims that "[the bill] interfere[s] with the municipal legislation of the states, with the relations existing exclusively between a State and its citizens, or between inhabitants of the same State" (lines 33-37), indicating that he believes its main effects are on local governments. He later states that the bill does that by "destroy[ing] [America's] federative system of limited powers" (lines 39-40). Choice A is incorrect because while Johnson does mention in lines 25-28 that this bill is unprecedented, he does not indicate that it is an overhaul of the status quo. The status quo has already been overhauled by liberation of former slaves at the national level and Johnson discusses that new relationship in the first paragraph. Choice B is incorrect because while Johnson does claim in the second paragraph that there are those who wish to promote discord between the races in order to extend their employment, that is not a primary outcome. Instead, it's just a qualm that Johnson has regarding the fact that the bill will interfere with the adjustment being made between "ownership capital and labor" (line 6). Choice C is incorrect because while Johnson states that the bill will increase the safeguards of black Americans, he does not claim that it will increase their political power. Furthermore, elevating safeguards above those of whites does not necessarily translate to an overall power increase.

Question 4: B
Choice B is the best answer because Johnson says that the bill will "break down the barriers which preserve the rights of the States" (lines 40-41), a negative consequence that the bill would impose on local, or State, governments. Choice A is incorrect because while Johnson claims that the bill is unprecedented, he does not attempt to clarify what that means for State governments. Choice C is incorrect because the claim Johnson makes in lines 42-44 is that the bill is a step towards centralized powers, but he does not say in that sentence that centralized powers are harmful for States. Choice D is incorrect because in lines 44-47 Johnson reveals that he believes that the bill should attempt to stop the progress of anything that stands in the way of the "States...bonds of union and peace" (lines 46-47) which is not what the bill does in actuality, nor would it be a negative consequence for the State governments.

Question 5: A
Choice A is the best answer because after Johnson says the tendency of the bill, he gives a clear goal: "to resuscitate the spirit of rebellion and to arrest the progress of those influences which are more closely drawing around the States the bonds of union and peace" (lines 44-47). This indicates that its "tendency" is its objective. Choice B is incorrect because Johnson could only be referring to a moral if the bill had already been passed and he was discussing its actual outcome. Choice C is incorrect because trajectory is used to refer to something while it is in action. Choice D is incorrect because the bill's method is the way that it works, and not what it does.

Question 6: A
Choice A is the best answer because in the evidence, Lawrence highlights that while a national law has declared equality, states have been allowed to strip people protected under that law of their means by which to exist. Choice B is incorrect because Johnson's support of the civil rights bill would not be used as justification for disharmony among people. Choice C is incorrect because if the national government has passed a law granting equality for blacks, it is not inherently disadvantaging them. The reason they are still at a disadvantage is because of either refusal to abide by the system or creation of superfluous laws. Choice D is incorrect because there is already a law to protect former slaves from discrimination at the federal level, as Lawrence points out in the first paragraph.

Question 7: B
Choice B is the best answer because the aim of the civil rights bill is to prevent states from either "[enacting] prohibitory laws, or…[failing] to protect any one of [the laws]" (lines 67-68), and in the first paragraph he asserts that state governments are doing just that by stripping former slaves of their means to exist. Therefore, it is Lawrence's view that Americans are not harmonious without the bill because states are allowed to put certain groups of people at a distinct disadvantage. Choice A is incorrect because lines 48-53 address the topic of earning a wage for doing work but none of the answers in question six mention that issue. Choice C is incorrect because while the ideas posed by Lawrence in lines 69-75 do highlight disharmony, racial progress is not brought up in this part of the text. Choice D is incorrect because although Lawrence does discuss disharmony in lines 89-93, it is that which is brought upon by citizens, not by state governments.

Question 8: B
Choice B is the best answer because Lawrence supports his main idea by claiming that while it is bad to deny men the right to a living, it is much worse to make them think they are equal citizens under the law and then allow them to be denied their rights by local governments. In this comparison, he uses the phrase "clothed by the national authority" (line 54) to mean that former slaves have national rights and the appearance of civil rights, or equal status under the law. Choice A is incorrect because identity is intrinsic, like natural rights, but these rights are civil, which are afforded by the government. Choice C is incorrect because while civil rights are privileges, the point being made by Lawrence is that former slaves have the appearance of equal status, meaning they can no longer be regarded as inferior under the law. Choice D is incorrect because while there are responsibilities that come along with having equal civil rights, in the specified context, Lawrence is discussing a factor that state authority has taken away.

Question 9: C
Choice C is the best answer because while Johnson does not make reference to naturalized citizens, Lawrence hypothesizes that "if the State should simply enact laws for native-born citizens and provide no law under which naturalized citizens could enjoy any one of these rights...that would be a denial of justice" (lines 75-80). Choices A, B, and D are incorrect because Johnson makes those points in passage one: "[the bill] establish[es] for the security of the colored race safeguards which go infinitely beyond any that the General Government has ever provided for the white race" (lines 28-31) (choice A); "[the bill] interfere[s] with the municipal legislation of the States" (lines 33-34) (choice B); and "[this bill] intervenes between capital and labor and attempts to settle questions of political economy through the agency of numerous officials" (lines 18-21) (choice D).

Question 10: A
Choice A is the best answer because Lawrence claims that were liberated slaves to not be protected under the civil rights bill, they would be "turn[ed] over...to the fury of their rebel masters, who deny them the benefit of all laws for the protection of their civil rights" (lines 89-93), clearly indicating that if the government does not protect the rights of all people, some will be subjected to harm. Choice B is incorrect because showing that this bill is unprecedented in nature would not further the main idea of the passage therefore it cannot be the primary purpose of the final paragraph. Choice C is incorrect because Lawrence cannot be reaffirming former slaves' loyalty to their government if he did not do that earlier in the passage. Choice D is incorrect because while Lawrence does differentiate between two concepts, it's between inalienable rights and rights afforded by the government, not between rights of the states and rights of the federal government.

Chapter
Five

Questions 1-10 are based on the following passage.

5.1

This passage is adapted from Theodore Roosevelt's "A Square Deal" speech delivered to farmers at the New York State Agricultural Association in 1903.

It cannot be too often repeated that in this country, in the long run, we all of us tend to go up or go down together. If the average of well-being is high, it means
Line that the average wage-worker, the average farmer, and
5 the average business man are all alike well-off. If the average shrinks, there is not one of these classes which will not feel the shrinkage.

It is all-essential to the continuance of our healthy national life that we should recognize this community
10 of interest among our people. We can keep our government on a sane and healthy basis, we can make and keep our social system what it should be, only on condition of judging each man, not as a member of a class, but on his worth as a man. It is an infamous thing
15 in our American life, and fundamentally treacherous to our institutions, to apply to any man any test save that of his personal worth, or to draw between two sets of men any distinction save the distinction of conduct. There are good citizens and bad citizens in
20 every class as in every locality, and the attitude of decent people toward great public and social questions should be determined, not by the accidental questions of employment or locality, but by those deep-set principles which represent the innermost souls of men.
25 The failure in public and in private life thus to treat each man on his own merits, the recognition of this government as being either for the poor as such or for the rich as such, would prove fatal to our Republic. A healthy republican government must rest upon
30 individuals, not upon classes or sections. As soon as it becomes government by a class or by a section, it departs from the old American ideal.

Our average fellow citizen is a sane and healthy man who believes in decency and has a wholesome
35 mind. He therefore feels an equal scorn alike for the man of wealth guilty of the mean and base spirit of arrogance toward those who are less well off, and for the man of small means who in his turn either feels, or seeks to excite in others the feeling of mean and base
40 envy for those who are better off. The two feelings, envy and arrogance, are but opposite sides of the same shield, but different developments of the same spirit.

Among ourselves we differ in many qualities of body, head, and heart; we are unequally developed,
45 mentally as well as physically. But each of us has the

right to ask that he shall be protected from wrong-doing as he does his work and carries his burden through life. Far and away the best prize that life offers is the chance to work hard at work worth doing; and
50 this is a prize open to every man. Surely from our own experience each one of us knows that this is true. To win success in the business world, to become a first-class mechanic, a successful farmer, an able lawyer or doctor, means that the man has devoted his best energy
55 and power through long years to the achievement of his ends. So it is in the life of the family, upon which in the last analysis the whole welfare of the nation rests. The man or woman who, as bread-winner and home-maker, or as wife and mother, has done all that
60 he or she can do, patiently and uncomplainingly, is to be honored.

You farmers, and wage-workers, and business men of this mighty and wonderful nation, are gathered together today, proud of your State and still prouder of
65 your nation, because your forefathers and predecessors have lived up to this creed. You have received from their hands a great inheritance, and you will leave an even greater inheritance to your children, provided only that you practice alike in your private and your
70 public lives the strong virtues that have given us as a people greatness in the past. We must possess the qualities which make us do our duty in our homes and among our neighbors -- the qualities of courage and hardihood, of individual initiative and yet of power to
75 combine for a common end, and above all, the resolute determination to permit no man and no set of men to sunder us one from the other by lines of caste or creed or section. We must act upon the motto of all for each and each for all. There must be ever present in our
80 minds the fundamental truth that in a republic such as ours the only safety is to stand neither for nor against any man because he is rich or because he is poor, because he is engaged in one occupation or another, because he works with his brains or because he works
85 with his hands. We must treat each man on his worth and merits as a man. We must see that each is given a square deal, because he is entitled to no more and should receive no less.

CONTINUE

1

The primary purpose of this passage is to

A) persuade Americans to work together so as to ensure the continued prosperity of the nation as a whole.

B) warn of the institutional damage that will result from the assessment of citizens based on anything other than behavior.

C) argue for more substantial equality that is based on treating each citizen according to his or her caliber and effort.

D) remind of the important lessons of the forefathers that Americans must do well to heed and ultimately pass on.

2

Which choice provides the best evidence for the answer to the previous question?

A) Lines 3-5 ("If the...well-off.")

B) Lines 14-17 ("It is...worth")

C) Lines 66-68 ("You have...children.")

D) Lines 85-88 ("We must...less.")

3

According to the passage, Roosevelt believes that the structure and foundation of America would be at risk if we

A) fail to foster rationality in our social systems and governments.

B) use arbitrary standards to measure man and partition society.

C) acknowledge the base differences between classes and creeds.

D) compartmentalize our efforts and ignore our commonalities.

4

It can most reasonably be inferred that the "old American ideal" referred to in line 32 is

A) the inherent morality of all men.

B) the valuable diversity of thought and belief.

C) the right to succeed through personal endeavor.

D) the desirable state of self-governance.

5

Which choice provides the best evidence for the answer to the previous question?

A) Lines 23-24 ("Those deep-set...men.")

B) Lines 25-26 ("The failure...merits")

C) Lines 29-30 ("A healthy...sections.")

D) Lines 43-44 ("Among ourselves...heart")

6

In the fourth paragraph, Roosevelt discusses "envy" and "arrogance" in order to

A) highlight the parallel pitfalls of those who succumb to ignoble opinions of their societal opposites.

B) reiterate his opinion that there is a direct correlation between the prosperity of the few and the many.

C) define the inauspicious traits that become rampant in a society that fails to value each of its members.

D) caution his listeners against inciting resentment toward those who are coincidentally more fortunate.

7

As used in line 50, "open to" most nearly means

A) attainable by.

B) extended to.

C) free for.

D) designated for.

8

The main purpose of Roosevelt's discussion of family life in lines 56-61 is to

A) emphasize the necessity of family to the production of honorable young men.

B) esteem the diligence and personal enterprise that should also exist in the home.

C) cite the patience and effort necessary to the successful navigation of parenthood.

D) situate a quotidian concern in the greater context of the passage as a whole.

CONTINUE

9

As used in line 77, "sunder" most nearly means

A) render.

B) divide.

C) evaluate.

D) assess.

10

Which choice best supports Roosevelt's belief that all are deserving of fair treatment despite the uneven distribution of attributes?

A) Lines 19-22 ("There are...determined")

B) Lines 33-35 ("Our average...mind.")

C) Lines 44-47 ("we are...doing")

D) Lines 80-82 ("the fundamental...poor")

CONTINUE

Questions 1-10 are based on the following passage.

5.2

This passage is adapted from Ho Chi Minh's 1946 appeal to the Governments of China, The United States of America, The Union of Socialist Soviet Republics, and Great Britain for their assistance in liberating Vietnam from the yoke of French colonial rule.

In August 1945, the Japanese surrendered to the Allies. The popular forces of Vietnam which, since 1940, had made incessant attacks on the Japanese
Line forces, and which had, in 1944, succeeded in creating
5 a "Free Zone" in Northern Indochina, went down to conquer the capital-city and the governing rule. The population, fired with democratic aspirations and spirit, enthusiastically welcomed them and manifested their desire to maintain their unity for the grandeur
10 of the Fatherland once lost and now found again. On September 2, 1945, the Democratic Republic of Vietnam was solemnly proclaimed, a factor of peace and progress in the reconstruction of the world.

But, on September 23, 1945, French troops
15 attacked Saigon, starting an invasion which is now in its fifth month. That invasion is menacing North Vietnam and French troops have begun to filter through our Chinese frontier. That aggression, carried on by an experienced and numerous army fully equipped
20 with the most recent inventions of modern warfare, has brought about the destruction of our towns and villages, the assassination of our civilian population, and the starving of a great part of our country. Untold atrocities have been committed, not as reprisals upon
25 our guerrilla troops, but on women and children and unarmed old people. These atrocities are beyond imagination and beyond words, and remind one of the darkest ages: assaults on the sanitary formations, on Red Cross personnel, bombing and machine-
30 gunning of villages, raping of women, looting and indiscriminate pillaging of Vietnam and Chinese houses, etc...

Yet, despite the maltreatments of the civilian population, we have, for 5 long months, mounted a
35 stubborn resistance, fought in the worst conditions, without food, medicine and without clothing. And we shall carry on, sustained by our faith in international honor and in our final victory. In the free zone of our national territory, especially in the area under Chinese
40 control, our civilians have set out to work, the results of which are most favorable and give rise to the brightest hopes.

Democracy has been established on solid foundations. On January 6 last, general elections were
45 organized with the greatest success. In a few days 400 representatives of the entire country will hold the first session of the Constituent National Assembly. A new administrative organization has replaced the old mandarinate system. The most unpopular taxes
50 have been abolished. The anti-illiteracy campaign has yielded unexpectedly optimistic results. The primary and secondary schools as well as the University have been reopened to numerous students. Peace and order are restored and smoothly maintained.
55 In the economic field, the situation is bettering every day. All the vexatory measures imposed by the French colonial economy have been abrogated. Commerce, production, and the transformation and consumption of raw materials, once subjected to very
60 strict regulations, are now operated on an entirely free basis. The shortage of rice, though still critical, has been relieved by the intensive production of other foodstuffs, and the price of rice has been reduced by some 40% of its 1945 figures. Cereals, matches,
65 salt, tobacco, once monopolized by speculators, are now offered on the normal markets at prices within reach of the common man. All public services have resumed their prewar activities, and the Vietnamese staff, under their Vietnamese Directors, are working
70 with industry and efficacy. Communications have been re-established, and the dam system has been not only mended but also fortified.

All these programs were carried out while, in the South, the French aggression has intensified every day.
75 We Vietnamese people, despite the difficulties of the present, and the heavy heritage of the last five years, have demonstrated our capacity to self-government and our desire to live free and independent.

For these reasons, we think it our duty to send this
80 note to the Great Powers which had led the anti-fascist crusade to final victory, and which had taken up the reconstruction of the world with a view to definitively outlawing war, oppression, exploitation, misery, fear and injustice.
85 We request that these Great Powers take all proper steps to stop, by an urgent interference, the bloodshed that is taking place in South Vietnam, and to arrive at an urgent and fair settling of the Indochinese issue. We are confident that, with their mediation, we may
90 be given a status worthy of a people that had fought and suffered for their democratic ideals. In so doing, the Great Powers will provide a solid foundation to peace and security in this part of the world, fulfilling the hopes that the oppressed peoples had placed in

CONTINUE

95 them. While waiting with confidence for a positive measure from the Governments of WASHINGTON, MOSCOW, LONDON, and CHUNGKING, we have determined to fight to our last drop of blood against the reestablishment of French imperialism.

1

The main purpose of the passage is to

A) inspire the Vietnamese to remain steadfast in their opposition to the French until aid has been received.

B) entreat the Great Powers to intervene on behalf of the Vietnamese people to free them from oppressive French colonial rule.

C) implore Vietnam's allies to aid in its struggle for independence which has had dire consequences for the Vietnamese people.

D) persuade the Great Powers to lend military aid to the Vietnamese guerilla forces and thereby check French violence in Southern Vietnam.

2

In the first paragraph, Ho Chi Minh enumerates Vietnam's colonial history in order to

A) praise the Vietnamese forces for their defense of liberty and democracy against the imperialist Japanese.

B) exemplify how the Vietnamese forces will once again be victorious over France by citing a former military victory.

C) clarify the true nature of the affront to Vietnam's valiant attempts at self-sovereignty and progress.

D) emphasize the disappointment of such rapid French invasion on the heels of Vietnam's apparent democratic success.

3

As used in line 27, "imagination" most nearly means
A) description.
B) perception.
C) thought.
D) belief.

4

Over the course of the passage, Ho Chi Minh shifts from

A) an impassioned denouncement of French conduct to a humbling solicitation of foreign militaries.

B) a composed account of French atrocities to a demonstration of Vietnam's democratic achievements.

C) a broad history of Vietnam's occupation to a specified explanation of its present struggles.

D) an illuminating discussion of colonial rule to a global contextualisation of such rule.

5

According to the passage, which best demonstrates the Vietnamese government's capability to rule the state?

A) Its commitment to democracy and a free market even in the face of hardship.

B) Its ability to meet the practical needs of its people despite French oppression.

C) Its stubborn and successful military resistance in spite of direct French pressure.

D) Its belief in the universal rights to basic necessities and military protection.

6

Which choice provides the best evidence for the answer to the previous question?

A) Lines 6-10 ("The population...again.")
B) Lines 33-38 ("Yet, despite...victory.")
C) Lines 64-70 ("Cereals, matches...efficacy")
D) Lines 73-78 ("All these...independent.")

7

In lines 80-81, Ho Chi Minh mentions "the anti-fascist crusade" primarily to

A) make the interference of the Great Powers a moral necessity.

B) call upon a historical precedent to further his political campaign.

C) show that Vietnam intends to take up that very same mantle.

D) parallel the struggle against fascism to that of Vietnamese independence.

CONTINUE

8

As used in line 88, "settling of" most nearly means

A) placating of.

B) conclusion to.

C) reconciliation of.

D) defraying of.

9

In establishing the current conflict between the French and the Vietnamese, Ho Chi Minh emphasizes the fact that the French

A) are arbitrarily committing human rights abuses in Vietnam.

B) have disregarded international law in their colonial incursions.

C) have an overpowering military advantage over the Vietnamese.

D) have rendered Vietnamese legislation ineffective through colonization.

10

Which choice provides the best evidence for the answer to the previous question?

A) Lines 11-15 ("On September … Saigon")

B) Lines 18-20 ("That aggression...warfare")

C) Lines 28-31 ("Assaults on … pillaging")

D) Lines 36-38 ("And we...victory")

CONTINUE

Questions 1-10 are based on the following passage.

5.3

Passage 1 is adapted from a speech by President Lynden Johnson, delivered at University of Michigan during his 1964 bid for re-election. Passage 2 is adapted from Ronald Reagan's 1964 "A Time for Choosing" speech in support of Johnson opponent Barry Goldwater.

Passage 1

The challenge of the next half century is whether we have the wisdom to use our wealth to enrich and elevate our national life, and to advance the quality of
Line our American civilization.
5   Your imagination, your initiative, and your indignation will determine whether we build a society where progress is the servant of our needs, or a society where old values and new visions are buried under unbridled growth. For in your time we have the
10 opportunity to move not only toward the rich society and the powerful society, but upward to the Great Society.

The Great Society rests on abundance and liberty for all. It demands an end to poverty and racial
15 injustice, to which we are totally committed in our time. The Great Society is a place where every child can find knowledge to enrich his mind and to enlarge his talents. It is a place where the city of man serves not only the needs of the body and the demands of
20 commerce but the desire for beauty and the hunger for community. It is a place where man can renew contact with nature. It is a place which honors creation for its own sake and for what it adds to the understanding of the race. It is a place where men are more concerned
25 with the quality of their goals than the quantity of their goods. But most of all, the Great Society is not a safe harbor, a resting place, a final objective, a finished work. It is a challenge constantly renewed, beckoning us toward a destiny where the meaning of our lives
30 matches the marvelous products of our labor.

I want to talk to you today about three places where we begin to build the Great Society—in our cities, in our countryside, and in our classrooms.

In the remainder of this century, urban population
35 will double, city land will double, and we will have to build homes, highways, and facilities equal to all those built since this country was first settled. So, in the next 40 years we must rebuild the entire urban United States. The catalog of ills is long: there is the decay of
40 the centers and the despoiling of the suburbs. There is not enough housing for our people or transportation for our traffic. Open land is vanishing and old landmarks are violated. Our society will never be great until our cities are great.

45   A second place where we begin to build the Great Society is in our countryside. We have always prided ourselves on being not only America the strong and America the free, but America the beautiful. Today that beauty is in danger. The water we drink, the food
50 we eat, the very air that we breathe, are threatened with pollution. Green fields and dense forests are disappearing. A few years ago, we were greatly concerned about the "Ugly American." Today we must act to prevent an ugly America.

55   A third place to build the Great Society is in the classrooms of America. There, your children's lives will be shaped. Our society will not be great until every young mind is set free to scan the farthest reaches of thought and imagination. We are still
60 far from that goal: In many places, classrooms are overcrowded and curricula are outdated. Most of our qualified teachers are underpaid, and many of our paid teachers are unqualified. So, we must give every child a place to sit and a teacher to learn from. Poverty must
65 not be a bar to learning, and learning must offer an escape from poverty.

These are three of the central issues of the Great Society. While our Government has many programs directed at those issues, I do not pretend that we have
70 the full answer to those problems. But I do promise this: We are going to assemble the best thought and the broadest knowledge from all over the world to find those answers for America. I intend to establish working groups to prepare a series of White House
75 conferences and meetings—on the cities, on natural beauty, on the quality of education, and on other emerging challenges. And from these meetings and from this inspiration and from these studies we will begin to set our course toward the Great Society.

Passage 2

80   One side in this campaign has been telling us that the issues of this election are the maintenance of peace and prosperity. In this vote-harvesting time, they use terms like the "Great Society," or as we were told a few days ago by the President, we must accept
85 a greater government activity in the affairs of the people. This was the very thing the Founding Fathers sought to minimize. They knew that governments can't control the economy without controlling people. They also knew that outside of its legitimate functions,
90 government does nothing as well or as economically as the private sector of the economy. This is the issue

CONTINUE

of this election: Whether we believe in our capacity for self-government or whether we abandon the American revolution and confess that a little intellectual elite in a
95 far-distant capitol can plan our lives for us better than we can plan them ourselves.

For three decades, we've sought to solve the problems of unemployment through government planning, and the more the plans fail, the more the
100 planners plan. We have so many people who can't see a fat man standing beside a thin one without coming to the conclusion the fat man got that way by taking advantage of the thin one. So, they're going to solve all the problems of human misery through government
105 planning. Well, now, if government planning and welfare had the answer—and they've had almost 30 years of it—shouldn't we expect government to read the score to us once in a while? Shouldn't they be telling us about the decline each year in the number
110 of people needing help? The reduction in the need for public housing?

No government ever voluntarily reduces itself in size. So, government programs, once launched, never disappear. Actually, a government bureau is the
115 nearest thing to eternal life we'll ever see on this earth. Federal employees number two and a half million. These proliferating bureaus with their thousands of regulations have cost us many of our constitutional safeguards. How many of us realize that today federal
120 agents can invade a man's property without a warrant? They can impose a fine without a formal hearing, let alone a trial by jury? And they can seize and sell his property at auction to enforce the payment of that fine.

Now it doesn't require expropriation or
125 confiscation of private property or business to impose socialism on a people. What does it mean whether you hold the deed to your business or property if the government holds the power of life and death over that business or property? And such machinery
130 already exists. The government can find some charge to bring against any concern it chooses to prosecute. Every businessman has his own tale of harassment. Somewhere a perversion has taken place. Our natural, unalienable rights are now considered to be a
135 dispensation of government, and freedom has never been so fragile.

1

Which choice best describes the developmental pattern of Passage 1?

A) A description of Johnson's utopia to a detailed enumeration of the ways in which that utopia would benefit Americans.

B) An explanation of a pressing challenge to an idealized depiction of a society which has overcome that challenge.

C) A portrayal of Johnson's aspirations for America to an outline of the implementation of his proposed policies.

D) An exaltation of American progress throughout recent history to an analysis of Johnson's intended developments.

2

Johnson suggests that all of the following are crucial in the creation of the Great Society EXCEPT

A) the accommodation of fundamental human needs so as to experience communal well-being.

B) the maximization of environmental action so as to conserve the land and promote its beauty.

C) the quality education of the youth so as to aid economic advancement and continue current progress.

D) the general promotion of affluence so as to encourage equality of opportunity for all people.

3

As used in line 7, "servant" most nearly means

A) catalyst.

B) resolution.

C) negation.

D) realization.

149

CONTINUE

4

Johnson warns of an "ugly America" (line 54) in order to emphasize the

A) visceral need for the natural world that is often overlooked.

B) importance of natural resources in an expanding society.

C) destruction of nature as a symbol of American prosperity.

D) irreplaceable role of nature in sustaining the American way of life.

5

As used in line 58, "scan" most nearly means

A) pursue.

B) explore.

C) reach.

D) comprehend.

6

The author of Passage 2 would most likely characterize the first passage's depiction of the "Great Society" as

A) a failed experiment that has been unnecessarily prolonged.

B) a misguided attempt to impose socialism on the American people.

C) an undemocratic fantasy promoted by politicians to gain popularity.

D) an overextension of social services on the part of the federal government.

7

Which choice provides the best evidence for the answer to the previous question?

A) Lines 80-87 ("One side...minimize")

B) Lines 91-96 ("This is… ourselves")

C) Lines 112-119 ("No government… safeguards")

D) Lines 130-136 ("The government… fragile")

8

The author of Passage 2 would most likely agree with which of the following statements about the relationship between the economy and the federal government?

A) Federal economic intervention will inevitably lead to the restriction of personal freedoms.

B) Federal legislation is fundamentally impotent in the furthering of social progress.

C) Economic self-sufficiency is the cornerstone of a truly democratic federal government.

D) Governmental economic intervention poses an arbitrary challenge to the superior private sector.

9

Which choice provides the best evidence for the answer to the previous question?

A) Lines 86-88 ("This was… people")

B) Lines 89-91 ("They also…economy")

C) Lines 97-100 ("For three...plan")

D) Lines 112-115 ("No government...earth")

10

Reagan uses an analogy in lines 100-103 ("We have… one") in order to underscore

A) the failure of large governments to ensure equality in spite of their extensive policies.

B) the false assumption that those who attain wealth have done so at another's expense.

C) the unjust discrimination faced by the wealthy from proponents of socialist agendas.

D) the misunderstanding of social inequality held by progressives in favor of large governments.

CONTINUE

Questions 1-10 are based on the following passage.

5.4

This passage is adapted from " David Walker's appeal to the colored citizens of the world, but in particular, and very expressly to those of the United States of America." Written in Boston, in the State of Massachusetts, Sept. 28, 1829.

Men of colour, who are also of sense, for you particularly is my appeal designed. Our more ignorant brethren are not able to penetrate its value. I call upon
Line you, therefore, to cast your eyes upon the wretchedness
5 of your brethren and to do your utmost to enlighten them—*go to work and enlighten your brethren!*—let the Lord see you doing what you can to rescue them and yourselves from degradation.

Do any of you say that you and your family are
10 free and happy and what have you to do with wretched slaves and other people? If any of you wish to know how free you are, let one of you go through the southern and western States of this country, and unless you travel as a slave to a white man or have your free
15 papers, if they do not take you up and put you in jail, and if you cannot give evidence of your freedom, sell you into eternal slavery, I am not a living man.

And yet some of you have the hardihood to say that you are free and happy! May God have mercy on
20 your freedom and happiness! I met a colored man in the street with a string of boots on his shoulder. We fell into conversation, and in course of which I said to him, "what a miserable set of people we are!" He asked why. Said I, "we are so subjected under the whites, that
25 we cannot obtain the comforts of life, but by cleaning their boots and shoes." Said he, "I am completely happy! I never want to live any better or happier than when I can get plenty of boots and shoes to clean!" Oh! how can those who are actuated by avarice only,
30 but think that our creator made us to be an inheritance to them forever, when they see that our greatest glory is centered in such mean and low objects? For if we are men, we ought to be thankful to the Lord for the past, and for the future. Be looking forward with
35 thankful hearts to higher attainments than *wielding the razor and cleaning boots and shoes.* The man whose aspirations are not *above* these is indeed ignorant and wretched enough.

There is a great work for you to do, as trifling
40 as some of you may think of it. You have to prove to the Americans and the world that we are men, and not *brutes* - as we have been represented and by millions treated. Remember to let the aim of your

labors among your brethren, and particularly the youth,
45 be the dissemination of education and religion. It is lamentable that many of our children leave school knowing but a little more about the grammar of their language than a horse does about handling a musket, and not a few of them are really so ignorant that
50 they are unable to answer a person correctly general questions in geography, and to hear them read would only be to disgust a man who has a taste for reading.

Some of our brethren are so very full of learning that you cannot mention any thing to them which
55 they do not know better than yourself! Nothing is strange to them! They knew everything years ago! If anything should be mentioned in company where they are, immaterial how important it is, respecting us or the world, if they had not divulged it, they make light
60 of it, and affect to have known it long before it was mentioned, and try to make all in the room believe that your conversation is not worth hearing!

I pray that the Lord may undeceive my ignorant brethren, and permit them to throw away pretensions,
65 and seek after the substance of learning. I would crawl on my hands and knees through mud and mire, to the feet of a learned man, where I would sit and humbly supplicate him to instill into me, that which neither devils nor tyrants could remove, only with my life. For
70 the Africans to acquire learning in this country, makes tyrants quake and tremble on their sandy foundation. The bare name of educating the coloured people scares our cruel oppressors almost to death. But if they do not have enough to be frightened for yet, it will be because
75 they can always keep us ignorant.

CONTINUE

1

What is the primary purpose of the passage?

A) To advocate for the advancement of African-Americans by securing their political and economic rights.

B) To encourage African-Americans to elevate members of their race by improving the quality of their education.

C) To argue for a higher standard of living among African-Americans by providing opportunities for higher paying jobs.

D) To accuse the institution of slavery of having conditioned African-Americans to expect little out of freedom.

2

As used in line 1, "of sense" most nearly means

A) sensible.

B) intelligent.

C) emotional.

D) respectable.

3

Walker characterizes true "freedom and happiness" (line 20) for members of his race as a condition that requires

A) the containment of slavery.

B) the acquisition of knowledge.

C) financial independence.

D) respect from white men.

4

In context of the passage as a whole, what is the purpose of the conversation between Walker and the man in the third paragraph?

A) It clarifies his argument by providing a relatable anecdote.

B) It highlights the tension that exists among African-Americans.

C) It illustrates a mindset among his people that he finds lamentable.

D) It details the hardships of African-Americans in the labor force.

5

As used in line 32, "mean" most nearly means

A) vile.

B) cruel.

C) rude.

D) worthless.

6

Which choice provides evidence for the claim that white men feel threatened by the prospect of an educated African-American populace?

A) Lines 13-15 ("unless you…jail")

B) Lines 24-26 ("Said I…shoes")

C) Lines 51-52 ("to hear…reading")

D) Lines 72-73 ("The bare…death")

7

What is the effect of the analogy in lines 47-48 ("knowing but…musket")?

A) It underscores the necessity of a particular course of action.

B) It belittles the efforts made by a segment of Americans.

C) It dramatizes the difficulty of teaching grammar to children.

D) It creates a humorous tone in an otherwise serious discussion.

8

How does Walker distinguish between the "learning" in line 53 and the "learning" in line 65?

A) The first is pretentious, while the second is noble.

B) The first is general, while the second is specific.

C) The first is praiseworthy, while the second is banal.

D) The first is accessible, while the second is elitist.

CONTINUE

9

What would the author consider to be a positive effect of African American learning?

A) It provides irremovable and fulfilling enrichment.

B) It advances the understanding of complex concepts.

C) It makes slave owners aware of their untenable position.

D) It unnerves white southerners into submission.

10

Which choice provides the best evidence for the answer to the previous question?

A) Lines 53-55 ("Some of...yourself")

B) Lines 63-65 ("I pray...learning")

C) Lines 67-69 ("I would...life")

D) Lines 69-71 ("For the...foundation")

CONTINUE

Questions 1-10 are based on the following passage.

5.5

The following passage is adapted from "Woman Man's Equal" (1873) by Reverend Thomas Webster.

We claim that women, being held equally responsible to the law with men, are as well entitled to have a voice in making that law. It is
Line a fundamental principle of all governments, not
5 despotic, that "taxation without representation" is a gross infringement upon the civil rights of the subject or citizen. When, in spite of the disadvantages under which women labor, they have, by unflagging industry and prudent management, acquired real estate, their
10 property is taxed according to the same rule by which the property of men is taxed, and still the elective franchise is denied them. Men, in legislating for men, know their wants and understand their particular needs because they have experience of them; however, in
15 legislating for women, they look at things from their own stand-point, and because it is impossible for them to experience the various annoyances and humiliations to which women are subjected, they do not realize the injustice toward women of the existing state of things.
20 It is contended that, if women were entitled to the franchise, it would make no difference with a party vote since as many women would vote on one ticket as on the other. What of it? The franchise has been extended from time to time for centuries to various
25 classes of men, and these classes did not, as a class, confine themselves to one particular ticket or party.

If women had a right to vote, say some, it would occasion family contention. Why should it? If a woman thinks as her husband, she will vote as he does;
30 if not, none but an unreasonable and overbearing man would insist that his wife must think as he does and vote in accordance with his views, whether they agree with her own or not. It would be quite as just and as reasonable to urge that, because the peace of families
35 is sometimes disturbed by fathers and sons voting for opposite parties, therefore, the sons should not be allowed to exercise the franchise during the life-time of their fathers.

The great objection, the one which rises above all
40 others with regard to women taking an active part in civil matters, is that they would thereby neglect their houses and families. This objection has some weight; it is not altogether so unreasonable as most of the others raised. But even here the event dreaded does
45 not necessarily follow any more than because men are

allowed to vote therefore their business and families must suffer in consequence. Prudent men, when they accept offices of public trust, so order their business arrangements that they shall be properly attended to
50 without allowing the one to interfere with the other. So too would prudent women. It might with as much propriety be argued that a farmer must not be permitted to accept any public office, not even that of juryman, because the acceptance of it might call him from home
55 either in springtime or harvest, nor a doctor to become a candidate for public honors lest someone might be sick while he was away, as to argue that a woman must not be permitted to take an active part in public affairs because the house is to be attended to, and the comfort
60 and well-being of her husband and children provided for. Are the recognized duties and ordinary occupations of women necessarily so all-engrossing as to be inconsistent with any other demand upon their time or thoughts, or of so much graver importance than the
65 duties which men owe to their business and families, as to require her constant presence and the entire devotion of all her energies?

The responsibility of regulating and ordering a household properly devolves equally upon both the
70 husband and wife. It cannot be a well-regulated house if either fails to share the responsibility equally. Is the careful wife and mother, then, to be cut off from the rights of citizenship because she is a wife and mother? There is no valid reason why an intelligent woman
75 should not be permitted to carry the weight of her judicious influence beyond the charmed circle of her home, any more than that she should not be permitted to exercise it there.

Though there is still much fierce opposition to
80 the movement for granting them equal civil rights and privileges, and though it may be expected that this opposition will be continued for some time to come, women have cause for thankful rejoicing, and may take courage. The long night of their bitter servitude
85 is nearly over, the dawn of better days is beginning to tinge the horizon, and hope may now be entertained that erelong they shall occupy the position to which they are entitled, as man's compeer—the position of equality with him in all the relations of life—and enjoy
90 the full rights and privileges of civilized citizenship.

The morning is breaking.

CONTINUE

1

Which choice best describes the developmental pattern of the passage?

A) A recognition of a fundamental aspect of democracy to a series of refutations to counterarguments.

B) An evocation of a founding American value to an admonishment of those against women's suffrage.

C) A criticism of male legislators to a detailed method of addressing the lack of representation.

D) A justification of women's suffrage to a comprehensive overview of injustices towards women.

2

As used in line 2, "responsible to" most nearly means

A) accountable for.

B) answerable to.

C) limited by.

D) entitled to.

3

Webster draws a comparison between men of different classes and women in order to

A) assert that the current civil state of women is lower than that of even the lowest class of men.

B) illustrate the flawed reasoning of men who assume that women's votes will not change the outcome of an election.

C) justify the need for women to counterbalance the multitudes of men who vote to preserve the status quo.

D) provide empirical evidence to show that women would not mishandle the right to suffrage.

4

Which choice provides the best evidence for Webster's claim that many women have achieved success despite institutionalized sexism?

A) Lines 7-11 ("When, in...taxed")

B) Lines 47-51 ("Prudent men...women")

C) Lines 61-64 ("Are the...thoughts")

D) Lines 85-88 ("the dawn...compeer")

5

Webster contends that male legislators have which of the following attitudes towards female empowerment?

A) Discriminatory, because they are intent on confining women's influence to the domestic sphere.

B) Oblivious, because they are ignorant about the societal and political injustices that women face.

C) Hostile, because they have a vested interest in maintaining the patriarchal status quo.

D) Skeptical, because they believe that women's suffrage will not affect elections in any significant way.

6

Which choice provides the best evidence for the answer to the previous question?

A) Lines 12-14 ("Men, who...them")

B) Lines 16-19 ("because it...things")

C) Lines 20-23 ("It is...other")

D) Lines 39-42 ("The great...families")

7

In context of the passage as a whole, the third paragraph (lines 27-38) primarily serves to

A) point out a double standard that challenges Webster's opponents.

B) raise and refute a potential counterargument of Webster's opponents.

C) anticipate and correct a possible misinterpretation of Webster's argument.

D) highlight a contrast that provides context for Webster's argument.

8

In lines 51-57 ("It might...away"), Webster refers to a "farmer", "juryman", and "doctor" primarily as examples of men who

A) are currently enfranchised with the right to vote.

B) have historically assumed masculine gender roles.

C) pursue careers that are laborious and unpredictable.

D) can balance their professional duties with their citizenry.

CONTINUE ➡

9

As used in line 74, "valid" most nearly means

A) credible.

B) compelling.

C) proven.

D) logical.

10

In lines 74-78 ("There is...there"), Webster refers to women's current role in the domestic sphere in order to

A) support the point that men are not uniquely capable of sensibly functioning within and outside the household.

B) demonstrate the good judgement of women to show their capacity for political participation.

C) illustrate yet another damaging double standard between men and women that is present in society.

D) highlight the abhorrent injustice in denying dutiful mothers and wives their rightful citizenship.

STOP

Please turn to next page for answer keys and explanations.

Answer Key: CHAPTER FIVE

5.1 | Roosevelt	5.2 | Ho Chi Minh	5.3 | Great Society	5.4 | Walker	5.5 | Webster
1: C	1: B	1: C	1: B	1: A
2: D	2: D	2: D	2: B	2: B
3: B	3: D	3: B	3: B	3: B
4: D	4: B	4: D	4: C	4: A
5: C	5: B	5: B	5: D	5: B
6: A	6: D	6: C	6: D	6: B
7: A	7: D	7: A	7: A	7: A
8: B	8: B	8: A	8: A	8: D
9: B	9: C	9: A	9: C	9: D
10: C	10: B	10: B	10: D	10: B

Answer Explanations

Chapter Five

Chapter 5.1 | Roosevelt

Question 1: C
Choice C is the best answer because Roosevelt highlights the importance of "[treating] each man on his worth and merits as a man" (lines 85-96), not based on the man's status "as a member of a class" (lines 13-14); Roosevelt can then be described as encouraging fair treatment based on "caliber and effort" instead of class and circumstance. Choice A is incorrect because Roosevelt does not prioritize "prosperity", but "the continuance of our healthy national life" (lines 8-9) and the collective well-being of the nation. Choice B is incorrect because Roosevelt does not primarily seek to "warn" his audience; although he characterizes inequality as an "infamous thing" that is "fundamentally treacherous to our institutions" (lines 14-16), he does not expand on these consequences throughout the remainder of the passage. Choice D is incorrect because Roosevelt indicates that his audience has inherited values from their forefathers, but does not state what these "strong virtues" (line 70) are.

Question 2: D
Choice D is the best answer because lines 85-88 reference the title of Roosevelt's speech—a "square deal"—and therefore reinforce the main claim or purpose of the passage. Choice A is incorrect because lines 3-5 contain context for Roosevelt's main purpose of his speech but do not indicate the main claim itself. Choice B is incorrect because lines 14-17 depict the problem that Roosevelt claims is "fundamentally treacherous" to our institutions, but does not address his solution to that problem. Choice C is incorrect because lines 66-68 describe privileges that Roosevelt's audience have received from actions in the past, while Roosevelt aims to guide his audience's actions in the future.

Question 3: B
Choice B is the best answer because Roosevelt claims that "the failure in public and in private life thus to treat each man on his own merits" (lines 25-26) in favor of judging others based on "accidental questions of employment or locality" (lines 22-23) "would prove fatal to our Republic" (line 28). Because Roosevelt calls the circumstances that create class divisions "accidental" and cautions against "the recognition of this government as being either for the poor...or for the rich" (lines 26-28), he thus sees such class divisions as unnecessary, or "arbitrary", in determining the attitudes of the government towards its people. Choice A is incorrect because Roosevelt does not characterize unequal treatment based on class differences as "irrational"; as such, he cannot be encouraging "rationality" throughout the passage. Choice C is incorrect because Roosevelt himself

acknowledges the differences among people in lines 43-45: "Among ourselves we differ in many qualities of body, head, and ehrt; we are unequally developed, mentally as well as physically." Therefore, Roosevelt does not believe that merely understanding the differences among groups of people are detrimental to society, but that unfair treatment based on those differences would be. Choice D is incorrect because Roosevelt does believe that we should "compartmentalize our efforts"; however, such discrimination should be based on work ethic and character, instead of on class and status.

Question 4: D
Choice D is the best answer because Roosevelt says in lines 29-30 that a healthy republican government "must rest upon individuals, not upon classes or sections": men should be judged by their characters, not by their affiliation to a group which is determined by arbitrary circumstances in life. Roosevelt thus encourages independence and individualism, which corresponds with "self-governance". Choice A is incorrect because morality is not a primary concern of Roosevelt throughout the passage, nor is it a necessary component of the "old American ideal": Roosevelt references the "principles" of men that should be the basis of their treatment by others (line 24), but does not specify the qualities of those principles. Choice B is incorrect because the "diversity of thought and belief" is seen as unnecessary to reach the American ideal: each American has the right to fair treatment and equal opportunity for success despite, not because of, their differences in "body, head, and heart" (line 44). Choice C is incorrect because Roosevelt does not believe that success is or should be guaranteed to all; therefore, he would disagree with its description as a "right".

Question 5: C
Choice C is the best answer because lines lines 29-30 describe the criteria for a "healthy republican government", which represents the ideal American government and therefore matches the topic of the previous question. Choices A, B, and D are off-topic: lines 23-24 reveal the characteristics by which Americans should be judged, lines 25-26 describe the failure of American government to judge by those characteristics, and lines 43-44 indicate the differences among different groups of Americans.

Question 6: A
Choice A is the best answer because Roosevelt states in the fourth paragraph that "the two feelings, envy and arrogance, are but opposite sides of the same shield" (lines 40-42), which indicates that there is a parallel between the two feelings. The elaboration of this point comes in the preceding lines, where Roosevelt repudiates both "the man of wealthy guilty of the mean and base spirit of arrogance toward those who are less well off" (lines 35-37) and "the man of small means who... feels...mean and base envy for those who are better off" (lines 38-40). So, Roosevelt is stating that those who think lowly of those who differ in wealth are similar in that their two feelings, envy and arrogance, are unfavorable. Choice B is incorrect because Roosevelt's point regarding the "direct correlation" in the first paragraph indicates that if one class of society does well, then the rest will. This statement doesn't apply to Roosevelt's discussion in the fourth paragraph, which talks about wealth differences between classes. All classes can prosper and falter at the same time, but that doesn't interact with the idea that they will still have base differences in their income and wealth. Choice C is incorrect because Roosevelt discusses the way in which individuals treat those of different socioeconomic statuses in this paragraph, whereas the answer choice refers to how society treats its members. Thus, Choice C is off-topic. Choice D is incorrect because Roosevelt

is not only discussing those who are resentful towards the more fortunate, but also those who look down on others for being less so. Additionally, Roosevelt is not cautioning his listeners; rather, he is expressing his opinion that both envy and arrogance are unfavorable.

Question 7: A
Choice A is the best answer because Roosevelt elaborates on the significance of "[this prize] open to every man" (line 50) in lines 52-56: "to win success...means that the man has devoted his best energy and power through long years to the achievement of his ends". He believes that every man should be able to access, or attain, success through hard work. "Attainable by" is the only answer choice that encapsulates the act of working towards success. Choices B, C, and D are incorrect because they all imply that success can be granted without hard work, which Roosevelt states is not the case.

Question 8: B
Choice B is the best answer because Roosevelt indicates that his description of success through hard work in lines 52-56 also applies to "the life of the family" (line 56). He then glorifies the work that men and women do "patiently and uncomplainingly" (line 60). In these lines, Roosevelt clearly expresses his belief that hard work, or "diligence" and "enterprise", ought to be valued, even when it takes place in the home. Choice A is incorrect because Roosevelt does not allude to the effects of family and home life on the next generation, which makes the phrase "the production of honorable young men" incorrect. Similarly, Choice C is incorrect because "parenthood" also emphasizes the next generation, or the children, whereas this concept is barely mentioned in lines 56-61. The only point at which "parenthood" is even referred to is when Roosevelt discusses that women can be mothers, but that is tangential to his overall point regarding the household. Choice D is incorrect because Roosevelt does not ever indicate that "the life of the family" is a "quotidian", or daily, concern. Additionally, the implication of a daily concern is that it is of lesser importance, whereas Roosevelt expresses that "the whole welfare of the nation rests" (lines 57-58) upon it.

Question 9: B
Choice B is the best answer because Roosevelt indicates that we must work towards a "common end" (line 75). His way for achieving this common end lies in "the resolute determination to permit no man and no set of men to sunder us one from the other by lines of caste or creed or section" (lines 75-78). These "lines", or class differences, cannot be considered while working towards unity; we must prevent divisions among us. Choice A is incorrect because to "render", or make, men distinct on the basis of class what Roosevelt is concerned with. Men are inherently distinct if they are of different classes; Roosevelt is advocating for us not letting these differences shape our behavior. Choices C and D are incorrect; their meanings are very close in this context, which would immediately eliminate both choices. Moreover, it is not the evaluation or assessment of the class differences that Roosevelt takes fault with. He believes that they can be acknowledged, as long as they do not divert the population from the "common end".

Question 10: C
Choice C is the best answer because lines 44-47 indicate that although Americans "are unequally developed" and therefore have an uneven distribution of advantages such as mental and physical strength, "each one of us has the right to ask that he shall be protected from wrong-doing". Roosevelt's description of equal treatment and protection from harm as a "right" underscores his belief that such treatment should be applied to all, regardless of one's station in life. Choice A is

incorrect because lines 19-22 indicate that an uneven distribution of attributes exists in a population ("there are good citizens and bad citizens"), but does not reveal Roosevelt's opinion about this issue. Choice B is incorrect because lines 33-35 describes the "average citizen" who "is a sane and healthy man" and therefore deserves fair treatment, but does not account for citizens who do not fit this ideal. Choice D is incorrect because lines 80-82 describe Roosevelt's claim that men should not "stand for or against" others; this supports Roosevelt's point that men should not perceive others differently because of their class, but does not make a claim about "treatment" or actions towards others.

Chapter 5.2 | Ho Chi Minh

Question 1: B
Choice B is the best answer because the whole passage, from the discussion of French atrocities to the enumeration of Vietnamese achievements, is framed as an appeal for help that is directed at the Great Powers. In the final paragraph, Ho Chi Minh writes, "We request that these Great Powers take all the proper steps...to stop the bloodshed...and to arrive at an urgent and fair settling of the Indochinese issue" (lines 85-88). Choice A is incorrect because it suggests that this passage is directed at the Vietnamese people with the hope of bolstering their resistance, when, as has been explained, Ho Chi Minh's intended audience are the Great Powers. Choice C is incorrect because it assumes that the Great Powers are already the allies of Vietnam, when the whole point it so enlist them as allies in the first place. Choice D is incorrect because Ho Chi Minh never actually specifies that the aid requested is of the military nature; he is also requesting aid for the aid to be directed at all of Vietnam and not just the guerilla forces.

Question 2: D
Choice D is the best answer because Ho Chi Minh takes care to provide a timeline of the affronts, as well as to emphasize the democratic fervor and general national hope that the initial establishment of the Democratic Republic gave the Vietnamese. He describes the people as being "fired with democratic aspirations and spirit" (lines 7-8) and says the Republic was "solemnly proclaimed" (line 12), which demonstrates the expectation and earnestness that was prevalent before Vietnam was again invaded. Choice A is incorrect because it implies that Ho Chi Minh is addressing the Vietnamese by giving praise, when in reality he is appealing to the Great Powers by clearly framing the devastation felt after the French invasion of Saigon. Choice B is incorrect because the military victory that Ho Chi Minh cites in the first paragraph is the victory they achieve over Japan, and not France. Choice C is incorrect because it implies that the French are being deceptive about their motives for invading Vietnam, when in reality the "true nature" of the invasion is clear: the French want to colonize.

Question 3: D
Choice D is the best answer because Ho Chi Minh hopes to emphasize that "the atrocities", while very real and able to be understood as actually happening, are hard to believe because of their extremely heinous nature. Choice A and C are incorrect for similar reasons as they both imply that the actions of the French cannot be described or thought about, while Ho Chi Minh goes on to do exactly that at the end of the second paragraph. Choice B is incorrect because it suggests that there is no way to become aware of the horrors through the senses, but they are clearly affronts that can be seen and felt.

Question 4: B
Choice B is the best answer because Ho Chi Minh takes a measured and logical approach throughout the passage, moving from a straightforward discussion of the colonial facts and French atrocities (lines 1-32) to a review of the positive political and economic programs that the Vietnamese government has enacted (lines 33-78). Choice A is incorrect because, while Ho Chi Minh does admit sadness and astonishment at the French conduct, he does not dwell on the emotional aspects or become overly passionate, and quickly moves on to more promising discussion of why Vietnam deserves support. Choice C is incorrect because the "struggles" are explained in the first half of the passage with regard to the colonizing powers and their actions, and the shift actually turns away from those "struggles" and toward Vietnamese achievements. Choice D is incorrect because, for a discussion to be "illuminating", a new perspective or clarifying realization about the broad topic would be expected, while Ho Chi Minh only provides a review of Vietnam's specific colonial history; it is further incorrect because the only "global contextualisation" that Ho Chi Minh engages in is the situation of the Vietnamese oppression in the greater context of the world fight against fascism (lines 79-84).

Question 5: B
Choice B is the best answer because showing that a government is able to take care of the things that are necessary to everyday life and keep its people healthy and happy is the most effective support for Vietnam's continued independence. Ho Chi Minh proves his ability to take care of these "practical needs" by explaining throughout the fourth and fifth paragraphs the democratic and economic programs that his government has already put in place. Choice A is incorrect because a "commitment" to certain ideals doesn't necessitate their actualization and could merely refer to a general intent to do something; Vietnam could intend to uphold democracy and a free market, yet not actually achieve that end, therefore failing to show their "capability". Choice C is incorrect because it suggests that Ho Chi Minh is appealing to the Great Powers by emphasizing the strength of their military, when in reality he focuses for the entire second half of the passage on their positive societal improvements. Choice D is incorrect because a belief in an ideal, as explained above, does not directly correlate to the execution of that ideal in practice; to demonstrate its ability for self-governance, the Vietnamese government needs to show the concrete ways they have already made change and succeeded in supporting their country.

Question 6: D
Choice D is the best answer because the previous question asks what proves Vietnam's ability to effectively rule itself, and the answer, that they have supported the needs of their people even during their fight against France, is best supported by Ho Chi Minh's statement that "[a]ll these programs were carried out while, in the South, the French aggression has intensified every day" (lines 73-74). Ho Chi Minh states that those programs "demonstrated our capacity to self-government" (line 77). Choice A is incorrect because it only states Vietnam's "democratic aspirations" while failing to reference how their will achieve that ideal. Choice B is incorrect because, while it discusses Vietnam's perseverance in the face of hardship, it focuses on their ability to continue to launch a military defence, and neglects to demonstrate how that will help them rule themselves. Choice C is incorrect because it only discusses one specific example of the ways that the government is helping their people, but again fails to connect that to the greater issue of how that example proves their ability to self govern.

Question 7: D
Choice D is the best answer because Ho Chi Minh hopes to situate the Vietnamese call for help within the global anti-fascist context, therefore proving that the Great Powers should come to their aid. He states, "For these reasons, we think it our duty to send this note to the Great Powers which had led the anti-fascist cruade" (lines 79-81), thereby implying that the "reasons" given about Vietnam qualify it as needing the same kind of aid that was given in the fight against fascism. Choice A is incorrect because it goes beyond what is discernible from the text and implies that, due to their previous actions, the Great Powers are morally obligated, by what they have established to be right and wrong, to intervene on behalf of Vietnam, but Ho Chi Minh is really just situating the two as similar issues deserving of similar responses. Choice B is incorrect because it suggests that Ho Chi Minh is trying to garner support for his personal political advancement or campaign, but that is never mentioned in the text. Choice C is incorrect because Vietnam is merely calling for help, not suggesting that they intend to launch their own fight against fascism.

Question 8: B
Choice B is the best answer because it clearly states the desire of Ho Chi Minh to gain help ridding his country of the French and ending the ongoing conflict. Choice A is incorrect because it implies that Ho Chi Minh is asking for the Great Powers to calm or appease the issue, rather than end it. Choice C is incorrect because reconciliation suggests that the two parties are going to come back into agreement or return to a previous state of friendly terms, yet there is no suggestion that Ho Chi Minh is interested in coming to an agreement with the French, only that he wants them out of his country. Choice D is incorrect because it suggests that a monetary factor is involved, but it is never stated what specific sort of aid Ho Chi Minh is asking for, and therefore we cannot assume that he is requesting money from the Great Powers.

Question 9: C
Choice C is the best answer because Ho Chi Minh focuses throughout the passage on emphasizing the advancements Vietnam has made even while holding off a much stronger military power, a point which is meant to further support their claim to a self governed state. Minh clearly emphasizes that the French army is "experienced and numerous" as well as "fully equipped" (line 19). Choice A is incorrect because the actions of the French are far from random or arbitrary, as they have a very clear objective: colonization. Choice B is incorrect because there is no international law forbidding colonialism that is discussed in this passage. Choice D is incorrect because, while the French have been an extra burden on the country as it tries to democratize, Minh takes care to make clear the litany of progressive steps the country has nevertheless been able to take.

Question 10: B
Choice B is the best answer because the answer to the previous question emphasizes the extreme disparity in military might that exists between Vietnam and France, and lines 18-20 expand on the nature of that disparity and of France's power. Choice A is incorrect because, while it underscores the rapid nature France's invasion, it doesn't discuss their overwhelming power. Choice C is incorrect because on the terrible nature of the French troops, and not the extent of their power as compared to Vietnam's. Choice D is incorrect because it simply clarifies the Vietnamese determination to persevere but doesn't mention the excessive power that they must persevere in the face of.

Chapter 5.3 | Great Society

Question 1: C

Choice C is the best answer because Johnson describes what "the Great Society rests on" throughout paragraph three (lines 13-30) before moving on to an explanation of his ideas for "where we begin to build the Great Society" (line 32) and his policies for how to do so throughout the rest of the passage. Choice A is incorrect because, while he acknowledges the benefits that can result from his proposed changes, the focus of the passage is on the changes that need to happen before any of the benefits can be realized; he concludes each of his discussions with a statement of what America must not allow to happen, not about what benefits his proposed actions will reap. Choice B is incorrect because it assumes that the challenge at hand has already been met, when, in reality, Johnson acknowledges that we do not "have the full answers to those problems" (lines 69-70), only a place to start attending to them. Choice D is incorrect because Johnson neither provides examples of progress in the past nor analysis of his plan, only an idealized example of what society can be and his idea of how to achieve that end.

Question 2: D

Choice D is the best answer because, while Johnson suggests that the country must work toward the eradication of poverty, he never suggests everyone should attain great wealth or that such attainment is a prerequisite for "equality of opportunity for all." Choice A is incorrect because Johnson believes fundamental needs are of importance, as he states that the Great Society "is a place where the city of man serves not only the needs of the body and the demands of commerce but the desire for beauty and the hunger for community" (lines 18-21); therefore, it is not a place where man should try to overcome fundamental needs but rather ensure that all are able to serve those needs so as to allow for greater enrichment elsewhere in life. Choice B is incorrect because Johnson believes that the protection of the countryside is an essential step toward building the Great Society, stating that "[t]he water we drink, the food we eat, the very air that we breathe, are threatened with pollution...Today we must act to prevent an Ugly America" (lines 49-54). Choice C is incorrect because Johnson states that "[p]overty must not be a bar to learning, and learning must offer an escape from poverty" (lines 64-66); he lists that achievement as essential to the building of a Great Society.

Question 3: B

Choice B is the best answer because it suggests that progress is the means by which a society works toward the resolution of its needs. Only through progress may a society alleviate and bring an end to its various needs. Choices A and D are incorrect for similar reasons as they both imply that progress causes or leads to needs. Choice C is incorrect because progress doesn't invalidate need or make it ineffective, as suggested by the word negation, but in reality attempts to find ways to fulfill needs.

Question 4: D

Choice D is the best answer because Johnson connects the need to protect the countryside with the idea that "[w]e have always prided ourselves on being not only America the strong and America the free, but America the beautiful" (lines 46-48), thus suggesting that beauty is as essential of an American guiding principle as the ideas of freedom and strength are. Choice A is incorrect because the word "visceral" suggests that there is a deep emotional or internal need for the natural world and, while that might be true, Johnson focuses instead on the outward beauty of the land and why it must be protected. Choice B is incorrect because, while he greatly emphasizes the importance of natural resources in paragraph six (lines 45-54), he doesn't connect that importance to a growing or expanding society. Choice C is incorrect because it suggests the exact opposite of what Johnson seems to believe, as he argues for the preservation of the American land and thus the prevention of its "destruction."

Question 5: B
Choice B is the best answer because Johnson suggests that all students should have the opportunity to roam in "the farthest reaches of thought and imagination" (lines 58-59), thus suggesting that thought and imagination are places that can be explored. Choice A is incorrect because it implies that the youth are going after or actively pursuing thought and imagination, while Johnson's implication is only that they must be able to survey those reaches. Choices C and D are incorrect for similar reasons as they both imply a conclusive attainment of thought and imagination, suggesting that all students must be able to get to and understand them, which is not what Johnson claims.

Question 6: C
Choice C is the best answer because, in the evidence for Question 7, Regan refers to the "Great Society" (line 83) and suggests that that means "greater government activity in the affairs of the people" (lines 85-86), which he believes to be "the very thing the Founding Fathers sought to minimize" (lines 86-87). That statement, coupled with the fact that he calls it a "vote-harvesting time" (line 82), supports the idea that the Great Society is being used to gain votes and promote socialism, which goes against the beliefs of the founding fathers and can therefore be considered undemocratic. Choice A is incorrect because the word "experiment" implies that the Great Society has already been enacted or attempted, when in reality it is just an idea for how Johnson would like the country to function. Choice B is incorrect because, while Regan does believe that socialism is wrong, he doesn't suggest that Johnson has been wrongly lead or misguided into the belief that it is right, only that the American people shouldn't want that outcome. Choice D is incorrect because Regan only argues that the government should stay out of the "affairs of the people" (lines 85-86), not that any specific social services have become too prominent and pervasive in people's lives.

Question 7: A
Choice A is the best answer because the answer to the previous question states that the Great Society is used by "[o]ne side" (line 80) of the campaign as an undemocratic attempt to gain votes, an idea which is supported by lines 80-87. Choices B and D are incorrect for similar reasons as, while they both claim that the people's power is being limited while the government's power is being expanded, they fail to connect that idea to the promotion of the Great Society, and therefore do not answer the question. Choice C is incorrect because, while it discusses the proliferation of government services, it too does not suggest that such an overextension is the result of Johnson's proposed Great Society, which is a necessary connection to make in order for the lines to answer the question.

Question 8: A
Choice A is the best answer because, in the evidence for Question 9, Regan states that the Founding Fathers "knew that governments can't control the economy without controlling the people" (lines 87-88), suggesting that greater federal control of the economy will lead to a greater infringement upon people's rights. Choice B is incorrect because it introduces the ideas of federal legislation and social progress which are both off-topic, as they don't provide any insight into the relationship between the government and the economy. Choice C is incorrect because it fails to specify whose "economic

166

self-sufficiency" is being referred to. Choice D is incorrect because, while Regan does claim that "the government does nothing as well or as economically as the private sector" (lines 90-91), he doesn't suggest that the challenge the government might pose to the private sector is random or without reason.

Question 9: A
Choice A is the best answer because the answer to the previous question states that government intervention in the economy will lead to a curtailment of personal freedom, which is supported by lines 86-88. The rest of the choices are incorrect because the general superiority of the private sector (Choice B), the failure of government planning (Choice C), and the longevity of government programs (Choice D) do not support the idea that government involvement in the economy will limit the freedom and choice of the people.

Question 10: B
Choice B is the best answer because the analogy comes in the paragraph that deals directly with the "problems of unemployment" (line 98) and "welfare" (line 106), therefore suggesting that the fat man is a metaphor for the wealthy man and the thin for the poor or unemployed. Choice A is incorrect because Regan states that "[w]e have so many people" who think in the way that is outlined in the analogy, and therefore the analogy refers to people and not to large governments. Choice C is incorrect because the analogy suggests how the thin man, or the poor man, is taken advantage of by the fat man, or wealthy man, and therefore cannot refer to discrimnation "faced by the wealthy." Choice D is incorrect because Regan never suggests that the view proposed in the analogy is representative of the view of "progressives," only that it is the view of "many people" (line 100).

Chapter 5.4 | Walker

Question 1: B
Choice B is the best answer because Walker attempts to persuade "men...of sense" (line 1) to "go to work and enlighten your brethren" (line 6), and he later says that "I pray that the lord may undeceive my ignorant brethren" (lines 63-64. By using the terms "sense", "enlighten", and "ignorant", Walker asserts that his concern is about mental capacity, thus supporting the idea of elevation through education. Choice A is incorrect because although Walker does advocate advancement of African-Americans, he does not mention rights. Choice C is incorrect because although Walker does share an anecdote regarding a job in lines 19-38, the purpose is to communicate a mindset he disagrees with, not the job itself. Choice D is incorrect because Walker's intention is to show these men that they have "great work...to do" rather than to make accusations aimed at the institution of slavery.

Question 2: B
Choice B is the best answer because Walker contrasts the "men" he addresses with "our more ignorant brethren" (line 2-3); "of sense" can thus be construed to mean the opposite of "ignorant", which would match with "intelligent". Choice A is incorrect because "sensible" refers to an intelligence that is applicable to more practical aspects of life, while the intelligence that Walker describes is more cerebral, abstract, and "enlightened". Choices C and D are incorrect because "emotional" and "respectable" are neither the opposite of nor mutually exclusive with "ignorance" and are thus off topic.

Question 3: B
Choice B is the best answer because Walker bases his argument on the claim that "men of color, who are also of sense" (line 1) must "go to work and enlighten your brethren" (line 6), a statement that supports that education is his primary concern. He claims that people who believe they "are free and happy" (line 19) while not realizing that their purpose is "centered in such mean and low objects" (line 32) are "indeed ignorant" (line 37), implying that they need to have higher aspirations in order to come out of their ignorance. Choice A is incorrect because the containment of slavery itself would not fix the problem that Walker's brethren need to "seek after the substance of learning" (line 65). Choice C is incorrect because while Walker does mention jobs in the third paragraph, he does so as a way of highlighting the absurdity of the viewpoint that one should not strive to attain higher goals. Choice D is incorrect because Walker's argument is about education and not about respect. He primarily asserts that African-Americans need to help each other, which does not concern white men.

Question 4: C
Choice C is the best answer because Walker claims that "the man whose aspirations are not above [wielding the razor and cleaning boots and shoes] is indeed ignorant and wretched enough". As Walker calls such people "wretched" and illustrates his desire for them to aspire to greater goals. Choice A is incorrect because the man with whom Walker had a conversation would not be "relatable" to his audience, as Walker primarily addresses "men of colour, who are also of sense" (line 1). Choice B is incorrect because Walker's disappointed reaction to the man's does not represent the perspective of any and thus cannot be representative of a "tension" that exists between groups of African-Americans. Choice D is incorrect because Walker's conversation with the man reveals African-Americans' reluctance to enter the workforce in a meaningful way, and does not imply that they would face "hardship" if they chose to pursue aspirations above menial labor.

Question 5: D
Choice D is the best answer because Walker parallels "mean" with "low" (line 32) to describe the objects on which men who are "actuated by avarice" are focused, indicating that those objects are essentially meaningless to anyone besides the "ignorant and wretched" "men whose aspirations are not above these [objects]" (lines 36-38). Choices A and B are incorrect because Walker does not describe the objects as being unpleasant; on the contrary, he admits that some men would even prefer these aspirations: "said he, 'I am completely happy! I never want to live any better or happier than when I can get plenty of boots and shoes to clean!" (lines 26-28). Choice C is incorrect because Walker's primary criticism of the man with whom he had conversation is not the "rudeness" of his occupation, but the fact that the man was content to continue his occupation without any higher aspirations.

Question 6: D
Choice D is the best answer because in lines 72-72, Walker asserts that "educating the coloured people scares our cruel oppressors". Throughout the passage, he makes it clear that the oppressor is the white man with statements such as "unless you travel as a slave to a white man" (lines 13-14) and "we are so subjected under the whites" (line 24). Choice A is incorrect because Walker says that men will be "put...in jail" (line 15) but not that anyone is fearful or educated. Choice B is incorrect because although being "subjected under the whites" (line 24) is mentioned, neither education nor threatened behavior are referenced. Choice C is incorrect because in this paragraph Walker aims to show that the work of educating African-Americans may be "trifling" (line 39) but it is necessary to

show "the world that [they] are men and not brutes" (lines 41-42). In the lines in question, 51-52, he states the reason that this task is so important.

Question 7: A
Choice A is the best answer because in the previous sentence, Walker advises his audience to "let the aim of your labors among your brethren, and particularly the youth, be the dissemination of education and religion" (lines 43-45), a mindset which Walker hopes other African-Americans will adopt. He then reveals why this is so important: children learn little information of consequence in school, leading to ignorance, which he finds "lamentable" (line 46). Because of this, it is essential that his audience "prove to the Americans and the world that [they] are men and not brutes" (lines 40-41), the course of action he is endorsing. Choice B is incorrect because Walker is not belittling the efforts to educate the youth; in fact, he is urging that these efforts continue. Choice C is incorrect because Walker makes no claim as to the difficulty of educating children, just that the outcome of this education leaves children knowing "little more ...than a horse does about handling a musket" (lines 47-48). Choice D is incorrect because Walker does not characterize this as a humorous task, rather he asserts its importance by referring to it as "great work...to do" (line 39).

Question 8: A
Choice A is the best answer because the learning Walker refers to in line 53 is that of men who claim to "[know] everything years ago!" (line 56) and he says those same men "make light of [anything]" that "they had not divulged" (line 59). Thus, Walker's use of exclamations and exaggeration serve to show the absurdity of his claims, supporting that the education of men in this paragraph is dubious. Later, Walker says, "I pray that the Lord may undeceive my ignorant brethren, and permit them to throw away pretensions" (lines 63-64), directly responding to the claims he made in the previous paragraph. Therefore, the learning he refers to in line 65 is one that is unpretentious, or noble. Choice B is incorrect because the two types of learning do not differ in the quantity of people who have them, just in their type. Choice C is incorrect because even if it is banal to have "the substance of learning" (line 65), it is not praiseworthy when men think there is nothing "which they do not know better than [others]" (lines 54-55) . Choice D is incorrect because it is not elitist to "throw away pretensions" (line 64).

Question 9: C
Choice C is the best answer because in the correct evidence for question 10, Walker states that "for the Africans to acquire learning...makes tyrants quake and tremble on their sandy foundation" (lines 70-71), evidence that he believes slave owners, or tyrants, become aware that they are not certain to remain in their societal position should African Americans further educate themselves. Choice A is incorrect because while in lines 67-69 Walker does state that learning can provide something "which neither devils nor tyrants could remove", he does not assert that education is "fulfilling enrichment". Choice B is incorrect because Walker does not refer to "complex concepts" in any of the evidence choices. Choice D is incorrect because although African American learning does unnerve slave owners, Walker neither states nor implies that they will yield their position as a result.

Question 10: D
Choice D is the best answer because the previous question asks for what Walker would consider to be a good outcome of the education of African-Americans. The answer, that it will make slave owners aware of the precarious nature of their power, is best supported by the reference to the slave

owners' "sandy foundation." Choice A is incorrect because in lines 53-56 Walker is making a snide comment about men who think they know more than they actually do: "you cannot mention any thing to them which they do not know better than yourself" (lines 54-55), which cannot translate to a positive consequence of learning as it is not something Walker endorses. Choice B is incorrect because it only states that learning is good while neglecting to explain why. Choice C is incorrect because, while it is a positive consequence of learning, it does not match to an adequate answer in the previous question.

Chapter 5.5 | Webster

Question 1: A
Choice A is the best answer because Webster begins his discussion by acknowledging that equal representation under the law that one is held accountable to is "a fundamental principle of all governments, not despotic" (lines 4-5), therefore suggesting it to be a fundamental aspect of democracy. He goes on to discuss all a series of arguments against allowing women the vote and why those arguments are not valid. Choice B and C are incorrect for similar reasons as this passage is not presented as an admonishment or criticism of anyone, but rather a clear-headed argument in favor of women's suffrage. Choice D is incorrect because the whole passage actually functions as a justification of women's suffrage, and Webster never dwells on or enumerates the injustices toward women, but rather the arguments against their enfranchisement.

Question 2: B
Choice B is the best answer because women must also adhere to the laws that govern them and thus answer to them just as men do. Choice A is incorrect because it implies that women are in charge of the law, when the primary point throughout the passage is that they are not. Choice C is incorrect because it implies being restrained or restricted by the law, which might be the case, but adds a connotation to the word that is not necessary in this context. Choice D is incorrect because it suggests that women are equally deserving of the law, which is tangential to the point that they must follow the law, yet have no say in the making of it.

Question 3: B
Choice B is the best answer because, in paragraph 2, Webster's aim is to refute the argument that "it would make no difference" (line 21) if women were allowed to vote, and he does so by referencing the "various classes of men" (lines 24-25) who have been given the vote over the years, despite the fact that they were not all going to "confine themselves to one particular ticket or party" (line 26) and therefore not going to make a difference in the outcome of elections. Choice A is incorrect because, while this assertion might be true, Webster only discusses the various other classes of men and never specifies that he is speaking of the lowest class. Choice C is incorrect because the conclusion Webster arrives at is that women might not influence the vote at all but, as historical precedent shows, that is no reason to keep them from it; therefore, they won't be counterbalancing anything. Choice D is incorrect because it implies that the men of different classes have misused their voting rights, which Webster never suggests.

170

Question 4: A
Choice A is the best answer because, in those lines, Webster emphasizes the fact that women have managed to "acquire real estate" (line 11) even "in spite of the disadvantages" (line 7) they face due to their sex, thus proving their achievements despite sexism. The rest of the choices are incorrect because they all fail to discuss the disadvantages women face, despite referencing the hypothetical success of a "prudent woman" (Choice B), the ability of women to balance their home and public life (Choice C), and the hope of equality and success in the future (Choice D).

Question 5: B
Choice B is the best answer because Webster argues that men, being incapable of experiencing "the various annoyances and humiliations to which women are subjected" (lines 17-18), are not aware of the changes that should be made to legislature in order to improve the lot of women. Choice A is incorrect because, while it might be extrapolated from the fact that men come up with reason after reason as to why women shouldn't be allowed the vote, Webster never states in the passage that the reason for that belief is the "discriminatory" desire to keep women in their place. Choice C is incorrect for a similar reason because, while men do have a vested interest in maintaining the status quo as they are the ones who benefit from it, Webster never goes so far as to suggest that they are attempting to do so in an antagonistic or hostile way. Choice D is incorrect because, while it is discussed as a potential argument against women's suffrage, it is not in direct connect to the way male legislators in particular think about the issue.

Question 6: B
Choice B is the best answer because the answer to the previous question is that men cannot experience women's reality and therefore are not aware of the legal changes that need to be made to aid them, which is supported by lines 16-19 that argue that male legislators "do not realize the injustice toward women of the existing state of things." Choice A is incorrect because the lines only encompass the fact that male legislators know what they themselves want, but fail to make the point that they don't know what women want and need. Choice C and D are incorrect for similar reasons because they only discuss general arguments against women's enfranchisement, it would be ineffectual (Choice C) and it would divert their attention from the home (Choice D), but they do not necessarily encompass the attitude of male legislators in particular.

Question 7: A
Choice A is the best answer because the third paragraph serves to demonstrate the fault in the opposition's argument that women shouldn't be allowed to vote because the potential for differing political opinions would create "family contention" (line 28). Webster does so by highlighting the fact that sons enjoy suffrage even though they might not vote according to their fathers wishes, thus underscoring the double standard that is present in his opponent's argument. Choice B is incorrect because the third paragraph, as well as the second and fourth paragraphs, all refute counterarguments that have already been argued, and thus aren't potential counterarguments but actual ones that have been launched against the fight for women's suffrage. Choice C is incorrect because it implies that Webster is conceding a point to the opposition, when in reality he is effectively arguing against their points. Choice D is incorrect because the third paragraph actually brings up a similar situation in order to provide the context for his argument for women's suffrage, not a contrasting one.

Question 8: D
Choice D is the best answer because Webster's aim in discussing men of important professions is that they are still able to attend to family life as well, thus negating the argument that women shouldn't be allowed to vote because they would neglect their domestic duties. He argues that "Prudent men...so order their business arrangements that they shall be properly attended to without allowing the one to interfere with the other. So too would prudent women" (lines 47-51). Choice A is incorrect because, while these men are currently allowed to vote, they are not brought up as examples of that fact. Choice B and C are incorrect for similar reasons as the masculine and laborious nature of certain jobs does not connect to the overarching point of the fourth paragraph which is to argue that women too can balance their home and civic lives and duties.

Question 9: D
Choice D is the best answer because Webster has shown throughout the whole passage that there is no argument for why a woman should not be allowed to vote that can't be refuted, and therefore no argument that is completely logical, or makes complete sense. Choice A and B are incorrect for similar reasons as the convincing nature of an argument does not necessarily mean that the argument makes logical sense; there are many ways for an argument to appear credible or compelling and still be flawed. Choice C is incorrect because it implies a step beyond even the logical nature of an argument, as an argument must be logical in order to be proven, and Webster's point is that they aren't even logical in the first place.

Question 10: B
Choice B is the best answer because the lines show Webster's opinion that the good judgement or "judicious influence" (line 76) of women in the house or "the charmed circle" (line 76) serve as further support of her mental competence and therefore her ability to engage in political affairs as well as domestic ones. Choice A is incorrect because it places the focus on men, when the lines are clearly focused on the role of women; it additionally discusses a point that was already proven in the previous paragraph (lines 39-67). Choice C is incorrect because, while the paragraph does highlight a double standard (lines 71-73), it isn't "yet another" one, but instead the same one that has been discussed throughout the entire passage. Choice D is incorrect because it suggests that the fight is over the citizenship status of mothers and wives when in fact it is over their voting status.

Chapter Six

Questions 1-10 are based on the following passage.

6.1

This passage is adapted from President Barack Obama's 2015 speech commending the Supreme Court's decision on same-sex marriage.

Our nation was founded on a bedrock principle that we are all created equal. The project of each generation is to bridge the meaning of those founding
Line words with the realities of changing times—a never-
5 ending quest to ensure those words ring true for every single American. Progress on this journey often comes in small increments, sometimes two steps forward, one step back, compelled by the persistent effort of dedicated citizens. And then sometimes there are days
10 like this, when that slow, steady effort is rewarded with justice that arrives like a thunderbolt.

This morning, the Supreme Court recognized that the Constitution guarantees marriage equality. In doing so, they have reaffirmed that all Americans are entitled
15 to the equal protection of the law; that all people should be treated equally, regardless of who they are or whom they love. In my second inaugural address, I said that if we are truly created equal, then surely the love we commit to one another must be equal as well.
20 It is gratifying to see that principle enshrined into law by this decision.

This decision will end the patchwork system we currently have. It will end the uncertainty hundreds of thousands of same-sex couples face of not knowing
25 whether their marriage, legitimate in the eyes of one state, will remain if they decide to move to or even visit another. It will strengthen all of our communities by offering to all loving same-sex couples the dignity of marriage across this great land. It's a victory for Jim
30 Obergefell and the other plaintiffs in the case. It's a victory for gay and lesbian couples who have so long fought for their basic civil rights. It's a victory for their children, whose families will now be recognized as equal to any other. It's a victory for the allies and
35 friends and supporters who spent years, even decades working and praying for change to come. And this ruling is a victory for America. This decision affirms what millions of Americans already believe in their hearts: when all Americans are treated as equal, we are
40 all more free.

My administration has been guided by that idea. It's why we stopped defending the so-called Defense of Marriage Act and why we were pleased when the court finally struck down the central provision of that
45 discriminatory law. It's why we ended, "Don't Ask,

Don't Tell." From extending full marital benefits to federal employees and their spouses to expanding hospital visitation rights for LGBT patients and their loved ones, we've made real progress in advancing
50 equality for LGBT Americans in ways that were unimaginable not too long ago.

I know a change for many of our LGBT brothers and sisters must have seemed so slow for so long. But compared to so many other issues, America's shift has
55 been so quick. I also know that Americans of good will continue to hold a wide range of views on this issue. Opposition, in some cases, has been based on sincere and deeply held beliefs. All of us who welcome today's news should be mindful of that fact, recognize different
60 viewpoints, and revere our deep commitment to religious freedom. But today should also give us hope that on the many issues with which we grapple, often painfully, real change is possible. A shift in hearts and minds is possible. And those who have come so far on
65 their journey to equality have a responsibility to reach back and help others join them, because, for all of our differences, we are one people, stronger together than we could ever be alone. That's always been our story.

We are big and vast and diverse, a nation of
70 people with different backgrounds and beliefs, different experiences and stories but bound by the shared ideal that no matter who you are or what you look like, how you started off or how and whom you love, America is a place where you can write your own destiny. We are
75 people who believe that every child is entitled to life, liberty, and the pursuit of happiness. There is so much more work to be done to extend the full promise of America to every American. But today, we can say in no uncertain terms that we've made our union a little
80 more perfect.

That's the consequence of a decision from the Supreme Court, but more importantly it is a consequence of the countless small acts of courage of millions of people across decades who stood up,
85 who came out, who talked to their parents, who were willing to endure bullying and taunts, who stayed strong and came to believe in themselves and who they were, and who slowly made an entire country realize that love is love. What an extraordinary achievement,
90 and what a vindication of the belief that ordinary people can do extraordinary things. What a reminder of what Bobby Kennedy once said about how small actions can be like pebbles thrown into a still lake, causing ripples of hope to cascade outwards and
95 change the world.

CONTINUE

1

The primary purpose of this speech is most likely to

A) claim a decisive victory over the opponents of LGBT rights in a historically contentious battle.

B) celebrate a culmination of a series of small but significant efforts towards the perfection of our democracy.

C) assure members of the LGBT community that the United States has now acquired the mantle of a safe haven.

D) explain the intricacies and significance of a newly published opinion by the Supreme Court.

2

As used in line 2, "project" most nearly means

A) purpose.

B) venture.

C) assignment.

D) endeavor.

3

Obama levels which criticism against the former status of marriage equality laws?

A) They rendered the legality of same-sex marriages inconsistent from state to state.

B) They accommodated the diversity of religious beliefs entrenched in American tradition.

C) They reflected a principle of the Constitution that would now be considered intolerant.

D) They restricted the power of state courts to overrule decisions from other states.

4

Which choice provides the best evidence for the answer to the previous question?

A) Lines 14-17 ("they have…love")

B) Lines 22-27 ("this decision…another")

C) Lines 46-51 ("From extending…ago")

D) Lines 55-61 ("I also…freedom")

5

Which technique does Obama use to describe the Supreme Court decision in the passage?

A) He emphasizes its disruptive nature by describing it as a pebble thrown into a still lake.

B) He illustrates its unexpected nature by describing it as having arrived like a thunderbolt.

C) He highlights its stable nature by describing it as being founded on a bedrock principle.

D) He underscores its haphazard nature by describing it as constituting a patchwork system.

6

Which choice provides the best evidence for Obama's claim that this Supreme Court decision was consistent with the policies of his presidency?

A) Lines 17-21 ("In my…decision")

B) Lines 37-40 ("This decision…free")

C) Lines 41-46 ("My administration…Tell")

D) Lines 81-84 ("That's the…people")

7

A central claim of the fifth paragraph (Lines 52-68) is that

A) LGBT community members must campaign aggressively in order to change the minds of those who oppose them.

B) the majority of Americans believe that the Supreme Court decision granting marriage equality was made in haste.

C) the reconciliation of opposing beliefs will require a concerted effort on an individual level.

D) supporters of LGBT rights have been historically intolerant of religious freedoms protected under the Constitution.

8

What device does Obama use to emphasize the variety of people who contributed to this landmark decision?

A) Metaphor

B) Allusion

C) Anecdote

D) Repetition

CONTINUE

9

As used in line 68, "story" most nearly means

A) narrative.

B) history.

C) principle.

D) reputation.

10

In context of the passage, lines 74-76 ("We are… happiness") primarily serve to

A) highlight the innocence of the children of LGBT parents who have been unfairly targeted.

B) sanctify the Supreme Court decision by connecting it to the nation's founding principles.

C) qualify the applicability of the Court decision by claiming only children are its intended beneficiaries.

D) appeal to the innate human sentiment to protect children in order to unify the country.

CONTINUE

Questions 1-10 are based on the following passage.

6.2

This passage is adapted from Lucy Stone's "Disappointment is the Lot of Women," delivered in 1848 at the Women's Rights Convention in Seneca Falls, New York.

From the first years to which my memory stretches, I have been a disappointed woman. When, with my brothers, I reached forth after the sources
Line of knowledge, I was reproved with "It isn't fit for
5 you; it doesn't belong to women." Then there was but one college in the world where women were admitted, and that was in Brazil. I would have found my way there, but by the time I was prepared to go, one was opened in the young State of Ohio—the
10 first in the United States where women and Negroes could enjoy opportunities with white men. I was disappointed when I came to seek a profession worthy an immortal being—every employment was closed to me, except those of the teacher, the seamstress, and
15 the housekeeper. In education, in marriage, in religion, in everything, disappointment is the lot of woman. It shall be the business of my life to deepen this disappointment in every woman's heart until she bows down to it no longer. I wish that women, instead of
20 being walking showcases, instead of begging of their fathers and brothers the latest and gayest new bonnet, would ask of them their rights.

The question of Woman's Rights is a practical one. The notion has prevailed that it was only an ephemeral
25 idea; that it was but women claiming the right to smoke cigars in the streets, and to frequent bar rooms. Others have supposed it a question of comparative intellect; others still, of sphere. Too much has already been said and written about woman's sphere. We are
30 told woman has all the rights she wants; and even women, I am ashamed to say, tell us so. They mistake the politeness of men for rights—seats while men stand in this hall tonight, and their adulations; but these are mere courtesies. We want rights. The flour
35 merchant, the house builder, and the postman charge us no less on account of our sex; but when we endeavor to earn money to pay all these, then, indeed, we find the difference. Man, if he have energy, may hew out for himself a path where no mortal has ever trod, held
40 back by nothing but what is in himself; the world is all before him, where to choose; and we are glad for you, brothers, men, that is so.

But the same society that drives forth the young man, keeps woman at home—a dependent—working

45 little cats on worsted, and little dogs on punctured paper; but if she goes heartily and bravely to give herself to some worthy purpose, she is out of her sphere and she loses caste. Women working in tailor shops are paid one-third as much as men. Someone in
50 Philadelphia has stated that women make fine shirts for twelve and a half cents apiece; that no woman can make more than nine a week, and the sum thus earned, after deducting rent, fuel, etc., leaves her just three and a half cents a day for bread. Female teachers in New
55 York are paid fifty dollars a year, and for every such situation there are five hundred applications. I know not what you believe of God, but I believe He gave yearnings and longings to be filled, and that He did not mean all our time should be devoted to feeding and
60 clothing the body. The present condition of woman causes a horrible perversion of the marriage relation. It is asked of a lady, "Has she married well?" "Oh, yes, her husband is rich." Woman must marry for a home, and you men are the sufferers by this; for a woman
65 who loathes you may marry you because you have the means to get money which she can not have. But when woman can enter the lists with you and make money for herself, she will marry you only for deep and earnest affection.

70 I am detaining you too long, many of you standing, that I ought to apologize, but women have been wronged so long that I may wrong you a little....I have seen a woman at manual labor turning out chair-legs in a cabinet shop, with a dress short enough not
75 to drag in the shavings. I wish other women would imitate her in this. It made her hands harder and broader, it is true, but I think a hand with a dollar and a quarter a day in it, better than one with a crossed ninepence....The widening of woman's sphere is to
80 improve her lot. Let us do it, and if the world scoff, let it scoff—if it sneer, let it sneer.

CONTINUE ➡

1

The main purpose of this passage is to

A) contend that neither women nor men can be content until there is true equality within the home and heart.

B) argue for the broadening of the feminine domain so as to provide women with the opportunity to attain economic autonomy.

C) provide an alternative definition of the women's sphere that will allow for greater acceptance of women among men.

D) maintain that women will only demand rights once their disappointment has become too great to endure any longer.

2

Which choice provides the best evidence for the answer to the previous question?

A) Lines 17-19 ("It shall...longer.")

B) Lines 27-29 ("Others have...sphere.")

C) Lines 64-66 ("you men...have.")

D) Lines 77-80 ("I think...lot.)

3

Throughout the first paragraph, Stone's rhetoric is notable for its use of

A) repetition that emphasizes the pervasiveness of women's dissatisfaction.

B) foreshadowing that prepares the audience for Stone's ultimate conclusion.

C) a personal anecdote that highlights the primary letdown in Stone's life.

D) an analogy that clarifies the divide between the lot of men and that of women.

4

As used in line 20, "showcases" most nearly means

A) mannequins.

B) spectacles.

C) ornaments.

D) advertisements.

5

According to the passage, what misleads some women into believing they have rights?

A) The ability to seek employment in select fields.

B) The emergence of greater educational opportunities.

C) The common respect and good manners of men.

D) The equal division of the various realms of life.

6

According to Stone, women become especially aware of their restricted rights when they

A) are confronted with their brothers' extensive privilege.

B) attempt to become economically self-sufficient.

C) finally ask for equality instead of material comforts.

D) realize they have married for money rather than love.

7

Which choice provides the best evidence for the answer to the previous question?

A) Lines 2-5 ("When, with...women.")

B) Lines 19-22 ("I wish...rights.")

C) Lines 34-38 ("The flour...difference.")

D) Lines 60-63 ("The present...rich.")

8

As used in line 44, "working" most nearly means

A) laboring.

B) employing.

C) designing.

D) stitching.

9

According to the passage, how would men benefit from women being allowed to work?

A) They would no longer be tasked with the burden of providing for their family alone.

B) They would have greater assurance that their wives married them for the right reasons.

C) Their happiness would be more honest and complete because their wives would have purpose.

D) They would receive greater affection because their wives would no longer be discontent.

CONTINUE

10

It can be most reasonably inferred that the "dress short enough not to drag in the shavings" (lines 74-75) serves

A) to underscore the lengths women must go to for acceptance in the man's world.

B) to accentuate women's capacity for ingenuity when given a fighting chance.

C) as an example of how women can find their place in traditionally male spheres.

D) as an indication of an emerging trend among female workers.

CONTINUE

Questions 1-10 are based on the following passage.

6.3

This speech was delivered to the full Congress by President Lyndon B. Johnson on March 15, 1965, a week after deadly racial violence had erupted in Selma, Alabama, as African Americans were attacked by police while preparing to march to Montgomery to protest voting rights discrimination.

At times, history and fate meet at a single time in a single place to shape a turning point in man's unending search for freedom. So it was at Lexington

Line and Concord. So it was a century ago at Appomattox.
5 So it was last week in Selma, Alabama. There, long suffering men and women peacefully protested the denial of their rights as Americans. Many of them were brutally assaulted. One good man--a man of God--was killed.
10 There is no cause for pride in what has happened in Selma. But there is cause for hope and for faith in our Democracy in what is happening here tonight. For the cries of pain and the hymns and protests of oppressed people have summoned into convocation all
15 the majesty of this great government to right wrong, to do justice, to serve man.

Rarely in any time does an issue lay bare the secret heart of America itself. Rarely are we met with a challenge, not to our growth or abundance, or our
20 welfare or our security, but rather to the values and the purposes and the meaning of our beloved nation. The issue of equal rights for American Negroes is such an issue. And should we defeat every enemy, and should we double our wealth and conquer the stars, and still
25 be unequal to this issue, then we will have failed as a people and as a nation.

There is no Negro problem. There is no Southern problem. There is no Northern problem. There is only an American problem. And we are met here tonight as
30 Americans--not as Democrats or Republicans--to solve that problem. This was the first nation in the history of the world to be founded with a purpose.

The great phrases of that purpose still sound in every American heart, North and South: "All men
35 are created equal." "Government by consent of the governed." "Give me liberty or give me death." And those are not just clever words, and those are not just empty theories. In their name Americans have fought and died for two centuries and tonight around
40 the world they stand there as guardians of our liberty risking their lives. Those words are promised to every

citizen that he shall share in the dignity of man. This dignity cannot be found in a man's possessions. It cannot be found in his power or in his position. It
45 really rests on his right to be treated as a man equal in opportunity to all others. It says that he shall share in freedom. He shall choose his leaders, educate his children, provide for his family according to his ability and his merits as a human being.
50 To apply any other test, to deny a man his hopes because of his color or race or his religion or the place of his birth is not only to do injustice, it is to deny Americans and to dishonor the dead who gave their lives for American freedom. Our fathers believed that
55 if this noble view of the rights of man was to flourish it must be rooted in democracy. This most basic right of all was the right to choose your own leaders.

Every device of which human ingenuity is capable, has been used to deny this right. The Negro
60 citizen may go to register only to be told that the day is wrong, or the hour is late, or the official in charge is absent. And if he persists and manages to present himself to the registrar, he may be disqualified because he did not spell out his middle name, or because he
65 abbreviated a word on the application. And if he manages to fill out an application, he is given a test. He may be asked to recite the entire Constitution, or explain the most complex provisions of state law.

And even a college degree cannot be used to prove
70 that he can read and write. For the fact is that the only way to pass these barriers is to show a white skin. Experience has clearly shown that the existing process of law cannot overcome systematic and ingenious discrimination. No law that we now have on the books,
75 and I have helped to put three of them there, can insure the right to vote when local officials are determined to deny it. In such a case, our duty must be clear to all of us.

We have all sworn an oath before God to support
80 and to defend the Constitution. We must now act in obedience to that oath. Wednesday, I will send to Congress a law designed to eliminate illegal barriers to the right to vote. After they have reviewed it, it will come here formally as a bill, known as a civil rights
85 bill. Its object is to open the city of hope to all people of all races, because all Americans must have the right to vote, and we are going to give them that right.

CONTINUE

1

Throughout the passage, Johnson's main goal is to

A) show support for the protestors in Selma.

B) condemn southern racism.

C) reflect on the history of protest in America.

D) justify the need for new legislation.

2

As used in line 15, "majesty" most nearly means

A) force.

B) authority.

C) glory.

D) sovereignty.

3

How does Johnson prioritize the achievement of civil rights in the broader context of American advancements?

A) He views it as the foundation without which all other success would be meaningless.

B) He deems it worthy of the highest praise possible for any national accomplishment.

C) He frames it as the culmination of America's longstanding progression towards equality.

D) He depicts it as analogous to the abolition of slavery for its moral and practical implications.

4

Which choice provides the best evidence for the answer to the previous question?

A) Lines 10-16 ("There is…man")

B) Lines 21-26 ("The issue…nation")

C) Lines 42-47 ("This dignity…freedom")

D) Lines 50-54 ("To apply…freedom")

5

In context of the passage as a whole, the fourth paragraph (lines 27-32) primarily serves to

A) assign blame for the current state of American politics.

B) expose the issue of civil rights on a national scale.

C) emphasize the need for unity in the face of a national challenge.

D) underscore the universal relevance of the civil rights movement.

6

How does Johnson frame his discussion in order to persuade congress to action?

A) He gives weight to his belief that support of voting rights equates to support for the Constitution by connecting the protests in Selma to significant moments in American history.

B) He chastises members of Congress for their previously lukewarm response to combating racism before demanding their unequivocal support for his proposed legislation.

C) He alludes to the political advantages to be gained by a Congress in support of his legislation by citing evidence of a rapidly expanding African-American voter bloc.

D) He reveals the blame shared by all Americans in creating an environment of racism that led to the events in Selma before urging Congress to break the cycle of oppression.

7

The inclusion of the quotations in lines 34-36 ("All men…death") has which effect?

A) It calls into question the patriotism of those who stood against the protesters in Selma.

B) It implies that the struggle for civil rights would have been supported by the founders of America.

C) It contends that race-based oppression violates the values expressed in the founding documents.

D) It demonstrates the continued relevance of America's founding principles in the fight for civil rights.

8

As used in line 37, "clever" most nearly means

A) witty.

B) brilliant.

C) shallow.

D) misleading.

181

CONTINUE

9

Throughout the passage, Johnson's focus shifts from

A) a description of an infringement on the voting rights of African-Americans to a prediction about its influence on American life.

B) a casting of the events in Selma as a seminal moment in the fight for democracy to the promotion of a new civil rights bill.

C) a description of the protests in Selma in context of American history to the introduction of a mandate directed at Southern officials.

D) a critical analysis of America's founding documents to the proposal of an amendment to those documents.

10

Which choice provides the best evidence for Johnson's claim that the voting tests are explicitly racist?

A) Lines 56-59 ("This most…right")

B) Lines 69-71 ("And even…skin")

C) Lines 74-77 ("No law…it")

D) Lines 83-87 ("After they…right")

CONTINUE

Questions 1-10 are based on the following passage.

6.4

In 1830, the federal government imposed taxes on the importation of manufactured goods. South Carolina, heavily dependent on these imports, attempted to nullify these tariffs through its own legislature. Passage 1 is adapted from a speech by Senator Robert Hayne. Passage 2 is adapted from Senator Daniel Webster's response to Hayne.

Passage 1

As to the doctrine that the federal government is the exclusive judge of the extent, as well as the limitations of its powers, it seems to me to be utterly
Line subversive of the sovereignty and independence of the
5 states. It makes but little difference, in my estimation, whether Congress or the Supreme Court are invested with this power. If the federal government, in all or any of its departments, are to prescribe the limits of its own authority, and the states are bound to submit
10 to the decision, and are not to be allowed to examine and decide for themselves, when the barriers of the Constitution shall be over-leaped, this is practically a government without limitation of powers. The states are at once reduced to mere petty corporations, and the
15 people are entirely at your mercy.

In all the efforts that have been made by South Carolina to resist the unconstitutional laws which Congress has extended over them, she has kept steadily in view the preservation of the Union by the only
20 means by which she believes it can be long preserved -- a firm, manly, and steady resistance against usurpation. The measures of the federal government have, it is true, prostrated her interests, and will soon involve the whole South in irretrievable ruin. But even
25 this evil, great as it is, is not the chief ground of our complaints. It is the principle involved in the contest -- a principle which, substituting the discretion of Congress for the limitations of the Constitution, brings the states and the people to the feet of the federal
30 government, and leaves them nothing they can call their own.

The South is acting on a principle she has always held sacred -- resistance to unauthorized taxation. These are the principles which induced the immortal
35 Hampden* to resist the payment of a tax of twenty shillings. Would twenty shillings have ruined his fortune? No! but the payment of half twenty shillings, on the principle on which it was demanded, would have made him a slave. If, in acting on these high
40 motives, if, animated by that ardent love of liberty

which has always been the most prominent trait in the Southern character, we should be hurried beyond the bounds of a cold and calculating prudence, who is there, with one noble and generous sentiment in his
45 bosom, that would not be disposed, in the language of Burke, to exclaim, "You must pardon something to the spirit of liberty!"

Passage 2

The proposition, that, in case of a supposed violation of the Constitution by Congress, the states
50 have a constitutional right to interfere and annul the law of Congress, is the proposition of the gentleman. I do not admit it. If the gentleman had intended no more than to assert the right of revolution for justifiable cause, he would have said only what all
55 agree to. But I cannot conceive that there can be a middle course, between submission to the laws, when regularly pronounced constitutional, on the one hand, and open resistance on the other. I admit that there is an ultimate violent remedy, above and in defiance of
60 the Constitution, which may be resorted to when a revolution is to be justified. But I do not admit that, under the Constitution and in conformity with it, there is any mode in which a state government, as a member of the Union, can interfere and stop the progress of the
65 general government, by force of her own laws, under any circumstances whatever.

This leads us to inquire into the origin of this government and the source of its power. Whose agent is it? Is it the creature of the state legislatures, or
70 the creature of the people? If the government of the United States be the agent of the state governments, then they may control it, provided they can agree in the manner of controlling it; if it be the agent of the people, then the people alone can control, modify, or
75 reform it. It is observable enough, that the doctrine for which the honorable gentleman contends leads him to the necessity of maintaining, not only that this general government is the creature of the states, but that it is the creature of each of the states severally, so that
80 each may assert the power for itself of determining whether it acts within the limits of its authority. It is the servant of four-and-twenty masters, of different wills and different purposes, and yet bound to obey all. This absurdity arises from a misconception as to the origin
85 of this government and its true character.

It is the people's Constitution, the people's government, made for the people, made by the people, and answerable to the people. The people of the United States have declared that the Constitution shall be the
90 supreme law. We must either admit the proposition, or dispute their authority. The states are, unquestionably,

CONTINUE

sovereign, so far as their sovereignty is not affected by this supreme law. But the state legislatures, as political bodies, however sovereign, are yet not sovereign over
95 the people.

The general government and the state governments derive their authority from the same source. Neither can, in relation to the other, be called primary, though one is definite and restricted, and the
100 other general and residuary. The national government possesses those powers which it can be shown the people have conferred on it, and no more. To make war, for instance, is an exercise of sovereignty; but the Constitution declares that no state shall make
105 war. To coin money is another exercise of sovereign power, but no state is at liberty to coin money. These prohibitions, it must be confessed, are a control on the state sovereignty of South Carolina, as well as on the other states, which does not arise "from her own
110 feelings of honorable justice." The opinion referred to, therefore, is in defiance of the plainest provisions of the Constitution.

* John Hampden was a member of Parliament whose challenge of and arrest by King Charles I sparked the English Civil War.

1

What choice best identifies a key difference in how Hayne and Webster view the Constitution?

A) Hayne suggests that the Constitution has been violated by the federal government, while Webster states that the Constitution inherently places federal power over that of state governments.

B) Hayne indicates that the Constitution in its current state must be amended to grant additional rights to state governments, while Webster advocates for greater restrictions on state power.

C) Hayne argues that the Constitution offers protections to state governments, while Webster claims that the Constitution renders states' rights ambiguous and subject to federal oversight.

D) Hayne implies that the Constitution is inadequate in curtailing the federal government's overreach, while Webster contends that the Constitution is an effective governing framework.

2

Based on the passages, Hayne and Webster would most likely agree with which of the following statements?

A) State and federal powers should be balanced.

B) Southern unrest is a threat to the federal government.

C) The Constitution is the supreme law of the land.

D) Governmental power rests in the hands of citizens.

3

Which of the following choices best describes Hayne's chief complaint in Passage 1?

A) The federal government's unilateral action without respect to the Constitution encroaches upon state sovereignty.

B) The economic legislation enacted by Congress has fostered conditions that favor some states at the expense of others.

C) South Carolina has faltered under the federal imposition of tariffs that do not value its role in the national economy.

D) The federal government's disregard for Southern values is in direct violation of states' Constitutional rights.

4

Which choice provides the best evidence to support Hayne's claim that the South has historically been opposed to unnecessary federal intervention?

A) Lines 18-20 ("she has...preserved")

B) Lines 32-33 ("The South...taxation")

C) Lines 34-36 ("These are...shillings")

D) Lines 40-42 ("animated by...character")

5

As used in line 23, "prostrated" most nearly means

A) subordinated.

B) suppressed.

C) subdued.

D) subsumed.

CONTINUE

6

The author of Passage 2 would most likely characterize Passage 1's description of Southern principles in lines 42-47 ("we should...liberty") as

A) understandable but misguided.

B) noble but unfounded.

C) illegitimate and subversive.

D) self-righteous and unconstitutional.

7

According to Webster, how is power divided between state and federal governments?

A) Federal power is unrestricted while state power is inherently limited in jurisdiction.

B) Federal power is more legitimate than state power as it directly represents the will of the people.

C) The authority of federal and state power is equal though the reach of their power is not.

D) The authority of the federal government is justified insofar as it does not encroach upon states' interests.

8

Which choice provides the best evidence for the answer to the previous question?

A) Lines 49-51 ("the states...Congress")

B) Lines 70-73 ("If the...it")

C) Lines 91-93 ("The states...law")

D) Lines 98-100 ("Neither can...residuary")

9

As used in lines 69 and 70, "creature" most nearly means

A) means.

B) will.

C) instrument.

D) embodiment.

10

In context of Passage 2 as a whole, lines 81-85 ("It is... character") primarily serve to

A) highlight the impracticality of conferring ultimate power to state governments.

B) lament the incompetence of state governments to unanimously agree on policies.

C) dismiss the threat against the nation on grounds of disunity among the states.

D) underscore the enormity of the problem posed by a group of rebellious states.

185

CONTINUE

Questions 1-10 are based on the following passage.

6.5

The following passage is adapted from "The Hypocrisy of American Slavery," a speech delivered at Rochester, N.Y. on July 4th, 1852 by Frederick Douglass.

Fellow citizens, allow me to ask, why am I called upon to speak here today? What have I or those I represent to do with your national independence? Are the great principles of political freedom embodied
5 in that Declaration of Independence extended to us? Am I called upon to bring our humble offering to the national altar and express devout gratitude for the blessings resulting from your independence to us?

The blessings in which you this day rejoice are not
10 enjoyed in common. The rich inheritance of justice, liberty, prosperity, and independence bequeathed by your fathers is shared by you, not by me. This Fourth of July is yours, not mine. You may rejoice, I must mourn.

15 Fellow citizens, above your tumultuous joy I hear the mournful wail of millions, whose chains, heavy and grievous, are today rendered more intolerable by the jubilant shouts that reach them. If I do forget, if I do not remember those bleeding children of sorrow this
20 day, "may my right hand forget her cunning, and may my tongue cleave to the roof of my mouth!" To forget them, to pass lightly over their wrongs and to chime in with the popular theme would be treason most scandalous and shocking.

25 My subject, then, fellow citizens, is "American Slavery." I shall see this day and its popular characteristics from the slave's point of view. Standing here, identified with the American bondman, I do not hesitate to declare that the character and conduct of
30 this nation never looked blacker to me than on this Fourth of July. I will, in the name of humanity, which is outraged, in the name of liberty, which is fettered, in the name of the Constitution and the Bible, which are disregarded and trampled upon, dare to call in question
35 and to denounce everything that serves to perpetuate slavery -- the great sin and shame of America!

But some of my audience say it is just in this circumstance that you and your brother Abolitionists fail to make a favorable impression on the public mind.
40 Would you argue more and denounce less your cause would be much more likely to succeed. But where all is plain there is nothing to be argued. What point in the anti-slavery creed would you have me argue? On what branch of the subject do the people of this country need

45 light?

Must I undertake to prove that the slave is a man? That point is conceded already. It is admitted in the fact that Southern statute books are covered with enactments, forbidding, under severe penalties, the
50 teaching of the slave to read and write. When you can point to any such laws in reference to the beasts of the field, then I may consent to argue the manhood of the slave.

Must I argue the wrongfulness of slavery? What!
55 Am I to argue that it is wrong to make men brutes, to rob them of their liberty, to work them without wages, to keep them ignorant of their relations to their fellow men, to beat them with sticks, to flay their flesh with the lash, to load their limbs with irons, to hunt them
60 with dogs, to sell them at auction, to sunder their families, to knock out their teeth, to burn their flesh, to starve them into obedience and submission to their masters? Must I argue that a system thus marked with blood is wrong? No - I will not. I have better
65 employment for my time than such arguments would imply.

At a time like this, scorching irony, not convincing argument, is needed. Oh! had I the ability, and could I reach the nation's ear, I would today pour out a fiery
70 stream of biting ridicule and stern rebuke. For it is not light that is needed, but fire; it is not the gentle shower, but thunder. The feeling of the nation must be quickened; the conscience of the nation must be roused; the propriety of the nation must be startled; the
75 hypocrisy of the nation must be exposed.

What to the American slave is your Fourth of July? I answer, a day that reveals to him more than all other days of the year, the gross injustice and cruelty to which he is the constant victim. To him your
80 celebration is a sham; your boasted liberty, unholy license; your national greatness, swelling vanity; your shouts of liberty and equality, hollow mock; your prayers and hymns, mere bombast and hypocrisy - a thin veil to cover up crimes which would disgrace a
85 nation of savages. Roam through all the monarchies and despotisms of the Old World, search out every abuse and when you have found the last, lay your facts by the side of the everyday practices of this nation, and you will say with me that, for revolting barbarity and
90 shameless hypocrisy, America reigns without a rival.

CONTINUE

1

Douglass' main purpose in the passage is to

A) admonish abolitionists for not having used sufficiently forceful methods to ensure the end of slavery.

B) rationally educate his audience about the wrongfulness of slavery and urge them to bring about its end.

C) evoke guilt in his audience for participating in a national day of celebration which ought to be one of mourning.

D) raise to the national conscience the fact that slavery is fundamentally inconsistent with American ideals.

2

Throughout the first paragraph (lines 1-8), Douglass uses rhetorical questions in order to

A) provoke the audience to ponder the significance of the Fourth of July.

B) embarrass the audience for its ignorance on the issue of slavery.

C) emphasize to his audience the necessity of criticizing the present celebration.

D) indicate to his audience the irony of his invitation to a Fourth of July event.

3

Which choice provides the best evidence for the claim that Douglass feels personally compelled to assert his beliefs on the Fourth of July?

A) Lines 9-13 ("The blessings…mine")

B) Lines 18-21 ("If I…mouth")

C) Lines 37-41 ("But some…succeed")

D) Lines 76-79 ("What to…victim")

4

In describing the current state of the abolitionist movement, Douglass expresses the need for

A) a more zealous and blunt expression of indignation.

B) a return to more traditional and religious values.

C) legislative reforms that guarantee universal civil rights.

D) increased efforts by abolitionists to gain popular support.

5

Which choice provides the best evidence for the answer to the previous question?

A) Lines 31-36 ("I will…America")

B) Lines 37-41 ("But some…succeed")

C) Lines 47-50 ("It is…write")

D) Lines 68-72 ("Oh! had…thunder")

6

In context of the passage as a whole, the fifth paragraph (lines 37-45) primarily serves to

A) point out the absurdity that abolitionists feel obligated to make their platform more palatable.

B) encourage fellow abolitionists to be less inflammatory as a means to attract more sympathizers.

C) pose questions that Douglass will answer by the end of the event at which the speech is given.

D) account for the lack of popular support for the abolitionist movement which he laments as obscure.

7

Douglass uses which of the following rhetorical devices in the seventh paragraph (lines 54-66) in order to illustrate the cruelty of slavery?

A) Irony

B) Imagery

C) Metaphor

D) Open-ended questions

8

As used in line 73, "quickened" most nearly means

A) hastened.

B) revitalized.

C) galvanized.

D) emancipated.

187

CONTINUE

9

Douglass makes which new claim in the last paragraph of the passage (lines 76-90)?

A) Slaves have no reason to celebrate the Fourth of July.

B) The Fourth of July does not absolve the nation of its guilt.

C) America is the last remaining nation to practice slavery.

D) America's record of human rights abuses is unparalleled.

10

As used in line 81, "license" most nearly means

A) privilege.

B) freedom.

C) permit.

D) right.

STOP

Please turn to next page for answer keys and explanations.

Answer Key: CHAPTER SIX

6.1 | Obama	6.2 | Stone	6.3 | LBJ	6.4 | Hayne / Webster	6.5 | F. Douglass
1: B	1: B	1: D	1: A	1: D
2: A	2: D	2: B	2: C	2: D
3: A	3: A	3: A	3: A	3: B
4: B	4: A	4: B	4: B	4: A
5: C	5: C	5: C	5: A	5: D
6: C	6: B	6: A	6: D	6: A
7: C	7: C	7: D	7: C	7: B
8: D	8: D	8: C	8: D	8: C
9: C	9: B	9: B	9: C	9: D
10: B	10: C	10: B	10: A	10: A

Answer Explanations

Chapter Six

Chapter 6.1 | Obama

Question 1: B
Choice B is the best answer because Obama states that the decision of the Supreme Court has "made our union a little more perfect" and representative of the democratic state envisioned in the Constitution (lines 79-80), but that it was also preceded by "the countless small acts of courage", or small but significant efforts, "of millions of people across decades who stood up" (lines 83-84). Choice A is incorrect because the opponents of LGBT rights are only mentioned in lines 57-58 ("opposition, in some cases, has been based on sincere and deeply held beliefs") and therefore cannot be the focal point of the passage. Choice C is incorrect because Obama emphasizes equality throughout the speech, not safety. Protection in the eyes of the law does not necessarily translate to the enforcement of that safety in real life. Choice D is incorrect; while Obama focuses on the significance of the Supreme Court decision for the vast majority of the speech, he does not focus on the actual content, or intricacies, of the decision.

Question 2: A
Choice A is the best answer because Obama describes the nation as being "founded on a bedrock principle that we are all created equal" (lines 1-2). Each generation is therefore responsible for upholding that "bedrock principle" by "bridging" that meaning with "the realities of changing times" (line 4); it is thus each generation's duty, or "purpose", to ensure that this standard of progress is maintained. Choice B is incorrect because "venture" implies a new project, whereas Obama describes the continued application of a founding principle. Choice C is incorrect because "assignment" suggests that a previous entity was responsible for forwarding democracy, which Obama never indicates. Choice D is incorrect because an "endeavor" is indicative of a singular attempt, but Obama describes this project as "a never-ending quest" (lines 4-5).

Question 3: A
Choice A is the best answer because lines 22-27 indicate that former marriage equality laws subjected same-sex couples to face "the uncertainty...of not knowing whether their marriage, legitimate in the eyes of one state, will remain if they decide to move to or even visit another"; if same-sex marriages are recognized in some states but not in others, their legality is therefore "inconsistent from state to state". Choice B is incorrect because Obama never indicates that former marriage equality laws accommodated any religious beliefs, only that current marriage laws might

challenge them (lines 55-61). Choice C is incorrect because Obama describes the Constitution as supporting marriage equality, not as intolerant of it: "the Constitution guarantees marriage equality" (line 13). Choice D is incorrect because Obama depicts the power of state courts to (within the borders of their state) overrule decisions from other states as negatively impacting same-sex couples; therefore, he would be unlikely to criticise marriage equality laws for restricting that power.

Question 4: B
Choice B is the best answer because lines 22-27 describe the "patchwork system" that was ended by the Supreme Court's decision, which matches with the topic of marriage equality laws' "former status" in the previous question. Choice A is incorrect because lines 14-17 explain the contents of the Supreme Court's decision to end the former status of marriage equality laws. Choice C is incorrect because lines 46-51 describe the efforts made by the Obama administration to correct former marriage equality laws. Choice D is incorrect because lines 55-61 depict the opposition to current marriage equality laws, not former ones.

Question 5: C
Choice C is the best answer because Obama begins the passage by stating that the United States "was founded on a bedrock principle that we are all created equal" (lines 1-2), before describing the Supreme Court decision as part of a "never-ending quest" (lines 4-5) to uphold that principle. Choice A is incorrect because Obama compares the "small actions" of "ordinary people" to further LGBT rights, not the Supreme Court decision, to "pebbles thrown into a still lake" (lines 89-95). Choice B is incorrect; although the Supreme Court decision was swift and sudden, it was not "unexpected", as "slow, steady effort" (line 10) had been made prior to the decision's enactment. Choice D is incorrect because former marriage laws, which the Supreme Court decision was meant to correct, was described as a "constituting a patchwork system" (line 22).

Question 6: C
Choice C is the best answer because Obama indicates in lines 41-46 that "[his] administration has been guided" by the idea that "when all Americans are treated as equal, we are all free" (lines 39-40). He then goes on to list the actions of his presidency ("stopped defending the so-called Defense of Marriage Act", "ended 'Don't Ask, Don't Tell'", etc) that have consistently shown his support of the LGBT community. Choice A is incorrect because lines 17-21 only describe Obama's intentions for his second term at his inaugural address, but does not indicate whether those ideas actually resulted in progressive policies. Choices B and D are incorrect because lines 37-40 and lines 81-84 describe the American people's support of LGBT rights, not Obama's.

Question 7: C
Choice C is the best answer because Obama reveals that those who have historically supported LGBT rights "have a responsibility to reach back and help others join them" (lines 64-66). "Concerted effort" by "those who have come so far on their journey" (lines 64-65) is thus needed in order to completely fulfill the "reconciliation" which was started by the Supreme Court decision. Choice A is incorrect because while members of the LGBT community have a duty to "help" those who oppose them, Obama also encourages them to be "mindful" and "recognize different viewpoints" (lines 59-61). "Campaigning aggressively in order to change minds" would therefore be too extreme to match Obama's advice in the passage. Choice B is incorrect because Obama never makes clear the magnitude of opposition to the Supreme Court decision; therefore, it cannot be said

that the "majority" of Americans were critical of the decision. Choice D is incorrect because the reactions of LGBT rights supporters towards religious opposition have not been mentioned in the passage, so they cannot be described as "historically intolerant".

Question 8: D
Choice D is the best answer because Obama uses repetition throughout the passage to emphasize the many people who contributed to the Supreme Court's decision: "it's a victory for Jim Obergefell and the other plaintiffs...it's a victory for gay and lesbian couples...it's a victory for their children... it's a victory for the allies...and this ruling is a victory for America" (lines 29-37). The repetition of the phrase "it's a victory" highlights the many people who stood in favor of marriage equality and the success of their movement. Choice A is incorrect because the instances in which Obama uses metaphor are not to emphasize the contributions to the Supreme Court's decision. For instance, Obama says draws the comparison between small actions and pebbles, stating that small actions can cause "ripples of hope to cascade outwards and change the world" (lines 94-95). Choice B is incorrect because Obama does not make any reference to literary or cinematic works. The only outside sources that Obama refers to are the Constitution, former legislation and the perspectives of those in society. Thus, he does not use allusion. Choice C is incorrect because Obama does not use anecdotes, or small, realistic narratives about people, especially not in the context of support for the Supreme Court decision.

Question 9: C
Choice C is the best answer because the "story" of Americans being "one people, stronger together than we could ever be alone" comes from the equality that is repeated throughout the passage; furthermore, Obama refers to equality as a "shared ideal" (line 71) and explicitly calls said equality a "principle" (line 20). Choices A and B are incorrect: stating that Americans have "always" (line 68) had a "narrative" or a "history" of equality would be incongruent with Obama's statement that "there is so much more work to be done" (lines 76-77). Choice D is incorrect because a "reputation" is concerned with how others perceive Americans, whereas Obama focuses on how Americans promote equality through their actions.

Question 10: B
Choice B is the best answer because Obama refers to "life, liberty, and the pursuit of happiness" in the given lines and follows this list of America's founding principles by stating that "today, we've made our union a little more perfect" (lines 78-80). The word "today" indicates that Obama is describing the Supreme Court decision bolstering the nation's founding principles. Choice A is incorrect because the only time in which the children of LGBT parents are mentioned is in lines 32-34, whereas the question asks us to evaluate lines 74-76 in context of the passage as a whole. Choice C is incorrect because lines 76-78, which follow lines 74-76, indicate that "there is so much more work to be done to extend the full promise of America to every American". The fact that Obama states that there is so much more work to be done to extend the "full promise of America" to everyone indicates that he strives for equality for all people; thus, it would be antithetical to restrict the applicability of the Supreme Court decision to only children. Moreover, the decision concerns marriage equality, and children cannot get married; if anything, the decision would not apply to children. Choice D is incorrect because one reference to children is insufficient for an appeal to human sentiment; the reference would have to be more drawn out and far more emotional than Obama presents.

Chapter 6.2 | Stone

Question 1: B
Choice B is the best answer because Stone laments throughout the passage that women's rights have been restricted through their economic dependence on men: "the same society that drives forth the young man, keeps woman at home—a dependent" (lines 43-44); moreover, women who try to work find themselves "out of [their] sphere" (lines 47-48) and are paid less than men doing the same work. To Stone, then, attaining equal rights would entail the "widening of woman's sphere" (line 79) so that women may work in previously male-dominated fields such as those involving "manual labor" (line 73). Choice A is incorrect because Stone concerns herself little with equality "within the home and heart": certain women already consider themselves to be equal to men, as Stone indicates that "[some women] mistake the politeness" (lines 31-32) and "adulations" (line 33) of men to be rights, whereas Stone believes that these are "mere courtesies" (line 34). Choice C is incorrect because Stone is not concerned with the "greater acceptance of women among men". In fact, Stone believes that women should not consider whether their stances will be well-received: "if the world scoff, let it scoff—if it sneer, let it sneer" (lines 80-81). Choice D is incorrect because Stone indicates that women have already attempted to gain rights, only to be let down: "when we endeavor to earn money to pay all these, then, indeed, we find the difference [in economic rights]" (lines 36-38).

Question 2: D
Choice D is the best answer because lines 77-80 illustrate Stone's main point—that women should seek economic independence through the "widening of [her] sphere". Choice A is incorrect because lines 17-19 describe the problem for which she provides a solution throughout the passage, but does not go into detail about the solution itself. Choice B is incorrect because lines 27-29 describe other people's perspectives of women's rights, as a "question of comparative intellect" or "of sphere". Because these phrases represent others' ideas, they cannot convey Stone's main point. Choice C is incorrect because lines 64-66 describe a situation that is a consequence of women's denial of rights but does not explain the problem as a whole nor its solution.

Question 3: A
Choice A is the best answer because Stone repeatedly refers to the disappointment, or "dissatisfaction", of women that exists across many aspects of life: "in education, in marriage, in religion, in everything, disappointment is the lot of woman" (lines 15-16) and "this disappointment in every woman's heart" (lines 17-18) are two examples of Stone highlighting the ubiquitous nature of women's disappointment. Choice B is incorrect because Stone's "ultimate conclusion", or the purpose of the passage, is mentioned in the first paragraph; it is not "foreshadowing", since Stone explicitly indicates that "disappointment is the lot of woman" (line 16), in addition to her hope that women will actively pursue equal rights. Choice C is incorrect because Stone does not highlight "a personal anecdote", or a singular story drawn from her personal life. Rather, she narrates a series of disappointing moments in her life to highlight the constant inequality that she faces. Similarly, Stone does not have a "primary letdown", as the overarching message of the first paragraph is that she has been disappointed many times. Choice D is incorrect because Stone does not incorporate "an analogy" in her explanation of the divide between man and woman; she explicitly highlights the opportunities that are exclusively available to men without figurative language.

Question 4: A

Choice A is the best answer because "mannequins" best conveys Stone's message that some women are currently nothing but idle displays for "the latest and gayest new bonnet", or different adornments. Choice B is incorrect because "spectacles" would indicate that these women are more striking than the average woman and warrant unique attention. However, Stone suggests that most women exist as "walking showcases" and that this condition is typical. Choice C is incorrect because the women are not the ornaments themselves; rather, they serve as displays, or "showcases", for ornaments such as bonnets. Choice D is incorrect because "advertisements" implies that these women exist with the purpose of selling products or promoting awareness, while Stone states that these women exist in a passive state and, as such, must demand rights.

Question 5: C

Choice C is the best answer because Stone indicates that some women "mistake the politeness of men for rights" (lines 31-32); however, she dismisses such "adulation" and respectful treatment as "mere courtesies" (line 34) that she contrasts with "true" rights such as that to be paid equally to men. Choice A is incorrect because Stone identifies the restriction of women from the workforce except in certain fields such as "those of the teacher, the seamstress, and the housekeeper" (lines 14-15) as a source of disappointment, not of empowerment. Choice B is incorrect because Stone does not believe that women are experiencing more educational opportunities: in fact, she emphasizes the rarity of colleges accepting women, with there being only "one [of such] college in the world...in Brazil" (lines 6-7) until "one was opened in...Ohio—the first in the United States" (lines 9-10). Stone further criticizes women's opportunities for education in lines 15-16: "in education...disappointment is the lot of woman". Choice D is incorrect because Stone does not imply that women and men are allotted equal divisions of the various realms of life, only that most women are restricted to one division—that of the home—while men have access to others.

Question 6: B

Choice B is the best answer because women are not subject to different prices due to their sex; their point of awareness comes when they attempt to enter the workforce and "endeavor to earn money to pay all [the costs of living]" (lines 36-37), only to find themselves paid less than men. Choice A is incorrect because Stone suggests that women are made aware of their inferior status when they are rejected for aiming to achieve economic autonomy, a process that would not necessarily involve their male cohorts. Moreover, Stone is not perturbed by men's apparent privilege: in fact, she states that "the world is all before [men]" (lines 40-41) and that "we are glad for you, brothers" (lines 41-42). Choice C is incorrect because Stone does not characterize equality and material comforts as contradictory; in fact, she indicates that for some women, equality consists of being able to afford the material comforts which they earn through hard work. Choice D is incorrect because Stone does not characterize women as having a sudden realization of why they married, but implies that women enter a marriage with the understanding that money is a factor: "woman must marry for a home, and you men are the sufferers by this" (line 63).

Question 7: C

Choice C is the best answer because lines 34-38 describe the point at which women "find the difference" between their perceived value in the economy and that of men, and thus the point at which they become aware of their restricted rights. Choice A is incorrect because lines 2-5 only address Stone's individual exclusion from learning opportunities that were available to men; they are insufficient to make a statement about women as a whole being "especially aware of their restricted rights". Choice B is incorrect because lines 19-22 depict women who are not yet aware of their lack of rights, as these women are still content with living as "walking showcases" who only aspire towards owning the latest fashion items. Choice D is incorrect because lines 60-63 describe an effect of women's lack of rights on their "marriage [relations]", but does not imply that women are conscious of the relationship between the two.

Question 8: D

Choice D is the best answer because Stone describes the material with which the woman works as "punctured paper" (lines 45-46). The world "puncture" indicates the nature of her work: stitching. Additionally, Stone refers to the tailor shop in her comparison of the woman at home and in the workforce, which further demonstrates that the woman is stitching. Choice A is incorrect; although the woman is working, the word "laboring" without a preposition cannot correctly describe the fact that the woman is working on the "little cats" and "little dogs" (line 45). Choice B is incorrect because "employing" in this context implies that the woman is giving the "little cats" and "little dogs" work; in reality, it is the "little cats" and "little dogs" that are keeping the woman preoccupied and working. Choice C is incorrect because Stone does not indicate that these "little cats" and "little dogs" are the original creation of the woman, which is what "designing" suggests.

Question 9: B

Choice B is the best answer because Stone claims that women who are economically self-sufficient and therefore would not need to marry for money can "marry [men] only for deep and earnest affection" (lines 68-69), which she sees as beneficial to men. Choice A is incorrect because Stone never discusses how women making money affects their ability to provide for their families; she only states that if women could make money, then men could be more assured that they were chosen out of love and not for other reasons. Choice C is incorrect because Stone does not discuss the happiness of men, nor how that happiness can increase from a healthy marriage. Choice D is incorrect because Stone does not imply that all women are discontent in their marriages, only that a rich man must always be aware of this risk; moreover, Stone indicates that women who marry for love will feel greater "affection" for their husbands, but does not guarantee that those husbands would receive more affectionate acts from their wives.

Question 10: C

Choice C is the best answer because Stone first describes the female worker as working in "manual labor turning out chair-legs in a cabinet shop" (lines 73-74), a stark contrast to acceptably feminine careers such as those of "the teacher, the seamstress, and the housekeeper" (lines 14-15). Stone then indicates that the worker was able to adapt to her more masculine environment, shortening her dress "not to drag in the shavings" (lines 74-75) and allowing her hands to become "harder and broader" (lines 76-77). These tactics enabled the worker to receive higher wages—a "dollar and a quarter a day" instead of "a crossed ninepence" (lines 77-79)—and "improve her lot" (line 80), thereby allowing her to become successful and "find her place". Choice A is incorrect because Stone implies that society would have a derisive reaction to the woman working as a manual laborer: "let us do it, and if the world scoff, let it scoff—if it sneer, let it sneer" (lines 80-81). Stone depicts the world as unaccepting of the women going to such radical lengths to be a part of the workforce, and she does not indicate alternative circumstances that would yield male acceptance. Choice B is incorrect because Stone encourages women to take matters into their own hands and claim economic equality without aid from society: "let us do it, and if the world scoff, let it scoff" (lines 80-81). It can then be reasonably inferred that the woman described in lines 72-75 was not "given a fighting chance" by society and became successful despite her lack of support from others. Choice D is incorrect because Stone expresses her wish for "other women [to] imitate" (lines 75-76) the worker whose "dress [is] short enough not to drag in the shavings", which implies that such a worker is an uncommon occurrence. Since this woman is characterized as an exception to societal standards, she cannot serve as an example of someone participating in an "emerging trend".

Chapter 6.3 | LBJ

Question 1: D
Choice D is the best answer because Johnson discusses critical events in United States' history, a current catalyst, and the founding principles of the country to culminate on the fact that "we must now act in obedience to that oath [to the constitution]" (lines 80-81) and "eliminate illegal barriers to the right to vote" (lines 82-83). The background Johnson provides supports this need to make laws ending discriminationatory voting practices. Choice A, B, and C are incorrect because although he does clearly support the protest in Selma, condemn racism, and discuss former protests, he does so with the intention of using that information as further cause to end illegal voting barriers.

Question 2: B
Choice B is the best answer because the "majesty" refers to the ability of the "government to right wrong, to do justice" (lines 15-16), corresponding to its authority to take legal action. Choice A is incorrect because although the government could use force to make this happen, it's not necessary. Choice C is incorrect because the glory of the government would not be used to refer to its power to create laws . Choice D is incorrect because while the country does have the ability to rule itself and make its own laws, using the word "sovereignty" indicates independence from rule by another country, which is not what Johnson is discussing in the passage.

Question 3: A
Choice A is the best answer because in the third paragraph, Johnson asserts that "we will have failed as a people and as a nation" (lines 25-26) should America make other achievements in the future yet neglect to cement equality for African Americans. Choice B is incorrect because while Johnson does say that other achievements are essentially worthless without equal rights, achieving fundamental rights isn't necessarily praiseworthy, it should be a general standard. Choice C is incorrect because a Johnson calls the right to "choose your own leaders" (line 57) the "most basic right" (line 54), or the baseline, and not the culmination of progress. Choice D is incorrect because Johnson does not make an analogy to abolition in any of the lines referenced in the following question.

Question 4: B
Choice B is the best answer because the previous question asks how the author prioritizes the achievement of civil rights in the broader context of American advancement. The answer, that Johnson says it is meaningless unless America achieves equality, is in the third paragraph. Choices A, C, and D are incorrect because the cited lines don't support the answer to the previous question. Instead, they characterize past pain the country has felt (choice A), define the meaning of the term "all men are created equal" (choice C), and condemn discrimination (choice D).

Question 5: C
Choice C is the best answer because the fourth paragraph is support for the main idea that America needs to remove voting barriers such that Johnson uses collective voice in these lines to unite his audience for the common cause. This supports that Americans need to be united if they are going to overcome the national challenge of eliminating barriers that prevent everyone from having the right to vote. Choice A is incorrect because he is not blaming anyone, hence saying it is everyone's problem. Choice B is incorrect because Johnson establishes the scale of the issue earlier in the passage when he says the "issue lay bare the secret heart of America itself" (lines 17-18), and as such that cannot be his primary purpose for paragraph four. Choice D is incorrect because "universal relevance" is too broad as it implies relevance to all, but this issue is only central to Americans; furthermore, his point in the fourth paragraph is centered on the problem of voting discrimination and not the civil rights movement in general.

Question 6: A
Choice A is the best answer because Johnson references the current problem as an "American problem" (line 29), which must be solved because the nation was "founded with a purpose" (line 32) to allow all men to "share in freedom" (lines 46-47). Then, in the fifth paragraph, Johnson alludes to the Constitution and well known events in history by citing the phrases "All men are created equal", "Give me liberty or give me death" and "Government by consent of the governed". He therefore is tying the events in Selma to both American patriotism and prior events in American history. Choice B is incorrect because Johnson does not reveal the former actions of Congress; he does talk about the past but only to refer to the events in Selma and other similarly important moments in American history. Choice C is incorrect because Johnson is focused on the government's duty to "support and defend the Constitution" (lines 79-80), not on political gain that can be had. Choice D is incorrect because Johnson focuses on the job of Congress to pass a civil rights bill, not on assigning blame.

Question 7: D
Choice D is the best answer because Johnson asserts that the phrases quoted in lines 34-36 "still sound in every American heart" (lines 33-34), indicating that although they originated at the founding of the country, they are still important to Americans at the time of the speech. Choice A is incorrect because Johnson does not discuss the protest at Selma beyond the second paragraph. Choice B is incorrect because Johnson clearly indicates that his reason for bringing up words of the founders is to show their relevance to the current problem by saying that "tonight around the world [those words] stand there as guardians of our liberty risking their lives" (lines 39-41). Choice C is incorrect because although those phrases are in the founding documents, those documents are not relevant to the point Johnson is making in the fifth paragraph about the importance that all men are treated equally as human beings.

Question 8: C
Choice C is the best answer because the key phrase in the sentence that is parallel to the word in context is "empty theories". In this sentence, Johnson is making the point that phrases such as "All men are created equal" (lines 34-35) are actually meaningful to the people, or not meaningless, most closely matching shallow. Choice A is incorrect because witty implies humor, which Johnson never brings up in the context of this word or the passage as a whole. Choice B is incorrect because Johnson might say the words are brilliant, but the word "not" is right before the word in context. Choice D is incorrect because although it's true that the words are not misleading, that is not supported by key words in the text.

Question 9: B
Choice B is the best answer because Johnson references the events in Selma as a primary catalyst for creating new laws that will "cause...hope and...faith in our Democracy" (lines 11-12) before going on to say that "[he] will send to Congress a new law designed to eliminate illegal barriers to the right to vote" (lines 81-83). Choice A is incorrect because Johnson does not make a "prediction" about the influence discrimination is having on American life. Furthermore, the claims Johnson does make about this reflect its effects on the mindset of Americans, not their lives. Choice C is incorrect because the proposed bill is not only directed at southern officials but at the entire Congress. Choice D is incorrect because Johnson does not critically analyze any founding documents, he merely references words from the founding documents in the fifth paragraph and an oath American politicians have sworn to defend the constitution in the ninth paragraph.

Question 10: B
Choice B is the best answer because Johnson states the "only way to pass these barriers is to show white skin" (lines 70-71), indicating that the barriers put up to block certain people from voting are premised on explicitly racist guidelines. Choice A is incorrect because in lines 56-59 Johnson references discrimination but not anything about voting tests. Choices C and D are incorrect because while Johnson does state that there are barriers between certain parties and their right to vote in lines 74-77 and 83-87, he does not mention that this denial is due to racism in these parts of the text.

Chapter 6.4 | Hayne / Webster

Question 1: A
Choice A is the best answer because Hayne argues that the states should be able "to examine and decide for themselves, when the barriers of the Constitution shall be over-leaped" (lines 10-12) and supports South Carolina in their resistance of "the unconstitutional laws which Congress has extended over them" (lines 17-18), implying that he thinks the federal government has ignored the Constitution and that the states should have the power to counteract that. In addition, Webster argues that, as stated in multiple places in the Constitution, the federal government is granted powers that the states are not; as proof, he cites the facts that "[t]o make war, for instance, is an exercise of sovereignty; but the Constitution declares that no state shall make war. To coin money is another exercise of sovereignty, but no state is at liberty to coin money" (lines 102-106). Choice B is incorrect because, despite Hayne's conviction that the states should have more say over the laws that dictate their actions, he never calls for any official amendments to the Constitution, only argues that the action of the south keeps with the "principle she has always held sacred" (lines 32-33) and that that principle of liberty is not in itself a violation of the Constitution. Choice C is incorrect because,

while Webster does believe that federal oversight is inherent in the Constitution, he would not argue that it is due to the ambiguity of states' rights; he claims that the "states are, unquestionably, sovereign, so far as their sovereignty is not affected by the supreme law" (lines 91-93), which suggests an unambiguous view of states' power. Choice D is incorrect because, while Hayne does believe that the federal government needs to be kept in check, he argues that it is the states which must undertake this task and not the Constitution; he says that, if "the states are bound to submit to the decision" (lines 9-10) of the federal government without having any say of their own, then "this is practically a government without limitation of powers" (lines 12-13).

Question 2: C
Choice C is the best answer because, even if the authors disagree on what constitutes a breach of the Constitution, they both agree that the Constitution has been breached, which suggests that they each believe the document to be the foremost law of the land and that it should not be broken. Hayne argues that "substituting the discretion of Congress for the limitations of the Constitution, brings the states and the people to the feet of the federal government, and leaves them nothing they can call their own" (lines 27-31), and Webster directly states that the "people of the United States have declared that the Constitution shall be the supreme law" (lines 88-90). Choice A is incorrect because Webster believes that, at a certain point, the federal government has the power to enact laws that the states should not be able to interfere with; he says, "I do not admit that, under the Constitution and in conformity with it, there is any mode in which a state government, as a member of the Union, can interfere and stop the progress of the general government" (lines 61-65). Choice B is incorrect because, while Webster might agree with this point, Hayne seems to believe that the right to dissent and resist, is an inherent and natural part of the system of checks and balances, and therefore would not characterize it as a threat. Choice D is incorrect because, while it presents the direct view of Webster as stated in lines 100-102, it is the opposite of Hayne's view as he suggests that power should rest with the states.

Question 3: A
Choice A is the best answer because Hayne argues that the actions of the federal government are "subversive of the sovereignty and independence of the states" (lines 4-5) and that to achieve those subversive actions "the discretion of Congress" was substituted "for the limitation of the Constitution" (lines 27-28). Choice B is incorrect because, while Hayne is primarily concerned with how the new taxation is detrimental to Southern states, he does not argue that it is beneficial to other states. Choice C is incorrect because Hayne argues that the new taxation is detrimental to the Southern economy, as it "will soon involve the whole South in irretrievable ruin" (lines 23-24), not that it is detrimental to the national economy. Choice D is incorrect because disregarding the South's values does not equate to disregarding the South's rights.

Question 4: B
Choice B is the best answer because it directly states that the South has "always" opposed "unauthorized taxation" (lines 32-33), which is the federally imposed intervention at issue in these passages. Choice A is incorrect because it only discusses the South's desire to preserve the Union. Choice C is incorrect because, while it is on the topic of resisting taxation, it does not connect that resistance to a greater history of resistance in the South. Choice D is incorrect because having a lasting love of liberty is not the equivalent of demonstrating consistent opposition to federal intervention.

Question 5: A

Choice A is the best answer because Hayne argues that the taxes imposed by the federal government, in effect, treat the interests of the South as less important, so much so that the taxation will cause "irretrievable ruin" (line 24) to the South. Choices B and C are incorrect for a similar reason as the interests of the South are not being prevented or defeated, but just marginalized by the federal government's general disregard. Choice D is incorrect because it implies that the interests of the South are being included, which is a positive outcome that Hayne does not think has been achieved.

Question 6: D

Choice D is the best answer because Webster argues that South Carolina professes "feelings of honorable justice" (line 110) that it does not deserve to profess, as it is only being prohibited from doing the same things that all "the other states" (line 109) are prohibited from doing as well. He further argues that the "opinion referred to, therefore, is in defiance of the plainest provisions of the Constitution" (lines 110-112). Choices A and B are incorrect for similar reasons as they both imply that Webster is sympathetic to or finds a positive view of the Southern Principles, but he is in direct opposition to Hayne and the views he represents. Choice C is incorrect because, while Webster does believe that it is unlawful or illegitimate for the the liberty of an individual state to take precedence over the benefit of the whole country, he doesn't say that such a principle is intended to be disruptive.

Question 7: C

Choice C is the best answer because, in the evidence for Question 8, Webster argues that neither the state nor the federal government "can, in relation to the other, be called primary, though one is definite and restricted, and the other general and residuary" (lines 98-100), which suggests the general equality of state and federal power despite the different extents to which that power can be exercised. Choice A is incorrect because Webster acknowledges that the general and state governments "derive their authority from the same source" (lines 97-98), which is the people; therefore, Webster thinks that federal power is indeed limited by the people, just not by the states. Choice B is incorrect because Webster argues, as cited above, that both the federal and state governments represent the will of the people, as their power comes from the people, and therefore the will of the people cannot serve as grounds for the heightened legitimacy of one form of government over another. Choice D is incorrect because it presents the view of Hayes from Passage 1, which Webster is opposing throughout Passage 2.

Question 8: D

Choice D is the best answer because the answer to the previous question argues that state and federal governments have the same amount of power but are differentiated by jurisdiction, which is supported by the idea that state power is "definite and restricted" and federal power is "general and residuary" (lines 98-100). Choice A is incorrect because it presents a summary of Hayne's view, but the question asks for an answer "according to Webster." Choices B and C are incorrect for similar reasons as their discussions are limited to state governments, therefore neglecting the essential discussion of federal governments and failing to answer the question.

Question 9: C
Choice C is the best answer because Webster argues that "[i]f the government of the United States be the agent of the state governments, then they may control it" (lines 70-72), which suggests that "creature" refers to something that is used or controlled by another party in order to enact its will. Choice A is incorrect because it refers to the way or method of controlling something, not the thing or instrument used to control it. Choice B is incorrect because it refers to intention or desire, and not that which is used to enact such intention. Choice D is incorrect because it implies that the United States government is the visible form or incarnation of either the people or the state, but Webster is actually trying to say that the government is the tool used by the people or the states to implement their beliefs.

Question 10: A
Choice A is the best answer because Webster argues that it is absurd to allow "each of the states severally" (line 79) to hold power because it would cause disunity, as all are "of different wills and different purposes" (lines 82-83). Choice B is incorrect because Webster is not expressing grief over the fact that the states cannot agree, but merely pointing out the impracticality of giving state governments supreme power and, therefore, the benefit of having a federal government that provides that needed unity. Choice C is incorrect because it implies that the lack of unity among the states is threatening the nation, but no direct threat is discussed in the passage and the catalyst of the problem that is discussed is one state's resistance to a new federally imposed law. Choice D is incorrect because, as mentioned above, the issue at hand stems from the actions of one state, South Carolina, alone and not a "group of rebellious states."

Chapter 6.5 | F. Douglass

Question 1: D
Choice D is the best answer because, throughout the passage, Douglass illustrates how the American ideal of freedom contradicts the institution of slavery: "the blessings in which you this day rejoice are not enjoyed in common. The rich inheritance of justice, liberty, prosperity, and independence bequeathed by your fathers is shared by you, not by me. This Fourth of July is yours, not mine" (lines 9-13). Here, Douglass highlights that American ideals such as "justice, liberty, prosperity, and independence" are not accessible to all Americans and are thus inconsistently applied. Choice A is incorrect because Douglass only admonishes those who claim that abolitionists must "make a favorable impression on the public mind" (line 39); while he later encourages abolitionists to be more forceful, he does not blame them for refraining from such force in the past. Choice B is incorrect because Douglass asserts that rationally proving the wrongfullness of slavery is not worth his time, as it is an obvious fact: "Must I argue that a system thus marked with blood is wrong? No—I will not. I have better employment for my time than such arguments would imply" (lines 63-66). Choice C is incorrect because Douglass does not seek to emotionally affect his audience; instead he wishes for radical action to combat the system of slavery. In addition, Douglas indicates that he himself mourns during the Fourth of July (lines 13-14), but does not imply that the holiday should transform into one of mourning. Instead, he recommends supporting the freedom of African-Americans so that celebration during the Fourth of July can become justified.

Question 2: D
Choice D is the best answer because Douglass poses the following questions: "What have I or those I represent to do with your national independence? Are the great principles of political freedom embodied in that Declaration of Independence extended to us?" These questions highlight the incongruence in the fact that Douglass, a black man who has been denied access to liberty, has been invited to give a speech on the Fourth of July, a day that is meant to celebrate freedom. Choice A is incorrect because Douglass' questions are not meant to "provoke the audience to ponder the significance of the Fourth of July". Douglass' questions are rhetorical and their answers are self-evident, which means that the audience need not debate his meaning. Choice B is incorrect because Douglass is not trying to elicit embarrassment from his audience; moreover, it is implied that Douglass' audience is not ignorant and is reasonably informed about slavery, given his rhetoric in lines 42-45: "there is nothing to be argued. What point in the anti-slavery creed would you have me argue? On what branch of the subject do the people of this country need light?" Choice C is incorrect because Douglass' goal in the first paragraph is not to criticize the celebration; he is still establishing the premise of his criticism by illustrating the ways that blacks are excluded from celebrating America's independence.

Question 3: B
Choice B is the best answer because lines 18-21 describe Douglass' belief that his punishment for neglecting to speak out about the injustice of slavery in the midst of Fourth of July celebrations should be his "right hand [forgetting] her cunning, and…[his] tongue [cleaving] to the roof of [his] mouth", thus showing an intense personal urge to "assert his beliefs". Choices A and D are incorrect because lines 9-13 and lines 76-79 highlight the hypocrisy of the Fourth of July, but do not express that such hypocrisy needed to be exposed. Choice C is incorrect because lines 37-41 do not describe Douglass' perspective, as they focus on the beliefs of "some of [his] audience".

Question 4: A
Choice A is the best answer because Douglass highlights in lines 68-72 the abolitionist movement's need for "biting ridicule and stern rebuke"; as he wishes for abolitionists to be more "biting" and "stern", he thus believes that the movement must adopt a more extreme or "blunt" method to express the wrongfulness of slavery. Choice B is incorrect because Douglass describes the "sin" of slavery as "[trampling] upon" (lines 31-34) the name of the Bible, but does not indicate the reverse: that the Bible must be utilized to fight slavery. Choice C is incorrect because Douglass argues against moderate reform, which he views as insufficiently radical; indeed, he states that "scorching irony, not convincing argument, is needed" (lines 67-68). Choice D is incorrect because only "some of [Douglass'] audience" believe that "abolitionists fail to make a favorable impression on the public mind" (lines 37-39); Douglass himself believes that such efforts to gain popularity are steeped in absurdity, since it should be of no debate that slavery is an evil that must be destroyed.

Question 5: D
Choice D is the best answer because lines 68-72 indicates that "it is not light that is needed, but fire; it is not the gentle shower, but thunder"; these lines thus express Douglass' opinion that the abolitionist movement is in need of greater fervor, which matches the topic of the previous question. Choice A is incorrect because lines 31-36 express Douglass' denunciation of slavery, but does not offer any solutions for the abolitionist movement. Choice B is incorrect because lines 37-41 describe what "some of [Douglass'] audience", not Douglass himself, feel is needed in the abolitionist movement. Choice C is incorrect because lines 47-50 describe the current state of laws regarding slavery and are thus off topic.

Question 6: A
Choice A is the best answer because Douglass indicates that some of his contemporaries argue that abolitionists "would be much more likely to succeed" if they "argue more and denounce less" (lines 40-41), before criticising that remark with the point that the injustice of slavery is patently clear and therefore does not need to be proved or "argued". The advice that abolitionists make their platform "more palatable" is thus absurd, since the abolitionist movement is already based on a fact that should already be widely accepted. Choice B is incorrect because Douglass encourages abolitionists to be more inflammatory, not less: "had I the ability, and could I reach the nation's ear,I would today pour out a fiery stream of biting ridicule and stern rebuke" (lines 68-70). Choice C is incorrect because the questions posed by Douglass—"what point in the anti-slavery creed would you have me argue?"— are answered within the same paragraph: "where all is plain there is nothing to be argued" (lines 41-42). Choice D is incorrect because Douglass does not indicate whether the abolitionist movement is obscure or popular, only that it is not as popular as some would like it to be.

Question 7: B
Choice B is the best answer because Douglass includes many detailed descriptions of slavery's cruelty in the seventh paragraph: "to beat them with sticks, to flay their flesh with the lash, to load their limbs with irons, to hunt them with dogs...to knock out their teeth, to burn their flesh, to starve them into obedience and submission" (lines 58-62). Choice A is incorrect because there is nothing ironic, or sarcastic, about the way in which Douglass describes the violence of slavery; his depiction of the horrors of slavery is genuine. Choice C is incorrect because Douglass does not use literal comparisons to characterize slavery; instead, he depicts what slavery is like by providing images and examples. Choice D is incorrect because the questions that Douglass poses in the paragraph are not open-ended; they are rhetorical questions to which everyone knows the answer. Indeed, Douglass presents his line of questioning as obvious, with no room for argument. "Must I argue the wrongfulness of slavery? What!" (line 54) yields only one answer: no.

Question 8: C
Choice C is the best answer because "galvanized" best matches "roused" (line 74) and "startled" (line 74), all of which Douglass uses to describe what must be done to the nation. Choice A is incorrect because to describe the feeling of the nation as "hastened" implies that zealous abolitionist activity already exists but at a slow pace, whereas Douglass' point is that it must be established. Choice B is incorrect because "revitalized" implies that the feeling once existed but no longer does, which is not the case. Choice D is incorrect because "emancipated" implies that the feeling is present but needs to be liberated, which is unsupported by the passage.

Question 9: D
Choice D is the best answer because Douglass states that America's crimes would "disgrace a nation of savages" (lines 84-85), which supports the inhumane aspect of "human rights abuses". Douglass furthers that "for revolting barbarity and shameless hypocrisy, America reigns without a rival" (lines 89-90); we are unmatched, or unparalleled, in our cruelty. Choice A is incorrect; while Douglass points out that slaves have no reason to celebrate the Fourth of July in the last paragraph, such as when he states that "[the Fourth of July] reveals to [the American slave] more than all other days of the year, the gross injustice and cruelty to which he is the constant victim" (lines 77-79), this point is repeated throughout the passage and is therefore not a "new claim". For instance, Douglass states that "the blessings in which you this day rejoice are not enjoyed in common" (lines 9-10) and that "above your tumultuous joy I hear the mournful wail of millions, whose chains, heavy and grievous, are today rendered more intolerable" (lines 15-17). Choices B and C are incorrect because Douglass does not indicate that the Fourth of July was meant to absolve guilt or discuss the status of slavery in the world.

Question 10: A
Choice A is the best answer because Douglas characterizes the "boasted liberty" (line 80) celebrated during the Fourth of July as only available to white Americans; because such "liberty" is only afforded to a few, it is actually a "privilege". Choice B is incorrect because Douglass claims that the "unholy license" is the opposite of true liberty; thus, it cannot be "freedom". Choice C is incorrect because "permit" is an overly literal synonym of "license". In addition, "permit" would imply that the deprevation of freedom to African-Americans was authorized by an authority, while Douglass depicts slavery as contradictory to the tenets of the Constitution (lines 31-36). Choice D is incorrect: African-Americans are not extended the freedoms that are enjoyed by white Americans, so such freedoms cannot be described as "rights" that are enforced by the government.

Chapter Seven

Questions 1-10 are based on the following passage.

7.1

The following passage is adapted from Senator Robert M. La Follette's "Free Speech in Wartime" address to the Senate on October 6, 1917 – six months after the United States had entered World War 1.

I have no intention of taking the time of the Senate with a review of the events which led to our entrance into the war except in so far as they bear upon the
Line question of personal privilege to which I am addressing
5 myself.

Six members of the Senate and fifty members of the House voted against the declaration of war. Immediately there was let loose upon those senators and representatives a flood of invective and abuse from
10 newspapers and individuals who had been clamoring for war, unequaled, I believe, in the history of civilized society. Prior to the declaration of war every man who had ventured to oppose our entrance into it had been condemned as a coward or worse. Since the declaration
15 of war the triumphant war press has pursued those senators and representatives who voted against the war with malicious falsehood and recklessly libelous attacks, going to the extreme limit of charging them with treason against their country.

20 But, sir, it is not alone members of Congress that the war party in this country has sought to intimidate. The mandate seems to have gone forth to the sovereign people of this country that they must be silent while those things are being done by their government
25 which most vitally concern their well-being, their happiness, and their lives. Today, and for weeks past, honest and law-abiding citizens of this country are being terrorized and outraged in their rights by those sworn to uphold the laws and protect the rights of the
30 people. I have in my possession numerous affidavits establishing the fact that people are being unlawfully arrested, thrown into jail, held incommunicado for days, only to be eventually discharged without even having been taken into court, because they have
35 committed no crime. Private residences are being invaded, loyal citizens of undoubted integrity and probity arrested, cross-examined, and the most sacred constitutional rights guaranteed to every American citizen are being violated. It appears to be the purpose
40 of those conducting this campaign to throw the country into a state of terror, to coerce public opinion, to stifle criticism, and suppress discussion of the great issues involved in this war.

It is the citizen's duty to obey the law until it is
45 repealed or declared unconstitutional. But he has the inalienable right to fight what he deems an obnoxious law or a wrong policy in the courts and at the ballot box. It is the suppressed emotion of the masses that breeds revolution. If the American people are to carry
50 on this great war, if public opinion is to be enlightened and intelligent, there must be free discussion. Congress, as well as the people of the United States, entered the war in great confusion of mind and under feverish excitement. The president's leadership was
55 followed in the faith that he had some big, unrevealed plan by which peace that would exalt him before all the world would soon be achieved. Gradually, reluctantly, Congress and the country are beginning to perceive that we are in this terrific world conflict, not only to
60 right our wrongs, not only to aid the allies, not only to share its awful death toll and its fearful tax burden, but, perhaps, to bear the brunt of the war. And so I say, if we are to forestall the danger of being drawn into years of war, perhaps finally to maintain imperialism and
65 exploitation, the people must unite in a campaign along constitutional lines for free discussion of the policy of the war and its conclusion on a just basis. It is said by many persons for whose opinions I have profound respect and whose motives I know to be sincere that
70 "we are in this war and must go through to the end.' That is true. But it is not true that we must go through to the end to accomplish an undisclosed purpose, or to reach an unknown goal.

I believe that whatever there is of honest
75 difference of opinion concerning this war, arises precisely at this point. There is, and of course can be, no real difference of opinion concerning the duty of the citizen to discharge to the last limit whatever obligation the war lays upon him. No, Mr. President;
80 it is on the other point suggested where honest differences of opinion may arise. Shall we ask the people of this country to shut their eyes and take the entire war program on faith? There are no doubt many honest and well-meaning persons who are willing
85 to answer that question in the affirmative rather than risk the dissensions which they fear may follow a free discussion of the issues of this war. With that position, I cannot agree. Have the people no intelligent contribution to make to the solution of the problems
90 of this war? I believe that they have, and that in this matter, as in so many others, they may be wiser than their leaders, and that if left free to discuss the issues of the war they will find the correct settlement of these issues.

CONTINUE

1

Which choice best represents the main idea of the passage?

A) Freedom of speech should be protected by the government even when the United States is at war.

B) The right to discourse must be granted to the citizenry to provide a check on abusive governance.

C) Citizens must be able to exercise their right to vote on the government's involvement in war.

D) The United States government is infringing upon citizens' right to prevent wartime involvement.

2

La Follette contends that, at the commencement of World War I, certain members of Congress were

A) deliberate traitors in their anti-war endeavors.

B) misunderstood defendants against charges of treason.

C) continued advocates for righteous peace initiatives.

D) innocent victims of irresponsible vilification.

3

According to La Follette, how has the general public been affected by World War I?

A) Its right to self-determination and freedom of expression in wartime has been infringed upon.

B) Its right to lawful judicial processes has been suspended for the purposes of national security.

C) Its Constitutional rights have been diminished by those who are responsible for protecting them.

D) Its right to responsible elected officials has been undercut by the abusiveness of their actions.

4

Which choice provides the best evidence for the answer to the previous question?

A) Lines 22-25 ("The mandate...well-being")

B) Lines 27-30 ("citizens of...people")

C) Lines 31-35 ("people are...crime")

D) Lines 35-37 ("Private residences...arrested")

5

In the context of the passage as a whole, lines 44-51 ("It is...discussion") primarily serve to

A) clarify the rights to which citizens are entitled during wartime.

B) demonstrate the significance of public opinion in wartime.

C) point out the consequences of suppressing indispensable rights.

D) warn of the danger that a complacent public poses to democracy.

6

As used in line 49, "breeds" most nearly means

A) cultivates.

B) promotes.

C) incites.

D) precedes.

7

As used in line 65, "campaign" most nearly means

A) strike.

B) resolution.

C) crusade.

D) movement.

8

Throughout the passage, La Follette draws a distinction between questioning wartime policies and supporting the war effort in order to

A) suggest that the process of questioning will yield answers that encourage the public to rally in favor of the war.

B) demonstrate that seeking to establish an objective through discourse is not the same as being unpatriotic.

C) characterize the American public as polarized with respect to opinions regarding participation in the war.

D) indicate that they are two fundamentally different principles that will divide the country when it can least afford it.

CONTINUE

9

Which choice provides the best evidence for the answer to the previous question?

A) Lines 70-73 ("we are...goal")

B) Lines 76-79 ("There is...him")

C) Lines 83-86 ("There are...dissensions")

D) Lines 88-92 ("Have the...leaders")

10

La Follette's question in lines 81-83 ("Shall we... faith?") primarily serves to

A) highlight the absurdity of the government encroaching upon the public's right to question wartime policies.

B) lend support to the argument that the United States' participation in the war cannot be logically justified.

C) express indignation in the government's assumption that citizens will unquestioningly support all military policies.

D) reveal that the public has been blindly following the government due to their fear of dissension.

CONTINUE

Questions 1-10 are based on the following passage.

7.2

This passage is adapted from Chief Justice Warren's opinion delivered as the culmination of the 1967 Supreme Court Case Loving v. Virginia. The opinion of the Court decides that it is unconstitutional to ban or punish marriages solely because they are interracial.

Virginia is now one of 16 States which prohibit and punish marriages on the basis of racial classifications. Penalties for miscegenation* arose as an incident to slavery, and have been common in Virginia since the colonial period. The present statutory scheme dates from the adoption of the Racial Integrity Act of 1924, passed during the period of extreme nativism which followed the end of the First World War.

The State argues that the meaning of the Equal Protection Clause, as illuminated by the statements of the Framers, is only that state penal laws containing an interracial element as part of the definition of the offense must apply equally to whites and Negroes in the sense that members of each race are punished to the same degree. Thus, the State contends that, because its miscegenation statutes punish equally both the white and the Negro participants in an interracial marriage, these statutes, despite their reliance on racial classifications, do not constitute an invidious discrimination based upon race.

The second argument advanced by the State assumes the validity of its equal application theory. The argument is that, if the Equal Protection Clause does not outlaw miscegenation statutes because of their reliance on racial classifications, the question of constitutionality would thus become whether there was any rational basis for a State to treat interracial marriages differently from other marriages. On this question, the State argues, the scientific evidence is substantially in doubt and, consequently, this Court should defer to the wisdom of the state legislature in adopting its policy of discouraging interracial marriages.

The State argues that statements in the Thirty-ninth Congress about the time of the passage of the Fourteenth Amendment indicate that the Framers did not intend the Amendment to make unconstitutional state miscegenation laws. Many of the statements alluded to by the State concern the debates over the Freedmen's Bureau Bill, which President Johnson vetoed, and the Civil Rights Act of 1866, 14 Stat. 27, enacted over his veto. While these statements have some relevance to the intention of Congress in submitting the Fourteenth Amendment, it must be understood that they pertained to the passage of specific statutes, and not to the broader, organic purpose of a constitutional amendment.

As for the various statements directly concerning the Fourteenth Amendment, we have said in connection with a related problem that, although these historical sources "cast some light" they are not sufficient to resolve the problem. We have rejected the proposition that the debates in the Thirty-ninth Congress or in the state legislatures which ratified the Fourteenth Amendment supported the theory advanced by the State, that the requirement of equal protection of the laws is satisfied by penal laws defining offenses based on racial classifications so long as white and Negro participants in the offense were similarly punished.

The clear and central purpose of the Fourteenth Amendment was to eliminate all official state sources of invidious racial discrimination in the States. There can be no question but that Virginia's miscegenation statutes rest solely upon distinctions drawn according to race. The statutes proscribe** generally accepted conduct if engaged in by members of different races. Over the years, this Court has consistently repudiated "distinctions between citizens solely because of their ancestry" as being "odious to a free people whose institutions are founded upon the doctrine of equality." At the very least, the Equal Protection Clause demands that racial classifications, especially suspect in criminal statutes, be subjected to the "most rigid scrutiny," and, if they are ever to be upheld, they must be shown to be necessary to the accomplishment of some permissible state objective, independent of the racial discrimination which it was the object of the Fourteenth Amendment to eliminate. Indeed, two members of this Court have already stated that they "cannot conceive of a valid legislative purpose which makes the color of a person's skin the test of whether his conduct is a criminal offense."

There is patently no legitimate overriding purpose independent of invidious racial discrimination which justifies this classification. The fact that Virginia prohibits only interracial marriages involving white persons demonstrates that the racial classifications must stand on their own justification, as measures designed to maintain White Supremacy. We have consistently denied the constitutionality of measures which restrict the rights of citizens on account of race. There can be no doubt that restricting the freedom to marry solely because of racial classifications violates the central meaning of the Equal Protection Clause.

211

CONTINUE

Marriage is one of the "basic civil rights of man," fundamental to our very existence and survival. To deny this fundamental freedom on so unsupportable
100 a basis as the racial classifications embodied in these statutes, classifications so directly subversive of the principle of equality at the heart of the Fourteenth Amendment, is surely to deprive all the State's citizens of liberty without due process of law. The
105 Fourteenth Amendment requires that the freedom of choice to marry not be restricted by invidious racial discriminations. Under our Constitution, the freedom to marry, or not marry, a person of another race resides with the individual, and cannot be infringed by the
110 State.

* **Interracial breeding**
** **outlaw**

1

Throughout the passage, Warren's main focus shifts from

A) A brief historical context of anti-miscegenation laws covering the time period between the colonial era and World War I to an affirmation of the right to marry regardless of race.

B) An outline of the State's contentions for anti-miscegenation to a Supreme Court deconstruction of the State's arguments as a means of invalidating its anti-miscegenation statutes.

C) A rejection of the perception that the Equal Protection Clause supports anti-miscegenation to a refutation based on a comprehensive understanding of the 14th Amendment.

D) A coverage of the State's arguments grounded in historical precedence and legislative interpretation to a dissension of the specific historical evidence advanced by the State.

2

As used in line 11, "illuminated" most nearly means

A) clarified.

B) stipulated.

C) evidenced.

D) revealed.

3

The State would most likely agree with which of the following claims regarding miscegenation?

A) The Equal Protection Clause's equal application theory supports the State's stance that no unjust discrimination has arisen from the Racial Integrity Act.

B) Miscegenation has equally punitive effects for all races and therefore is not discriminatory towards blacks in the slightest.

C) There are no inherently racist mechanisms involved in making interracial marriage illegal because both blacks and whites have the same punishment.

D) The State and its citizenry ought to be the parties voting against or in favor of miscegenation statutes because they are the groups that are being impacted.

4

Which choice provides the best evidence for the answer to the previous question?

A) Lines 10-16 ("The State...degree")

B) Lines 16-21 ("Thus, the...race")

C) Lines 24-29 ("the Equal...marriages")

D) Lines 29-34 ("On this...marriages")

5

What is the purpose of the State's mention of the "Freedmen's Bureau Bill" and the "Civil Rights Act of 1866" in paragraph 4 (lines 35-48)?

A) To demonstrate how Andrew Johnson's discriminatory executive veto against the two bills is evidence in favor of the State's right to arbitrate its own legislation.

B) To specify two instances in which the premises of the bills support anti-miscegenation laws to provide a legislative precedent.

C) To illustrate the benevolent legislation that the Thirty-ninth Congress put forth in order to align the State's stance with one that is typically seen as more benign.

D) To evoke the Congressional resistance to the two bills in order to demonstrate that the Framers of the 14th Amendment did not intend to make anti-miscegenation laws illegal.

CONTINUE

6

As used in line 47, "organic" most nearly means

A) natural.

B) holistic.

C) original.

D) unaltered.

7

Warren's claim in lines 69-72 ("Over the...equality") can be best characterized as

A) an emphasis of the judicial precedent that exists regarding the matter at hand to support the Court's ruling.

B) a quotation of the language of previous Court rulings to lend credibility to the current ruling.

C) an advocacy for the lack of distinction between ethnic groups to align the Court with ideals of liberty and equality.

D) a demonstration of the Court's designs to sustain crucial elements of American democracy.

8

Which choice best describes Warren's ultimate justification for his ruling against anti-miscegenation laws?

A) Anti-miscegenation laws are discriminatory because they violate the intent of the 14th Amendment and the Equal Protection Clause.

B) Anti-miscegenation laws are unjust because they are only applied to interracial marriages which include whites.

C) Anti-miscegenation laws are racist because they were designed to maintain White Supremacy.

D) Anti-miscegenation laws are unconstitutional because they use race as a determiner of whether or not typically benign conduct is legal.

9

Which choice provides the best evidence for the answer to the previous question?

A) Lines 64-68 ("There can...races")

B) Lines 76-80 ("if they...eliminate")

C) Lines 87-91 ("The fact...Supremacy")

D) Lines 91-96 ("We have...Clause")

10

Warren's mention of "due process of law" in line 104 primarily serves to

A) elucidate another unfortunate consequence that will arise from subverting inherent liberties on the basis of race.

B) suggest that the removal of civil liberties can only be justified if achieved by the application of due process.

C) claim that racial classifications undermine the requirement of due process by restricting liberties based on race.

D) reinforce the fact that it is the right of the individual and not the state to decide whom the individual will marry.

CONTINUE

Questions 1-10 are based on the following passage.

7.3

The following passage is adapted from a work by Wilford Horace Smith, a lawyer who specialized in constitutional law and who fought against state laws that discriminated against African-Americans. He was the first African-American lawyer to have won a case against the U.S. Supreme Court.

The statutory enactments and recent Constitutions of most of the former slave-holding States, show that they have never looked with favor upon the
Line amendments to the national Constitution. They rather
5 regard them as war measures designed by the North to humiliate and punish the people of those States lately in rebellion. While in the main they accept the 13th amendment and concede that the negro should have personal freedom, they have never been altogether in
10 harmony with the spirit and purposes of the 14th and 15th amendments.

The 13th amendment provides that neither slavery nor involuntary servitude, except as a punishment for crime, whereof the party shall have been duly
15 convicted, shall exist in the United States or any place subject to their jurisdiction.

The 14th amendment provides in section one, that all persons born or naturalized in the United States and subject to the jurisdiction thereof, are citizens of the
20 United States, and of the State wherein they reside. No State shall make or enforce any law which shall abridge the privileges or immunities of citizens of the United States, nor shall any State deprive any person of life, liberty or property without due process of law,
25 nor deny to any person within its jurisdiction the equal protection of the law.

The 15th amendment provides that the right of citizens of the United States to vote shall not be denied or abridged by the United States, or by any State
30 on account of race, color, or previous condition of servitude.

There seems to be a distinct and positive fear on the part of the South that if the negro is given a man's chance, and is accorded equal civil rights with white
35 men on the juries, on common carriers, and in public places, that it will in some way lead to his social equality.

To be taxed without representation is a serious injustice in a republic whose foundations are laid upon
40 the principle of "no taxation without representation." But serious as this phase of the case must appear,

infinitely more serious is the case when we consider the fact that they are likewise excluded from the grand and petit juries in all the State courts, with the fewest
45 and rarest exceptions. The courts sit in judgment upon their lives and liberties, and dispose of their dearest earthly possessions. They are not entitled to life, liberty or property if the courts should decide they are not, and yet in this all-important tribunal they are denied
50 all voice, except as parties and witnesses, and here and there a negro lawyer is permitted to appear. One vote on the grand jury might prevent an indictment, and save disgrace and the risk of public trial; while one vote on the petit jury might save a life or a term
55 of imprisonment, for an innocent person pursued and persecuted by powerful enemies.

With no voice in the making of the laws, which they are bound to obey, nor in their administration by the courts, thus tied and helpless, the negroes
60 were proscribed by a system of legal enactments intended to wholly nullify the letter and spirit of the war amendments to the national organic law. This crusade was begun by enacting a system of Jim-Crow car laws in all the Southern States, so that now the
65 Jim-Crow cars run from the Gulf of Mexico into the national capital. They are called, "Separate Car Laws," providing for separate but equal accommodations for whites and negroes. Though fair on their face, they are everywhere known to discriminate against the colored
70 people in their administration, and were intended to humiliate and degrade them.

If these statutes were not especially aimed at the negro, an arrangement of different fares, such as first, second and third classes, would have been far more
75 just and preferable, and would have enabled the refined and exclusive of both races to avoid the presence of the coarse and vicious, by selecting the more expensive fare. Still these laws have been upheld by the Federal Supreme Court, and pronounced not in conflict with
80 the amendments to the Constitution of the United States.

With the population of the South distinctly divided into two classes, not the rich and poor, not the educated and ignorant, not the moral and immoral, but simply
85 whites and blacks, all negroes being generally regarded as inferior and not entitled to the same rights as any white person, it is bound to be a difficult matter to obtain fair and just results, when there is any sort of conflict between the races. The negro realizes this, and
90 knows that he is at an immense disadvantage when he is forced to litigate with a white man in civil matters, and much more so when he is charged with a crime by a white person.

CONTINUE

1

What is a central claim of the passage?

A) There should be African-American judges serving on the Supreme Court.

B) The 13th, 14th, and 15th amendments have failed.

C) The 13th, 14th, and 15th amendments are being undermined by Southern state laws.

D) The South fears African-American voters.

2

It can be reasonably inferred from the passage that Smith believes that

A) local courts have the most direct impact on the lives of African-Americans.

B) the right to vote is more important than the right to serve on a jury.

C) class divides are not a sufficient replacement for racial divides.

D) the legal system at the federal level is corrupt and irreparably broken.

3

As used in line 10, the word "purposes" most nearly means

A) motives.

B) goals.

C) justifications.

D) outcomes.

4

Smith makes which point about the relationship between African-Americans and White Southerners?

A) African-Americans are resented by White Southerners for their involvement in the Civil War.

B) African-Americans are distrustful of the policies implemented by White Southerners.

C) White Southerners feel threatened by the potential upward mobility of African-Americans.

D) White Southerners believe that African-Americans are not intellectually equipped to receive equal rights.

5

Which choice provides the best evidence for the claim that African Americans are legally barred from the benefits of the constitution?

A) Lines 32-37 ("There seems to be…social equality.")

B) Lines 38-40 ("To be taxed…without representation.")

C) Lines 45-47 ("The court sits…earthly possessions.")

D) Lines 57-62 ("With no voice…national organic law.")

6

According to the author, the Supreme Court has taken which position on the issue of African-American rights?

A) The Supreme Court has become the driving force of protection for African-American rights.

B) The Supreme Court has become the primary block to equal access for African-Americans.

C) The Supreme Court is complicit in the efforts of Southern states to undermine the new constitutional amendments.

D) The Supreme Court is attempting to fight against Jim Crow car laws put in place by southern states.

7

Which choice provides the best evidence for the answer to the previous question?

A) Lines 47-51 ("They are not entitled…permitted to appear")

B) Lines 57-62 ("With no voice…national organic law")

C) Lines 62-66 (This crusade…national capital")

D) Lines 78-81 ("Still, these…the United States")

215

CONTINUE

8

How does Smith support his claim that Southern states do not have appropriate respect for the new constitutional amendments?

A) He describes the amendments and the current legal system before discussing concrete examples of Southern laws meant to undercut equal rights.

B) He describes the amendments in detail before explaining how they have been exploited by the legal system to support racism.

C) He describes the current legal environment on the federal level before providing examples of how it leaves African-Americans vulnerable to racist litigation.

D) He describes the punishments inflicted on Southern states following the civil war before describing segregation practices on trains.

9

As used in line 88, the word "just" most nearly means

A) impartial.

B) equal.

C) suitable.

D) honest.

10

According to the author, equal legal protection for African-Americans rests on

A) the existence of more black members on juries.

B) enforcement of the new amendments by the Supreme Court.

C) separate juries for black and white defendants.

D) a repeal of the new amendments.

CONTINUE

Questions 1-10 are based on the following passage.

7.4

The following passage is adapted from "A Crisis of Confidence" delivered by President Jimmy Carter on July 15, 1979.

Good evening.

During the past three years I've spoken to you on many occasions about national concerns, the energy
Line crisis, reorganizing the Government, our Nation's
5 economy, and issues of war and especially peace. But over those years the subjects of the speeches, the talks, and the press conferences have become increasingly narrow, focused more and more on what the isolated world of Washington thinks is important.
10 Gradually, you've heard more and more about what the Government thinks or what the Government should be doing and less and less about our Nation's hopes, our dreams, and our vision of the future.

But after listening to the American people I have
15 been reminded again that all the legislation in the world can't fix what's wrong with America. So, I want to speak to you first tonight about a subject even more serious than energy or inflation. I want to talk to you right now about a fundamental threat to American
20 democracy.

I do not mean our political and civil liberties. They will endure. And I do not refer to the outward strength of America, a nation that is at peace tonight everywhere in the world, with unmatched economic
25 power and military might.

The threat is nearly invisible in ordinary ways. It is a crisis of confidence. It is a crisis that strikes at the very heart and soul and spirit of our national will. We can see this crisis in the growing doubt about the
30 meaning of our own lives and in the loss of a unity of purpose for our Nation.

In a nation that was proud of hard work, strong families, close-knit communities, and our faith in God, too many of us now tend to worship self-indulgence
35 and consumption. Human identity is no longer defined by what one does, but by what one owns. But we've discovered that owning things and consuming things does not satisfy our longing for meaning. We've learned that piling up material goods cannot fill
40 the emptiness of lives which have no confidence or purpose.

The confidence that we have always had as a people is not simply some romantic dream or a proverb in a dusty book that we read just on the Fourth of July.
45 It is the idea which founded our Nation and has guided our development as a people. Confidence in the future has supported everything else – public institutions

and private enterprise, our own families, and the very Constitution of the United States. Confidence has
50 defined our course and has served as a link between generations. We've always had a faith that the days of our children would be better than our own.

Our people are losing that faith, not only in government itself but in the ability as citizens to serve
55 as the ultimate rulers and shapers of our democracy. We were sure that ours was a nation of the ballot, not the bullet, until the murders of John Kennedy and Robert Kennedy and Martin Luther King, Jr. We were taught that our armies were always invincible and
60 our causes were always just, only to suffer the agony of Vietnam. We respected the Presidency as a place of honor until the shock of Watergate. We remember when the phrase "sound as a dollar" was an expression of absolute dependability, until 10 years of inflation
65 began to shrink our dollar and our savings.

These wounds are still very deep. They have never been healed. The gap between our citizens and our Government has never been so wide. The people are looking for honest answers, not easy answers;
70 clear leadership, not false claims and evasiveness and politics as usual. What you see too often in Washington and elsewhere around the country is a system of government that seems incapable of action. You see a Congress twisted and pulled in every direction
75 by hundreds of well-financed and powerful special interests. Often you see paralysis and stagnation and drift. You don't like it, and neither do I. What can we do?

We simply must have faith in each other, faith in
80 our ability to govern ourselves, and faith in the future of this Nation. Restoring that faith and that confidence to America is now the most important task we face. It is a true challenge of this generation of Americans. We know the strength of America. We can regain our unity.
85 We can regain our confidence. We are the heirs of generations who survived threats much more powerful and awesome than those that challenge us now. Our fathers and mothers were strong men and women who shaped a new society during the Great Depression,
90 who fought world wars, and who carved out a new charter of peace for the world. We ourselves are the same Americans who just 10 years ago put a man on the Moon. We are the generation that dedicated our society to the pursuit of human rights and equality.
95 Little by little we can and we must rebuild our confidence. We can spend until we empty our treasuries, and we may summon all the wonders of science. But we can succeed only if we tap our greatest resources – America's people, America's values, and
100 America's confidence.

Thank you and good night.

CONTINUE

1

Carter's main purpose in this speech is to

A) accuse fellow government officials of overlooking the plight of ordinary American citizens.

B) argue that the way out of America's existing crisis is through the adoption of a strict and moral way of life.

C) make the case that, due to an erosion of public confidence in the government, the outlook for America is bleak.

D) acknowledge a problem and address it by attempting to restore a sense of national pride to Americans.

2

Which choice best supports the claim that Americans no longer feel empowered by their rights?

A) Lines 36-38 ("But we've … meaning.")

B) Lines 53-55 ("Our people … democracy.")

C) Lines 67-68 ("The gap … so wide.")

D) Lines 71-73 ("What you ... action.")

3

In context of the passage, lines 53-65 serve to

A) outline a series of events that has shaped the course of American history.

B) summarize a viewpoint that is critical of the American government.

C) provide background helpful in explaining a particular American attitude.

D) list common grievances that will be addressed by the U.S. government.

4

Which statement provides the best description of a technique Carter uses throughout his speech to establish a connection with his audience?

A) He criticizes the complacency of the current generation by juxtaposing it with the hard-working character of former generations.

B) He distances himself from the behavior of the current government by drawing attention to its isolation from the people.

C) He aligns himself with ordinary Americans by sharing their dismay over government conduct and by referencing patriotic values.

D) He acknowledges the disenchantment of Americans by using pessimistic language to describe the current state of affairs.

5

As used in line 55, "rulers" most nearly means

A) influencers.

B) leaders.

C) governors.

D) custodians.

6

Carter implies that Congress has become ineffective because

A) it lacks a clear and convincing leadership.

B) its divided loyalties make it untrustworthy.

C) it is subjected to conflicting interests.

D) it makes misleading representations.

7

Which choice provides the best evidence for the answer to the previous question?

A) Lines 6-9 ("But over...important.")

B) Lines 10-13 ("Gradually...the future.")

C) Lines 68-71 ("The people...as usual.")

D) Lines 73-76 ("You see...interests.'")

CONTINUE

8

As used in line 77, "drift" most nearly means

A) indecision.

B) disloyalty.

C) corruption.

D) digression.

9

Which choice would Carter most likely choose to summarize the "crisis of confidence" (line 27) he sees in America?

A) Americans no longer control the direction of their government.

B) Americans see no progress or bright future for their children.

C) Americans are losing faith in the ideals of their democracy.

D) Americans are aggrieved by the gradual erosion of their civil rights.

10

In his attempt to restore confidence to Americans, Carter draws attention to the fact that

A) Americans have a proven capacity for overcoming economic and political challenges.

B) Americans have always prevailed in war due to having the most powerful military in the world.

C) Americans are inevitably unified by a glorious history and shared traditions.

D) American scientific prowess and fiscal might are sufficient to stimulate the economy.

CONTINUE

Questions 1-10 are based on the following passage.

7.5

The following passages are adapted from the Supreme Court decision in Roe V. Wade in which a majority ruling declared that the Texas anti-abortion laws were in violation of the Constitution. Passage 1 is adapted from the Court's Opinion as delivered by Justice Blackmun. Passage 2 is adapted from the dissenting opinion as delivered by Mr. Justice Rehnquist.

Passage 1

    The principal thrust of appellant's attack on the Texas statutes is that they improperly invade a right, said to be possessed by the pregnant woman, to choose

Line to terminate her pregnancy. Appellant would discover
5 this right in the concept of personal "liberty" embodied in the Fourteenth Amendment's Due Process Clause; or in personal, marital, familial, and sexual privacy said to be protected by the Bill of Rights.

    The right of privacy, whether it be founded in
10 the Fourteenth Amendment's concept of personal liberty and restrictions upon state action, as we feel it is, or, as the District Court determined, in the Ninth Amendment's reservation of rights to the people, is broad enough to encompass a woman's
15 decision whether or not to terminate her pregnancy. The detriment that the State would impose upon the pregnant woman by denying this choice altogether is apparent. Specific and direct harm medically diagnosable even in early pregnancy may be involved.
20 Maternity, or additional offspring, may force upon the woman a distressful life and future. Psychological harm may be imminent. Mental and physical health may be taxed by child care. There is also the distress, for all concerned, associated with the unwanted
25 child, and there is the problem of bringing a child into a family already unable, psychologically and otherwise, to care for it. In other cases, as in this one, the additional difficulties and continuing stigma of unwed motherhood may be involved. All these are
30 factors the woman and her responsible physician necessarily will consider in consultation. We conclude that the right of personal privacy includes the abortion decision, but that this right is not unqualified, and must be considered against important state interests as to
35 protection of health, medical standards, and prenatal life.

    Texas urges that, apart from the Fourteenth Amendment, life begins at conception and is present

throughout pregnancy, and that, therefore, the State
40 has a compelling interest in protecting that life from and after conception. We need not resolve the difficult question of when life begins. When those trained in the respective disciplines of medicine, philosophy, and theology are unable to arrive at any consensus,
45 the judiciary, at this point in the development of man's knowledge, is not in a position to speculate as to the answer. We do not agree that, by adopting one theory of life, Texas may override the rights of the pregnant woman that are at stake. We repeat, however, that the
50 State does have an important and legitimate interest in preserving and protecting the health of the pregnant woman, whether she be a resident of the State or a nonresident who seeks medical consultation and treatment there, and that it has still another important
55 and legitimate interest in protecting the potentiality of human life. These interests are separate and distinct.

Passage 2

    I have difficulty in concluding, as the Court does, that the right of "privacy" is involved in this case. Texas, by the statute here challenged, bars the
60 performance of a medical abortion by a licensed physician on a plaintiff such as Roe. A transaction resulting in an operation such as this is not "private" in the ordinary usage of that word. Nor is the "privacy" that the Court finds here even a distant relative of the
65 freedom from searches and seizures protected by the Fourth Amendment to the Constitution, which the Court has referred to as embodying a right to privacy.

    If the Court means by the term "privacy" no more than that the claim of a person to be free from
70 unwanted state regulation of consensual transactions which may be a form of "liberty" protected by the Fourteenth Amendment, there is no doubt that similar claims have been upheld in our earlier decisions on the basis of that liberty. I agree that the "liberty,"
75 against deprivation of which, without due process, the Fourteenth Amendment protects, embraces more than the rights found in the Bill of Rights. But that liberty is not guaranteed absolutely against deprivation, only against deprivation without due process of law.
80 The test traditionally applied in the area of social and economic legislation is whether or not a law such as that challenged has a rational relation to a valid state objective.

    As in cases applying substantive due process
85 standards to economic and social welfare legislation, the adoption of the compelling state interest standard will inevitably require this Court to examine the legislative policies and pass on the wisdom of these

CONTINUE

policies in the very process of deciding whether a
90 particular state interest put forward may or may not be
"compelling." The decision here to break pregnancy
into three distinct terms and to outline the permissible
restrictions the State may impose in each one, for
example, partakes more of judicial legislation than it
95 does of a determination of the intent of the drafters of
the Fourteenth Amendment. The fact that a majority of
the States reflecting, after all, the majority sentiment
in those States, have had restrictions on abortions for
at least a century is a strong indication, it seems to me,
100 that the asserted right to an abortion is not "so rooted
in the traditions and conscience of our people as to be
ranked as fundamental." Even today, when society's
views on abortion are changing, the very existence of
the debate is evidence that the "right" to an abortion
105 is not so universally accepted as the appellant would
have us believe.

1

The primary purpose of both passages is to

A) persuade the Court to review how abortion rights relate to the Constitution and to amend it if necessary.

B) argue that the Constitution may be interpreted by the Court in order to pass a ruling on abortion rights.

C) specify how the Amendments and relevant precedents should be interpreted regarding abortion rights.

D) evaluate the rulings of lower courts in the historical context of women's healthcare and the American family.

2

The list in lines 20-29 ("Maternity, or…involved") of Passage 1 serves to

A) delineate the potential breaches of privacy and liberty of unborn children.

B) illustrate the contexts in which a right to choose could be beneficial.

C) criticize the State of Texas for imposing undue burdens on its pregnant citizens.

D) catalog the considerations taken by physicians in every case of abortion.

3

As used in line 33, "unqualified" most nearly means

A) unofficial.

B) unchartered.

C) unconditional.

D) unlicensed.

4

The statement in lines 47-49 ("We do not … stake") indicates that one theory of life

A) is impossible to determine based on current scientific and philosophical evidence.

B) has absolutely no place in questions about the rights of pregnant women.

C) should never be used to legislate the rights of citizens in general.

D) is an insufficient basis on which to deny rights to pregnant women.

5

Based on the passages, how might the author of Passage 1 view the statement in line 96-102 (The fact … fundamental) of Passage 2?

A) With skepticism, because it is impossible for the majority sentiment to account for a true consensus on the question of when life begins.

B) With disapproval, because the States are placing restrictions on pregnant women that violate their Constitutional right to privacy.

C) With tolerance, because the ambiguity of the Constitution makes matters of this sort open to interpretation by the States.

D) With scorn, because the majority sentiment only reflects the beliefs held by those whose individual rights are not at stake.

6

Which choice provides the best evidence for the answer to the previous question?

A) Lines 4-6 ("Appellant would … Clause")

B) Lines 9-15 ("The right … pregnancy")

C) Lines 37-41 ("Texas urges … conception")

D) Lines 42-47 ("When those … answer")

221

CONTINUE

7

As used in lines 40 and 86, "compelling" most nearly means

A) valid.

B) plausible.

B) feasible.

D) important.

8

In discussing legislation, the author of Passage 2 implies that the Supreme Court is

A) abusing its power to the highest degree.

B) correcting prior omissions of rights.

C) complicating laws already in place.

D) straying from its intended purpose.

9

The authors of both Passage 1 and Passage 2 would agree that

A) the States have had too much power over individuals for too long.

B) pregnant women have not enjoyed the same rights as other citizens.

C) the State has some legitimate duty in the question of abortion rights.

D) the life of a pregnant woman is a core consideration in an abortion case

10

Which choice identifies how each passage uses the Amendments in arguments?

A) Passage 2 argues that the Fourteenth and the Ninth are not broad enough to encompass the right to choose without due process, while Passage 1 argues that Fourteenth and the Fourth have always included the right to choose.

B) Passage 2 argues that the Due Process Clause in the Fourth is sufficient protection for the right of pregnant women to abortion, while Passage 1 argues that Due Process Clause in the Fourteenth guarantees the right to choose.

C) Passage 2 argues that neither the Fourth nor the Fourteenth constitute the right to privacy as it pertains to abortion, while Passage 1 argues that the Ninth and the Fourteenth constitute the right to privacy as it pertains to abortion.

D) Passage 2 argues that the Fourteenth and the Fourth are the primary basis for all legal questions regarding abortion, while Passage 1 argues that the Fourteenth and the Fourth are secondary to the one theory of life.

STOP

Please turn to next page for answer keys and explanations.

Answer Key: CHAPTER SEVEN

7.1 | La Follette	7.2 | Loving V. Virginia	7.3 | Horace Smith	7.4 | Carter	7.5 | Roe V. Wade
1: A	1: B	1: C	1: D	1: C
2: D	2: B	2: A	2: B	2: B
3: C	3: C	3: B	3: C	3: C
4: B	4: B	4: C	4: C	4: D
5: C	5: D	5: D	5: A	5: B
6: C	6: B	6: C	6: C	6: B
7: D	7: A	7: D	7: D	7: A
8: B	8: D	8: A	8: A	8: C
9: A	9: A	9: A	9: C	9: C
10: A	10: C	10: A	10: A	10: A

Answer Explanations

Chapter Seven

Chapter 7.1 | La Follette

Question 1: A
Choice A is the best answer because La Follette establishes a sense of urgency from the outset of his speech to address that "a flood of invective and abuse from newspapers and individuals" (lines 9-10) is being directed at members of congress and "the sovereign people of this country" (lines 22-23) for not supporting America's involvement in the war. He later reveals that this is a problem because if the right to freedom of speech is not upheld, "suppressed emotion of the masses...breeds revolution" (lines 48-49). Choice B is incorrect because while the right to discourse is La Follette's primary concern, he does not imply that the government is abusive, he specifically cites newspapers, police, and individuals as the problematic parties. Choice C and D are incorrect because the right to vote for or against war is only incidental to the passage. War has already begun and La Follette even states that he has "no intention of taking the time of the Senate with a review of the events which led to our entrance into the war" (lines 1-3), making it clear that his primary issue is something other that involvement in war, specifically freedom of speech regarding agreeing or disagreeing with the war.

Question 2: D
Choice D is the best answer because La Follette deems the "invective and abuse" (line 9) being "let loose upon...senators and representatives (lines 8-9) "malicious falsehoods and recklessly libelous attacks", indicating that the attacks are both slanderous and misguided. Choice A is incorrect because the author asserts in the first paragraph that he is not addressing whether anyone is right or wrong in their support for or opposition to the war. Choice B is incorrect because La Follette never describes these members of congress as "defendants"; in fact, he later reveals that people are "eventually discharged...because they have committed no crime" (lines 33-35), which is as much as the audience learns about what happens after people are charged with crimes regarding the issues in the passage. Choice C is incorrect because La Follette does not make any claim as to what these congressmen's beliefs are at the time of the passage.

Question 3: C
Choice C is the best answer because La Follette shows the effects on the general public as being diminished by saying the public is "terrorized and outraged in their rights" (line 28) and he specifically accuses "those sworn to uphold the laws and protect the rights of the people" (lines 28-30) as the parties responsible. Choice A is incorrect because La Follette does not mention the

public's right to control their own lives as having been infringed upon, only their right to voice their opinion on wartime matters. Choice B is incorrect because none of the lines in the next question mention national security or the judicial process, only infringement of rights. Choice D is incorrect because La Follette does not state that "responsible elected officials" is a right of the public.

Question 4: B
Choice B is the best answer because La Follette states that the atrocities being committed against the public are being done by "those sworn to uphold the laws and protect the rights of the people" (lines 28-29). Choices A, C, and D are incorrect because while all three choices detail violations committed against the general public, none of the lines explicitly state that those responsible for protecting the public are the same people committing the offenses.

Question 5: C
Choice C is the best answer because La Follette distinguishes between obeying the law and fighting to repeal a law that is not right in the beginning of the paragraph before going on to say that people must be allowed to fight for what they believe in or "the suppressed emotion of the masses...breeds revolution" (lines 48-49), warning of a possible negative outcome should the government not heed his advice. Choice A is incorrect because La Follette discusses rights of the citizens during wartime prior to this part of the text, and he only discusses one specific right in lines 44-51. Choice B is incorrect because the significance of public opinion La Follette is discussing in these lines extends beyond just wartime. This is a general statement about the rights of the citizens that applies at all times in all situations. Choice D is incorrect because while La Follette is warning of danger that could arise, it is due to an engaged public, not a complacent one.

Question 6: C
Choice C is the best answer because in the previous sentence, La Follette states that a citizen must be free to "fight what he deems an obnoxious law" (lines 46-47) because if this right to exercise power is removed, the country is vulnerable to revolt, supporting that revolution is "incited", or "stirred up". Choice A is incorrect because cultivate implies something happening over time and becoming more refined or honed, and is generally used to refer to a skill or to crops/land/plants. Choice B is incorrect because to promote is to raise or to further something but La Follette does not indicate that the hypothetical revolution that would be bred is already in progress. Choice D is incorrect because while oppression of freedom of speech could precede revolution, in this instance La Follette is referring to the cause of a possible uprising, not clarifying the timeline.

Question 7: D
Choice D is the best answer because La Follette asserts earlier in the sentence that people need to "unite...for free discussion" (lines 65-66) and what they unite into is a "coalition", indicative of banding together, or starting a movement. Choice A is incorrect because La Follette calls for the campaign to come together for "free discussion" (line 66), and not to oppose or refuse anything. Choice B is incorrect because while the campaign may come to a resolution, the reason La Follette uses that particular word in line 65 is to emphasize the togetherness of the people. Choice C is incorrect because while crusade and movement both indicate people coming together for a common social or political cause, crusade is used in more aggressive situations whereas La Follette merely states that this campaign is to maintain free discussion.

Question 8: B

Choice B is the best answer because La Follette asserts that it is important to be patriotic and support the war: "we are in this war and must go through to the end" (line 70); but he also states that people may at the same time ask questions to better understand the goal of the war: "it is not true that we must go through to...accomplish an undisclosed purpose" (lines 71-72). Choice A, C, and D are incorrect because while La Follette does suggest that Americans should question the war, he does not make any claims about the way Americans in general feel (nor does he make predictions regarding future consequences) other than that they want their right to freedom of speech to be upheld.

Question 9: A

Choice A is the best answer because in lines 70-73, La Follette distinguishes between supporting the war, "we are in this war and must go through to the end" (line 70), and asking questions to better understand the goal of the war, "it is not true that we must go through to...accomplish an undisclosed purpose" (lines 71-72). Choice B is incorrect because there is no distinction in lines 76-79; instead, La Follette details a fact that is true of all people: that they all know their "duty...to discharge to the last limit whatever obligation the war lays upon [them]" (lines 77-79). Choice C is incorrect because in lines 83-86 La Follette merely details a fear of the people about questioning wartime policies but does not mention supporting the war effort. Choice D is incorrect because La Follette does not address questioning wartime policies in lines 88-92.

Question 10: A

Choice A is the best answer because in lines 81-83 La Follette poses a rhetorical question that has an obvious answer: no. By asking this question to the audience, La Follette makes it obvious how absurd it would be for the public to act on blind faith regarding matters of the country. Choice B is incorrect because La Follette never claims that war can not be justified; in fact, he states that "it is said by many persons for whose opinions [he has] profound respect and whose motives [he knows] to be sincere" (lines 67-69) that America must continue its duty to the wartime efforts, and he agrees by saying "that is true" (line 71). Choice C is incorrect because while La Follette is indignant about treatment of citizens who oppose the Vietnam war, he makes no claims about all wars. Choice D is incorrect because the author reveals that members of the public are blindly following due to fear of repercussions in another part of the passage when he says "there are...many...persons who are willing to answer...in the affirmative rather than risk the dissensions which they fear may follow a free discussion" (lines 83-87).

Chapter 7.2 | Loving V. Virginia

Question 1: B

Choice B is the best answer; Warren begins by outlining the State's arguments for anti-miscegenation. In lines 10-15, Warren explains the State's interpretation of the Equal Protection Clause, which it then uses to justify its anti-miscegenation statutes. Warren continues with his explanation of the State's arguments: "the State argues, the scientific evidence is substantially in doubt and...this Court should defer to...the state legislature" (lines 30-32). Warren then proceeds to explain that the State's arguments are invalid. When the State argues that the 39th Congress' debates express the Framers' lack of intent to make anti-miscegenation unconstitutional (lines 35-43), Warren refutes these points, stating that "these historical sources...are not sufficient to resolve the problem" (lines 52-53). Moreover, Warren claims that "the clear...purpose of the Fourteenth Amendment was to eliminate all official state sources of invidious racial discrimination...There can be no question but that Virginia's miscegenation statutes rest solely upon distinctions drawn according to race" (lines 62-67). Choice A is incorrect. Referencing colonial origins of penalizing miscegenation and the current statute's origin in the interwar period does not constitute "a brief historical context of anti-miscegenation laws"; it is far too sparse to contextualize the broad category of anti-miscegenation laws. Additionally, even if one could argue that the two references to origin suffice as "a brief historical context", the timeline is inaccurate: the time period would extend beyond World War I to at least 1924, which the passage indicates "followed the end of the First World War" (lines 8-9). Choice C is incorrect; there is no rejection of the fact that the Equal Protection Clause supports anti-miscegenation at the forefront of the passage because Warren is outlining the State's arguments, which use the Equal Protection Clause to support its anti-miscegenation statute. Choice D is incorrect. Although the State's arguments are indeed "grounded in historical precedence and legislative interpretation", Warren moves beyond just "a dissension of the specific historical evidence advanced by the State". He also challenges its legislative interpretation: "the clear and central purpose of the Fourteenth Amendment was to eliminate all official state sources of invidious racial discrimination in the States" (lines 62-64).

Question 2: B
Choice B is the best answer because the State argues that "the statements of the Framers" outline the meaning of the Equal Protection Clause. As such, the Framers "stipulated" the Equal Protection Clause through their statements. Choice A is incorrect because the Framers could not have "clarified", or specified, the Equal Protection Clause; it did not exist prior to their conception of it. Choice C is incorrect because the statements of the Framers cannot be taken as proof or evidence of the meaning of the Equal Protection Clause; the statements of the Framers are what constitute the Equal Protection Clause in its entirety. Choice D is incorrect because, once again, the meaning of the Equal Protection Clause cannot be "revealed" by the statements of the Framers, since it is the statements themselves that make up the Equal Protection Clause.

Question 3: C
Choice C is the best answer because the State argues that anti-miscegenation laws are not racist because both whites and blacks are equally penalized, meaning that there is no violation of the Equal Protection Clause. Choice A is incorrect because the primary issue is that the equal application theory is not an inherent part of the Equal Protection Clause; it is the State's interpretation of the Equal Protection Clause that is called the "equal application theory". Choice B is incorrect because miscegenation is indeed discriminatory towards blacks, in that there is a distinction based on race. However, the State argues that since this differentiation is also extended to whites, the discrimination is not racist. Choice D is incorrect because the State believes that anti-miscegenation laws ought to be under the jurisdiction of the state legislatures, but that does not necessarily translate to the citizenry "voting against or in favor of miscegenation statutes". Additionally, the State never explicitly states that the rationale for the citizenry voting stems from the fact that "[it is the group] being impacted".

Question 4: B

Choice B is the best answer; although all of the choices describe parts of the State's argument, which means that the State would agree with all of them, Choice B is the only choice that accurately matches a choice in Question 3. Warren indicates in lines 16-21 that "the State contends that, because its miscegenation statutes punish equally both the white and the Negro participants in an interracial marriage, these statues, despite their reliance on racial classifications, do not constitute an invidious discrimination based upon race". As such, the State would agree that anti-miscegenation statutes are not racist because both whites and blacks are equally penalized for their participation in an interracial marriage. Choice A is incorrect because lines 10-16 only establish the State's interpretation of the Equal Protection Clause, which is known as the equal application theory. The only choice that mentions the equal application theory in Question 3 is Choice A, but lines 10-16 do not address the latter part of the choice, which is that "no unjust discrimination has arisen". Choice C is incorrect because lines 24-29 bring up the constitutionality of distinguishing between interracial marriages and other marriages. There is no choice in Question 3 that brings up this distinction, which means that Choice C cannot be matched to a choice in Question 3. Choice D is incorrect because lines 29-34 indicate that anti-miscegenation laws ought to fall under the jurisdiction of state legislatures. The only choice in Question 3 that addresses the State being able to dictate anti-miscegenation statutes is Choice D. However, the State and its citizenry cannot be equated to the state legislature. Additionally, lines 29-34 do not include the rationale that "the State and its citizenry" should vote "because they are the groups that are being impacted". Lines 29-34 actually state that the state legislature should have jurisdiction because "the scientific evidence is substantially in doubt" (lines 30-31).

Question 5: D

Choice D is the best answer; "the State argues that statements in the Thirty-ninth Congress about the time of the passage of the Fourteenth Amendment indicate that the Framers did not intend the Amendment to make unconstitutional state miscegenation laws" (lines 35-39) is the topic sentence of paragraph 4. The statements in question refer to "the debates over the Freedmen's Bureau Bill" (lines 40-41) and "the Civil Rights Act of 1866" (line 42). The State is highlighting "Constitutional resistance", or "the debates", to demonstrate the Framers' intent at the time of the 14th Amendment's passing. Choice A is incorrect because the Freedmen's Bureau Bill and the Civil Rights Act of 1866 are not mentioned to demonstrate Andrew Johnson's executive veto. Any mention of Johnson's veto is tangential to the State's overarching point regarding the 14th Amendment. Furthermore, the passage does not indicate that Johnson's veto "is evidence in favor of the State's right to arbitrate its own legislation". Indeed, there is no mention of state legislatures in this paragraph. Choice B is incorrect because the passage does not indicate the premises of the two bills, so it cannot be ascertained that they support anti-miscegenation laws. They are merely discussed to discern the Framers' intent. Additionally, there is no precedent that is illustrated, mainly because the passage indicates that the debates about the bills occurred at "the time of the passage of the Fourteenth Amendment" (lines 36-37). A precedent requires that one bill come before the other, which is not the case here. Choice C is incorrect; both the description of the legislation as "benevolent" and the State positioning itself with a "more benign" one are unsupported by the passage.

Question 6: B

Choice B is the best answer because Warren argues that the scope of Congressional debates is limited to "specific statutes" (line 47), whereas the 14th Amendment has a "broader, organic purpose" (lines 47-48). Holistic best matches the description of the 14th Amendment's purpose as "broad", especially when juxtaposed with the description of the bills as "specific". Choice A is incorrect because a constitutional amendment cannot have a natural, or innate, purpose. A constitutional amendment is meant to be interpreted, which is exactly what is being done throughout the passage. Choices C and D are incorrect because, in addressing Congress' intent at the time of the amendment's passing in lines 43-45, it is already implied that the "original" or "unaltered" intent is in question. Additionally, because "original" and "unaltered" are synonyms, it can reasonably be inferred that neither can be the correct answer.

Question 7: A

Choice A is the best answer because Warren is elucidating a trend in the Court's actions: "over the years, this Court has consistently repudiated". In placing this statement after his thesis, "there can be no question but that Virginia's miscegenation statutes rest solely upon distinctions drawn according to race" (lines 64-67), it is clear that Warren is trying to lend support to his argument. Choice B is incorrect because Warren does not indicate that the quotations are from "previous Court rulings"; he only indicates that the Court has acted in a manner that is consistent with the values emphasized in the quotations, regardless of the quotations' origin. Choice C is incorrect because Warren is not advocating for a total absence of distinction between ethnic groups. Warren understands that ethnicities are, by definition, distinct. He only takes fault with these distinctions when they exist in the legislative statutes to perpetuate racial discrimination. Choice D is incorrect because Warren's motivation is to establish his ruling's legitimacy and denounce racial classifications, not to convince his audience of the fact that the Court is the protector of American democracy.

Question 8: D

Choice D is the best answer because Warren explains in lines 64-68 that the miscegenation statutes use race to determine whether typically acceptable conduct is legal, which makes them racially discriminatory and antithetical to the Constitution's intent. Choice A is incorrect because it is off topic; there is no line reference that includes both the 14th Amendment and the Equal Protection Clause. Moreover, violating the 14th Amendment and the Equal Protection Clause in and of itself is not what makes the anti-miscegenation statutes discriminatory; their use of race to determine whether the marriage is valid is what makes them discriminatory. Violating the 14th Amendment and the Equal Protection Clause, both of which were made with the intent to reduce discrimination, only serves to further underscore the statutes' discriminatory nature. Choice B is incorrect because Warren's reference to the statutes' double standards is meant to highlight the fact that the racial classifications involved are meant to maintain white supremacy. Warren is illustrating the intent behind the statutes, not providing overarching justification for his ruling. Choice C is incorrect; although it is accurate to state that anti-miscegenation laws are racist and were designed to maintain white supremacy, Warren does not cite these as reasons for ruling against said laws. He repudiates them for these characteristics, but selects very specific elements of the laws (such as their use of race to distinguish between legal and illegal actions) to justify his ruling.

Question 9: A

Choice A is the best answer because Warren states that the miscegenation statutes "rest solely upon distinctions drawn according to race" (lines 66-67) and that "the statutes proscribe generally accepted conduct if engaged in by members of different races" (lines 67-68), thereby indicating that race is the determining factor in whether the marriage is legal. Choice B is incorrect because Warren is illustrating a specific condition under which racial classifications would be deemed acceptable by the Equal Protection Clause, which is tangential to his overall point and is not a justification for his ruling against anti-miscegenation laws. Choice C is incorrect because Warren is repudiating Virginia's double standards regarding interracial marriage and their contributions to white supremacy, but that does not explain his specific justification for ruling against anti-miscegenation laws. Choice D is incorrect because Warren is referring to judicial precedent in lines 91-96, but that can only be taken as further support for the reason for his ruling; he does not actually explicitly state the reason for his ruling in these lines.

Question 10: C

Choice C is the best answer because Warren states that "to deny [marriage] on...racial classifications embodied in these statutes...is surely to deprive all the State's citizens of liberty without due process of law" (lines 98-104). Warren indicates in these lines that restricting liberty on the basis of race violates due process, which refers to the judicial requirement of respecting each citizen's legal rights and liberties. Choice A is incorrect because subverting each citizen's liberties on the basis of race is a deprivation of due process in and of itself; violating due process is not a consequence of subverting legal liberties, but the very definition of doing so. Choice B is incorrect because Warren does not unequivocally state that due process is the only acceptable means of removing civil liberties; rather, he states that racial classifications deprive citizens of liberty without due process, which merely implies that due process is one way of depriving citizens of their rights. Choice D is incorrect because Warren is illustrating another reason as to why racial classifications are antithetical to Constitutional ideals and practices by invoking due process; he never directly relates the violation of due process to the right of the individual to marry.

Chapter 7.3 | Horace Smith

Question 1: C

Choice C is the best answer because Smith asserts his stance in the first paragraph, stating that "[former slave-holding States] have never looked with favor upon the amendments to the national Constitution" (lines 2-4). He then details the purpose of each amendment (paragraphs 2-5), his speculation as to why this is happening (paragraph 6), and the explicit reasons this is detrimental to African-Americans. The latter reasons are that "to be taxed without representation is a serious injustice in a republic whose foundations are laid upon the principle of 'no taxation without representation'" (lines 38-41), Jim-Crow laws "are everywhere known to discriminate against the colored people" (lines 68-69), and "it is bound to be a difficult matter to obtain fair and just results, when there is any sort of conflict between the races" (lines 87-89). Choice A is incorrect because Smith mentions that "[African-Americans] are likewise excluded from the grand and petit juries in all the State courts" (lines 43-44), but does not mention their exclusion as judges on the Supreme court. Choice B is incorrect because the stated problem is not the failure of the amendments themselves but the failure of their application caused by the Jim-Crow laws that were created to evade upholding the laws established by these amendments. Choice D is incorrect because the south

231

fearing "if the negro is given a man's chance" (lines 33-34) is only part of the argument. Smith wants to establish all of the issues that this causes with regards to the 14th and 15th amendment.

Question 2: A
Choice A is the best answer because Smith indicates that State courts "sit in judgment upon [African-Americans'] lives and liberties" (lines 45-46) and that "[African-Americans] are not entitled to life, liberty or property if the courts should decide they are not" (lines 47-48), demonstrating the significance of local courts on the lives of African-Americans. Choice B is incorrect because Smith states that representation on a jury is extremely important, as "one vote...might save a life or a term of imprisonment, for an innocent person pursued and persecuted by powerful enemies" (lines 54-56). Choice C is incorrect due to Smith's statement (lines 72-78) that the Separate Car Laws would have been acceptable had they instead been predicated on the price of fare. Choice D is incorrect because it suggests that there is no way to fix the current injustices in the legal system, while Smith believes that allowing for accurate representation on juries would be a crucial step on the way to repairing the system (lines 51-56).

Question 3: B
Choice B is the best answer because Smith claims that the South is "not in harmony" with the message set forth in the 14th and 15th amendment. The primary issue he makes is of the "spirit and purposes" of these amendments, supporting that the South does not agree with the aims or goals intended to be upheld by these amendments. Notably, he states that people of the South have a "distinct and positive fear" (line 32) regarding African-Americans ability to have due process of law and the right to vote. Choices A and C are incorrect because although "motive" and "justification" could refer to the reasons for the South not wanting these laws to be fully applied, it could not be used to describe the laws themselves. Choice D is incorrect because "outcomes" implies the amendments' end results rather than their intended purposes, which is what Smith suggests the South is namely against.

Question 4: C
Choice C is the best answer because Smith states that "there seems to be a distinct and positive fear on the part of the South that if the negro is given a man's chance...that it will in some way lead to his social equality" (lines 32-37). As African-Americans had lower social standing than white Southerners at this time, gaining equality implies upward mobility. Choice A is incorrect because the war is only mentioned in the first paragraph. Smith states that white Southerners regard the amendments as "war measures...to humiliate and punish the people of those States lately in rebellion" (lines 5-7), implying that perhaps people of the North resent people of the South for their rebellion, not that white people of the South resent African-Americans of the South. Choice B is incorrect because Smith asserts that African-Americans are "bound to obey" the laws and are "tied and helpless" but not how they assess the policies behind the laws prescribed to them. Choice D is incorrect because Smith makes no claim regarding how white Southerners feel about the intellectual capabilities of African-Americans.

Question 5: D

Choice D is the best answer because Smith states that African-Americans are condemned by a system of laws that in effect negate the constitution, or the "national organic law" (line 62), thereby ensuring that African-Americans are unable to benefit from it. The other choices are incorrect because they describe Southern whites' fear of equal civil rights leading to social equality (choice A), a violation of an American principle (choice B), and State courts (choice C), not the constitution.

Question 6: C

Choice C is the best answer because the evidence states that "the Federal Supreme Court... pronounced [Jim Crow Laws] not in conflict with...the Constitution" (lines 78-81), indicating the Supreme Court is in agreement that the 14th and 15th amendments don't necessarily need to be upheld in their current forms. Choice A is incorrect because it is in direct opposition to what Smith says the Supreme Court is doing with regards to African-American rights, i.e. endorsing "separate but equal accommodations" (line 68), which "were intended to humiliate and degrade [African-Americans]" (lines 70-71). Choice B is incorrect because the primary block to equal access is Jim Crow Laws, which are created by the state courts and the Supreme Court only chooses not to shoot them down. Choice D is incorrect because the Supreme Court did not fight against Jim Crow Laws; in fact, it allowed state courts to maintain their position on these laws.

Question 7: D

Choice D is the best answer because in it, Smith discusses matters "upheld by the Federal Supreme Court" (lines 78-79), thereby addressing the topic of question six. Choice A, B, and C are incorrect because they are about the "grand and petit juries in all the State courts" (lines 43-44), not the Supreme Court.

Question 8: A

Choice A is the best answer because Smith first explains the purposes of the 13th, 14th, and 15th amendments (lines 12-31) and the workings of the petit and grand juries (lines 43-44), before then discussing Jim-Crow Laws, specifically the Separate Car Laws which "were intended to humiliate and degrade" (line 70-71) African-Americans. Choices B and C are both incorrect because they neglect to show a clear connection to the Southern states in particular. Choice D is incorrect because, although Smith acknowledges the South's belief that the new amendments were meant to "punish the people of those states lately in rebellion" (line 6-7), punishment of the South is not the intended aim of these amendments, and Smith does not describe them as such.

Question 9: A

Choice A is the best answer because the word just is referring to the results obtained under the current circumstances that "all negroes [are] generally regarded as inferior and not entitled to the same rights as any white person" (lines 85-87). Smith is making the point that "the negro...knows that he is at an immense disadvantage" (lines 90-91), stemming from the fact that courts of law cannot be impartial or fair. Choice B is incorrect because "equal" implies that the "results" (line 88) must be alike or comparable across the board, as opposed to being unbiased. Choice C is incorrect because while "suitable" suggests that the results fit the crime, it does not address the added element of bias. Choice D is incorrect because "honest" suggests that truth and sincerity are important factors, while Smith states that the division is not, in fact, between "the moral and immoral" (line 84), but between "whites and blacks" (line 85), thus implying that the problem stems from prejudice.

Question 10: A

Choice A is the best answer because the culmination of Smith's argument is that "the negro...knows that he is at an immense disadvantage when he is fored to litigate with a white man in civil matters" (lines 89-91). Choice B is incorrect because according to Smith, "the courts sit in judgment upon [African-American's] lives and liberties" (lines 45-46), implying that without representation on these courts, their lives and liberties will not equally protected, and this happens on the state level regardless of decisions made by the Supreme Court. Choice C is incorrect because Smith maintains that separate but equal laws are "known to discriminate against the colored people...and were intended to humiliate and degrade them" (lines 69-71). Choice D is incorrect because the issue Smith takes with the amendments is that the South is not "altogether in harmony with the spirit and purposes of the 14th and 15th amendments" (lines 9-11), and he does not make the claim that the amendments themselves are problematic; in fact, Smith details the aim of each amendment, making it clear that the amendments in of themselves are intended to be beneficial to African-Americans.

Chapter 7.4 | Carter

Question 1: D

Choice D is the best answer because it touches upon the main themes of the passage: Carter's concern about the "threat" of America's "crisis of confidence" (lines 26-27) before his reassuring the audience that they are the "heirs of generations who survived threats much more powerful and awesome" (lines 85-87). Choice A is incorrect because the word "accuse" is overly negative; in addition, Carter focuses on the effects of the crisis of confidence on the American public, but never on the causes of the crisis itself. Choice B is incorrect because Carter identifies the solution to America's crisis of confidence as a change of perception ("[having] faith in each other, faith in our ability to govern ourselves, and faith in the future of this Nation", lines 79-81), not a change in lifestyle. Choice C is incorrect because the word "bleak" is contradicted by Carter's optimistic tone in the last paragraph, in which he indicates his belief that Americans "can and must rebuild [their] confidence" (lines 95-96).

Question 2: B

Choice B is the best answer because lines 53-55 indicate that citizens are losing faith in their ability to "serve as the ultimate rulers and shapers of our democracy": in short, their civil right to participate in government. Choice A is incorrect because lines 36-38 do not mention American rights; instead, Carter discusses Americans' disillusionment with consumerism ("owning things and consuming things does not satisfy our longing"). Choice C is incorrect because Carter does not discuss the reaction of citizens towards the lack of trust between them and the government. Additionally, the lack of trust does not qualify as a "right" and therefore does not answer the question. Choice D is incorrect because, like lines 67-68, lines 71-73 do not express American citizens' reaction to the actions of their government and therefore cannot indicate their feeling of "disempowerment".

Question 3: C
Choice C is the best answer because lines 53-65 start with the description of "a particular American attitude": a lack of faith. Carter then explains the events that fostered that attitude, thereby providing a "background" for his claim. Choice A is incorrect because the events described in the line references do not encompass the hundreds of years during which the United States has been a country, nor do the historical events serve to indicate the most important events throughout American history. Choice B is incorrect because Carter merely seeks to objectively present information to the reader, not express a particular opinion regarding such events. Choice D is incorrect because the word "grievances" is overly negative; in addition, Carter believes that these problems will be solved not by the government, but by the American people.

Question 4: C
Choice C is the best answer because Carter repeatedly uses the first person to indicate his solidarity with the American public and his disapproval of governmental actions: "You don't like it, and neither do I. What can we do?" (line 77-78). Additionally, in the following paragraph, Carter continues to use collective voice to express his faith in American values: "We know the strength of America... We ourselves are the same Americans who just 10 years ago pub a man on the Moon" (lines 83-93). Choice A is incorrect because Carter does not accuse his audience's generation of being complacent; on the other hand, he praises their dedication to "the pursuit of human rights and equality" (line 94). Choice B is incorrect because Carter never makes an attempt to separate himself from governmental behavior, nor does he discuss governmental isolation. Choice D is incorrect because the word "pessimistic" does not correctly express the hopeful tone throughout the passage.

Question 5: A
Choice A is the best answer because it represents Carter's belief that American citizens have a "[shaping]" role in the democracy, because they are "influencers" of it. Choices B and C are incorrect because Carter's vision of American citizenship entails maintaining American democracy through the "ballot" (line 56); in that sense, citizens have the capacity to elect the "leaders" and "governors" of the country, but will not become those leaders and governors themselves. Choice D is incorrect because Carter never places the responsibility of safeguarding the democracy upon the citizens; thus, they cannot be "custodians".

Question 6: C
Choice C is the best answer because Carter blames the state of a "government incapable of action" and Congress' "paralysis and stagnation" (line 73-76) on the conflicting interests of the "hundreds of well-financed and powerful" organizations that influence Congress. Choice A is incorrect because Carter does not mention the existence of a Congressional leader, let alone the role of such a leader in creating government policies. Choice B is incorrect because Carter never addresses the differing loyalties within Congress itself nor states that its inefficacy is due to its untrustworthiness. Choice D is incorrect because Carter indicates that Congress is so paralyzed by its indecisiveness that it is unable to make decisions at all; therefore, the "misleading representations" of policies never occur.

Question 7: D
Choice D is the best answer because lines 73-76 are the only lines that mention Congress, which is the subject of the previous question. Choices A, B, and C all mention the "Government" or "leaders", but Carter never specifically criticizes Congress or the legislative branch.

Question 8: A
Choice A is the best answer because it parallels Carter's description of a Congress that is "[paralyzed] and [stagnant]". Choice B is incorrect because Carter never accuses Congress of being disloyal to either the American people or the other institutions in American government. Choices C and D are similarly off topic: Carter's main grievance with Congress is their tendency to be "pulled in every direction" (line 74), not their abuses of power ("corruption") or their tangential discussions ("digression").

Question 9: C
Choice C is the best answer because Carter presents the "crisis of confidence" as the American public's newfound doubts about their ability to exercise influence in their democracy after having experienced events such as the "murders of John Kennedy and Robert Kennedy and Martin Luther King, Jr", the "agony of Vietnam", and the "shock of Watergate" (lines 56-62), thereby supporting "losing faith in the ideals of their democracy". Choice A is incorrect because total "control" of the government has never been a goal for either Carter or the American public: the closest reference to "control" of democracy is in his discussion of the decreased "influence" of the citizenry in democracy. Choice B is incorrect because Carter depicts the crisis of confidence as "growing doubt" (line 29) and "losing...faith" (line 53), making the phrase 'no progress' too definite. Choice D is incorrect because Americans are not frustrated with their "gradually eroding" rights; instead, they are becoming disillusioned with the exercise of power that their still-intact rights provide.

Question 10: A
Choice A is the best answer because Carter cites the "the Great Depression" and "world wars" (lines 89-90) as examples of economic and political challenges that have been overcome, thereby demonstrating the "proven capacity" of Americans. Choice B is incorrect because Carter never specifies that the United States military is the most powerful in the world, nor is it true that "America has always prevailed in war": in fact, Carter explicitly mentions the "agony of Vietnam" (lines 60-61) prior in the passage, which is an example of the United States' failure in a war. Choice C is incorrect because Carter does not discuss "shared traditions" nor how they cause unity among Americans. Choice D is incorrect because "[stimulating] the economy" is never mentioned in the passage, thus making the answer choice off-topic.

Chapter 7.5 | Roe V. Wade

Question 1: C
Choice C is the best answer because both passages make frequent reference to the Bill of Rights and the Fourteenth Amendment, though the author of Passage 1 argues that they should be interpreted as "broad enough to encompass a woman's decision whether or not to terminate her pregnancy" (lines 14-15), while the author of Passage 2 argues that they provide some liberty of choice but that it "is not guaranteed absolutely against deprivation" (line 78). Additionally, they both cite precedents from previous cases (lines 27-29 and 72-74). Choice A is incorrect because the Court has already made its decision, and these speeches are simply the arguments as held by each side; this suggests that there is no room for persuasion. Choice B is incorrect because it suggests that the point of each passage is to prove that the court is allowed to interpret the Constitution, when what is at issue isn't the legality of interpretation but the dissenting opinions about which interpretation is accurate. Choice D is incorrect because neither the rulings of lower, non-federal courts are cited nor the broad historical context of women's healthcare.

Question 2: B
Choice B is the best answer because the cited list provides examples of when "specific and direct harm medically diagnosable even in early pregnancy may be involved" (lines 18-19), thus providing clear cases in which abortion might be necessary or extremely beneficial for the woman mentally and physically. Choice A is incorrect because, while it does mention the potential mental harm to the unborn child, the list is primarily focused on the harm that could befall the pregnant woman should she be forced to keep a child. Choice C is incorrect because the examples in the list are neither situated as circumstances that necessarily occurred in Texas nor as an admonishment of Texas specifically, but merely as general examples of why abortion could have a beneficial side. Choice D is incorrect because, while the author of Passage 1 argues that such considerations should be taken into account, he by no means suggests that physicians always take them into account; the fact that he is bringing these particular examples up at all suggests that they are not taken into account as often as they should be, or potentially at all.

Question 3: C
Choice C is the best answer because it suggests that there are certain conditions which must be taken into account when allowing for the right to abortion, which is supported by the statement that the right to abortion "must be considered against important state interests as to protection of health, medical standards, and prenatal life" (lines 33-36). The rest of the choices are incorrect because, in context, they all suggest that the right to abortion is, in some way, officially permitted, which doesn't fit with the following lines that explain what the author means by the word "unqualified."

Question 4: D
Choice D is the best answer because the author of Passage 1 argues that if the majority of learned people are "unable to arrive at any consensus" about the one theory of life, then "the judiciary, at this point in the development of man's knowledge, is not in the position to speculate as to the answer" (lines 44-47). This suggests that the author of Passage 1 does not believe that adopting a specific theory of life, due to the uncertainty of its validity, can serve as grounds for denying abortion. Choice A is incorrect because the author of Passage 1 only suggests that philosophers and scientists haven't yet been able to come to a conclusion about when life begins, which doesn't mean that it is an impossible feat. Choice B is incorrect because it subscribes an overly strong opinion to the author of Passage 1, who actually goes on to say that the state not only has an interest in protecting the pregnant woman, but to a certain extent also has an interest in "protecting the potentiality of human life" (lines 55-56), which suggests that there might be some place for the discussion of when exactly life comes to be. Choice C is incorrect because it extrapolates the discussion and assumes that it has to do with people's rights in general, when the question at hand should remain situated in the very specific context of abortion.

Question 5: B
Choice B is the best answer because the author of Passage 1 believes that the right to abortion is covered under the right to privacy, which, "whether it be founded in the Fourteenth Amendment's concept of personal liberty and restrictions upon state action...or...in the Ninth Amendment's reservation of rights to the people" (lines 9-14), has been supported and enshrined in law since the Constitution was framed. He would, therefore, disapprove of the statement in Passage 2, as it suggests that abortion is not a fundamental right and that the majority sentiment has long been against it. Choice A is incorrect because it refers to the varying theories of life, which are beside

the current point and not discussed by Passage 2. Choice C is incorrect because it suggests that the author of Passage 1 holds the same ideas on states rights as the author of Passage 2 does, when in reality they are on opposing sides of this argument and the author of Passage 1 does not think the states should be able to interpret the Constitution however they would like. Choice D is incorrect because, while the statement might be true, the problem of representation is not discussed in either of the two passages.

Question 6: B
Choice B is the best answer because the answer to the previous question states that the author of Passage 1 believes that the right to abortion is protected under the Consitution and that the states should not able to circumscribe that right. This is supported by lines 9-15, which state that abortion falls under the right to privacy and that the right to privacy is protected by the Constitution in many ways. Choice A is incorrect because it is too limited in that it only discusses one of the ways in which this right is protected and doesn't directly draw the connection between the right being protected and the right to an abortion as lines 9-15 do. Choices C and D are incorrect for similar reasons as they both center on the discussion of when life begins, which is unrelated to the cited lines that the author of Passage 1 is supposed to be responding to; they, additionally, do not state that the right to abortion is protected under the Constitution, or even mention that such a right has been protected in the past.

Question 7: A
Choice A is the best answer because it implies that there is a justifiable reason for a state to involve itself with the problem of abortion, and can be supported by the idea that the state has a "legitimate interest" (line 50) in these cases. Choices B and C are incorrect for similar reasons as they both suggest the potentiality or possibility of something happening, but not the validity of it. Choice D is incorrect because the importance of a matter doesn't necessitate the right of a certain party to involve itself in that matter, and therefore "important" does not encompass the idea that the State has a convincing or compelling right to legislate on abortion.

Question 8: C
Choice C is the best answer because the author of Passage 2 writes that the "decision here to break pregnancy into three distinct terms and to outline the permissible restrictions the State may impose in each one, for example, partakes more of judicial legislation than it does of a determination of the intent of the drafters of the Fourteenth Amendment" (lines 91-96), which suggests that the Supreme Courts expansion of the Constitutional amendments is making the amendments more complicated, rather than just interpreting them to fit the case. Choice A is incorrect because, while the author of Passage 2 might disagree with the conclusion that the Supreme Court reached, he does not go so far as to suggest that the discussion represents the highest abuse of power. Choice B is incorrect because it suggests that the Supreme Court decision is achieving something positive, in the form of a correction, but the author of Passage 2 is presenting the dissenting opinion and thus doesn't agree with their ruling. Choice D is incorrect because, while the author of Passage 2 might not agree with the decision arrived at, he does not suggest that the Supreme Court is getting involved where it shouldn't, as it is directly serving its purpose of determining the final ruling on a case.

Question 9: C

Choice C is the best answer because the author of Passage 1 argues that the "State does have an important and legitimate interest in preserving and protecting the health of the pregnant woman... and that it has still another important and legitimate interest in protecting the potentiality of human life" (lines 50-56), while the author of Passage 2 concurrs, stating that "a majority of the States... have had restrictions on abortions for a least a century" (lines 96-99) and suggesting that such a fact gives a "strong indication" (line 99) that state involvement in abortion rights is legitimate. Choice A is incorrect because the author of Passage 2 argues for Texas to have the continued right to restrict abortion and thus have power over individuals, suggesting that he does not think that states are encroaching on personal liberty. Choice B is incorrect because the issue at hand has to do specifically with pregnant women alone, and therefore does not relate to the rights of other citizens. Choice D is incorrect because, while the life of the pregnant woman is of importance for both authors, they also acknowledge the need to consider the life of the child, which is especially true for the author of Passage 2.

Question 10: A

Choice A is the best answer because the author of Passage 2 states that he agrees "that the 'liberty,' against deprivation of which, without due process, the Fourteenth Amendment protects, embraces more than the rights found in the Bill of Rights. But that liberty is not guaranteed absolutely against deprivation" (lines 74-78), suggesting that due process is necessary if the amendments are going to be used to protect the right to abortion. Further, the author of Passage 1 argues that the Bill of Rights (the first ten amendments) and the Fourteenth Amendment are both "broad enough to encompass a women's decision whether or not to terminate her pregnancy" (lines 14-15). Choice B is incorrect because the author of Passage 2 clearly states that he does not believe "the 'privacy' that the Court finds here [to be] even a distant relative of the freedom from searches and seizures protected by the Fourth Amendment" (lines 63-66); it is also incorrect because it suggests that the two authors are in agreement. Choice C is incorrect because, while the author of Passage 2 does not believe that the Fourth can be called upon here, he does allow for the fact that the Fourteenth can be more encompassing, though it must be contingent upon due process. Choice D is incorrect because the author of Passage 2, as has been shown above, patently does not believe that the Fourth pertains to abortion, and the author of Passage 1 does not believe that the "one theory of life" does either, stating that "we do not agree that, by adopting one theory of life, Texas may override the rights of the pregnant woman that are at stake" (lines 47-49).

Chapter
Eight

Questions 1-10 are based on the following passage.

8.1

This passage is adapted from the First Inaugural Address of President Lincoln, March 4th, 1861.

A disruption of the Federal Union, heretofore only menaced, is now formidably attempted. I hold that in the contemplation of universal law and of the
Line Constitution, the Union of these States is perpetual.
5 Perpetuity is implied, if not expressed, in the fundamental law of all national governments. It is safe to assert that no government proper ever had a provision in its organic law for its own termination. Continue to execute all the express provisions of
10 our national Constitution, and the Union will endure forever, it being impossible to destroy it, except by some action not provided for in the instrument itself.

Again, if the United States be not a government proper, but an association of States in the nature of
15 a contract merely, can it, as a contract, be peaceably unmade by less than all the parties who made it? One party to a contract may violate it, but does it not require all to lawfully rescind it? Descending from these general principles we find the proposition that in
20 legal contemplation the Union is perpetual, confirmed by the history of the Union itself.

It follows from these views that no State, upon its own mere motion, can lawfully get out of the Union; that resolves and ordinances to that effect, are
25 legally void; and that acts of violence within any State or States against the authority of the United States, are insurrectionary or revolutionary, according to circumstances. I therefore consider that, in view of the Constitution and the laws, the Union is unbroken,
30 and, to the extent of my ability, I shall take care, as the Constitution itself expressly enjoins upon me, that the laws of the Union shall be faithfully executed in all the States. Doing this, which I deem to be only a simple duty on my part, I shall perfectly perform it, so far as is
35 practicable, unless my rightful masters, the American people, shall withhold the requisition, or in some authoritative manner direct the contrary.

To those who really love the Union, may I not speak, before entering upon so grave a matter as the
40 destruction of our national fabric, with all its benefits, its memories, and its hopes? Would it not be well to ascertain why we do it? Will you hazard so desperate a step, while any portion of the ills you fly from, have no real existence? Will you, while the certain ills you fly
45 to, are greater than all the real ones you fly from? Will you risk the commission of so fearful a mistake? All

profess to be content in the Union if all constitutional rights can be maintained.

Is it true, then, that any right, plainly written in
50 the Constitution has been denied? I think not. Think, if you can, of a single instance in which a plainly-written provision of the Constitution has ever been denied. If, by the mere force of numbers, a majority should deprive a minority of any clearly-written
55 constitutional right, it might, in a moral point of view, justify revolution; it certainly would, if such right were a vital one. But such is not our case. All the vital rights of minorities and of individuals are so plainly assured to them by affirmations and negations, guaranties and
60 prohibitions in the Constitution, that controversies never arise concerning them. But no organic law can ever be framed with a provision specifically applicable to every question which may occur in practical administration. No foresight can anticipate, nor any
65 document of reasonable length contain, express provisions for all possible questions. Shall fugitives from labor be surrendered by national or by State authorities? The Constitution does not expressly say. Must Congress protect slavery in the Territories? The
70 Constitution does not expressly say. From questions of this class, spring all our constitutional controversies, and we divide upon them into majorities and minorities.

If the minority will not acquiesce, the majority
75 must, or the government must cease. There is no alternative for continuing the government but acquiescence on the one side or the other. If a minority in such a case, will secede rather than acquiesce, they make a precedent which in turn will ruin and divide
80 them, for a minority of their own will secede from them whenever a majority refuses to be controlled by such a minority. For instance, why not any portion of a new confederacy, a year or two hence, arbitrarily secede again, precisely as portions of the present Union
85 now claim to secede from it? All who cherish disunion sentiments are now being educated to the exact temper of doing this. Is there such perfect identity of interests among the States to compose a new Union as to produce harmony only, and prevent renewed
90 secession? Plainly, the central idea of secession is the essence of anarchy. A majority held in restraint by constitutional check and limitation, and always changing easily with deliberate changes of popular opinions and sentiments, is the only true sovereign of
95 a free people. Whoever rejects it, does, of necessity, fly to anarchy or to despotism.

CONTINUE

1

Lincoln's main aim in writing this passage is to

A) argue for the maintenance of the United States as one unified country.

B) persuade the governors of the southern states not to secede.

C) request that the southern states abandon the practice of slavery in order to preserve the nation's integrity.

D) enumerate the benefits and drawbacks of both unification and southern secession.

2

Which choice provides the best evidence that, at the time of Lincoln's first inaugural address, some Union supporters were not confident in the longevity of the Union?

A) Lines 1-4 ("A disruption of...is perpetual.")

B) Lines 22-28 ("It follows...circumstances.")

C) Lines 42-46 ("Will you...a mistake?")

D) Lines 91-96 ("A majority...despotism.")

3

As used in line 14, "association" most nearly means

A) acquaintanceship.

B) connection.

C) coalition.

D) partnership.

4

To what sorts of questions does Lincoln believe the Constitution cannot provide answers?

A) Those pertaining to contracts between two private entities.

B) Those linked to disagreements between two states.

C) Those centered on voting rights for minority populations.

D) Those related to highly specific or unusual situations the Founding Fathers might not have predicted.

5

Which choice provides the best evidence for the answer to the previous question?

A) Lines 13-18 ("Again, if...rescind it?")

B) Lines 28-33 ("I therefore...the States.")

C) Lines 57-61 ("All the vital...them.")

D) Lines 64-70 ("No foresight...expressly say.")

6

As used in line 31, the phrase "enjoins upon" most nearly means

A) allies with.

B) begs for.

C) asks of.

D) forbids.

7

How does Lincoln develop his argument about secession as an "insurrectionary" act over the course of the passage?

A) He claims the act is an immoral one and then stresses the need for an alternative solution.

B) He characterizes the act as localized and then demonstrates its relevance to the nation as a whole.

C) He argues that the act is inconsistent with the precepts of a social contract and that it might entail dire consequences.

D) He describes the act as threatening to the civil rights of all Americans and invites his audience to challenge it.

CONTINUE

8

With which of the following would Lincoln most likely agree?

A) A nation formed by seceding states is destined to fall apart.

B) The majority of a democratic nation must respect the rights of racial minorities.

C) The United States will eventually be destroyed should slavery continue to be practiced anywhere within it.

D) The Constitution must continue to expand in breadth as new political controversies arise.

9

It can be reasonably inferred from the passage that at the time the passage was written

A) the first battles of the American Civil War were already underway.

B) all southern states were politically organized as a confederacy.

C) former slaves were aligned with political minorities.

D) the process of secession had already begun.

10

In this passage, Lincoln's stance is most analogous to that of

A) a schoolteacher explaining classroom rules to his pupils.

B) a United Nations diplomat negotiating a peace settlement.

C) a mayor formally responding to escalating tensions in her city.

D) a political candidate explaining her platform.

CONTINUE

Questions 1-10 are based on the following passage.

8.2

This passage is adapted from "Atlanta Compromise," delivered by Booker T. Washington in 1895.

Mr. President, Gentlemen of the Board of Directors and Citizens:

A ship lost at sea for many days suddenly sighted
Line a friendly vessel. From the mast of the unfortunate
5 vessel was seen the signal: "Water, water, we die of
thirst." The answer from the friendly vessel at once
came back, "Cast down your bucket where you are."
The captain of the distressed vessel, at last heeding the
injunction, cast down his bucket and it came up full of
10 fresh, sparkling water from the mouth of the Amazon
River. To those of my race who depend on bettering
their condition in a foreign land, or who underestimate
the importance of cultivating friendly relations with the
Southern white man who is their next-door neighbor, I
15 would say cast down your bucket where you are; cast
it down in making friends in every manly way of the
people of all races by whom we are surrounded.

Cast it down in agriculture, in mechanics, in
commerce, in domestic service and in the professions.
20 And in this connection, it is well to bear in mind that
whatever other sins the South may be called upon to
bear, that when it comes to business pure and simple,
it is in the South that the Negro is given a man's
chance in the commercial world, and in nothing is this
25 Exposition more eloquent than in emphasizing this
chance.

Our greatest danger is, that in the great leap
from slavery to freedom we may overlook the fact
that the masses of us are to live by the productions
30 of our hands, and fail to keep in mind that we shall
prosper in proportion as we learn to dignify and
glorify common labor and put brains and skill into the
common occupations of life... No race can prosper
till it learns that there is as much dignity in tilling a
35 field as in writing a poem. It is at the bottom of life we
must begin and not the top. Nor should we permit our
grievances to overshadow our opportunities.

To those of the white race who look to the
incoming of those of foreign birth and strange tongue
40 and habits for the prosperity of the South, were I
permitted, I would repeat what I say to my own race.
"Cast down your bucket where you are." Cast it down
among the 8,000,000 Negroes whose habits you know,
whose loyalty and love you have tested in days when
45 to have proved treacherous meant the ruin of your

firesides.

Cast it down among these people who have
without strikes and labor wars tilled your fields,
cleared your forests, built your railroads and cities,
50 and brought forth treasures from the bowels of the
earth and helped make possible this magnificent
representation of the progress of the South. Casting
down your bucket among my people, helping and
encouraging them as you are doing on these grounds,
55 and to the education of head, hand, and heart, you
will find that they will buy your surplus land, make
blossom the waste places in your fields, and run your
factories.

While doing this, you can be sure in the future, as
60 you have been in the past, that you and your families
will be surrounded by the most patient, faithful, law-
abiding and unresentful people that the world has seen.
As we have proven our loyalty to you in the past, in
nursing your children, watching by the sick bed of your
65 mothers and fathers, and often following them with
tear dimmed eyes to their graves, so in the future in
our humble way, we shall stand by you with a devotion
that no foreigner can approach, ready to lay down our
lives, if need be, in defense of yours, interlacing our
70 industrial, commercial, civil and religious life with
yours in a way that shall make the interests of both
races one. In all things that are purely social we can
be as separate as the fingers, yet one as the hand in all
things essential to mutual progress.

75 There is no defense or security for any of us
except in the highest intelligence and development of
all. If anywhere there are efforts tending to curtail the
fullest growth of the Negro, let these efforts be turned
into stimulating, encouraging and making him the
80 most useful and intelligent citizen. Effort or means so
invested will pay a thousand per cent interest. These
efforts will be twice blessed: "Blessing him that gives
and him that takes."

CONTINUE

1

What is a central claim of the passage?

A) Disenfranchised African-Americans will only achieve upward mobility through gaining acceptance from the white community.

B) African-Americans should seek empowerment through economic development rather than through acquisition of rights.

C) Although the present white community bears no blame for the atrocities of slavery, they nevertheless hold a responsibility to empower African-Americans.

D) Slavery has created economic dependence between the White and Black communities, which African-American manual laborers should exploit.

2

Which of the following claims does Washington NOT make in the passage?

A) White southerners should choose to employ former slaves over recent immigrants.

B) African-Americans in the South are not yet ready to receive full political rights.

C) Black and White Americans need to recognize their economic interdependence

D) White Americans should benefit from the relationships they nurtured during slavery.

3

By repeating the phrase "Cast down your bucket where you are" throughout the passage, Washington advises both Black and White Americans to

A) take advantage of opportunities that are readily accessible.

B) seek opportunities for a better life and economic status.

C) take the necessary steps to reconcile their differences.

D) develop skills that can be used in a variety of industries.

4

Which of the following literary devices does Washington utilize in this passage?

A) Rhetorical questions

B) Satire

C) Hyperbole

D) Analogy

5

Which choice provides the best evidence for the answer to the previous question?

A) Lines 3-11 ("A ship…River")

B) Lines 21-26 ("whatever other…chance")

C) Lines 38-41 ("To those…race")

D) Lines 63-72 ("As we…one")

6

As used in line 37, "overshadow" most nearly means

A) hinder.

B) cloud.

C) belittle.

D) darken.

7

What is the main idea of the fourth paragraph (lines 27-37)?

A) Access to prestigious employment comes from education.

B) African-Americans are inherently suited to farming.

C) The path to prosperity rests on pride in one's work.

D) Former slaves must learn to overcome their past.

8

Which choice provides the best evidence for Washington's claim that Black slaves experienced emotional bonds with their masters?

A) Lines 47-50 ("Cast it…treasures")

B) Lines 63-66 ("As we…graves")

C) Lines 67-69 ("we shall…yours")

D) Lines 72-74 ("In all…progress")

CONTINUE

9

As used in line 52, "representation" most nearly means

A) embodiment.
B) depiction.
C) enactment.
D) manifestation.

10

Washington would find which of the following most consistent with "efforts tending to curtail the fullest growth of the Negro" (lines 77-78)?

A) The federal government refusing to grant voting rights to African-Americans.
B) A state passing a law allowing businesses to discriminate against African-Americans.
C) A White factory owner advertising a job opening that excludes African-Americans.
D) A White family systematically refusing to socialize with African-American families.

CONTINUE

Questions 1-10 are based on the following passage.

8.3

On March 12, 1947, President Harry S. Truman devised an economic assistance program, known as the Truman Doctrine, in order to prevent the worldwide spread of communism. Passage 1 is adapted from Truman's address to Congress requesting funds to initiate the program. Passage 2 is adapted from a speech given by Henry A. Wallace in response to the program.

Passage 1

Mr. President, Mr. Speaker, Members of the Congress of the United States:

I am fully aware of the broad implications
Line involved if the United States extends assistance
5 to Greece and Turkey, and I shall discuss these implications with you at this time.

At the present moment in world history nearly every nation must choose between alternative ways of life. The choice is too often not a free one.
10 One way of life is based upon the will of the majority, and is distinguished by free institutions, representative government, free elections, guarantees of individual liberty, freedom of speech and religion, and freedom from political oppression. The second
15 way of life is based upon the will of a minority forcibly imposed upon the majority. It relies upon terror and oppression, a controlled press and radio; fixed elections, and the suppression of personal freedoms.

I believe that it must be the policy of the United
20 States to support free peoples who are resisting attempted subjugation by armed minorities or by outside pressures. I believe that we must assist free peoples to work out their own destinies in their own way. I believe that our help should be primarily
25 through economic and financial aid which is essential to economic stability and orderly political processes.

It is necessary only to glance at a map to realize that the survival and integrity of the Greek nation are of grave importance in a much wider situation.
30 If Greece should fall under the control of an armed minority, the effect upon its neighbor, Turkey, would be immediate and serious. Confusion and disorder might well spread throughout the entire Middle East. Moreover, the disappearance of Greece as an
35 independent state would have a profound effect upon those countries in Europe whose peoples are struggling against great difficulties to maintain their freedoms and their independence while they repair the damages of war.
40 It would be an unspeakable tragedy if these countries, which have struggled so long against overwhelming odds, should lose that victory for which they sacrificed so much. Collapse of free institutions and loss of independence would be disastrous not
45 only for them but for the world. Discouragement and possibly failure would quickly be the lot of neighboring peoples striving to maintain their freedom and independence. The seeds of totalitarian regimes are nurtured by misery and want. They spread and grow in
50 the evil soil of poverty and strife. They reach their full growth when the hope of a people for a better life has died. We must keep that hope alive.

Passage 2

President Truman, in the name of democracy and humanitarianism, proposed a military lend-lease
55 program. He proposed a loan of $400 million to Greece and Turkey as a down payment on an unlimited expenditure aimed at opposing Communist expansion. He proposed, in effect, that America police Russia's every border. There is no regime too reactionary for us,
60 provided it stands in Russia's expansionist path. There is no country too remote to serve as the scene of a contest which may widen until it becomes a world war.

I say that this policy is utterly futile. No people can be bought. America cannot afford to spend billions
65 and billions of dollars for unproductive purposes. The world is hungry and insecure, and the peoples of all lands demand change. President Truman cannot prevent change in the world any more than he can prevent the tide from coming in or the sun from
70 setting. But once America stands for opposition to change, we are lost. America will become the most-hated nation in the world.

Russia may be poor and unprepared for war, but she knows very well how to reply to Truman's
75 declaration of economic and financial pressure. All over the world Russia and her ally, poverty, will increase the pressure against us. Who among us is ready to predict that in this struggle American dollars will outlast the grievances that lead to communism?
80 I certainly don't want to see communism spread. I predict that Truman's policy will spread communism in Europe and Asia. You can't fight something with nothing.

When President Truman proclaims the world-wide
85 conflict between East and West, he is telling the Soviet leaders that we are preparing for eventual war. They will reply by measures to strengthen their position in the event of war. Then the task of keeping the world at peace will pass beyond the power of the common
90 people everywhere who want peace. Certainly, it will not be freedom that will be victorious in this

CONTINUE

struggle. Psychological and spiritual preparation for war will follow financial preparation; civil liberties will be restricted; standards of living will be forced
95 downward; families will be divided against each other; none of the values that we hold worth fighting for will be secure.

1

Which choice best identifies the distinction in how Truman and Wallace characterize the Truman Doctrine?

A) Truman views it as endorsing the Middle East and bolstering the economic power of Greece, while Wallace views it as undermining the spread of peace and directly kindling a subsequent world war.

B) Truman views it as curtailing communist tendencies and promoting freedom and prosperity, while Wallace views it as priming Russia for war and therefore instigating further constraints on civil liberties.

C) Truman views it as the only way to protect the will of the majority and stop the financial oppression of communism, while Wallace views it as protecting the will of the minority and causing opposition to change.

D) Truman views it as preventing widespread tragedy and assisting the development of democracy, while Wallace views it as upending the sovereignty of freedom and the hope for reconciliation in Europe.

2

In Passage 1, Truman suggests that the "profound effect" (line 35) of Greece succumbing to communism is

A) the spread of communism throughout Europe.

B) the destabilization of the world economy.

C) the rise of undesirable social orders.

D) the general demoralization of free societies.

3

Which choice provides the best evidence for the answer to the previous question?

A) Lines 24-26 ("I believe...processes.")

B) Lines 30-32 ("If Greece...serious.")

C) Lines 43-45 ("Collapse of...world.")

D) Lines 45-48 ("Discouragement and...independence.")

4

The figurative language in lines 48-52 ("The seeds... hope alive.") serves mainly to suggest that

A) the rapid spread of totalitarianism is dependent upon the adherence of the United States to the policy that Truman is putting forth.

B) the promotion of hope among nations at risk of communist subversion is the greatest defense against Russian expansion.

C) there are specific circumstances that foster the rise of communism and must be alleviated in order to arrest its further development.

D) there will no longer be the promise of a better future if America continues to allow evil to spread throughout the countries of Europe.

5

As used in line 58, "in effect" most nearly means

A) in theory.

B) in practice.

C) in this case.

D) in essence.

6

Truman and Wallace would most likely agree on which statement about communism?

A) Its expansion is an unfortunate and undesirable result of poverty.

B) Its influence cannot be diminished through American intervention alone.

C) The Truman Doctrine is the only way to mitigate its swift proliferation.

D) The foremost method of prevention is through monetary mediation.

7

In Passage 2, Wallace suggests that the Truman Doctrine

A) ignores the inevitability of change and the strength of the people's desire for it.

B) will drain American funds due to the inexhaustible nature of the proposed aid.

C) supports authoritarian governments under the guise of thwarting Russia.

D) is a declaration of war against the East and will lead to unknowable tragedy.

CONTINUE

8

Which choice provides the best evidence for the answer to the previous question?

A) Lines 55-57 ("He proposed...expansion.")

B) Lines 59-62 ("There is...war.")

C) Lines 67-70 ("President Truman...setting.")

D) Lines 84-86 ("When President...war.")

9

As used in line 89, "pass beyond" most nearly means

A) exceed.

B) overshadow.

C) overwhelm.

D) upstage.

10

How does Wallace think Russia will respond to the Truman Doctrine?

A) By imposing further constraints on the desires and needs of its citizens.

B) By mentally and economically preparing for a perceived threat of war.

C) By lashing out at neighboring countries as a sign of indirect retaliation.

D) By pressuring the United States to repeal its policy by escalating poverty.

CONTINUE

Questions 1-10 are based on the following passage.

8.4

This passage is adapted from President Dwight Eisenhower's Farewell Address delivered on January 20th, 1961.

Throughout America's adventure in free government, our basic purposes have been to keep the peace; to foster progress in human achievement, and to enhance liberty, dignity and integrity among people and among nations. To strive for less would be unworthy of a free and religious people.

Progress toward these noble goals is persistently threatened by the conflict now engulfing the world. It commands our whole attention, absorbs our very beings. We face a hostile ideology-global in scope, atheistic in character, ruthless in purpose, and insidious in method. Unhappily, the danger it poses promises to be of indefinite duration. To meet it successfully, there is called for not so much the emotional and transitory sacrifices of crisis, but rather those which enable us to carry forward steadily, surely, and without complaint the burdens of a prolonged and complex struggle, with liberty at stake.

Crises there will continue to be. In meeting them, whether foreign or domestic, great or small, there is a recurring temptation to feel that some spectacular and costly action could become the miraculous solution to all current difficulties. A huge increase in newer elements of our defense; development of unrealistic programs to cure every ill in agriculture; a dramatic expansion in basic and applied research - these and many other possibilities, each possibly promising in itself, may be suggested as the only way to the road we wish to travel.

But each proposal must be weighed in the light of a broader consideration: the need to maintain balance in and among national programs, balance between the private and the public economy, balance between cost and hoped for advantage, balance between the clearly necessary and the comfortably desirable, balance between our essential requirements as a nation and the duties imposed by the nation upon the individual, balance between action of the moment and the national welfare of the future. Good judgment seeks balance and progress; lack of it eventually finds imbalance and frustration.

A vital element in keeping the peace is our military establishment. Our arms must be mighty, ready for instant action, so that no potential aggressor may be tempted to risk his own destruction. Our military organization today bears little relation to that known by any of my predecessors in peace time, or indeed by the fighting men of World War II or Korea. Until the latest of our world conflicts, the United States had no armaments industry. American makers of plowshares could, with time and as required, make swords as well. But now we can no longer risk emergency improvisation of national defense; we have been compelled to create a permanent armaments industry of vast proportions. Added to this, three and a half million men and women are directly engaged in the defense establishment. We annually spend on military security more than the net income of all United States corporations.

This conjunction of an immense military establishment and a large arms industry is new in the American experience. The total influence - economic, political, even spiritual-is felt in every city, every state house, every office of the Federal government. We recognize the imperative need for this development. Yet we must not fail to comprehend its grave implications. Our toil, resources and livelihood are all involved, so is the very structure of our society.

In the councils of government, we must guard against the acquisition of unwarranted influence, whether sought or unsought, by the military-industrial complex. The potential for the disastrous rise of misplaced power exists and will persist. We must never let the weight of this combination endanger our liberties or democratic processes. We should take nothing for granted; only an alert and knowledgeable citizenry can compel the proper meshing of huge industrial and military machinery of defense with our peaceful methods and goals, so that security and liberty may prosper together.

CONTINUE

1

Which choice best describes the developmental pattern of the passage?

A) A description of the specific threats to American democracy followed by a detailing of potential solutions to those threats.

B) A characterization of America's role in upholding democracy followed by a consideration of the issues and difficulties that accompany such a role.

C) An overview of recent changes to national military policies followed by an analysis of the impact those changes will have on the nation.

D) An discussion of previous administrations' positions on American foreign policy followed by the author's own plans for the future.

2

Which choice provides the best evidence for the author's claim that the protection of both national and personal freedom rests primarily on the actions of ordinary people?

A) Lines 2-6 ("our basic…people")

B) Lines 13-17 ("To meet…struggle")

C) Lines 69-72 ("In the…complex")

D) Lines 76-80 ("only an...together")

3

As used in line 13, "meet" most nearly means

A) defeat.

B) endure.

C) experience.

D) encounter.

4

Throughout the third paragraph (lines 19-29), Eisenhower implies that

A) acts of heroism are rarely required for the protection of worldwide democracy.

B) some individuals are far too rash in seeking instant and radical change.

C) America is currently in imminent danger of invasion by outside forces.

D) miracles are impossible in matters that concern the national interest.

5

As used in line 21, "spectacular" most nearly means

A) impressive.

B) extravagant.

C) ambitious.

D) stunning.

6

Throughout lines 42-68 ("A vital…society"), Eisenhower's primary focus shifts from

A) the advantages of America's currently small-scale industrial system to the risks of increasing its military might.

B) the recent expansion in America's military strength and spending to the potential consequences of such changes.

C) the formerly modest status of America's military in the international scene to its current standing as a superpower.

D) the increased government investment in the military to an explanation of how this will positively impact the economy.

7

Which choice best describes the overall tone of the passage?

A) Concerned

B) Pessimistic

C) Alarmist

D) Indignant

252

CONTINUE

8

In context of the fifth paragraph, lines 50-52 ("American makers...well") primarily serve to

A) warn citizens that large-scale industrialization could lead to the manufacture of weapons by untrained civilians.

B) imply that previous generations' methods of manufacturing weapons were superior to modern solutions.

C) contrast the relatively low stakes of past military conflicts with the urgency of the current threat to America.

D) provide context for the author's argument about the unprecedented nature of the current military climate.

9

Eisenhower warns that the increase in military power could have which unwanted consequence?

A) Power will shift from the citizenry to the military.

B) Americans will become dependent on the military.

C) The military will be in a position to overthrow the government.

D) Americans will develop a penchant for war and conquest.

10

Which choice provides the best support for the answer to the previous question?

A) Lines 52-55 ("But now...proportions")

B) Lines 62-64 ("The total...government")

C) Lines 66-68 ("Yet we...society")

D) Lines 72-75 ("The potential...processes")

CONTINUE

Questions 1-10 are based on the following passage.

8.5

Passage 1 is adapted from a 1964 report by Secretary of Defense Robert McNamara. Passage 2 is adapted from Eugene McCarthy's 1967 campaign speech.

Passage 1

At the Third National Congress of the Communist Party in Hanoi, September 1960, North Vietnam's belligerency was made explicit. Ho Chi Minh stated,
Line "The North is becoming more consolidated into a firm
5 base for the struggle for national reunification," and that the party's new task was "to liberate the South from the atrocious rule of the U.S. imperialists and their henchmen." To the communists, 'liberation' meant sabotage, terror, and assassination: attacks
10 on innocent hamlets and villages and the murder of thousands who had the misfortune to oppose the communist version of 'liberation.' This aggression against South Vietnam was meticulously planned and relentlessly pursued by the government in Hanoi.
15 In 1961 the Republic of (South) Vietnam, unable to contain the menace by itself, appealed to the United States to honor its unilateral declaration of 1954. President Kennedy responded promptly and affirmatively by sending to that country additional
20 American advisers, arms, and aid.

I turn now to a consideration of United States objectives in South Vietnam. They are: first, to answer the call of the South Vietnamese, a member nation of our free-world family, to help them save their country
25 for themselves; second, to help prevent the strategic danger which would exist if communism absorbed Southeast Asia's people and resources; and third, to prove in the Vietnamese test case that the free-world can cope with communist 'wars of liberation.'
30 First, South Vietnam, a member of the free world, is striving to preserve its independence from communist attack. The Vietnamese have asked our help. We have given it. We shall continue to give it. We do so in their interest; and we do so in our
35 own clear self-interest. For basic to the principles of freedom and self-determination which have sustained our country for almost two centuries is the right of peoples everywhere to live and develop in peace. Our own security is strengthened by the determination of
40 others to remain free, and by our commitment to assist them. We will not let this member of our family down, regardless of its distance from our shores.

Second, Southeast Asia has great strategic significance in the forward defense of the United
45 States. Its location across east-west air and sea lanes flanks the Indian subcontinent on one side and Australia, New Zealand, and the Philippines on the other and dominates the gateway between the Pacific and Indian Oceans. In communist hands this area
50 would pose a most serious threat to the security of the United States and to the family of free-world nations to which we belong. To defend Southeast Asia, we must meet the challenge in South Vietnam.

And third, South Vietnam is a test case for the new
55 communist strategy. In January 1961, Soviet Chairman Khrushchev stated: "In modern conditions, the following categories of wars should be distinguished: world wars, local wars, liberation wars and popular uprising." He ruled out what he called 'world wars'
60 and 'local wars' as being too dangerous for profitable indulgence in a world of nuclear weapons. But with regard to what he called 'liberation wars,' he referred specifically to Vietnam. He said, "It is a sacred war. We recognize such wars." Today in Vietnam, we are
65 not dealing with factional disputes or the remnants of a colonial struggle against the French but rather with a major test case of communism's new strategy. That strategy has so far been pursued in Cuba, may be beginning in Africa, and failed in Malaya and
70 the Philippines only because of a long and arduous struggle by the people of these countries with assistance provided by the British and the United States.

Passage 2

Instead of the language of promise and of hope,
75 we have in politics today a new vocabulary in which the critical word is "war": war on poverty, war on ignorance, war on crime, war on pollution. None of these problems can be solved by war. But we do have one war which is properly called a war-- the war in
80 Vietnam, which is central to all of the problems of America.

It is a war of questionable legality and questionable constitutionality. A war which is diplomatically indefensible; the first war in this century
85 in which the United States, which at its founding made an appeal to the decent opinion of mankind in the Declaration of Independence, finds itself without the support of the decent opinion of mankind. What is necessary is a realization that our role is not to police
90 the planet but to use military strength with restraint and within limits, while at the same time we make available to the world the great power of our economy, of our knowledge, and of our good will.

CONTINUE

It is a war which is not defensible even in
95 military terms, which runs contrary to the advice
of our greatest generals. Estimate after estimate as
to the time of success and the military commitment
necessary to success has had to be revised -- always
upward: more troops, more extensive bombing, a
100 widening and intensification of the war. With the
escalation of our military commitment has come a
parallel of overleaping of objectives: from protecting
South Vietnam, to nation building in South Vietnam,
to protecting all of Southeast Asia, and ultimately to
105 suggesting that the safety and security of the United
States itself is at stake.

Finally, it is a war which is morally wrong. The
most recent statement of objectives cannot be accepted
as an honest judgment as to why we are in Vietnam. It
110 has become increasingly difficult to justify the methods
we are using and the instruments of war which we
are using as we have moved from limited targets and
somewhat restricted weapons to greater variety and
more destructive instruments of war, and also have
115 extended the area of operations almost to the heart of
North Vietnam. Even assuming that both objectives
and methods can be defended, the war cannot stand
the test of proportion and of prudent judgment. It is no
longer possible to prove that the good that may come
120 with what is called victory is proportionate to the loss
of life and property and to other disorders that follow
from this war.

1

Throughout Passage 1, McNamara's primary objective is
to

A) outline the goals of the United States' campaign in
South Vietnam.

B) call upon American values to garner support for the
Vietnam War.

C) warn of the impending danger that a communist
Vietnam poses.

D) challenge the notion that the war is without objective or
merit.

2

McNamara primarily characterizes the uprising against
South Vietnam as

A) an effort to curtail imperialism in defense of a
consolidated and free Vietnam.

B) an insurgency marked by indiscriminate violence and
insubordination.

C) an operation precisely strategized and conducted by a
remote authority.

D) an offensive that has been a needless financial burden
on the United States.

3

Which choice provides the best evidence for the answer
to the previous question?

A) Lines 2-5 ("North Vietnam's...reunification")

B) Lines 8-12 ("To the...liberation")

C) Lines 12-14 ("This aggression...Hanoi")

D) Lines 18-20 ("President Kennedy...aid")

4

As used in line 26, "absorbed" most nearly means

A) engrossed.

B) assimilated.

C) monopolized.

D) integrated.

5

As used in line 36, "sustained" most nearly means

A) defended.

B) motivated.

C) preserved.

D) advanced.

CONTINUE

6

Which choice best describes a central difference between how McNamara (Passage 1) and McCarthy (Passage 2) view the founding principles of the United States?

A) McNamara views the propagation of these values as critical to national security, whereas McCarthy argues that these values are being violated through American actions in Vietnam.

B) McNamara cites these values as justification for American intervention in Vietnam, whereas McCarthy states that these values have led to a tyrannical use of force abroad.

C) McNamara calls upon these values to rally the American people in favor of the war, whereas McCarthy sees these values as supporting his isolationist policies toward Vietnam.

D) McNamara describes these values as common to all peace-loving nations, whereas McCarthy believes that these values are actually leading the nation towards war.

7

It can be most reasonably inferred from Passage 2 that McCarthy would criticize the narrative of the United States as the world protector that McNamara puts forth in Passage 1 for being

A) idealistic, since it is based on false assumptions about the need for freedom and civil rights globally.

B) misguided, since global influence is better asserted through economic and intellectual advancement.

C) precarious, since there is little international public support for America's involvement in Vietnam.

D) impractical, since military strength alone is not enough to preserve democracy throughout the world.

8

Which choice from Passage 2 provides the best evidence for the answer to the previous question?

A) Lines 74-78 ("Instead of...war")
B) Lines 82-84 ("It is...indefensible")
C) Lines 88-93 ("What is...will")
D) Lines 94-96 ("It is...generals")

9

In context of Passage 2 as a whole, lines 100-106 ("With the...stake") primarily serve to

A) characterize the United States' defense of its participation in Vietnam as empty rhetoric.

B) repudiate the narrative of American participation in Vietnam for its inconsistency.

C) depict American intervention in Vietnam as potentially enabling an authoritarian agenda.

D) highlight the absurdity of invoking the national defense as a justification for war.

10

The fourth paragraph (lines 107-122) indicates which potential consequence of America's continued participation in Vietnam?

A) An erosion of public support, given the United States' inability to justify a war that is immoral at its core.

B) An unending war, given the ability of North Vietnam to endure continued American attacks on its territory.

C) A certain defeat of the American forces, given the flawed judgement of their military planners.

D) A questionable victory, given the expanding scope and increasing destructiveness of the war.

STOP

Please turn to next page for answer keys and explanations.

Answer Key: CHAPTER EIGHT

8.1 | Lincoln	8.2 | B.T. Washington	8.3 | Truman Doctrine	8.4 | Eisenhower	8.5 | Vietnam War
1: A	1: B	1: B	1: B	1: A
2: C	2: B	2: D	2: D	2: B
3: C	3: A	3: D	3: A	3: B
4: D	4: D	4: C	4: B	4: D
5: D	5: A	5: D	5: B	5: B
6: C	6: C	6: A	6: C	6: A
7: C	7: C	7: A	7: A	7: B
8: A	8: B	8: C	8: D	8: C
9: D	9: D	9: A	9: A	9: B
10: C	10: C	10: B	10: D	10: D

Answer Explanations

Chapter Eight

Chapter 8.1 | Lincoln

Question 1: A
Choice A is the best answer because Lincoln primarily seeks to convince his audience that according to the "contemplation of universal law and of the Constitution, the Union of these States is perpetual" (lines 3-4), indicating that the Union should remain undivided. Choice B is incorrect; while Lincoln is urging the states to not secede, this plea is not specifically directed to the "governors" of the states, but towards the country as a whole during his inauguration. Choice C is incorrect because Lincoln never explicitly mentions "slavery" as the reason behind the nation's divide. Assuming that slavery is the main point of the passage would be using outside knowledge; on the SAT, all the information needed to answer the questions is in the passage. Choice D is incorrect; while Lincoln describes the drawbacks of secession at length, as well as the benefits of unification, he does not discuss the drawbacks of unification and the benefits of secession. His viewpoint is decidedly pro-unification, and there is no enumeration of the counterargument to his stance.

Question 2: C
Choice C is the best answer because lines 42-46 indicate that some who "really love the Union" (line 38) have been contemplating "so desperate a step, while any portion of the ills [they] fly from have no real existence", implying that some supporters of the Union have felt the necessity to avoid an imaginary "ill" and highlighting a lack of confidence in the Union. Choice A is incorrect because lines 1-4 stress that the Union will be "perpetual", or longstanding, but does not indicate that Lincoln is responding to the potential counterargument that the Union would not be so. Choice B is incorrect because while lines 22-28 indicate that the longevity of the Union is in danger by Southern states' insurrection, Lincoln never indicates that these views have been declared by those who support the Union. Choice D is incorrect because lines 91-96 describe a hypothetical conditional statement: those who reject a restrained but empowered majority "fly to anarchy". However, Lincoln never actually states that the Union is currently heading down that path; furthermore, lines 91-96 describe the views of Lincoln, not of other Union supporters.

Question 3: C
Choice C is the best answer; the word "association" refers to a "coalition" of states, which is indicated by the word "parties" (line 16) in the same question that contains "association". Choices A, B and D are incorrect because "acquaintanceship", "connection", and "partnership" would imply

a personal relationship on some level among the states, which Lincoln does not indicate. Lincoln's point about contracts places a greater emphasis on the states as entities in and of themselves, and he does not focus on them having ties with one another at this point in the passage.

Question 4: D
Choice D is the best answer because lines 64-70 indicate that "the Constitution does not say" anything about issues such as "fugitives from labor" or "slavery in the Territories", which Lincoln lists as examples of problems that "no foresight [could] anticipate"; therefore, he claims that the Constitution is unable to provide answers for unusual situations which would not have been predicted, or "anticipated", by its authors, or the Founding Fathers. Choice A is incorrect because the "contracts" mentioned are among states, not businesses or "private entities". Choice B is incorrect because Lincoln is primarily concerned with the relationships of states to the Union as a whole, not those of states with other states. Choice C is incorrect; although the Constitution did not include voting rights for minority populations at that point in time, selecting Choice C for that reason would be mistakenly using outside knowledge. The "minority" that Lincoln refers to in the passage is solely based on sheer numbers, whereas Lincoln does not focus on "minority populations", or marginalized demographics.

Question 5: D
Choice D is the best answer because lines 64-70 address questions for which "no foresight can anticipate, nor any document of reasonable length contain, express provisions". Lincoln then specifies the Constitution as one of those documents, indicating that there are certain questions which it cannot answer. Choice A is incorrect because lines 13-18 are off-topic; they do not refer to the Constitution at all. Choice B is incorrect; although Lincoln refers to the Constitution, he states that it "expressly enjoins upon [him]" the right to see that "the laws of the Union" are "executed". Thus, there is no mention of what the Constitution does not address or "provide answers" to. Choice C is incorrect because lines 57-61 actually indicate which matters are squarely covered by the Constitution, to the point where there is no controversy or lack of clarity whatsoever regarding them. This sentiment is the opposite of one that expresses matters for which the Constitution cannot provide, thereby making it false.

Question 6: C
Choice C is the best answer because Lincoln describes himself as performing a "simple duty" and following the Constitution, therefore doing what is "[asked] of" him by the document. Choices A and B are incorrect because "[allying] with" and "[begging]" can only be done by people, not an inanimate object like the Constitution. Choice D is incorrect because "forbids" would imply that Lincoln feels compelled to not "faithfully [execute]" the laws of the Union in all the states, which is contradictory to his intentions throughout the passage.

Question 7: C
Choice C is the best answer because Lincoln characterizes the association of the different states as a "contract" that cannot be "peaceably unmade by less than all the parties who made it"; one or more parties seceding from the Union would thus be "[violating]" that contract (lines 13-18). Furthermore, Lincoln emphasizes that any violation of such a social contract would be considered "insurrectionary or revolutionary" (line 27) and would, if left unfettered, lead to the "destruction of our national fabric" (line 40). Choice A is incorrect because Lincoln calls secession unconstitutional and unwise,

but never criticizes it from a "moral" standpoint. Choice B is incorrect because Lincoln calls the movement of secession "a minority" (line 77), but never specifies that it is "localized". Choice D is incorrect because Lincoln's grievances with Southern secession are primarily based upon its violation of the social contract set out in the Constitution, and not upon its disruption of Americans' "civil rights"; assuming that Lincoln was concerned with the rights and treatment of slaves would be using outside information.

Question 8: A
Choice A is the best answer because Lincoln imagines that a nation formed by seceding states would "make a precedent which in turn will ruin and divide them" (lines 79-80), since a minority population which refused to be controlled by the majority would feel motivated to "arbitrarily secede again" (lines 83-84), furthering a vicious cycle. Choice B is incorrect because Lincoln indicates that a violation of the rights of minorities would justify revolution, but never specifically points out the need for the protection of racial minorities. Choice C is incorrect because Lincoln identifies secession as the destructive force within the United States, not slavery. Choice D is incorrect because Lincoln indicates that the Constitution is unable to respond to such an unprecedented situation, but never offers any solutions (such as "[continuing] to expand its breadth") for remedying this problem.

Question 9: D
Choice D is the best answer because Lincoln states in lines 1-2 that "a disruption of the Federal Union...is now formidably attempted", which indicates that the South has already attempted to secede, hence the need for Lincoln's response. Choice A is incorrect because Lincoln does not mention the Civil War at all; thus, there is no chronological context to determine whether or not a battle has taken place. Choice B is incorrect because we cannot ascertain that all of the southern states had formed a confederacy at this point in time; at best, we can only conclude that some states have begun the process of doing so. Furthermore, Lincoln does not refer to any state or states in particular. His lack of specificity is another reason why it is impossible to conclude that all the states have organized as a confederacy. Choice C is incorrect; the only context in which "majority" and "minority" are referred to is that of Constitutional controversy. There is no reference to "political minorities", which are implied to be people, and whether or not "former slaves" are members of this demographic. Furthermore, the phrase "former slave" is not mentioned in the passage, thereby making this answer choice off-topic.

Question 10: C
Choice C is the best answer. Lincoln, the president, is attempting to resolve the problems that the secession movement has brought upon the country. A mayor responding to rising tensions is analogous to Lincoln's stance, as the president is a member of the executive branch of the federal government, while the mayor is a member of the executive branch of a city; in addition, both are attempting to resolve a situation that has escalated. Choice A is incorrect because Lincoln indicates that the secession crisis is an unprecedented situation (for which the Constitution cannot adequately provide a solution). Thus, "rules" cannot apply in these circumstances. Choice B is incorrect; while it is true that Lincoln wants reunification because he believes it will bring about peace, he is not attempting to compromise with the South and therefore is being inherently undiplomatic. Choice D is incorrect because Lincoln is not running for office and therefore cannot be promoting his own policies like a "candidate" would.

Chapter 8.2 | B.T. Washington

Question 1: B

Choice B is the best answer because Washington emphasizes that regardless of the social relationship between whites and blacks in the South, "when it comes to business pure and simple, it is in the South that the Negro is given a man's chance in the commercial world" (lines 22-24); throughout the passage, Washington stresses that the metaphorical bucket should be cast down in "agriculture, in mechanics, in commerce, in domestic service, and in the professions" (lines 18-19), an indication that the way to quench their thirst referenced in paragraph one is through economical means. Choice A is incorrect because the word "only" makes the answer too narrow. Washington's main advice to African-Americans is to focus on making the most of their employment opportunities, but he also advocates "cultivating friendly relations" (line 13) and "the highest intelligence and development of all" (lines 76-77). Choice C is incorrect because Washington implies that white Americans in the South do possess some "sins" from the past that they "may be called upon to bear" (lines 21-22) and therefore are not completely free from blame for slavery; moreover, he encourages whites to empower African Americans out of practicality, not out of responsibility or guilt. Choice D is incorrect because Washington only implies that the relationship he recommends is not codependent, but mutually beneficial.

Question 2: B

Choice B is the best answer because Washington prioritizes economic growth over the acquisition of political rights but does not question the intellectual or moral ability of African Americans: in fact, he believes that blacks would be fully capable of effectively exercising their political rights, if given the opportunity. Choice A is incorrect because Washington advises white southerners who "look to the incoming of those of foreign birth and strange tongue and habits for the prosperity of the South" to instead "cast [down their bucket] among the 8,000,000 Negros whose habits [they] know" (lines 38-43) and employ former slaves over immigrants. Choice C is incorrect because Washington indicates that "in all things that are purely social" white and black Americans can "be as separate as the fingers", but must be "one as the hand in all things essential to mutual progress" (lines 72-74), implying that such progress entails economic development. Choice D is incorrect because one of the main advantages to employing African Americans cited by Washington is the longstanding relationship that was created during slavery: "as we have proven our loyalty to you in the past...we shall stand by you with a devotion that no foreigner can approach" (lines 59-68). '

Question 3: A

Choice A is the best answer because Washington repeats the phrase "cast down your bucket" when encouraging black Americans to cultivate friendly relations with their white neighbors (lines 12-17) and to seek employment from white employers (lines 18-26); in addition, he uses the phrase while urging white Americans to hire former slaves instead of foreigners (lines 38-46). In each case, Washington highlights the proximity of each opportunity for economic advancement and thus advises both white and black Americans to "take advantage" of circumstances that are "readily accessible". Choices B and D are incorrect because "seeking opportunities for a better life and economic status" and "developing skills that can be used in a variety of industries" are pieces of advice that Washington only gives to black Americans and therefore cannot also be directed towards whites. Choice C is incorrect because "reconciling differences" would entail members of both races apologizing for any harbored animosity, while the advice that Washington offers is more practical than emotional.

Question 4: D
Choice D is the best answer because Washington uses the image of a boat lost at sea to represent the African American population, and the act of casting down a bucket for it to rise with "fresh, sparkling water from the mouth of the Amazon River" (lines 10-11) to represent the potential reaping of wealth that would follow from establishing business relationships with white Americans. Choice A is incorrect because Washington does not ask any questions to his audience throughout the passage, let alone any rhetorical ones. Choice B is incorrect because satire is primarily intended to criticize, while Washington aims to promote and encourage his audience. Choice C is incorrect because the facts that Washington uses to support his point have not been grossly exaggerated or

Question 5: A
Choice A is the best answer because lines 3-11 present an indirect representation of Washington's argument through the extended description of a boat at sea, and therefore match the topic of "a literary device used by Washington" in the previous question. Choices B, C, and D are incorrect because lines 21-26, lines 38-41, and lines 63-72 all contain direct statements, claims, or suggestions by Washington and as such are not considered examples of literary devices or figurative language.

Question 6: C
Choice C is the best answer because Washington suggests that former slaves must not let their "opportunities" (line 37) be diminished by or "overlook[ed]" (line 28) due to a preoccupation with other problems; "belittle" therefore matches as it suggests that one thing is taking precedence over or is minimizing another. Choice A is incorrect because "hinder" implies that opportunities are being impeded or obstructed by "grievances" (line 37), while Washington just suggests that they are being upstaged. Choices B and D are incorrect for similar reasons, as "cloud" and "darken" both imply that the opportunities have become confusing or negative.

Question 7: C
Choice C is best because Washington introduces the paragraph by noting the danger of "[overlooking] the fact that the masses of us are to live by the productions of our hands" (lines 28-30), emphasizing his concern regarding African-Americans overlooking their ability to "dignify and glorify common labor" (lines 21-32), thus having pride in their work. Choice A is incorrect because he makes no claim about education, only about production and prosperity. Choice B is incorrect because although Washington does reference "tilling a field" (lines 34-35), he does not mention that this skill is inborn in anyone, just that "the masses of us are to live by the productions of our hands" (lines 29-30). Choice D is incorrect because Washington advises his audience that

Question 8: B
Choice B is the best answer because Washington states several examples of the bond formed between African-Americans and white southerners with the examples of "nursing your children, watching by the sick bed of your mothers and fathers, and often following them with tear dimmed eyes to their graves" (lines 64-66). Choice A is incorrect because in lines 47-50 Washington is recalling his advice to white southerners to "cast down [their] bucket" (line 42), but not stating that this has already happened. Choice C is incorrect because in lines 67-69 Washington is making a prediction of what will happen "in the future" (line 66), not something that has been experienced yet. Choice D is incorrect because in lines 72-74, Washington claims that the two races are "as separate as the fingers" (line 73), not bonded together as indicated in the question.

Question 9: D

Choice D is the best answer because Washington describes the progress which blacks "[made] possible" through their tilling of fields, clearing of forests, building of railroads, etc. (lines 47-51); "manifestation" therefore matches something that is done or created. Choice A is incorrect because "embodiment" would imply that what Washington describes is an example of the South's progress, not progress itself. Choices B and C are incorrect for similar reasons: "depiction" and "enactment" both suggest that blacks have portrayed or imitated Southern progress, as one would depict or enact a character in a play, but does not actually suggest that they created the progress themselves.

Question 10: C

Choice C is the best answer because Washington believes it is through acquiring jobs and valuing manual labor that former slaves will better their lot, as "the masses of us are to live by the productions of our hands" (lines 29-20). It is due to this belief that he calls for the "white race" (line 38) to "Cast down your bucket where you are" (line 42) and hire former slaves rather than turn to those of "foreign birth" (line 39). Choices A and B are incorrect for similar reasons, as they both refer to the government and imply that legislature is necessary to the advancement of former slaves, while Washington's primary concern in the passage is work. D is incorrect because it suggests that social integration is important to bettering conditions, while again, Washington's ultimate concern is the opportunity to get a job and work for a living.

Chapter 8.3 | Truman Doctrine

Question 1: B

Choice B is the best answer because Truman outright declares his interest in supporting "free peoples who are resisting attempted subjugation by armed minorities" (lines 20-21) and this is best achieved through financial aid to ensure "economic stability and orderly political processes" (line 26). In contrast, Wallace claims that Russia "will replay by measures to strengthen their position in the event of war" (lines 86-87) and that "civil liberties will be restricted" (lines 93-94). Choice A is incorrect because the written intent of the doctrine to financially bolster Greek and Turkey is not denied by Wallace, and therefore cannot be considered a distinction in how the two authors characterize the program. Choice C is incorrect because Wallace asserts that the doctrine defines America as a nation that "stands for opposition to change", not that it will cause this opposition. Choice D is incorrect because Wallace never mentions any risk to reconciling European nations.

Question 2: D

Choice D is the best answer because lines 45-48 describe how the fall of one country to communism will discourage the efforts of the surrounding nations to "maintain their freedom and independence". Choice A is incorrect because while Truman highlights the susceptibility of nations recovering from the recent war to totalitarianism, he does not at any point suggest that the rest of Europe is at equal risk. Choice B is incorrect because Truman does not focus on the global economy at any point in the passage. The few mentions of economic stability are tied to the greater concept of political democracy. Choice C is incorrect because the "undesirable social orders" that Truman seeks to curtail already exist within Europe; Greece being overtaken by a Communist government would increase the rate of expansion, not cause it.

Question 3: D
Choice D is the best answer because only lines 45-48 directly refer to the negative effect on the morale of unstable and recovering countries seeking to maintain democratic governance. Choice A is incorrect because lines 24-26 discuss Truman's belief that the United States can best provide aid to struggling free societies financially. Choice B is incorrect because lines 30-32 only address the impact of Greece's collapse on its immediate neighbor, Turkey. Choice C is incorrect because while lines 43-45 do suggest negative consequences arising from the situation addressed in the previous question, it does not describe a specific effect.

Question 4: C
Choice C is the best answer because the illustration of totalitarianism as a plant that requires certain conditions to thrive, such as the "evil soil of poverty and strife", suggests that should these conditions be eliminated through financial aid, its growth can be halted. Choice A is incorrect because the policy that Truman is proposing seeks to prevent the growth of communism, not encourage it. Choice B is incorrect because while the loss of hope is mentioned as a factor in the flourishing of totalitarianism, the emphasis of the language here also states the contribution of poverty and conflict. Hope is incidental to these concerns. Choice D is incorrect because the imagery here specifically describes the phenomenon of Communism, not a vague and ill-defined evil.

Question 5: D
Choice D is the best answer because in line 58, Wallace is claiming this is the perceived intent of the doctrine, when considering its most fundamental aspects. Choice A is incorrect because "in theory" suggests that what he is describing is what the doctrine is intended to achieve. Choice B is incorrect because the Truman Doctrine has yet to be enacted. Choice C is incorrect because Wallace is not referring to a particular application of the doctrine, but rather his impression of the bill as a whole.

Question 6: A
Choice A is the best answer because Truman's claim that the "seeds of totalitarian regimes…spread and grow in the evil soil of poverty" (lines 48-50) is in accord with Wallace's belief in lines 76-79 that poverty is the grievance that encourages the spread of communism throughout Europe and Asia. Choices B, C, and D are incorrect because Wallace repeatedly asserts that American interventionism, particularly in the form of economic stimulus, will fail due to the inability of money alone to either change the ideology of entire peoples or outpace the spread of a deep-rooted and difficult to reverse societal flaw such as poverty. This in direct contrast to Truman's implementation of his doctrine to financially support nations he deems susceptible to totalitarianism.

Question 7: A
Choice A is the best answer because lines 67-70 describe how Wallace believes that President Truman seeks to block change itself with this doctrine, and that he "cannot prevent change in the world", comparing it to halting the movement of the tides and the sun, a clearly impossible action. Choice B is incorrect because while Wallace does mention that America cannot afford to spend billions of dollars for a fruitless endeavor, at no point is it stated the proposed aid is limitless. Choice C is incorrect because Wallace claims that the doctrine will enable any regimes, no matter how violent, in the interest of halting Soviet expansion, not that Russia will be used as a cover for supporting these authoritarian governments. Choice D is incorrect because Wallace very clearly defines what he believes are the consequences of agitating Russia, namely the deterioration of the current state of freedoms for its people; "unknowable tragedy" is an inaccurate description.

Question 8: C
Choice C is the best answer because lines 67-70 clearly state the futility of trying to act as a barrier against global change, which best supports "inevitability of change". Choice A is incorrect because lines 55-57 are simply a description of the literal contents of the doctrine. Choice B is incorrect because lines 59-62 are framed as unintentional but inevitable consequences of the Truman Doctrine, not as desired goals. Choice D is incorrect because lines 84-86 describe what Wallace believes the Russian response to the doctrine will be, not an actual stated goal of the program itself.

Question 9: A
Choice A is the best answer because Wallace claims that Russia preparing for war will make maintaining peace an issue too difficult to be achieved by the "power" of the people, supporting "exceed". Choice B and Choice D are incorrect because to "overshadow" is to appear much more prominent or important than something, while "upstage" is draw attention away from someone towards oneself, both of which are irrelevant to a discussion of ability. Choice C is incorrect because "overwhelm" implies that the task itself will somehow defeat the people of the world rather than no longer be within their control.

Question 10: B
Choice B is best because Wallace asserts that Truman's policy effectively declares that the United States is "preparing for eventual war" (line 86) and that Russia will respond in like, as "[p]sychological and spiritual preparation for war will follow financial preparation" (lines 92-93). Choice A is incorrect because while Wallace does describe the restriction of civil liberties as one of Russia's responses to the Truman Doctrine, this is only part of the preparation, which is more completely defined in choice B. Choices C and D are incorrect because Wallace makes no mention of either of these reactions; the neighboring countries are discussed only tangentially when he describes how the Truman Doctrine aims to prop up regimes to block Communist expansion, and for the latter, Wallace claims that poverty itself will pressure the United States by acting as an ideological tool in spreading Communism.

Chapter 8.4 | Eisenhower

Question 1: B
Choice B is the best answer because Eisenhower indicates that America's "basic purposes have been to keep the peace, to foster progress in human achievement, and to enhance liberty, dignity and integrity among people and among nations" (lines 2-5), thus establishing the United States' position as the safeguard of freedom. Eisenhower then describes the "crises" that the United States currently faces and will face in the future (line 19), as well as "the potential for the disastrous rise of misplaced power" that accompanies American remedies to such crises. Choice A is incorrect because there is only one threat to American democracy: the hostile ideology" (line 10). As such, Eisenhower cannot be describing all of the specific "threats" that endanger the United States. In addition, the threat is not specified; it is described as "global in scope, atheistic in character, ruthless in purpose, and insidious in method" (lines 10-12), but Eisenhower never names the threat for what it is: communism. Choice C is incorrect because Eisenhower's description of the recent changes to national military policies are only first mentioned in line 46, and therefore cannot encompass the developmental pattern of the passage as a whole. Choice D is incorrect because Eisenhower never specifies previous administrations' foreign policies, nor states that the growth of the military-industrial complex is part of his own administration's foreign policy.

Question 2: D

Choice D is the best answer because lines 76-80 are the only line references that allude to "an alert and knowledgeable citizenry", thus indicating that ordinary people are instrumental to the prosperity of "security and liberty". Choices A, B, and C are incorrect because lines 2-6, lines 13-17, and lines 69-72 refer to ways of progressing democracy or addressing the danger of the "hostile ideology" (line 10) that are generalized: the words "we" and "our" are used, but Eisenhower does not suggest that only non-governmental figures—i.e. ordinary citizens—are the only group indicated through those pronouns.

Question 3: A

Choice A is the best answer because in lines 7-13, Eisenhower states that "progress...is persistently threatened by...conflict...we face a hostile ideology...the danger it poses promises to be of indefinite duration". He promotes eliminating this danger through "sacrifices of crisis" (line 16) and indicates that "liberty [is] at stake" (line 18). Because Eisenhower uses the ideal of "liberty" to rouse Americans to action, he wants them to fight or "defeat" the conflict. Choice B is incorrect because Eisenhower is not suggesting that Americans passively wait for the danger to end, which is what "endure" implies; rather, he urges them to make these sacrifices in the name of liberty. Choice C is incorrect because Eisenhower does not want Americans to "experience" danger; he views it as incompatible with American citizens and wants them to live in a world without it. Choice D is incorrect because Eisenhower states that the conflict "commands our whole attention" (line 9) and "absorbs our very beings" (lines 9-10). As such, "encounter" would be incorrect, because to encounter something means to meet it for the first time, and Americans have already been exposed to the threat.

Question 4: B

Choice B is the best answer because Eisenhower describes people's tendency to "feel that some spectacular and costly action could become the miraculous solution to all current difficulties" (lines 21-23). These individuals seek out instant change, as Eisenhower indicates that "miraculous [solutions]" are proposed for "current difficulties". These proposed changes are also radical, as Eisenhower describes them "a huge increase" (line 23) and "a dramatic expansion" (lines 25-26). Choice A is incorrect because "heroism" implies that there is some degree of bravery and honor, which are positive characteristics; however, Eisenhower has an unfavorable perspective toward advocates for radical change. Choice C is incorrect because the third paragraph discusses a tendency for people to expect miracles when approaching crises; it is critiquing a potential route of solvency for the danger, but does not discuss a danger in and of itself. Also, there is no mention of the danger being a physical invasion in the paragraph, let alone in the passage; Eisenhower explicitly states that the danger is an ideological one. Choice D is incorrect because Eisenhower never states that "miracles are impossible"; he only criticizes the fact that people have a predisposition to seek them out as solutions in all circumstances.

Question 5: B

Choice B is the best answer because Eisenhower primarily takes issue with the unnecessary cost of the proposed solutions; this is evident in the modifier "costly" when describing the solutions that he describes as unnecessary. Choices A, C, and D are incorrect because Eisenhower does not take fault with solutions being "impressive", "ambitious", or "stunning", which are all positive modifiers which indicate a desire to solve the crises at hand. These qualities are all independently acceptable; Eisenhower only disapproves of them when they are paired with unnecessary spending.

Question 6: C

Choice C is the best answer because Eisenhower describes the state of the previous American military establishment in lines 49-52: "until the latest of our world conflicts, the United States had no armaments industry. American makers of plowshares could, with time and as required, make swords as well". Eisenhower then outlines the current state of the military-industrial complex, stating that "this conjunction of an immense military establishment and a large arms industry is new" (lines 60-61). The United States military's superpower status is evident in Eisenhower calling it "a permanent armaments industry of vast proportions" (lines 54-55). Choice A is incorrect; although Eisenhower expresses his concerns with increased military influence, America does not currently have a "small-scale industrial system", but rather one of "vast proportions" (line 55). Choice B is incorrect; while Eisenhower does indicate an increase in American military strength and spending, he does not discuss the potential consequences in lines 42-68. Within these lines, he only discusses the current consequences of the military-industrial complex: "the total influence-economic, political, even spiritual-is felt in every city, every state house, every office of the Federal government" (lines 62-64). It is only in the last paragraph where Eisenhower discusses the potential consequences, but that paragraph is not included in the lines indicated by the question. Choice D is incorrect; although Eisenhower mentioned that increased investment in the military has an economic influence across the nation, he does not elaborate on this economic influence, nor does he state that said influence will be positive. So, there is no "explanation of how [this investment] will positively impact the economy".

Question 7: A

Choice A is the best answer because Eisenhower identifies a "hostile ideology" (line 10) that threatens the United States' progress towards a free government, before explaining how American people can "meet [the conflict] successfully" (line 13) and indicating that such developments also have "grave implications" (lines 66-67) and that "liberty [is] at stake" (line 18). Because Eisenhower is appropriately worried about the threat at hand and approaches the problem seriously, he can be described as "concerned". Choice B is incorrect because Eisenhower believes that freedom and democracy can still be preserved; while this goal is being "threatened", the threat can also be "[met] successfully", and Eisenhower advocates for different channels through which this can be done. Choice C is incorrect because "alarmist" suggests that the threat Eisenhower identifies is not significant or valid; however, Eisenhower seems appropriately worried about the danger that seems to be "now engulfing the world" (line 8). Choice D is incorrect because "indignant" implies anger at an unjust situation, while Eisenhower is not so much concerned about morality as he is about the practical safety of American citizens.

Question 8: D

Choice D is the best answer because Eisenhower reveals that the United States' "military organization today bears little relation to that known by any of my predecessors in peace time, or indeed by the fighting men of World War II or Korea" (lines 45-48), before indicating that before this conflict, "the United States had no armaments industry" (lines 49-50). Eisenhower's reference to a makers of plowshares making their own swords thus provides an example of how the armaments industry has changed drastically over the past few years, and provides support for his claim that "this conjunction of an immense military establishment and a large arms industry is new in the American experience" (lines 60-62). Choice A is incorrect because the "manufacture of weapons by untrained civilians" was a mark of the old approach to armament, as "American makers of plowshares", or farmers, would make their own swords; Eisenhower thus cannot "warn" against something that already happened. Choice B is incorrect because Eisenhower suggests that previous generations' methods of manufacturing weapons were actually inferior to that of today: he describes the manufacture of arms in the past as "emergency improvisation" and indicates that industrialization has made armaments more "mighty [and] ready for instant action" (lines 43-44). Choice C is incorrect because Eisenhower does not suggest that the current conflict is more or less concerning than past military struggles like the Civil War, World War II, and the Revolutionary War; what he contrasts is not the level of danger involved in each conflict but the level of economic investment the United States has devoted to its military establishment.

Question 9: A
Choice A is the best answer. Since Choice D in Question 10 is the only line reference that addresses an unwanted consequence of the military-industrial complex, the answer to Question 9 must match that line reference. Choice A is the only answer choice that addresses the power shift addressed in lines 72-75; Eisenhower clearly indicates in the topic sentence of the paragraph that he is discussing the military-industrial complex gaining unnecessary power when he addresses that power shift. Choices B, C, and D are incorrect because they do not match the only viable line reference in Question 10. Choice B is also incorrect because Eisenhower advises against dependence on the military but does not actually believe that this is a likely possibility. Choice C is also incorrect because Eisenhower never specifies that the military will overthrow the current government; he merely states that democratic values could be endangered, but it would be incorrect to equate endangering these values with the eradication of the entire democratic government. Choice D is also incorrect because Eisenhower does not address how the military-industrial complex will change the character of the citizenry; he only states that they may experience a decrease in power, which would unfavorably hinder their ability to hold the complex accountable.

Question 10: D
Choice D is the best answer because Eisenhower highlights a potential shift in power toward the military and the threat that it may pose to American democratic values in lines 72-75: "the potential for the disastrous rise of misplaced power exists...we must never let [the military-industrial complex] endanger our liberties or democratic processes". Choices A, B, and C are incorrect because they do not describe an unwanted consequence for the increase in military power. Eisenhower describes the reason for creating the military-industrial complex in lines 52-55, but does not address any consequences of the complex's creation. Eisenhower describes a consequence of the military-industrial complex in lines 62-64, but does not indicate that the consequence is unwanted. Additionally, the question asks us to consider which unwanted consequence could arise, which implies that only a potential consequence could be the answer; on the other hand, lines 62-64 describe a consequence that has already happened. In lines 66-68, Eisenhower warns the people that they must consider the consequences of the military-industrial complex, but does not indicate what these consequences are nor if they're unwarranted.

Chapter 8.5 | Vietnam War

Question 1: A
Choice A is the best answer because after providing background of the current situation in Vietnam (paragraph 1), McNamara goes on to list and elaborate on three "objectives in South Vietnam" (line 22) in the remainder of the passage. Choice B is incorrect because while McNamara does all upon American values when he references liberation and America's free-world family, he does not intend to garner support, as America is already in the war and it's unclear whether he's addressing Americans or only the government. Choice C is incorrect because McNamara does reference the "danger which would exist if communism absorbed Southeast Asia's people and resources" (lines 25-26), that's only one of three objectives he lists in that paragraph and elaborates on throughout the passage. Choice D is incorrect because in order to challenge a notion, it would have to be stated or clearly implied in the passage, but McNamara makes no reference to people who believe the war is without objective.

Question 2: B
Choice B is the best answer because McNamara characterizes the war as rife with "sabotage, terror, and assasination: attacks on innocent hamlets...and the murder of thousands" (lines 9-11). Choice A is incorrect because while McNamara does indicate that the uprising of the Communist Party in Vietnam aims to "liberate the South from the atrocious rule of the U.S. imperialists and their henchmen", he does so in lines 6-8, which are not an option to use as evidence in question three. Choice C is incorrect because the uprising is not by a remote authority, it's by North Vietnam. Choice D is incorrect because McNamara does not mention finances in any of the reference lines in question three.

Question 3: B
Choice B is the best answer because the answer to the previous question suggests that McNamara views the Communist attack on South Vietnam as filled with violence and misconduct, which is supported by lines 8-12. Choice A is incorrect because, while it acknowledges the impending "struggle for national unification" (line 5), it fails to demonstrate how that struggle is viewed by McNamara. Choice C is incorrect because the fact that the aggression was "meticulously planned and relentlessly pursued" (lines 13-14) doesn't suggest that it was necessarily violent or achieved through insubordination. Choice D is incorrect because it only discusses America's actions and not those of South Vietnam or McNamara's perspective on them.

Question 4: D
Choice D is the best answer because it refers to the action of "Southeast Asia's people and resources" (line 27) becoming part of the Communist world, and therefore being integrated or immersed in such an ideology. Choice A is incorrect because it refers to one's attention being focused specifically on a certain thing, and thus cannot refer to Southeast Asia's "resources." Choice B is incorrect because Communism taking over a country does not necessarily mean that the conquered people decide to fully act in accordance and agree with the ideas of the new ideology; additionally, the word "assimilated" cannot refer to resources. Choice C is incorrect because it is a highly economical term that refers to the domination of a certain industry, and therefore does not match to a discussion of the way an ideology takes over a people and their resources.

Question 5: B
Choice B is the best answer because McNamara is citing the interest America has in aiding Vietnam, the basic principles of freedom and self-determination, which have guided America in its quest to protect "member[s] of the free world" (lines 30-31). Therefore, "sustained" refers to America's motivation in the fight for freedom. Choice A is incorrect because freedom and self-determination cannot defend the nation; they could be cited as reasons for America to defend itself. Choice C is incorrect because while freedom and self-determination have been preserved because America sends aid to countries like Vietnam, they haven't preserved the nation itself. Choice D is incorrect because the nation is not being advanced by its basic principles-- the principles are being advanced throughout the world.

Question 6: A
Choice A is the best answer because McNamara believes that "basic to the principles of freedom and self-determination...is the right of peoples everywhere to live and develop in peace" (lines 35-38), and that "our own security is strengthened...by our commitment to assist them" (lines 38-41). It is additionally correct because McCarthy calls upon the fact that America "made an appeal to the decent opinion of mankind in the Declaration of Independence" (lines 86-87) and through its actions in Vietnam has found itself for the first time without the support of that decent opinion, suggesting that there has been a violation of the principles laid out in the Declaration of Independence. Choice B is incorrect because, while McNamara does use the values to support his belief that America is justified in its presence in Vietnam, McCarthy only suggests that American is no longer upholding the principles, not that it has gone in direct opposition to them by using oppressive or dictatorial force. Choice C is incorrect because McCarthy is not supporting isolationist policies toward Vietnam; in fact, he states that we should get involved, just in a different way: by "us[ing] military strength with restraint...while...mak[ing] available...the great power of [America's] economy, of [America's] knowledge, and of [America's] good will" (lines 90-94). Choice D is incorrect because McCarthy, while believing that the founding principles are being wrongly used to justify America's presence in Vietnam, he doesn't go so far as to suggest that America's belief in such principles is causing the country's involvement or guiding it toward a war.

Question 7: B
Choice B is the best answer because in lines 88-93 McCarthy states that America does not need to be the police of the planet, instead it should aid other countries by "mak[ing] available to the world the great power of [America's] economy, of [America's] knowledge, and of [America's] good will". This statement supports the idea that McCarthy would rather assert influence in domains other than war. Choice A is incorrect because McCarthy would not agree or disagree that there is a need for freedom globally; the issues he takes with America's involvement in the war relate to unjustifiable destruction and killing. Choice C is incorrect because McCarthy does not mention international support for America's involvement in the war although he does.

Question 8: C
Choice C is the best answer because in lines 88-93, McCarthy correctly addresses the topic of the previous question: America's role as the police of the planet. Choices A, B, and D are not the right answers because they incorrectly address the language of politics (choice A) and justification for the Vietnam war (choices B and D).

Question 9: B
Choice B is the best answer because the primary point of paragraph three in the second passage is that the war is indefensible even in military terms. Therefore, later, when McCarthy asserts that the United States keeps escalating its objectives, he is supporting that there is no defense for the war and as a result the nation needs to keep changing its justification. Choice A is incorrect because McCarthy doesn't claim to know whether or not those who make these defenses for being in war are sincere or disingenuous. Choice C is incorrect because America's changing defenses for war are in defense of Vietnam and Southeast Asia, which would hinder authoritarian agenda, not enable it. Choice D is incorrect because the defenses McCarthy claims people are making relate to safety of Vietnam and Southeast Asia as well as the United States. Furthermore, he uses these examples to show that the alleged "need" for security is growing from one place to the next, highlighting its absurdity in general, not just because the United States was used as a defense.

Question 10: D
Choice D is the best answer because McCarthy's primary objective in the last paragraph is to support the idea that the war "is morally wrong" (line 107). He does this by saying that America can on longer "prove that the good that may come with what is called victory is proportionate to the loss of life and property and other disorders that follow" (lines 19-22). By manipulating his word choice to highlight that he disagrees with calling winning the war a victory, McCarthy makes it clear that he disagrees with this view. He also points out that "we have moved from limited targets...to greater variety and more destructive instruments" (lines 112-114), indicating that the scope of the war is expanding. Choice A is incorrect because McCarthy does not mention the public's support in the last paragraph. Choice B is incorrect because while McCarthy does state that America is continuously attacking Vietnam, he doesn't state whether they can withstand those attacks; in fact, he alludes to the possibility that Vietnam may lose the war when he mentions victory in line 120.

Chapter Nine

Questions 1-10 are based on the following passage.

9.1

Adapted from "Iron Curtain" a speech delivered in 1946 by British Prime Minister Winston Churchill, at Westminster College, Missouri. There, in attendance and to introduce Churchill, was U.S President Harry S. Truman.

From Stettin in the Baltic to Trieste in the Adriatic, an iron curtain has descended across the continent. Behind that line lie all the capitals of the
Line ancient states of Central and Eastern Europe. Warsaw,
5 Berlin, Prague, Vienna, Budapest, Belgrade, Bucharest and Sofia, all these famous cities and the populations around them lie in what I must call the Soviet sphere, and all are subject in one form or another, not only to Soviet influence but to a very high and, in some
10 cases, increasing measure of control from Moscow. The Russian-dominated Polish Government has been encouraged to make enormous and wrongful inroads upon Germany, and mass expulsions of millions of Germans on a scale grievous and undreamed-of are
15 now taking place. The Communist parties, which were very small in all these Eastern States of Europe, have been raised to pre-eminence and power far beyond their numbers and are seeking everywhere to obtain totalitarian control. Police governments are
20 prevailing in nearly every case, and so far, except in Czechoslovakia, there is no true democracy.

If now the Soviet Government tries to build up a pro-Communist Germany in their areas, this will cause new serious difficulties in the American and
25 British zones, and will give the defeated Germans the power of putting themselves up to auction between the Soviets and the Western Democracies. Whatever conclusions may be drawn from these facts, this is certainly not the Liberated Europe we fought to build
30 up. Nor is it one which contains the essentials of permanent peace.

The safety of the world requires a new unity in Europe, from which no nation should be permanently outcast. It is from the quarrels of the strong parent
35 races in Europe that the world wars we have witnessed, or which occurred in former times, have sprung. Twice in our own lifetime we have seen the United States, against their wishes and their traditions, drawn by irresistible forces into these wars in time to secure
40 the victory of the good cause, but only after frightful slaughter and devastation had occurred. Twice the United States has had to send several millions of its young men across the Atlantic to find the war; but

now war can find any nation, wherever it may dwell
45 between dusk and dawn. Surely, we should work with conscious purpose for a grand pacification of Europe, within the structure of the United Nations and in accordance with our Charter. That I feel is an open cause of policy of very great importance.
50   I do not believe that Soviet Russia desires war. What they desire is the fruits of war and the indefinite expansion of their power and doctrines. But what we have to consider here today while time remains, is the permanent prevention of war and the establishment
55 of conditions of freedom and democracy as rapidly as possible in all countries. Our difficulties and dangers will not be removed by closing our eyes to them. They will not be removed by mere waiting to see what happens, nor will they be removed by a policy of
60 appeasement.

From what I have seen of our Russian friends and Allies during the war, I am convinced that there is nothing they admire so much as strength, and there is nothing for which they have less respect than for
65 weakness, especially military weakness. For that reason, the old doctrine of a balance of power is unsound. We cannot afford, if we can help it, to work on narrow margins, offering temptations to a trial of strength. If the Western Democracies stand together
70 in strict adherence to the principles of the United Nations Charter, their influence for furthering those principles will be immense and no one is likely to molest them. If the population of the English-speaking Commonwealths be added to that of the United States
75 with all that such co-operation implies in the air, on the sea, all over the globe and in science and in industry, and in moral force, there will be no quivering, precarious balance of power to offer its temptation to ambition or adventure. On the contrary, there will be
80 an overwhelming assurance of security. If we adhere faithfully to the Charter of the United Nations and walk forward in sedate and sober strength seeking no one's land or treasure, seeking to lay no arbitrary control upon the thoughts of men, if all British moral
85 and material forces and convictions are joined with your own in fraternal association, the high-roads of the future will be clear, not only for us but for all, not only for our time, but for a century to come.

CONTINUE

1

The stance taken by Churchill in this passage is one of

A) a pacifist seeking a diplomatic solution.

B) a war-weary critic of military expansion.

C) a concerned politician urging a show of strength.

D) a historian cautioning against a rising trend.

2

Which characterization of the region behind the "iron curtain" (line 2) is most central to Churchill's overall argument?

A) It is the former battleground of many European wars.

B) It is a zone coming increasingly under Russian control.

C) It is an area that was wrongfully seized from Germany.

D) It is where the great ancient cities of Europe are found.

3

According to Churchill, which consequence of Soviet expansion poses the greatest threat to Europe?

A) The outbreak of another world war.

B) The humiliation of a defeated Germany.

C) The proliferation of oppressive regimes.

D) The disruption to a fragile balance of power.

4

Which choice provides the best evidence for the answer to the previous question?

A) Lines 13-15 ("mass expulsions … place.")

B) Lines 15-19 ("The Communist … control")

C) Lines 52-56 ("But what … countries")

D) Lines 65-67 ("For that … unsound")

5

In the third paragraph, Churchill refers to the recent U.S. participation in two European wars most likely to

A) underscore his caution against an all-powerful Europe.

B) frame his stance against Russia as a moral necessity.

C) dramatize the threat posed by Russia to the United States.

D) point to a possible outcome of a policy of inaction.

6

In urging an alliance with the U.S., Churchill implies that Russia,

A) despite its overwhelming military might, can be defeated in a war.

B) despite its apparent aggressiveness, can be dissuaded from advancing further.

C) despite its incursions into Europe, will not spread its influence globally.

D) despite its military advantage, will yield to international consensus.

7

Which choice provides the best evidence for the answer to the previous question?

A) Lines 32-34 ("The safety … outcast")

B) Lines 45-48 ("Surely, we … Charter")

C) Lines 61-65 ("From what … weakness.")

D) Lines 73-79 ("If the population … adventure.")

8

As used in line 46, "conscious purpose" most nearly means

A) dedicated intent.

B) keen insight.

C) deep understanding.

D) clear meaning.

CONTINUE

9

As used in line 78, "temptation" most nearly means

A) seduction.

B) invitation.

C) opportunity.

D) inclination.

10

It can reasonably be inferred from the last paragraph that Churchill believes that

A) the recent escalation of tension between the West and Russia will inevitably lead to war.

B) Russia will interpret a lack of Western resolve as a justification for expanding its influence.

C) Russia will renew its alliance with the West if the right conditions are met.

D) Communist forces are equal in strength to the combined powers of Britain and the U.S.

CONTINUE

Questions 1-10 are based on the following passage.

9.2

This passage is adapted from President William McKinley's War Message to Congress, delivered in 1898.

The present revolution is but the successor of other similar insurrections which have occurred in Cuba against the dominion of Spain, extending over
Line a period of nearly half a century, each of which has
5 subjected the United States to great effort and expense in enforcing its neutrality laws, caused enormous losses to American trade and commerce, caused irritation, annoyance, and disturbance among our citizens, and, by the exercise of cruel, barbarous,
10 and uncivilized practices of warfare, shocked the sensibilities and offended the humane sympathies of our people.

Our people have beheld a once prosperous community reduced to comparative want, its lucrative
15 commerce virtually paralyzed, its exceptional productiveness diminished, its fields laid waste, its mills in ruins, and its people perishing by tens of thousands from hunger and destitution. We have found ourselves constrained, in the observance of that strict
20 neutrality which our laws enjoin, and which the law of nations commands, to police our own waters and watch our own seaports in prevention of any unlawful act in aid of the Cubans.

The war in Cuba is of such a nature that, short
25 of subjugation or extermination, a final military victory for either side seems impracticable. The forcible intervention of the United States as a neutral to stop the war, according to the large dictates of humanity and following many historical precedents
30 where neighboring states have interfered to check the hopeless sacrifices of life by internecine conflicts beyond their borders, is justifiable on rational grounds.

First, in the cause of humanity and to put an end to the barbarities, bloodshed, starvation, and horrible
35 miseries now existing there, and which the parties to the conflict are either unable or unwilling to stop or mitigate. It is no answer to say this is all in another country, belonging to another nation, and is therefore none of our business. It is specially our duty, for it is
40 right at our door.

Second, we owe it to our citizens in Cuba to afford them that protection and indemnity for life and property which no government there can or will afford, and to that end to terminate the conditions that deprive
45 them of legal protection.

Third, the right to intervene may be justified by the very serious injury to the commerce, trade, and business of our people, and by the wanton destruction of property and devastation of the island.

50 Fourth, and which is of the utmost importance, the present condition of affairs in Cuba is a constant menace to our peace, and entails upon this government an enormous expense. With such a conflict waged for years in an island so near us and with which our people
55 have such trade and business relations; when the lives and liberty of our citizens are in constant danger and their property destroyed and themselves ruined; where our trading vessels are liable to seizure and are seized at our very door by warships of a foreign nation, the
60 expeditions of filibustering that we are powerless to prevent altogether, and the irritating questions and entanglements thus arising - all these and others that I need not mention, with the resulting strained relations, are a constant menace to our peace, and compel us to
65 keep on a semi-war footing with a nation with which we are at peace.

These elements of danger and disorder already pointed out have been strikingly illustrated by a tragic event which has deeply and justly moved the American
70 people. I have already transmitted to Congress the report of the Naval Court of Inquiry on the destruction of the battleship Maine in the harbor of Havana during the night of the 15th of February. The destruction of that noble vessel has filled the national heart with
75 inexpressible horror. Two hundred and fifty-eight brave sailors and marines and two officers of our Navy, reposing in the fancied security of a friendly harbor, have been hurled to death, grief and want brought to their homes, and sorrow to the nation.

80 The long trial has proved that the object for which Spain has waged the war cannot be attained. The fire of insurrection may flame or may smolder with varying seasons, but it has not been, and it is plain that it cannot be, extinguished by present methods. The
85 only hope of relief and repose from a condition which can no longer be endured is the enforced pacification of Cuba. In the name of humanity, in the name of civilization, in behalf of endangered American interests which give us the right and the duty to speak and to
90 act, the war in Cuba must stop.

In view of these facts and of these considerations, I ask the Congress to authorize and empower the President to take measures to secure a full and final termination of hostilities between the government
95 of Spain and the people of Cuba, and to secure in the island the establishment of a stable government, capable of maintaining order and observing its international obligations, insuring peace and tranquility and the security of its citizens as well as our own, and
100 to use the military and naval forces of the United States as may be necessary for these purposes.

CONTINUE

1

The main purpose of the passage is to

A) catalogue the atrocities of the Spanish-Cuban war.

B) explain why Americans in Cuba have been targeted.

C) justify the need for U.S. military involvement in Cuba.

D) argue for the annexation of Cuba by the United States.

2

The passage states that Cuba, prior to the outbreak of war,

A) experienced rapid economic growth.

B) harbored a vibrant business community.

C) relied primarily on agricultural exports.

D) was a highly developed industrial society.

3

As used in line 3, "dominion" most nearly means

A) territory.

B) control.

C) mastery.

D) government.

4

In the passage, which justification does McKinley NOT give for wanting to involve the United States in the Cuban war?

A) To protect American commercial interests.

B) To curtail Spain's global influence.

C) To address a growing humanitarian crisis.

D) To eliminate a threat to U.S. security.

5

Which choice provides evidence in support of McKinley's claim that the war in Cuba has caused "enormous losses to American trade" (lines 6-7)?

A) Lines 9-12 (" by the exercise … our people.")

B) Lines 18-23 ("We have … Cubans")

C) Lines 39-40 ("It is … door")

D) Lines 57-59 (where our … nation")

6

In context of his overall message, McKinley alludes to the sinking of the battleship Maine most likely because

A) the incident highlights to what degree the relations between the United States and Spain have become strained by the Cuban war.

B) the incident should be interpreted as an unequivocal declaration of war on the United States by Spain.

C) the incident has galvanized the American people to rally behind in the United States' stance on the war in Cuba.

D) the incident highlights the danger posed to the United States even as a neutral party in an ongoing conflict.

7

As used in line 74, "heart" most nearly means

A) vibe.

B) core.

C) spirit.

D) essence.

8

McKinley makes which prediction about the Cuban war, were it allowed to continue without U.S. intervention?

A) Spain will eventually give up because the war will become too costly to sustain.

B) The war will drag on because Spain and Cuba are locked in a permanent stalemate.

C) The Cubans will lose in the long run from the effects of attrition and starvation.

D) The war will inspire other parts of the Spanish Empire to fight for their independence.

9

Which choice provides the best evidence for the answer to the previous question?

A) Lines 1-4 ("The present … century")

B) Lines 24-26 ("The war … impracticable")

C) Lines 80-81 ("The long … attained")

D) Lines 84-87 ("The only … Cuba")

CONTINUE

10

It can be inferred from the last paragraph that McKinley's ultimate goal is to

A) help Cuba win its independence from Spain.

B) end the rebellion and bring order to Cuba.

C) spread American democratic values in Cuba.

D) form an alliance with the government in Cuba.

CONTINUE

Questions 1-10 are based on the following passage.

9.3

This passage is adapted from U.S. President William Harrison's 1841 Inaugural Address

As was to be expected from the defect of language and the necessarily sentential manner in which the Constitution is written, disputes have arisen as to the
Line amount of power which it has actually granted or was
5 intended to grant. This is more particularly the case in relation to that part of the instrument which treats of the legislative branch, and not only as regards the exercise of powers claimed under a general clause giving that body the authority to pass all laws
10 necessary to carry into effect the specified powers, but in relation to the latter also. It is, however, consolatory to reflect that most of the instances of alleged departure from the letter or spirit of the Constitution have ultimately received the sanction of a majority of the
15 people.

But the great danger to our institutions does not appear to me to be in a usurpation by the Government of power not granted by the people, but by the accumulation in one of the departments of that which
20 was assigned to others. Limited as are the powers which have been granted, still enough have been granted to constitute a despotism if concentrated in one of the departments. This danger is greatly heightened, as it has been always observable that men are less
25 jealous of encroachments of one department upon another than upon their own reserved rights.

When the Constitution of the United States first came from the hands of the Convention which formed it, many of the sternest republicans of the day
30 were alarmed at the extent of the power which had been granted to the Federal Government, and more particularly of that portion which had been assigned to the executive branch. There were in it features which appeared not to be in harmony with their ideas
35 of a simple representative democracy or republic, and knowing the tendency of power to increase itself, particularly when exercised by a single individual, predictions were made that at no very remote period the Government would terminate in virtual monarchy.
40 It would not become me to say that the fears of these patriots have been already realized; but as I sincerely believe that the tendency of measures and of men's opinions for some years past has been in that direction, it is, I conceive, strictly proper that I should take this
45 occasion to repeat the assurances I have heretofore given of my determination to arrest the progress of that

tendency if it really exists and restore the Government to its pristine health and vigor, as far as this can be effected by any legitimate exercise of the power placed
50 in my hands.

I proceed to state in as summary a manner as I can my opinion of the sources of the evils which have been so extensively complained of and the correctives which may be applied. Some of the former
55 are unquestionably to be found in the defects of the Constitution; others, in my judgment, are attributable to a misconstruction of some of its provisions. Of the former is the eligibility of the same individual to a second term of the Presidency. The sagacious mind of
60 Mr. Jefferson early saw and lamented this error, and attempts have been made, hitherto without success, to apply the amendatory power of the States to its correction. As, however, one mode of correction is in the power of every President, and consequently in
65 mine, it would be useless, and perhaps invidious, to enumerate the evils of which, in the opinion of many of our fellow-citizens, this error of the sages who framed the Constitution may have been the source and the bitter fruits which we are still to gather from it if it
70 continues to disfigure our system.

It may be observed, however, as a general remark, that republics can commit no greater error than to adopt or continue any feature in their systems of government which may be calculated to create
75 or increase the lover of power in the bosoms of those to whom necessity obliges them to commit the management of their affairs; and surely nothing is more likely to produce such a state of mind than the long continuance of an office of high trust. Nothing
80 can be more corrupting, nothing more destructive of all those noble feelings which belong to the character of a devoted republican patriot. When this corrupting passion once takes possession of the human mind, like the love of gold it becomes insatiable. It is the never-
85 dying worm in his bosom, grows with his growth and strengthens with the declining years of its victim. If this is true, it is the part of wisdom for a republic to limit the service of that officer at least to whom she has entrusted the management of her foreign relations,
90 the execution of her laws, and the command of her armies and navies to a period so short as to prevent his forgetting that he is the accountable agent, not the principal; the servant, not the master. Until an amendment of the Constitution can be effected public
95 opinion may secure the desired object. I give my aid to it by renewing the pledge heretofore given that under no circumstances will I consent to serve a second term.

CONTINUE

1

Harrison's main goal throughout the passage is to

A) make the public aware of flaws in the United States Constitution.
B) argue for a moderation in the power of the executive branch.
C) inform his audience that he will not seek a second term in office.
D) chastise Congress for straying too far from the Constitution.

2

Throughout the passage, Harrison's focus shifts from a conversation of historical concerns and their present-day manifestations to

A) a detailed plan of how to remedy the current power imbalance.
B) a call for a Congressional amendment limiting presidential terms.
C) an explanation of their potential causes and a proposed solution.
D) an admonition of their inevitable role in the erosion of democracy.

3

In the second paragraph (lines 16-27), Harrison makes a distinction between

A) legitimate power and illegitimate power.
B) constructive power and destructive power.
C) democratic power and federal power.
D) centralized power and decentralized power.

4

Harrison would agree with which potential solution to the issues he sees within the Executive branch of the government?

A) Executive power should never be vested in only one individual; in an ideal government, the office of president would be split among multiple people.
B) The Executive branch threatens an eventual monarchy; as such, it should be fall completely under the control of the Legislative branch.
C) There is danger inherent in any one individual holding power for too long; therefore, the power of the Executive branch should be restricted through term limits.
D) The Executive branch needs to be more accountable to the citizenry; to that end, major Executive decisions should be subjected to a public referendum.

5

Which choice provides the best evidence for the answer to the previous question?

A) Lines 16-20 ("But the...others")
B) Lines 54-59 ("Some of...Presidency")
C) Lines 63-68 ("As, however...source")
D) Lines 87-93 ("it is...master")

6

As used in line 25, "jealous" most nearly means

A) defensive.
B) cynical.
C) envious.
D) wary.

7

Which lines provide the best evidence to show that Harrison believes that the American democracy is suffering as a result of political overreach?

A) Lines 29-33 ("many of...branch")
B) Lines 38-43 ("predictions were...direction")
C) Lines 44-50 ("I conceive...hands")
D) Lines 59-63 ("The sagacious...correction")

CONTINUE

8

In context of the passage as a whole, Harrison's discussion of fears among the early republican government officials serves which purpose?

A) It criticizes the fact that this concern was not properly addressed at the time the Constitution was written.

B) It demonstrates that the Constitution and, as a result, the American government were flawed from the outset.

C) It shows that an inequitable division of power between the Legislative and Executive branches is a recurring theme in American history.

D) It reveals that the excessive accumulation of Executive power was anticipated by some members of the founding government.

9

Throughout the passage, Harrison depicts the Constitution as

A) a sacrosanct document that must not be altered to increase the power of the Executive branch.

B) a malleable text that must be updated to address concerns that have been realized since its initial writing.

C) a tool used by the Executive branch to nullify unlawful decisions made by Congressional overreach.

D) a remedy available to Congress to define and limit the powers afforded to the Executive branch.

10

Which technique does Harrison use to characterize the corrupting effect of power?

A) He highlights its destructive nature by likening it to a parasite which thrives as its host weakens.

B) He illustrates its delusional nature by suggesting that powerful men tend to forget their place.

C) He underscores its lucrative nature by comparing it to an insatiable desire for gold.

D) He emphasizes its immoral nature by describing it as erosive to a noble patriotic sentiment.

CONTINUE

Questions 1-10 are based on the following passage.

9.4

In June 1971, a secret report detailing a systematic pattern of government efforts to conceal from the public and Congress that a war against Vietnam was unwinnable, was leaked to The New York Times and The Washington Post. President Nixon immediately sought a court injunction to block publication of the report. However, The Supreme Court ruled that the right to publish was protected under the First Amendment, and so it was that this report, dubbed the "Pentagon Papers," was published. Passage 1 is adapted from Mr. Justice Black's concurring opinion. Passage 2 is adapted from Mr. Justice Blackmun's dissenting opinion.

Passage 1

In seeking injunctions against these newspapers, and in its presentation to the Court, the Executive Branch seems to have forgotten the essential purpose
Line and history of the First Amendment. Madison and
5 the other Framers of the First Amendment wrote in language they earnestly believed could never be misunderstood: "Congress shall make no law . . . abridging the freedom . . . of the press. . . ." The Founding Fathers gave the free press the protection it
10 must have to fulfill its essential role in our democracy. The Government's power to censor the press was abolished so that the press would remain forever free to censure the Government. The press was protected so that it could bare the secrets of government and inform
15 the people.

Only a free and unrestrained press can effectively expose deception in government. And paramount among the responsibilities of a free press is the duty to prevent any part of the government from deceiving the
20 people and sending them off to distant lands to die of foreign fevers and foreign shot and shell. In revealing the workings of government that led to the Vietnam war, the newspapers nobly did precisely that which the Founders hoped and trusted they would do.
25 The Government's case here is based on premises entirely different from those that guided the Framers of the First Amendment. It argues in its brief that, in spite of the First Amendment, "the authority of the Executive Department to protect the nation
30 against publication of information whose disclosure would endanger the national security stems from two interrelated sources: the constitutional power of the President over the conduct of foreign affairs and his authority as Commander-in-Chief." In other words, we

35 are asked to hold that, despite the First Amendment's emphatic command, the Executive Branch, Congress, and the Judiciary can make laws enjoining publication of current news and abridging freedom of the press in the name of "national security."
40 The word "security" is a broad, vague generality whose contours should not be invoked to abrogate the fundamental law embodied in the First Amendment. The guarding of military and diplomatic secrets at the expense of informed representative government
45 provides no real security for our Republic. The Framers of the First Amendment, fully aware of both the need to defend a new nation and the abuses of the English and Colonial governments, sought to give this new society strength and security by providing
50 that freedom of speech, press, religion, and assembly should not be abridged. This thought was eloquently expressed in 1937 by Mr. Chief Justice Hughes when the Court held that a man could not be punished for attending a meeting run by Communists. "The greater
55 the importance of safeguarding the community from incitements to the overthrow of our institutions by force and violence, the more imperative is the need to preserve inviolate the constitutional rights of free speech, free press and free assembly in order to
60 maintain the opportunity for free political discussion, to the end that government may be responsive to the will of the people and that changes, if desired, may be obtained by peaceful means. Therein lies the security of the Republic, the very foundation of constitutional
65 government."

Passage 2

The New York Times clandestinely devoted a period of three months to examining the 47 volumes that came into its unauthorized possession. Once it had begun publication of material from those volumes, the
70 New York case now before us emerged. It immediately assumed a frenetic pace and character. Seemingly, once publication started, the material could not be made public fast enough. Seemingly, from then on, every deferral or delay, by restraint or otherwise, was
75 abhorrent, and was to be deemed violative of the First Amendment and of the public's "right immediately to know."

The First Amendment is only one part of an entire Constitution. Article II of the great document
80 vests in the Executive Branch primary power over the conduct of foreign affairs, and places in that branch the responsibility for the Nation's safety. Each provision of the Constitution is important, and I cannot subscribe to a doctrine of unlimited absolutism for the
85 First Amendment at the cost of downgrading other

CONTINUE

provisions.

What is needed here is a weighing, upon properly developed standards, of the broad right of the press to print and of the very narrow right of the Government
90 to prevent. The parties here are in disagreement as to what those standards should be. But even the newspapers concede that there are situations where restraint is in order and is constitutional. Mr. Justice Holmes gave us a suggestion when he said, "It is a
95 question of proximity and degree. When a nation is at war, many things that might be said in time of peace are such a hindrance to its effort that their utterance will not be endured so long as men fight and that no Court could regard them as protected by any
100 constitutional right."

I strongly urge that these two newspapers be fully aware of their ultimate responsibilities to the United States of America. Judge Wilkey concluded that there were a number of examples of documents
105 that, if in the possession of the Post and if published, "could clearly result in great harm to the nation," and he defined "harm" to mean "the death of soldiers, the destruction of alliances, the greatly increased difficulty of negotiation with our enemies, the inability of our
110 diplomats to negotiate," to which list I might add the factors of prolongation of the war and of further delay in the freeing of United States prisoners.

1

Which choice best describes a central tension between the passages?

A) Whether the press is responsible for keeping the government in check.

B) Whether there are limits to rights granted by the First Amendment.

C) Whether the government may deceive the public about the Vietnam War.

D) Whether the Supreme Court may pass a ruling on the Pentagon Papers.

2

Justice Black indicates that the Framers wrote the First Amendment in language "they earnestly believed could never be misunderstood" (lines 6-7) primarily to emphasize the

A) degree to which the Framers were unable to predict the escalation of global tensions.

B) extent to which the government has manipulated the Constitution to support its agenda.

C) severity of the repudiation to the Framers that was committed through restriction of the press.

D) patent violation of the Constitution that resulted from the government's lawsuit against the press.

3

Justice Black would most likely respond to the claims made by Justice Blackmun in the last paragraph of Passage 2 by asserting that

A) repression of the press predisposes the government to further violate the agency of the people.

B) victory in the Vietnam War will only be achieved with the informed involvement of the people.

C) the security of the nation has been compromised by the government's betrayal of the people.

D) the press has an obligation to expose the government's dishonesty for the safety of the people.

4

Which choice provides the best evidence for the answer to the previous question?

A) Lines 17-21 ("And paramount...shell")

B) Lines 25-27 ("The Government's...Amendment")

C) Lines 40-45 ("The word...Republic")

D) Lines 63-65 ("Therein lies...government")

5

As used in line 41, "contours" most nearly means

A) rigid assignation.

B) unclear delineation.

C) expansive definition.

D) undefined scope.

CONTINUE

6

In the context of Passage 2 as a whole, the words "clandestinely" and "frenetic" in the first paragraph (lines 66 and 71) have which effect?

A) They create a skeptical tone to show the author's doubts about the authenticity of the confidential source material used by the New York Times.

B) They create a grave tone to show the author's dismay at the irreparable damage done overseas by the publication of confidential material.

C) They create a sarcastic tone to show the author's disapproval of the way in which the publication of material was executed by the New York Times.

D) They create a critical tone to show the author's belief that the press was extremely careless in publishing confidential material.

7

Which choice best identifies a key difference in how Justices Black and Blackmun make use of the concept of security to advance their arguments?

A) Black states that national security is conditional upon the opportunity for unrestricted political discussion, whereas Blackmun contends that military security is of paramount importance in times of armed conflict.

B) Black suggests that national security is already maintained by the involvement of an informed citizenry, whereas Blackmun implies that military security is endangered when it enters the purview of the public.

C) Black asserts that security is malleable to the interests and needs of the citizenry, whereas Blackmun maintains that national security is an invariable necessity that must be imposed independently of popular opinion.

D) Black indicates that the security of the republic rests upon strict adherence to the Constitution, whereas Blackmun claims that security must be upheld through responsible exercising of judgments by the press.

8

Justice Blackmun would most likely characterize Justice Black's interpretation of the Constitution as

A) rigid, because it ascribes excessive regard to the intentions of the Founding Fathers.

B) reactionary, because it diminishes the significance of executive power in wartime.

C) revisionist, because it attempts to reallocate the responsibility of security from the government to the press.

D) reductionist, because it fails to account for the role of the First Amendment as only one part of a greater system.

9

Which choice provides the best evidence for the answer to the previous question?

A) Lines 79-82 ("Article II...safety")

B) Lines 82-86 ("Each provision...provisions")

C) Lines 87-91 ("What is...be")

D) Lines 103-106 ("Judge Wilkey...nation")

10

As used in line 112, "factors" most nearly means

A) risks.

B) causes.

C) elements.

D) consequences.

CONTINUE

Questions 1-10 are based on the following passage.

9.5

The following passage is adapted from Justice John Marshall Harlan's dissenting opinion on the Supreme Court decision in Plessy v. Ferguson in which the Court held that the state of Louisiana did not violate the Fourteenth Amendment by establishing and enforcing a policy of racial segregation in its railway system.

In respect of civil rights, common to all citizens, the Constitution of the United States does not, I think, permit any public authority to know the race of those
Line entitled to be protected in the enjoyment of such
5 rights. Every true man has pride of race, and under appropriate circumstances which the rights of others, his equals before the law, are not to be affected, it is his privilege to express such pride and to take such action based upon it as to him seems proper. But I deny that
10 any legislative body or judicial tribunal may have regard to the race of citizens which the civil rights of those citizens are involved. Indeed, such legislation as that here in question is inconsistent not only with that equality of rights which pertains to citizenship,
15 national and state, but with the personal liberty enjoyed by everyone within the United States.

It was said in argument that the statute of Louisiana does not discriminate against either race but prescribes a rule applicable alike to white and
20 colored citizens. But this argument does not meet the difficulty. Everyone knows that the statute in question had its origin in the purpose not so much to exclude white persons from railroad cars occupied by blacks as to exclude colored people from coaches
25 occupied by or assigned to white persons. Railroad corporations of Louisiana did not make discrimination among whites in the matter of accommodation for travelers. The thing to accomplish was, under the guise of giving equal accommodations for whites
30 and blacks, to compel the latter to keep to themselves while travelling in railroad passenger coaches. No one would be so wanting in candor as to assert the contrary. The fundamental objection, therefore, to the statute is that it interferes with the personal freedom of citizens.
35 If a white man and a black man choose to occupy the same public conveyance on a public highway, it is their right to do so, and no government, proceeding alone on grounds of race, can prevent it without infringing the personal liberty of each.
40 The white race deems itself to be the dominant race in this country. And so it is in prestige, in

achievements, in education, in wealth, and in power. So, I doubt not, it will continue to be for all time, if it remains true to its great heritage and holds fast to the
45 principles of constitutional liberty. But in the view of the Constitution, in the eye of the law, there is in this country no superior, dominant, ruling class of citizens. There is no caste here. Our Constitution is color-blind and neither knows nor tolerates classes among citizens.
50 In respect of civil rights, all citizens are equal before the law. The humblest is the peer of the most powerful. The law regards man as man and takes no account of his surroundings or of his color when his civil rights as guaranteed by the supreme law of the land are
55 involved.

The arbitrary separation of citizens, on the basis of race, while they are on a public highway, is a badge of servitude wholly inconsistent with the civil freedom and the equality before the law established by the
60 Constitution. It cannot be justified upon any legal grounds. If evils will result from the commingling of the two races upon public highways established for the benefit of all, they will be infinitely less than those that will surely come from state legislation regulating the
65 enjoyment of civil rights upon the basis of race.

We boast of the freedom enjoyed by our people above all other peoples. But it is difficult to reconcile that boast with the state of the law which, practically, puts the brand of servitude and degradation upon a
70 large class of our fellow citizens, our equals before the law. The thin disguise of "equal" accommodations for passengers in railroad coaches will not mislead anyone, nor atone for the wrong this day done.

CONTINUE

1

The main purpose of the passage is to

A) prove that there is no clear superiority of the white race and show how the law supports this absence of hierarchy.

B) argue that the legislation at hand cannot be justified because it infringes upon citizens' personal liberties.

C) explain that the existence of the law in question proves the inability of the Fourteenth Amendment to fulfill its claims.

D) present a dissenting opinion about a controversial court case and suggest an alternate legal route.

2

As used in line 4, "enjoyment" most nearly means

A) indulgence.

B) gratification.

C) exercising.

D) ownership.

3

The author believes that "pride of race" (line 5) is acceptable on the condition that

A) all honest men possess this particular form of egotism.

B) it does not infringe upon the legal liberties of others.

C) the white race remains the most dominant in America.

D) civil rights violations are not a topic of discussion.

4

With which of the following statements about the role of racial identity in the law would Harlan most strongly DISAGREE?

A) Racial identity should be a source of personal pride that empowers citizens to take part in civil society.

B) Racial identity is a fair basis for laws on the condition that all races are equally provided for in such laws.

C) Racial identity is not addressed in the Constitution and therefore cannot form the foundation of any law.

D) Racial identity is the true basis of state laws providing separate but supposedly equal accommodations.

5

Which lines provide the best evidence for the answer to the previous question?

A) Lines 17-20 ("It was...citizens")

B) Lines 28-31 ("The thing...coaches")

C) Lines 37-39 ("no government...each")

D) Lines 48-51 ("Our Constitution...law")

6

As used in line 32, "wanting" most nearly means

A) desirous.

B) craving.

C) inadequate.

D) lacking.

7

What purpose do lines 40-45 ("The white...liberty") serve in Harlan's argument?

A) They give voice to the reasoning of the Louisiana railroad company executives for separating black and white passengers.

B) They appeal to the racial pride white Americans hold and suggest that the court decision made was against their own self-interest.

C) They appeal to the morals of Louisiana railroad company executives so that they might change the policies on their own.

D) They explain to black Americans the reasoning behind other Supreme Court justices' votes in favor of segregated facilities.

8

In line 48, Harlan characterizes the Constitution as "color-blind" primarily to

A) show that racial discrimination is wrong because the Constitution is unaware of such differences between people.

B) present the claim that the goal of racial tolerance was not considered when the Constitution was written.

C) personify the Constitution as a way of keeping his audience engaged in and persuaded of his argument.

D) further clarify his point that the differences between races are irrelevant in the realm of civil rights.

CONTINUE

9

Which lines provide the best evidence for Harlan's claim that by designating separate classes of citizenry, the Supreme Court decision is in conflict with previously granted legal freedoms?

A) Lines 52-55 ("The law…involved")

B) Lines 56-61 ("The arbitrary…grounds")

C) Lines 61-65 ("If evils…race")

D) Lines 66-71 ("We boast…law")

10

Throughout the passage, Harlan's focus shifts from

A) a reflection on different types of transportation methods to a discussion of American Constitutional ideals.

B) a conclusion about a specific court case to an evaluation of its potential ramifications on American values.

C) a summary of the current state of transportation law to an analysis of its contribution to institutional racism.

D) a censure of the Supreme Court for enabling racist policies to a promotion of racial equality laws.

STOP

Please turn to next page for answer keys and explanations.

Answer Key: CHAPTER NINE

9.1 | Churchill	9.2 | McKinley	9.3 | Harrison	9.4 | First Amendment	9.5 | Harlan
1: C	1: C	1: B	1: B	1: B
2: B	2: B	2: C	2: D	2: C
3: C	3: B	3: D	3: D	3: B
4: B	4: B	4: C	4: A	4: B
5: B	5: D	5: D	5: B	5: D
6: B	6: D	6: D	6: D	6: D
7: D	7: C	7: B	7: D	7: B
8: A	8: B	8: D	8: D	8: D
9: C	9: B	9: B	9: B	9: B
10: B	10: B	10: A	10: A	10: B

Answer Explanations

Chapter Nine

Chapter 9.1 | Churchill

Question 1: C
Choice C is the best answer because Churchill, the British prime minister, is warning his audience about the threat posed by communism. In response, he suggests that the United States and Britain come together to cooperate "in the air, on the sea, all over the globe and in science and in industry" (lines 75-77) and intimidate the Russians. He states that this response will, in turn, provide security (lines 79-80) that appeasement cannot accomplish (lines 58-60). Choice A is incorrect because Churchill's advocacy for a show of force contradicts the values of pacifism and diplomacy. Choice B is incorrect because Churchill's tone throughout the passage is primarily one of urgency and encouragement, not critique; "criticism" is therefore overly negative. Choice D is incorrect because Churchill's speech is contemporary to the issues it discusses and is therefore a primary source; by this same logic, Churchill cannot be a historian, as he is responding to these issues as they are happening.

Question 2: B
Choice B is the best answer because Churchill states that, beyond the "iron curtain", there are famous cities and populations that make up "the Soviet sphere" (line 8) and "are subject ... to Soviet influence" (lines 8-9). Churchill cites these places as a demonstration of the increase in Soviet power; in doing so, he is able to advocate for the military solution that he presents later on in the passage. Choice A is incorrect because Churchill does not specify any European wars in the passage, nor does he state that they took place in the cities that he lists. Choice C is incorrect because Germany is merely an example of one of the places in which Soviet influence is taking hold; Churchill does not indicate that all of the places listed were previously German. Choice D is incorrect because Churchill refers to the states of Eastern Europe as "ancient", not the cities. Furthermore, even if he had referred to the cities, the fact that they are "great" or "ancient" would be tangential in proving his overall point regarding the compromise of freedom as the result of Soviet encroachment.

Question 3: C
Choice C is the best answer because Churchill indicates in lines 15-19 that the popularity of the Communist party in many Eastern European states has given the Soviets an opportunity to "[seek] everywhere to obtain totalitarian control"; thus corresponding with "proliferating" and "oppressive

regimes". Choice A is incorrect because Churchill warns of increased world tensions and "new serious difficulties in the American and British zones" as a result of increased Communist power, but never indicates that such tensions will escalate into a full-blown world war. Choice B is incorrect because the "humiliation" of a subjugated Germany is never a concern of Churchill, who stresses instead the threat to democracy that Soviet control of Germany proposes. Choice D mistakenly interprets a "balance of power" between the Communist and Democratic powers as ideal; instead, Churchill promotes a "showing of strength", a disruption to the balance of power that would actually protect, not threaten, Europe.

Question 4: B
Choice B is the best answer because lines 15-19 directly refer to the results of the Communist parties' expansion of "power far beyond their numbers": the momentum to "[seek] everywhere to obtain totalitarian control". Choice A is incorrect because lines 13-15 only describe the effects of Soviet rule on Germans, not Europe as a whole. Choice C is incorrect because lines 52-55 discuss Churchill's proposed response to the consequences of Soviet expansion, not the consequences themselves. Similarly, choice D is incorrect because lines 65-67 consider and dismiss a potential plan of action, neglecting the events that necessitated that plan of action (i.e. Soviet expansion of power).

Question 5: B
Choice B is the best answer because it calls for European unity in the name of global security (lines 32-34). Churchill warns that, when Europe was divided in the past, the United States had to enter the war "to secure the victory of the good cause". Churchill's delineation of the causes' moralities is implicit in his description of certain causes as "good", thereby framing European conflicts in a moral context. His reference to the United States' participation is therefore a message to other countries that they must take up their rightful responsibility. Choice A is incorrect because Churchill does not mention European omnipotence. At best, he discusses how certain European great powers have conflicted in the past, but these countries are not representative of Europe as a whole. Furthermore, a powerful Europe is not relevant to his ultimate desire of European peace. Choice C is incorrect because Russia is not mentioned in the third paragraph, making that answer choice off-topic. Choice D is incorrect because Churchill's recommendation for unity is in light of what happened in the past, but he does not use these events to explicitly state that a similar outcome will happen again if Europe is inactive. In fact, Churchill actually indicates that these circumstances are different than those of World War I and II when he states that "twice the United States has had to send several millions ... to find the war; but now war can find any nation" (lines 41-44), which means that the events that informed previous proceedings no longer apply.

Question 6: B
Choice B is the best answer because lines 73-79 indicate that a coalition of Western Democracies would tip the "quivering, precarious balance of power" away from the Soviet Union, therefore preventing them from "advancing further" into Europe. Choice A is incorrect because Churchill suggests intimidating Russia through a showing of economic and intellectual strength, not through direct military action such as a "war". Choice C is incorrect because "incursions" suggests a literal Soviet invasion of European states, while the Soviet Union has merely exercised indirect power through the political influence of the Communist Party. Choice D wrongly implies that if the Russians have the upper hand with regard to its military, they would still respond to international

consensus. Churchill claims in lines 63-65 that Russia respects military might the most and has the least respect for weakness. If Russia were to have the best military, then it would not yield because of its own definition of superiority. Also, Churchill advocates for military unity of multiple countries, which is a far more active policy than a consensus, in which countries merely agree on a stance or perspective.

Question 7: D
Choice D is the best answer because lines 73-79 explicitly refer to the British-United States alliance, when it states that "if the population of the English-speaking Commonwealths be added to that of the United States", and states that this "co-operation" and "moral force" will prevent the possibility of a "quivering, precarious balance of power". Churchill indicates that this "balance of power", though, is "unsound" because it might give way to further Russian attempts at aggression earlier in the paragraph (lines 65-69). Thus, an alliance can halt current Russian aggression, which matches with choice B in the previous question. Choice A is incorrect because lines 32-34 state that unity is required for safety, which is a general statement that does not indicate action that will stop Russian aggression. In fact, neither the British-United States alliance nor Russia is mentioned whatsoever in these lines or in the paragraph that contains these lines. Choice B is incorrect because lines 45-48 indicate that working within the United States should be with the goal of peace in mind. But there is no allusion to Russia, the subject of the question, which makes the line references off-topic. Choice C is incorrect because lines 61-65 merely establish what the Russians value when interacting with foreign powers. It does not specify a means of deterring Russia from pursuing an expansionist policy. These lines also do not discuss the implication of a British-United States alliance, making them off-topic.

Question 8: A
Choice A is the best answer because it expresses that steps will be taken to realize Churchill's goal of a peaceful Europe. The necessity of action is implied in the phrase "an open cause of policy", since driving factors of policy indicate that there is work being done to achieve a goal. In Choice A, the phrase "dedicated intent" demonstrates his willingness and desire to have peace prevail in the region. It is the only choice that implies that some degree of action being undertaken. Choices B, C, and D include the words "insight", "understanding", and "meaning", but these only express cognizance of what needs to be done and not a willingness to do so, which Choice A does.

Question 9: C
Choice C is the best answer because Churchill describes a potential "balance of power" which would "offer" the ability to seek ambition or adventure; the offer is therefore an "opportunity". Choice A is incorrect because "seduction" is an overly literal interpretation of "temptation". Choice B is incorrect because "invitation" would suggest some agency or conscious thought on the part of the balance of power, which is not possible. Choice D is incorrect because an "inclination" is a tendency or proclivity, which only a person can have.

Question 10: B
Choice B is the best answer because Churchill indicates that the Russians admire strength and have no respect for military weakness. Thus, he advocates for the unification of Western Democracies in order to prevent the "quivering, precarious balance of power" from "[offering] its temptation to ambition or adventure" (lines 77-79). According to Churchill, it is only when there is resolve, or no

"quivering", that the "temptation" of Russian expansion can be quelled. Therefore, if the democratic powers do not put on a show of strength, they will lend themselves to a lack of Russian respect that would prompt further expansion. Choice A is incorrect because Churchill indicates that British and American unity will result in "the high-roads of the future [being] clear", but does not indicate that not doing so will guarantee, or make "inevitable", the occurrence of war. Choice C is incorrect because Churchill is focused on matters of security, not on the criteria for gaining back old alliances; in fact, there is no language to suggest that there is a chance of gaining back the previous wartime alliance, nor is there language to indicate that there is even a willingness to reconcile. Choice D is incorrect because Churchill implies that the combination of British and American powers will be stronger than Soviet forces and will create "an overwhelming assurance of security" (line 80).

Chapter 9.2 | McKinley

Question 1: C
Choice C is the best answer because McKinley states in lines 26-33 that "the forcible intervention of the United States as a neutral to stop the war...is justifiable on rational grounds" and proceeds in the following paragraphs to list the "grounds" that would warrant American military involvement (lines 34-66). Choice A is incorrect because discussion of the atrocities committed during the Spanish-Cuban war are limited to lines 13-18 ("Our people...destitution) and lines 33-35 ("First, in...there"), and therefore cannot be considered the main focus or goal of the passage; furthermore, McKinley's description of the war's destruction of Cuba only serves as context and justification for American military intervention. Choice B is incorrect because while McKinley briefly cites a duty to protect "our [American] citizens in Cuba" (line 41), he never indicates that they are being targeted separately from Cuban citizens, nor does he explain that they are being targeted for a specific reason. Choice D is incorrect because "annexation" of Cuba is not part of McKinley's plans; he aims to use American military and naval force to stop the war and implement a stable government, but never indicates that such a government would be American or that Cuba would be under American control.

Question 2: B
Choice B is the best answer because McKinley discusses "a once prosperous community", "lucrative commerce", and "exceptional productiveness" in lines 13-16 and laments that these no longer exist because of the war. All of these phrases support the claim that there was a "vibrant business community". Choice A is incorrect; although it is possible that there was rapid economic growth from the business sector, there are no details in the passage that describe the speed of the growth. In fact, the passage does not even indicate that there was growth; it only describes the success and prosperity before the war. There is no timeline or description of the business community's previous successes to use as a point of comparison; thus, it cannot be assumed that there was growth before the war. Choice C is incorrect; while the passage describes "fields laid waste", "mills in ruins", and "people perishing...from hunger and destitution" (lines 16-18), these phrases cannot be used to support the claim that there was a heavy reliance on agriculture. Making this statement would require a breakdown of exports across all sectors of the economy and establishing that agriculture has the largest role. But the ruin of what previously was the agriculture sector and people dying of starvation does not necessarily mean that the Cuban population primarily relied on that sector. Choice D is incorrect because McKinley does not qualify Cuba's stage of development nor does he comment on their industry; this choice is off-topic.

Question 3: B

Choice B is the best answer because Cuba is staging an "insurrection" against the political "authority" or "jurisdiction" that Spain has exercised over the country; "control" is therefore the closest synonym. Choice A is incorrect because Cuba rebelling against the "territory" of Spain would entail travelling to Spain and waging a physical war there. Choice C is incorrect because one can only have "mastery" over a skill, not a country. Choice D is incorrect; while Cubans are technically rebelling against the "government" of Spain, the government itself is not "extending over a period of nearly half a century", which would create a misplaced modifier. The Cubans' grievance with Spain is not the government itself, but the oppression (or "control") the government has inflicted upon its citizens.

Question 4: B

Choice B is the best answer because McKinley mentions the "dominion of Spain" which has "[extended] over a period of nearly half a century" (lines 3-4) as justification for Cuba's uprising against Spain, but not for the United States' intervention in the conflict. Choice A is incorrect because McKinley cites the interconnectedness of Cuban and American economics in lines 6-7 ("caused enormous...commerce") and explicitly indicates that "the right to intervene may be justified by the very serious injury to the commerce, trade, and business of our [American] people" (lines 46-48). Choice C is incorrect because McKinley calls intervention in the Spanish-Cuban war a duty "in the cause of humanity and to put an end to the barbarities, bloodshed, starvation, and horrible miseries" (lines 33-35), therefore characterizing the situation in Cuba as a "humanitarian crisis". Choice D is incorrect because McKinley argues that "the present condition of affairs in Cuba is a constant menace to our [American] peace" (lines 51-52), therefore implying that chaos in Cuba would present a threat to the national security of the United States.

Question 5: D

Choice D is the best answer because McKinley establishes in lines 57-59 that other countries are seizing American "trading vessels", thereby providing the reason for why trade is suffering. Choice A discusses the effect of the Cuban war on "the sympathies of the people", thereby making the answer choice off-topic. Choice B is incorrect because it discusses American neutrality; these lines similarly do not provide an explanation for why there are losses to American trade. At best, these lines would explain how America is currently unable to step in to aid Cuban trade (based on the topic sentence of the paragraph), Choice C is incorrect because McKinley merely asserts that it is the United States' right to assume the role that he is advocating for; this sentence does not detail the reasons behind trade suffering.

Question 6: D

Choice D is the best answer because McKinley begins his recounting of the sinking by stating that it is an example of the danger inherent in the United States' position at the time the passage was written. Since the question is asking about the allusion in context of McKinley's overall message, his stance opposing American neutrality can be taken as evidence for the fact that he does not believe America's current status as a "neutral party" is beneficial. Choice A is incorrect because McKinley never specifies that Spain attacked the battleship Maine; thus, it cannot be concluded that he is referring to the United States' relations with Spain, especially because tensions with Spain are not mentioned anywhere else in the passage. Spain is only ever mentioned in the context of its role as one of the motivating factors for the Cuban revolution. Choice B is incorrect; again, the identity of the attacker is not mentioned, which means that the sinking cannot be interpreted as a declaration of war by Spain. Choice C is incorrect; while McKinley states that "the destruction of [the battleship Maine] has filled the national heart with inexpressible horror" (lines 73-75), there is no mention of how that event has resulted in increased support for the United States government's position regarding the war. Even if the American people were emotionally affected by the event, there is no mention of the impact on their perspective of the war.

Question 7: C
Choice C is the best answer because the phrase "national spirit" encompasses the emotional effect of the sinking of the battleship, as well as the common ground that he states all Americans shared as a result of the event. Choice A is incorrect because the word "vibe" has a greater emphasis on the national atmosphere that is being established by the event, rather than the way that all Americans felt as a result of it. Thus, it does not stress the emotional aspect of the situation, which is the reason that McKinley alludes to the event in the first place. Choices B and D are incorrect because the words "core" and "essence" emphasize the physical nature of what connects the citizens of a nation, but do not take into account the emotional nature of the sinking that McKinley stresses.

Question 8: B
Choice B is the best answer because McKinley claims that "short of subjugation or extermination" (lines 24-25) of the conflict by the United States, a final military victory of either side would be "impracticable" (line 26); McKinley cannot imagine a final victory or a final battle, and therefore implies that the war would continue or "drag on" without American intervention. Choice A is incorrect because McKinley never mentions that the cost of the war is of concern to Spain, nor that the war in Cuba has financially deprived the country. Choice C is incorrect because McKinley states in lines 24-26 that he cannot foresee a victory by either side, including Spain; therefore, "the Cubans [losing]" cannot be a part of his prediction. Choice D is incorrect because other colonies of Spain are not a focus of the passage and are thus not mentioned throughout the line references.

Question 9: B
Choice B is the best answer because lines 24-26 reveal McKinley's thoughts about "a final military victory for either side", thus matching the topic of the previous question (a prediction about the fate of the Cuban war); the following lines introduce "the forcible intervention of the United States" (lines 26-28) as a potential solution, implying that the prediction made by McKinley would occur under the circumstances of American non-intervention. Choice A is incorrect because lines 1-4 describe the events that have led up to the current conflict and do not mention a potential consequence of the war. Choice C is incorrect because lines 80-81 describe a prediction about the end of the Cuban war, but do not place it in the context of American non-intervention. Choice D is incorrect because lines 84-87 describe McKinley's suggestion for how the United States should act, not a speculation of what would happen if the United States did not intervene.

Question 10: B
Choice B is the best answer because McKinley states his intention to "secure a full and final termination of hostilities between the government of Spain and the people of Cuba" (lines 93-95), which correlates with "ending the rebellion", and to "secure in the island the establishment of a stable government" (lines 95-96), which corresponds with "bringing order to Cuba". Choice A is incorrect because McKinley prioritizes ending the conflict in Cuba regardless of whether

Cubans attain independence. Choice C is incorrect because McKinley only indicates that the new government would provide security and stability, none of which would not be considered exclusively "American democratic values". Choice D is incorrect because McKinley plans to supplant the existing Cuban government with one that is "capable of maintaining order and observing its international obligations" (lines 96-97); thus, he would not be "forming an alliance" with the government in Cuba so much as replacing it with another.

Chapter 9.3 | Harrison

Question 1: B
Choice B is the best answer because the particular issues Harrison draws attention to are discussed within the context of limiting presidential terms. Choice A is incorrect because even though he does state flaws, his purpose is to persuade rather than instruct or "make the public aware". Choice C is incorrect because his goal in stating he will not seek a second office is to show that he believes in his larger goal of limiting terms. Choice D is incorrect because Congress is not the focus of his critique.

Question 2: C
Choice C is the best answer because paragraphs 4 and 5 comprise Harrison's solution to overreaching executive power. Choices A and B are incorrect because he does not elaborate on the steps necessary to limiting presidential terms, and only mentions amending the Constitution twice in the last two paragraphs (lines 62 and 94) in passing. Choice D is incorrect because, even though Harrison makes reference to the erosion of democracy when he warns of "the bitter fruits which we are still to gather from it if it continues to disfigure our system" (lines 69-70), he does not fully focus on this role.

Question 3: D
Choice D is the best answer because Harrison first draws a distinction between "usurpation" (line 16) and "accumulation" (line 19) of power, then points out that "enough [powers] have been granted to constitute a despotism if concentrated in one of the departments"; therefore, he shows the difference between concentrated (accumulated) power and decentralized power. Choice A is incorrect because he does not explicitly discuss the source of these "granted" powers, and so does not say whether they are legitimate or not. Choice B is incorrect because he does not mention either creation or destruction. Choice C is incorrect because he does not state that there is a difference between democratic and federal power.

Question 4: C
Choice C is the best answer because the main goal of Harrison's speech is to show that term limits can curb executive overreach; more specifically, in lines 87-93 he states that it is imperative "to limit that service of [the President]" in order to "prevent [the President's] forgetting that he is the accountable agent, not the principal; the servant, not the master." Choice A is incorrect because he never discusses expanding the executive office in the interest of splitting the power among more people. Choice B is incorrect because putting the executive branch under the power of the legislative branch would lead to the accumulation of power that he argues against. Choice D is incorrect because he never puts forth the idea that the public referendum is a suitable balance to executive overreach.

Question 5: D
See above for further clarification of the best answer. Choice D is correct because it is the only choice that clearly contains a solution as required by the previous question. Choices A and B are both incorrect because they outline the issues that need solving, but do not provide a solution. Choice C is incorrect because in those lines Harrison says that he will work to amend the problem rather than how he will do so.

Question 6: D
Choice D is the best answer because toward the end of the second paragraph, Harrison describes how people react to "encroachments" (line 25) on the rights of branches of the government versus those on their own rights. He means that people tend to be less concerned, worried or "wary" of the encroachments that do not have personal meaning. Choices A and C are incorrect because the words "defensive" and "envious" would mean that people defend or envy those encroachments. Choice B is incorrect because even if "cynical" describes acting in self-interest or the belief that people only act in self-interest, it does not describe the "worried" response to an immediate threat to rights.

Question 7: B
Choice B is the best answer because in lines 38-43, Harrison states that "the tendency of measures... and opinions for some years past has been in [the direction of virtual monarchy]," which shows that American democracy has felt some degree of the negative effects of political overreach." Choices A and C are incorrect because while they show that there is a perceived problem of political overreach, they do not give direct or indirect evidence of actual damage to American democracy. Choice D is incorrect because it shows that attempts have been made and will be made to fix damage done, but does not give strong enough evidence of that damage.

Question 8: D
Choice D is the best answer because in the third paragraph, Harrison discusses the "[alarm] at the extent of the power which had been granted to the Federal Government" (lines 30-31) as well as the "predictions" of a future "virtual monarchy" (line 39). Choice A is incorrect because he does not suggest that immediate action was never taken to address these issues. Choice B is incorrect because he does not say that the flaws were so absolute as to render the entire American government so. Choice C is incorrect because he does not discuss recurring themes of American history so much as he refers to one specific period of time.

Question 9: B
Choice B is the best answer because Harrison immediately begins his speech by pointing out that "disputes have arisen as to the amount of power which [the Constitution] has actually granted or was intended to grant" (line 3-5). Later, he notes that "Some of the [evils] are unquestionably to be found in the defects of the Constitution; others, in my judgment, are attributable to a misconstruction of some of its provisions" (lines 54-57). Choice A is incorrect because he shows that the Constitution can and should be altered, though not to increase the power of the Executive branch. Choice C is incorrect because he does not discuss nullifying unlawful decisions. While he does discuss limiting Executive power by an amendment passed through Congress, choice D is still incorrect because Harrison explicitly mentions this only once rather than throughout the passage.

Question 10: A

Choice A is the best answer because Harrison describes the love of power as "the never-dying worm in his bosom, grows with his growth and strengthens with the declining years of its victim" (lines 84-86). Choice B is incorrect because he does not say that there is an innate tendency to forget one's place or that, even if that happens, it is a delusion. Choice C is incorrect because he does not discuss whether power is lucrative (profitable). Choice D is incorrect because he does not connect immorality with the loss of patriotism.

Chapter 9.4 | First Amendment

Question 1: B

Choice B is the best answer because all points of disagreement from both passages revolve around the First Amendment's establishment of the freedom of the press and whether there are circumstances, such as war, in which this right does not apply. Choice A is incorrect because both passages (lines 13-15 and lines 88-89) acknowledge that the press can publish content criticizing and effectively "checking" the government; the main argument lies in the limits of the said responsibility. Choice C is incorrect because both passages do not pass explicit judgment on any wrongdoing or deception on the government's part but rather argue about the press's reaction to it (lines 21-24 and lines 66-68). Choice B is incorrect because the passages themselves are part of the ruling that the Supreme Court has passed on the Pentagon Papers (with Passage 1 being a concurring opinion and Passage 2 being a dissenting opinion); their own existence answers the question as to whether the Supreme Court may decide on the Pentagon Papers.

Question 2: D

Choice D is the best answer because by highlighting the clear language of the First Amendment, Justice Black can emphasize how the government has so obviously violated it and "have forgotten [its] essential purpose and history" (lines 3-4). Choice A is incorrect because Passage 1 later underscores that the Framers had actually anticipated circumstances, such as the Vietnam War, in which the press would be forced to exercise their freedom and "[do] precisely that which the Founders hoped and trusted they do." (lines 23-24). Choice B is incorrect because the government is not shown to be "manipulating" the Constitution but simply arguing that "national security" and the authority of the Executive Branch trump the First Amendment. Choice C is incorrect because Justice Black is not concerned with how the restriction of the press personally contradicts the Framers (and their ideals) but rather how it technically violates the Constitution that the American government is built upon.

Question 3: D

Choice D is the best answer because Justice Black's assertion of the press's duty to provide the people with truth directly responds to Justice Blackmun's assertion (in Passage 2's last paragraph) that the press has "ultimate responsibilities to the United States of America" (lines 102-103) that force them to sometimes withhold information that "could clearly result in great harm to the nation" (line 106). Choice A is incorrect there is no suggestion made by Justice Black that the American government might begin restricting more freedoms. Choice B is incorrect because the Pentagon Papers have already established that the Vietnam War is unwinnable for the United States (lines 19-21) so any type of "victory" is out of the question. Choice C is incorrect because it focuses on the government's actions threatening the nation's security rather than responding to Justice Blackmun's assertions that the press's actions threaten the nation's security.

Question 4: A

Choice A is the best answer because it explicitly states that the press has "the duty to prevent any part of the government from deceiving the people..." (lines 18-20). Choice B, Choice C, and Choice D (lines 25-27, lines 40-45, lines 63-65) are incorrect because they do not clearly mention any responsibilities of the press in ensuring the safety of the people.

Question 5: B

Choice B is the best answer because it expresses the inability for the term "national security" to be described precisely and thus, allows the government to justify any restriction of free press based upon it. Choice A is incorrect because it calls the term inflexible in its meaning, which stops it from being used by the government in imprecise means. Choice C is incorrect because it indicates that the term actually has a definition, which (similarly to Choice A) stops the government from capitalizing on its "vague" quality. Choice D is incorrect because, while Justice Black believes that the term is "broad" and "vague" (line 40) which suggests that it isn't defined clearly enough, he never suggests that the term is not defined at all.

Question 6: D

Choice D is the best answer because it exhibits how the author expresses his disapproval of press's publication process using negative adjectives that characterize it as hasty and hurried ("Seemingly, once publication started, the material could not be made public fast enough." [lines 71-73]). Choice A is incorrect because the author never exhibits serious doubts on the validity of the Pentagon Papers as they are primary sources from the government. Choice B is incorrect because there is no mention of the published materials evidently causing any damage outside of the United States, only the possibility of more documents being leaked and endangering the nation (lines 103-106). Choice C is incorrect because there is no sarcasm in the first paragraph (or Passage 2, in general); all of the author's statements are straightforward and direct.

Question 7: D

Choice D is the best answer because Black's belief that the First Amendment (including the freedom of press) is inflexible and should never be abandoned (lines 4-10) contrasts with Blackmun's assertions that in certain cases, the amendment should be limited. Choice A is incorrect because Black simply discerns that the term "national security" can be used by the government to justify restriction of First Amendment freedoms, he never states that national security itself is subject to any conditions. Choice B is incorrect because Blackmun only states that there are specific military documents whose publication may cause harm to the nation (lines lines 103-106), he never generalizes that military security is endangered by the public's knowledge of it. Choice C is incorrect because it implies that Black sees national security as conditional based on the public's views while he actually says national security is used conditionally by the government (lines 36-39).

Question 8: D

Choice D is the best answer because it references Blackmun's belief that other parts of the constitution must be taken into account just as much as the First Amendment is when deciding on matters of freedom and national security (lines . This directly rebuts the main crux of Black's argument that the First Amendment should be followed exactly as it is written in the Constitution, without exception. Choice A is incorrect because while Black does focus on the Framers' intentions about the First Amendment, it does not constitute "excessive regard" since he spends far greater time expanding on his own logical arguments about the First Amendment. Choice B is incorrect because the term "reactionary" (meaning conservative, right-wing) does not correlate with Black's relatively liberal stance on First Amendment. Choice C is incorrect because Black doesn't reassign the responsibility of the nation's security to the press, instead he simply states that an unrestricted press is fundamental in maintaining it (lines 57-63).

Question 9: B
Choice B (lines 82-86) is the best answer because it directly contradicts Black's interpretation of the Constitution which emphasizes the supremacy/rigidity of the First Amendment. Choice A (lines 79-82) is incorrect as it provides examples and descriptions of specific parts of the Constitution, however, does not express a specific argument about their interpretation in regards to the First Amendment. Choices C and D (lines 87-91 and lines 103-106) are incorrect since they do not directly address the relationship between the First Amendment and the rest of the Constitution.

Question 10: A
Choice A is the best answer because the word "risks" is appropriate in describing potential problems, such as the mentioned "prolongation of the war" (line 112). Choice B and Choice D are incorrect because there is no explicit cause-and-effect relationship in line 112 and thus, their terms do not properly apply. Choice C is incorrect because it is too vague and neutral to be describing negative issues such as the "further delay in the freeing of the United States prisoners" (line 112-113).

Chapter 9.5 | Harlan

Question 1: B
Choice B is the best answer. Justice Harlan is writing a dissenting opinion on a Supreme Court decision that upheld the legality of Louisiana's policy of racial segregation; he opposes the notion that the policy is constitutional. The reason that it cannot be justified is in lines 12-16: "Such legislation...is inconsistent...with the personal liberty enjoyed by everyone within the United States". Choice A is incorrect because Harlan's ultimate concern is the legality of Louisiana's policy; he acknowledges that "in the eye of the law, there is in this country no superior, dominant, ruling class of citizens" (lines 46-47). Harlan does not address the existence of racial hierarchy; he only states that it is unconstitutional. Choice C is incorrect; Harlan does not critique the Fourteenth Amendment's validity throughout the passage. He merely believes that the legislation in question is antithetical to the Fourteenth Amendment, thereby making it unconstitutional, but he does not take fault with the Amendment itself. Choice D is incorrect; the passage does not indicate anything regarding the controversial nature of the case. Moreover, there is no suggestion of an "alternate legal route" or different course of action that should be sought out. The passage is not recommending action; it is simply expressing disagreement with the Court's ruling.

Question 2: C
Choice C is the best answer. In lines 1-5, Harlan states that civil rights are common to all citizens and that all citizens are entitled to these rights, one of which is the right to equal treatment regardless of race. Since these rights have already been established, "exercising" is the best word because it describes the act of putting the rights to use, thereby ensuring their widespread applicability. Choices A and B are incorrect because "indulgence" and "gratification" imply that the rights are a privilege and that to use them is somehow pleasurable or rewarding. This notion is contradictory to

Harlan's affirmation that each person is unconditionally entitled to their rights. Choice D is incorrect; since these rights are meant to be universal for all United States citizens, no individual can claim "ownership" of the rights. These rights are not exclusively belonging to one person; the collective is entitled to access these rights. Moreover, to use the word "ownership" implies that there is an object or physical entity in question, whereas rights are intangible.

Question 3: B
Choice B is the best answer. Harlan states that "the pride of race" exists within "every true man" and that it is his "privilege to express such pride" (lines 5-10). The only qualification that Harlan includes is that "the rights of others...are not to be affected" (lines 6-7). Choice A is incorrect; while Harlan states that this pride exists within "every true man" (line 5), it is not the basis or condition upon which the pride is acceptable. Choice C is incorrect because "the pride of race", as described by Harlan in the first paragraph (lines 1-16), is not contingent upon how it affects different races or demographics. Indeed, there is no mention of "the white race" or its continual dominance in the paragraph. Choice D is incorrect because Harlan states that "the pride of race" ought not have bearing on being able to exercise civil rights. Even if civil rights violations are not being discussed, "the pride of race" cannot affect civil rights or result in violations either.

Question 4: B
Choice B is the best answer. Harlan explicitly states that racial identity, regardless of whether or not the provision is equally applied to all races, is an unjust basis for laws: "the statute...prescribes a rule applicable alike to white and colored citizens. But this argument does not meet the difficulty. Everyone knows that the statute...had its origin in the purpose not so much to exclude white persons...as to exclude colored people" (lines 17-24). Even in instances where the law is applied for both whites and blacks, the intent is inherently exclusionary, racist, and unjust. Choice A is incorrect; Harlan never discusses the implications of racial identity on citizens performing their civic duties and engaging in government. Choice C is incorrect because Harlan would not disagree with the notion that "racial identity...cannot form the foundation of any law", based on the same logic for why Choice B is correct. Choice D is incorrect because Harlan actually states that racial identity is the basis of "separate but equal" in lines 17-24 (see above) and in lines 28-31: "the thing to accomplish was, under the guise of giving equal accommodations for whites and blacks, to compel the latter to keep to themselves while travelling in railroad passenger coaches".

Question 5: D
Choice D is the best answer. It expresses the sentiment that taking race into consideration is unjust because "our Constitution is color-blind and neither knows nor tolerates classes among citizens. In respect of civil rights, all citizens are equal before the law". Any consideration of race therefore violates the constitutional premise that there should not be classes. Choice A is incorrect because the phrase "the statute...does not discriminate...but prescribes a rule applicable alike" is not Harlan's viewpoint. He includes this sentence to invalidate it. Choice B is incorrect because, in lines 28-31, Harlan is making a specific argument that pertains to Louisiana's policy; it cannot support a general statement about the role of racial identity in the law. Choice C is incorrect because lines 37-39 address the topic of racial identity in the law but do not directly contradict any of the choices in the previous question.

Question 6: D
Choice D is the best answer. Harlan states that "the thing to accomplish, under the guise of giving equal accommodations for whites and blacks, to compel the latter to keep to themselves while travelling in railroad passenger coaches. No one would be so wanting in candor as to assert the contrary" (lines 28-32). Since Harlan believes that the concept of "equal accommodations" is false and that to say otherwise would indicate an absence of truthfulness, or "candor", "lacking" is the best choice. Choices A and B are incorrect; although "desirous", "craving", and "wanting" are synonyms in context of an urge or a wish, they do not convey Harlan's intent to say that one would be untruthful to suggest that the Louisiana railroad corporations had any intention to provide equal accommodations. Choice C is incorrect because Harlan is not saying that perpetuating the notion of "equal accommodations" would make the truth "inadequate", or not enough. He is stating that to believe that concept is to be wholly devoid of truth, since there is not one part of the railroad corporation's intent that he finds truthful or correct. Since the truth does not exist, it cannot be "inadequate".

Question 7: B
Choice B is the best answer. Harlan states that "the white race deems itself to be the dominant race... So, I doubt not, it will continue to be for all time, if it remains true to its great heritage and holds fast to the principles of...liberty". In addressing whites' feelings of racial pride with respect to their dominance, Harlan reveals that the best way to uphold their superiority is through abiding by the United States' founding values. Thus, Harlan would say that the majority opinion, or the opinion that Harlan is criticizing, is not in whites' self-interest because it contradicts the core American principle of liberty. Choice A is incorrect because Harlan indicates that the actual reasoning of the executives for separating whites and blacks is "to exclude colored people from coaches occupied by or assigned to white persons" (lines 24-25). To state that this reasoning was influenced by ideas of white supremacy would be factually correct; however, because Harlan does not state that within his dissenting opinion, selecting Choice A would be using outside knowledge. Choice C is incorrect because the Louisiana railroad company executives are not Harlan's target audience in these lines. Rather, he is suggesting that all white people uphold constitutional values, not just the executives in question. Moreover, the "morals" of the executives are unclear; the passage only indicates their policy of segregation and that the reason for said policy was to segregate blacks, but it does not indicate the executives' morality or lack thereof. Lastly, Harlan is not advocating for any policy change within his dissenting opinion, least of all a policy change from the corporations themselves. He is merely expressing the lack of constitutionality in the current policy. Choice D is incorrect because the "other Supreme Court justices' votes" are not mentioned in the passage and their reasoning cannot be assumed.

Question 8: D
Choice D is the best answer. In lines 45-51, Harlan states that "in the view of the Constitution, in the eye of the law, there is in this country no superior, dominant, ruling class of citizens...In respect of civil rights, all citizens are equal before the law". Thus, he is emphasizing that race should have no bearing on exercising civil rights and supports this claim with the Constitution. Choice A is incorrect because Harlan never indicates that the Constitution is "unaware" of racial differences; instead, he believes that the Constitution does understand race but does not recognize it as a meaningful basis for one's treatment. Choice B is incorrect because Harlan uses the Constitution to further his argument that racial tolerance is critical; thus, he would not state that racial tolerance was not the

goal of the Constitution. Choice C is incorrect because Harlan is not making an attempt to engage his audience in describing the Constitution as "color-blind". He is merely reinforcing his point that it is unconstitutional to consider race with respect to civil rights.

Question 9: B

Choice B is the best answer. Harlan indicates in lines 56-60 that "the arbitrary separation of citizens, on the basis of race...is...wholly inconsistent with the civil freedom and equality before the law established by the Constitution". Separating citizens by race constitutes as "designing separate classes of citizenry", and Harlan indicates that this segregation is incongruous with the Constitution, or "previously granted legal freedoms". Choice A is incorrect because lines 52-55 merely state that the law does not take race into account; there is no contradiction with "previously granted legal freedoms" that is presented. Choice C is incorrect because lines 61-65 present the point that, even if segregation were bad, restricting civil rights on the basis of race would be far worse. Once again, Harlan does not present a conflict with previously granted freedoms; he is speaking in support of granting legal freedom to blacks. Choice D is incorrect because lines 66-71 indicate that it is "difficult to reconcile" "the state of the law" with "[our boasts] of freedom". Although Harlan mentions freedom, he does not state that this freedom is a "previously granted legal freedom", as opposed to freedom as an ideal or core American value.

Question 10: B

Choice B is the best answer. Harlan begins his dissenting opinion by outlining the argument of the majority opinion: "it was said in argument that the statute of Louisiana does not discriminate against either race but prescribes a rule applicable alike to white and colored citizens" (lines 17-20). He furthers that "the fundamental objection, therefore, to the statute is that it interferes with the personal freedom of citizens" (lines 33-34). After indicating his perspective on Plessy v. Ferguson, Harlan highlights the dangers inherent in the majority opinion: "the arbitrary separation of citizens, on the basis of race...is...wholly inconsistent with the civil freedom and equality before the law established by the Constitution" (lines 56-60). Harlan is taking a stand for American values of freedom and equality, which is mirrored in lines 66-67: "we boast of the freedom enjoyed by our people above all other peoples". But, he warns that "it is difficult to reconcile that boast with the state of the law" (lines 67-68). Harlan presents that the majority decision in Plessy v. Ferguson has the potential to erode the American value of liberty. Choice A is incorrect because there is no mention of "different types of transportation methods" anywhere in the passage; this answer choice is off-topic. Choice C is incorrect because Harlan does not shift from "the current state of transportation law" to "an analysis of its contribution to institutional racism"; he starts by discussing the racial implications of the transportation law and ends with an explanation of how the law is the antithesis of American values. Also, "transportation law" is far too general, in that it refers to that type of law as a whole; on the other hand, Harlan centers his argument around Louisiana railroad corporations' policies of segregation. Choice D is incorrect because Harlan never explicitly states that the Supreme Court is racist; he merely argues that the policy of racial segregation upheld by the majority opinion "[infringes] the personal liberty of [white men and black men]" (lines 38-39). Additionally, Harlan does not conclude his dissenting opinion with a "promotion of racial equality laws"; he is not advocating for a policy change.

Chapter Ten

Questions 1-10 are based on the following passage.

10.1

The following passage is adapted from President John F. Kennedy's Tribute to American poet Robert Frost.

This day, devoted to the memory of Robert Frost, offers an opportunity for reflection which is prized by politicians as well as by others and even by poets. For
Line Robert Frost was one of the granite figures of our time
5 in America. He was supremely two things: an artist and an American.

A nation reveals itself not only by the men it produces but also by the men it honors, the men it remembers. In America, our heroes have customarily
10 run to men of large accomplishments. But today this college and country honor a man whose contribution was not to our size but to our spirit; not to our political beliefs but to our insight; not to our self-esteem but to our self-comprehension. In honoring Robert Frost we
15 therefore can pay honor to the deepest sources of our national strength.

The men who create power make an indispensable contribution to the nation's greatness, but the men who question power make a contribution just as
20 indispensable, especially when that questioning is disinterested, for they determine whether we use power or power uses us. Our national strength matters; but the spirit which informs and controls our strength matters just as much. This was the special significance
25 of Robert Frost. He brought an unsparing instinct for reality to bear on the platitudes and pieties of society. His sense of the human tragedy fortified him against self-deception and easy consolation. "I have been," he wrote, "one acquainted with the night." And because
30 he knew the midnight as well as the high noon, because he understood the ordeal as well as the triumph of the human spirit, he gave his age strength with which to overcome despair. At bottom he held a deep faith in the spirit of man. And it is hardly an accident that Robert
35 Frost coupled poetry and power, for he saw poetry as the means of saving power from itself.

When power leads man towards arrogance, poetry reminds him of his limitations. When power narrows the areas of man's concern, poetry reminds him of
40 the richness and diversity of his existence. When power corrupts, poetry cleanses, for art establishes the basic human truths which must serve as the touchstones of our judgement. The artist, however faithful to his personal vision of reality, becomes the
45 last champion of the individual mind and sensibility against an intrusive society and an officious state. The great artist is thus a solitary figure. He has, as Frost said, "a lover's quarrel with the world." In pursuing his perceptions of reality he must often sail against
50 the currents of his time. This is not a popular role. If Robert Frost was much honored during his lifetime, it was because a good many preferred to ignore his darker truths. Yet, in retrospect, we see how the artist's fidelity has strengthened the fiber of our national life.

55 If sometimes our great artists have been the most critical of our society, it is because their sensitivity and their concern for justice, which must motivate any true artist, make them aware that our nation falls short of its highest potential. I see little of more importance to
60 the future of our country and our civilization than full recognition of the place of the artist. If art is to nourish the roots of our culture, society must set the artist free to follow his vision wherever it takes him.

In free society art is not a weapon, and it does
65 not belong to the sphere of polemics and ideology. Artists are not engineers of the soul. It may be different elsewhere, but in a democratic society the highest duty of the writer, the composer, the artist, is to remain true to himself and to let the chips fall where they may. In
70 serving his vision of the truth, the artist best serves his nation. And the nation which disdains the mission of art invites the fate of Robert Frost's hired man—the fate of having "nothing to look backward to with pride, And nothing to look forward to with hope."

75 I look forward to a great future for America—a future in which our country will match its military strength with our moral strength, its wealth with our wisdom, its power with our purpose. I look forward to an America which will not be afraid of grace
80 and beauty, which will protect the beauty of our national environment, which will preserve the great old American houses and squares and parks of our national past, and which will build handsome and balanced cities for our future. I look forward to an
85 America which will reward achievement in the arts as we reward achievement in business or statecraft. I look forward to an America which will steadily raise the standards of artistic accomplishment and which will steadily enlarge cultural opportunities for all our
90 citizens. And I look forward to an America which commands respect throughout the world, not only for its strength but for its civilization as well.

CONTINUE

1

Kennedy's main purpose in this passage is to

A) ensure that Frost is appropriately remembered as an American hero.

B) urge Americans to consider art to be a greater power than strength.

C) argue that Frost has been the moralizing and energizing spirit of America.

D) eulogize a famous poet by emphasizing the crucial value of art to the nation.

2

As used in line 15, "sources" most nearly means

A) informants.

B) references.

C) origins.

D) springs.

3

As used in line 21, "disinterested" most nearly means

A) equitable.

B) unbiased.

C) indifferent.

D) apathetic.

4

According to the passage, the main role of the artist in the national community is to

A) temper society's tendency for blind acceptance of truisms with strict adherence to empirical reality.

B) aid in the freedom of society by making certain that creation remains divorced from propaganda.

C) serve as the country's cautionary voice that nurtures civilization and guides it toward truth.

D) be the watchman of the state and fortify it against the corrupting influence of excessive power.

5

Which choice provides the best evidence for the answer to the previous question?

A) Lines 25-26 ("He brought...society.")

B) Lines 37-38 ("When power...limitations.")

C) Lines 41-43 ("for art...judgement.")

D) Lines 64-65 ("In free...ideology.")

6

By dubbing the artist "a solitary figure" (line 47), Kennedy is emphasizing

A) the loneliness that is inherent in pursuing a creative lifestyle.

B) the singularizing obligation of the artist to challenge the norms of his society.

C) that Robert Frost, like most artists, was introverted and individualist.

D) that the artist alone can be our Nation's pillar of culture and justice.

7

Which choice provides the best evidence for the answer to the previous question?

A) Lines 9-12 ("In America...spirit")

B) Lines 43-46 ("The artist...state.")

C) Lines 50-53 ("This is...truths.")

D) Lines 53-54 ("Yet, in...life.")

8

Kennedy cites the quote in lines 73-74 ("nothing to... with hope.") most likely to

A) reflect on the potential fate of those hired by Frost had they failed to learn respect for the artistic undertaking.

B) utilize the poetry of Frost to signal a turn away from mere fact and toward idealistic conjecture.

C) offer a didactic adage about destiny to ensure that America continues down the path that Frost suggested.

D) caution against the restriction of the artist and shift focus toward the excellence of a nation that heeds that advice.

CONTINUE

9

According to Kennedy, what is the relationship between power and poetry?

A) It is the obligation of poetry to investigate the presumptuous power of politicians and the self-importance of the state.

B) It is through Frost's juxtaposition of both poetry and power that the limitations of each value are analyzed and clarified.

C) It is through the qualifying guidance of poetry that man is reminded of the corrupting influence of power.

D) It is the aim of poetry to serve as a platform for the essential discussions that are born of man's insatiable desire for power.

10

In the final paragraph, Kennedy uses which rhetorical device to further his point?

A) Comparison, in order to juxtapose the failings of the country with the promise that Frost believed it to have.

B) Repetition, in order to emphasize the foreseeable potential of America to bridge the gap between what the Nation is and what it can be.

C) Allusion, in order to reference the dichotomy between the value of our achievements and the respect they garner around the world.

D) Imagery, in order to paint a picture of the beauty and strength that America possesses due to the poetic counsel of Frost.

CONTINUE

Questions 1-10 are based on the following passage.

10.2

This passage is adapted from President Garfield's 1881 inaugural address.

The elevation of the negro race from slavery to the full rights of citizenship is the most important political change we have known since the adoption of
Line the Constitution of 1787. No thoughtful man can fail
5 to appreciate its beneficent effect upon our institutions and people. It has freed us from the perpetual danger of war and dissolution. It has added immensely to the moral and industrial forces of our people. It has liberated the master as well as the slave from a relation
10 which wronged and enfeebled both. It has surrendered to their own guardianship the manhood of more than 5,000,000 people, and has opened to each one of them a career of freedom and usefulness. It has given new inspiration to the power of self-help in both races by
15 making labor more honorable to the one and more necessary to the other. The influence of this force will grow greater and bear richer fruit with the coming years.

No doubt this great change has caused serious
20 disturbance to our Southern communities. This is to be deplored, though it was perhaps unavoidable. But those who resisted the change should remember that under our institutions there was no middle ground for the negro race between slavery and equal citizenship.
25 There can be no permanent disfranchised peasantry in the United States. Freedom can never yield its fullness of blessings so long as the law or its administration places the smallest obstacle in the pathway of any virtuous citizen.
30 The emancipated race has already made remarkable progress. They are rapidly laying the material foundations of self-support, widening their circle of intelligence, and beginning to enjoy the blessings that gather around the homes of
35 the industrious poor. They deserve the generous encouragement of all good men. So far as my authority can lawfully extend they shall enjoy the full and equal protection of the Constitution and the laws.

The free enjoyment of equal suffrage is still in
40 question, and a frank statement of the issue may aid its solution. It is alleged that in many communities negro citizens are practically denied the freedom of the ballot. In so far as the truth of this allegation is admitted, it is answered that in many places honest
45 local government is impossible if uneducated negroes are allowed to vote. These are grave allegations. So

far as the latter is true, it is the only palliation that can be offered for opposing the freedom of the ballot. Bad local government is certainly a great evil which
50 ought to be prevented, but to violate the freedom and sanctities of the suffrage is more than an evil. It is a crime which, if persisted in, will destroy the Government itself. It has been said that unsettled questions have no pity for the repose of nations. It
55 should be said with the utmost emphasis that this question of the suffrage will never give repose or safety to the States or to the nation until each, within its own jurisdiction, makes and keeps the ballot free and pure by the strong sanctions of the law.
60 But the danger which arises from ignorance in the voter cannot be denied. It covers a field far wider than that of negro suffrage and the present condition of the race. It is a danger that lurks and hides in the sources and fountains of power in every state. We have no
65 standard by which to measure the disaster that may be brought upon us by ignorance and vice in the citizens when joined to corruption and fraud in the suffrage.

The voters of the Union, who make and unmake constitutions, and upon whose will hang the destinies
70 of our governments, can transmit their supreme authority to no successors save the coming generation of voters, who are the sole heirs of sovereign power. If that generation comes to its inheritance blinded by ignorance and corrupted by vice, the fall of the
75 Republic will be certain and remediless.

The census has already sounded the alarm in the appalling figures which mark how dangerously high the tide of illiteracy has risen among our voters and their children. To the South this question is of supreme
80 importance. But the responsibility for the existence of slavery did not rest upon the South alone. The nation itself is responsible for the extension of the suffrage, and is under special obligations to aid in removing the illiteracy which it has added to the voting population.
85 For the North and South alike there is but one remedy: all the constitutional power of the nation and of the States and all the volunteer forces of the people should be surrendered to meet this danger by the savory influence of universal education.
90 It is the high privilege and sacred duty of those now living to educate their successors and fit them, by intelligence and virtue, for the inheritance which awaits them. In this beneficent work sections and races should be forgotten and partisanship should be
95 unknown. Let our people find a new meaning in the divine oracle which declares that "a little child shall lead them," for our own little children will soon control the destinies of the Republic.

CONTINUE

1

Throughout the passage, the main focus shifts from

A) a discussion of both the positive and negative consequences of emancipation to the identification of a specific issue which requires a comprehensive solution.

B) an overview of the ways in which black citizens have been affected by their transition from slavery to freedom to a discussion of the resulting impact on white Americans.

C) a critique of Southern governments' undermining of policies aimed to empower newly freed black citizens to an urgent call for more progressive legislative reform.

D) an exaltation of the greater civil rights afforded to black citizens after emancipation to a reminder of the obstacles they may face in the difficult journey ahead.

2

In the first paragraph, the author states that the emancipation of slaves has benefited the country in all of the following ways **EXCEPT**

A) by minimizing the risk of internal conflict.

B) by increasing the size of the workforce.

C) by eliminating a mutually unhealthy relationship.

D) by bestowing a mantle of dignity to work.

3

The author characterizes the "middle ground...between slavery and equal citizenship" (lines 23-24) as a condition that

A) cannot persist because it is not the fullest expression of freedom.

B) reflects a positive step towards the enfranchisement of black citizens.

C) will facilitate a harmonious coexistence between whites and blacks.

D) represents a precarious compromise in the struggle for sovereign power.

4

Which choice provides the best evidence for the answer to the previous question?

A) Lines 13-16 ("It has...other")

B) Lines 25-29 ("There can...citizen")

C) Lines 30-35 ("The emancipated...poor")

D) Lines 36-38 ("So far...laws")

5

According to Garfield, the next generation of citizens has a responsibility to

A) regularly participate in the political processes to which they are entitled.

B) ensure that the nation is adequately literate and informed to preserve democracy.

C) support the equality and economic self-sufficiency of all citizens regardless of race.

D) expand sovereign power by removing all literacy prerequisites at the ballot box.

6

It can be reasonably inferred from the passage that Garfield perceives the consequence of an uninformed citizenry as being

A) a source of weakness for Southern governments that will subsequently damage the wellbeing of the entire Union.

B) a representation of a longstanding flaw in the school system that has been exacerbated in a new political situation.

C) an imminent threat to the national interest that will lead to irreversible destruction if it is not immediately addressed.

D) a legislative oversight resulting from a history of uneven application of rights throughout the country.

7

Which choice provides the best evidence for the answer to the previous question?

A) Lines 43-46 ("In so...vote")

B) Lines 52-54 ("It is...nations")

C) Lines 64-67 ("We have...suffrage")

D) Lines 73-75 ("If the...remediless")

8

As used in line 72, "heirs" most nearly means

A) beneficiaries.

B) recipients.

C) administrators.

D) replacements.

CONTINUE

9

As used in line 88, "surrendered" most nearly means

A) relinquished.

B) mobilized.

C) united.

D) renounced.

10

In the last paragraph, Garfield's citation from the divine oracle (lines 96-97) has the effect of

A) predicting the potential leadership capabilities of an educated and enfranchised black citizenry.

B) highlighting the moral righteousness that he believes is needed for an effective governance of the Union.

C) reinforcing his point about the importance of educating the next generation as the future leaders of the nation.

D) eliciting sympathy for a new generation of free black citizens who will benefit from the reforms he proposes.

311

CONTINUE

Questions 1-10 are based on the following passage.

10.3

The following passage is adapted from a speech by Soviet General Secretary Mikhail Gorbachev, addressed at the United Nations General Assembly on December 7, 1988.

The history of the past centuries and millennia has been a history of almost ubiquitous wars, and sometimes desperate battles, leading to mutual
Line destruction. They occurred in the clash of social and
5 political interests and national hostility, be it from ideological or religious incompatibility. All that was the case, and even now many still claim that this past -- which has not been overcome -- is an immutable pattern. However, parallel with the process of wars,
10 hostility, and alienation of peoples and countries, another process was in motion and gaining force: the emergence of a mutually connected and integral world.

Further world progress is now possible only through the search for a consensus of all mankind, in
15 movement toward a new world order. We have arrived at a frontier at which controlled spontaneity leads to a dead end. The world community must learn to shape and direct the process in such a way as to preserve civilization, to make it safe for all and more pleasant
20 for normal life. It is a question of cooperation that could be more accurately called "co-creation" and "co-development." The formula of development "at another's expense" is becoming outdated. In light of present realities, genuine progress by infringing upon
25 the rights and liberties of man and peoples, or at the expense of nature, is impossible.

It is evident that freedom of choice is a universal principle to which there should be no exceptions. The increasing varieties of social development in different
30 countries are becoming an ever more perceptible feature of these processes. This relates to both the capitalist and socialist systems. This fact presupposes a respect for other people's views and a preparedness to see phenomena that are different as not necessarily bad
35 or hostile, and an ability to learn to live side by side while remaining different and not agreeing with one another on every issue.

We are not giving up our convictions, philosophy, or traditions. Neither are we calling on anyone else to
40 give up theirs. Yet we are not going to shut ourselves up within the range of our values. That would lead to spiritual impoverishment, for it would mean renouncing so powerful a source of development as sharing all the original things created independently
45 by each nation. In the course of such sharing, each

should prove the advantages of his own system, his own way of life and values, not through words or propaganda alone, but through real deeds as well. That is, indeed, an honest struggle of ideology, but it
50 must not be carried over into mutual relations between states. Otherwise we simply will not be able to solve a single world problem; arrange broad, mutually advantageous and equitable cooperation between peoples; manage rationally the achievements of the
55 scientific and technical revolution; transform world economic relations; protect the environment; overcome underdevelopment; or put an end to hunger, disease, illiteracy, and other mass ills. Finally, in that case, we will not manage to eliminate the nuclear threat and
60 militarism.

Relations between the Soviet Union and the United States of America span five and a half decades. The world has changed, and so have the nature, role, and place of these relations in world politics. For too
65 long they were built under the banner of confrontation, and sometimes of hostility, either open or concealed. But in the last few years, throughout the world people were able to heave a sigh of relief, thanks to the changes for the better in the substance and atmosphere
70 of the relations between Moscow and Washington. The U.S.S.R. and the United States created the biggest nuclear missile arsenals, but after objectively recognizing their responsibility, they were able to be the first to conclude an agreement on the reduction and
75 physical destruction of a proportion of these weapons, which threatened both themselves and everyone else. We value this.

We are not inclined to oversimplify the situation in the world. Yes, the tendency toward disarmament has
80 received a strong impetus, and this process is gaining its own momentum, but it has not become irreversible. Yes, the striving to give up confrontation in favor of dialogue and cooperation has made itself strongly felt, but it has by no means secured its position forever
85 in the practice of international relations. Yes, the movement toward a nuclear-free and nonviolent world is capable of fundamentally transforming the political and spiritual face of the planet, but only the very first steps have been taken. Moreover, in certain influential
90 circles, they have been greeted with mistrust, and they are meeting resistance. The inheritance of inertia of the past are continuing to operate. Profound contradictions and the roots of many conflicts have not disappeared.

The fundamental fact remains that the formation
95 of the peaceful period will take place in conditions of the existence and rivalry of various socioeconomic and political systems. However, the meaning of our international efforts, and one of the key tenets of the

CONTINUE

new thinking, is precisely to impart to this rivalry the
100 quality of sensible competition in conditions of respect
for freedom of choice and a balance of interests. In
this case, it will even become useful and productive
from the viewpoint of general world development;
otherwise; if the main component remains the arms
105 race, as it has been till now, rivalry will be fatal.
Indeed, an ever greater number of people throughout
the world, from the man in the street to leaders, are
beginning to understand this.

1

Which choice best describes the main idea of the passage?

A) The United States and the Soviet Union must cooperate
to diversify their interests to ensure that the arms race
does not define the two countries' relationship.

B) The United States and the Soviet Union must respect
each other's sovereign interests to prevent others from
bearing the consequences of their conflict.

C) The United States and the Soviet Union must learn to
tolerate their ideological differences to maintain global
peace and prosperity.

D) The United States and the Soviet Union must
understand the necessity of mutual respect in their
ideological rivalry to further global development.

2

Gorbachev hails which development as resulting from
recent changes in the global social-political order?

A) The adherence to a policy of inclusiveness.

B) The obsolescence of a zero-sum mentality.

C) The reaffirmation of ideological beliefs.

D) The systematic elimination of social blights.

3

Which choice provides the best evidence for the answer to
the previous question?

A) Lines 22-26 ("The formula...impossible")

B) Lines 28-31 ("The increasing...processes")

C) Lines 54-58 ("manage rationally...ills")

D) Lines 63-66 ("The world...concealed")

4

Gorbachev characterizes the "freedom of choice" (line
27) as

A) an admirable quality which nations have lamentably
failed to universally maintain up until this point.

B) an indisputable tenet of democracy which works best
when it is understood that disagreement is inevitable.

C) an overarching principle of society which necessitates
the tolerance of divergent opinions.

D) an essential aspect of the economy which allows
for interconnectivity enabled by the acceptance of
differences.

5

Gorbachev believes that individual countries must

A) maintain their contrasting qualities to enrich wordly
diversity.

B) advocate for their own ideologies to promote their
legitimacy.

C) not permit their differences to interfere in their
intentions towards other states.

D) not demand that other countries enact change to
ensure that sovereignty is maintained.

6

Which choice provides the best evidence for the answer
to the previous question?

A) Lines 38-40 ("We are...theirs")

B) Lines 40-42 ("Yet we...impoverishment")

C) Lines 45-48 ("In the...well")

D) Lines 49-51 ("That is...states")

7

As used in line 42, "impoverishment" most nearly
means

A) deprivation.

B) dispossession.

C) distress.

D) destitution.

313

CONTINUE

8

As used in line 73, "responsibility" most nearly means

A) accountability.

B) authority.

C) charge.

D) duty.

9

Throughout the sixth paragraph (lines 78-93), Gorbachev expresses his concern regarding which of the following threats to global security?

A) The complacency of both governments brought on by slight improvements in nuclear disarmament.

B) The reversal of the current course of action if diplomatic and cooperative strategies should fail.

C) The perception of current progress as being anything other than mere diplomatic niceties.

D) The resistance to continued progressive dialogue that is weakened by a legacy of confrontation.

10

Throughout the last paragraph (lines 94-108), Gorbachev primarily underscores which of the following distinctions?

A) A competition that is productive and fair versus one that is dangerous and irresponsible.

B) An arms race that is contained versus one that has proliferated into foreign territories.

C) A rivalry centered around socio-political standards versus one based on military might.

D) A world heading towards peace versus one that is heading towards catastrophe.

CONTINUE

Questions 1-10 are based on the following passage.

10.4

The following passage is adapted from William Jennings Bryan's 'Cross of Gold' speech, delivered at the 1896 Democratic National Convention. In it, he argues against the gold standard and in favor of the free coinage of silver, or 'bimetallism', as a way to relieve restrictions on the money supply.

On the 4th of March, 1895, a few Democrats, most of them members of Congress, issued an address to the Democrats of the nation asserting that the
Line money question was the paramount issue of the hour;
5 concluding with the request that all believers in free coinage of silver should organize and take charge of and control the policy of the Democratic Party. Our silver Democrats went forth from victory unto victory, until they are assembled now, not to discuss, not to
10 debate, but to enter up the judgment rendered by the plain people of this country.

We do not come as individuals. I say it was not a question of persons; it was a question of principle; and it is not with gladness, my friends, that we find
15 ourselves brought into conflict with those who are now arrayed on the other side.

When you come before us and tell us that we shall disturb your business interests, we reply that you have disturbed our business interests by your action.
20 We say to you that you have made too limited in its application the definition of a businessman. The man who is employed for wages is as much a businessman as his employer. The attorney in a country town is as much a businessman as the corporation counsel in
25 a great metropolis. The merchant at the crossroads store is as much a businessman as the merchant of New York. The farmer who goes forth in the morning and toils all day and by the application of brain and muscle to the natural resources of this country creates
30 wealth, is as much a businessman as the man who goes upon the Board of Trade and bets upon the price of grain. The miners who go 1,000 feet into the earth or climb 2,000 feet upon the cliffs and bring forth from their hiding places the precious metals to be poured
35 in the channels of trade are as much businessmen as the few financial magnates who in a backroom corner the money of the world. We come to speak for this broader class of businessmen. They are as deserving of the consideration of this party as any people in this
40 country. We do not come as aggressors. Our war is not a war of conquest. We are fighting in the defense of our homes, our families, and posterity.

There are two ideas of government. There are those who believe that if you just legislate to make the
45 well-to-do prosperous, that their prosperity will leak through on those below. The Democratic idea has been that if you legislate to make the masses prosperous their prosperity will find its way up and through every class that rests upon it. You come to us and tell us
50 that the great cities are in favor of the gold standard. I tell you that the great cities rest upon these broad and fertile prairies. Burn down your cities and leave our farms, and your cities will spring up again as if by magic. But destroy our farms and the grass will grow
55 in the streets of every city in the country.

The gentleman from New York says that he wants this country to try to secure an international agreement for the adoption of bimetallism. Why doesn't he tell us what he is going to do if they fail to
60 secure an international agreement? They have tried for thirty years to secure an international agreement, and those are waiting for it most patiently who don't want it at all. No private character, however pure, no personal popularity, however great, can protect from
65 the avenging wrath of an indignant people the man who will either declare that he is in favor of fastening the gold standard upon this people, or who is willing to surrender the right of self-government and place legislative control in the hands of foreign potentates.
70 My friends, we shall declare that this nation is able to legislate for its own people on every question without waiting for the aid or consent of any other nation on earth, and upon that issue we expect to carry every single state in the Union. When citizens are
75 confronted with the proposition, "Is this nation able to attend to its own business?" it is the issue of 1776 over again. Our ancestors, when but 3 million, had the courage to declare their political independence of every other nation upon earth. Shall we, their descendants,
80 when we have grown to 70 million, declare that we are less independent than our forefathers?

If they say bimetallism is good but we cannot have it till some nation helps us, we reply that, instead of having a gold standard because England has, we
85 shall restore bimetallism, and then let England have bimetallism because the United States has. If they dare to come out in the open field and defend the gold standard as a good thing, we shall fight them to the uttermost, having behind us the producing masses
90 of the nation and the world. Having behind us the commercial interests and the laboring interests and all the toiling masses, we shall answer their demands for a gold standard by saying to them, you shall not press down upon the brow of labor this crown of thorns. You
95 shall not crucify mankind upon a cross of gold.

CONTINUE

1

The primary purpose of this passage is to

A) instigate a bipartisan debate over the validity of bimetallism as a monetary policy.

B) criticise the opposition party for its lack of genuine interest in the working classes.

C) argue that the introduction of silver into the money supply would benefit the masses.

D) contend that proponents of the gold standard have disregarded the needs of the people.

2

As used in line 16, "arrayed" most nearly means

A) revealed.

B) outfitted.

C) aligned.

D) empaneled.

3

How does the third paragraph (lines 17-42) contribute to the passage as a whole?

A) It attempts to make a definition more comprehensive so as to show that the Democratic party promotes the rights of the overlooked masses.

B) It enumerates the various classes of businessmen with the aim of clarifying the Convention's understanding and use of the term.

C) It explains the duties and goals of various occupations in order to elicit sympathy from politicians traditionally opposed to aiding laborers.

D) It positions Democratic leaders among the working public with the intent of gaining support in the fight for the free coinage of silver.

4

As used in line 21, "application" most nearly means

A) implementation.

B) scope.

C) relevance.

D) industry.

5

Bryan mentions the "issue of 1776" (line 76) mainly to

A) guilt Republicans into supporting bimetallism by calling upon the memory of the forefathers.

B) cite historical precedent as a defense against the opposition's request for an international accord.

C) use the hallowed history of the nation to argue for increased independence of thought and action.

D) illuminate the international stance that the Framers would have expected the United States to take.

6

Which choice provides the best evidence to support Bryan's claim that acting in the interest of the "toiling masses" (line 92) is in turn acting in the interest of the nation as a whole?

A) Lines 17-19 ("When you...action.")

B) Lines 49-52 ("You come...prairies")

C) Lines 52-55 ("Burn down...country")

D) Lines 70-73 ("My friends...earth")

7

How do the phrases "crown of thorns" (line 94) and "cross of gold" (line 95) further Bryan's point?

A) They are direct references to the suffering that humanity will face in the event of its continued dismissal of bimetallism.

B) They serve as poignant allusions to the threat of widespread hardship resulting from America's adherence to the gold standard.

C) They act as religious metaphors in order to heighten the stakes of the debate and sanctify the Democratic opinion.

D) They offer historical points of reference so as to relate to the nation's workers and show empathy for their plight.

CONTINUE

8

Based on the passage, how would Bryan characterize the opponents of the gold standard?

A) As purveyors of equality and saviours of the masses.

B) As proponents of independence and economic isolationists.

C) As the voice of the people and the executors of their will.

D) As champions of morality and guardians of the collective future.

9

Which choice provides the best evidence for the answer to the previous question?

A) Lines 14-16 ("it is...side.")

B) Lines 40-42 ("We do...posterity.")

C) Lines 46-49 ("The Democratic...it.")

D) Lines 77-79 ("Our ancestors...earth.")

10

How does Bryan rebut the view of the "gentleman from New York" (line 56)?

A) He laments that the desired outcome will never be achieved.

B) He argues that America should be the exemplar rather than the follower.

C) He calls upon the productive strength and governing power of the majority.

D) He deems the gentleman's view weak and lacking the proper initiative.

CONTINUE

Questions 1-10 are based on the following passage.

10.5

Passage 1 is adapted from *Émile* (1762), a novel on sexual differences and women's nature by philosopher Jean-Jacques Rousseau. Passage 2 is adapted from a section in *The Vindication of the Rights of Woman* (1792) in which Mary Wollstonecraft responds directly to Rousseau.

Passage 1

Once it is demonstrated that man and woman are not, and should not be, constituted the same, either in character or in temperment, it follows that they should
Line not have the same education.
5   Women, for their part, are always complaining that we raise them only to be vain and coquettish*, that we keep them amused with trifles so that we may more easily remain their masters; they blame us for the faults we attribute to them. What stupidity! And since when
10 is it men who concern themselves with the education of girls? Well then, decide to raise them like men; the men will gladly agree; the more women want to resemble them, the less women will govern them, and then men will truly be the masters.
15   All the faculties common to the two sexes are not equally divided; but taken as a whole, they offset one another. Woman is worth more as a woman and less as a man; whenever she makes her rights valued, she has the advantage; whenever she wishes to usurp ours, she
20 remains inferior to us.
Hence it follows that the system of woman's education should in this respect be the opposite of ours. On the good constitution of mothers depends primarily that of the children; on the care of women depends
25 the early education of men; and on women, again, depends their morals, their passions, their tastes, their pleasures, and even their happiness. Thus the whole education of women ought to be relative to men. To please them, to be useful to them, to make themselves
30 loved and honored by them, to educate them when young, to care for them when grown, to counsel them, to console them, and to make life agreeable and sweet to them--these are the duties of woman at all times, and should be taught them from their infancy. Unless we
35 are guided by this principle, we shall miss our aim, and all the precepts we give them will accomplish nothing either for their happiness or for our own.

Passage 2

I may be accused of arrogance; still I must declare what I firmly believe, that all the writers
40 who have written on the subject of female education and manners, from Rousseau to Dr. Gregory, have contributed to render women more artificial, weak characters, than they would otherwise have been - and consequently, more useless members of society.
45   Rousseau declares that a woman should never, for a moment, feel herself independent, that she should be governed by fear to exercise her natural cunning, and made a coquettish slave in order to render her a more alluring object of desire, a sweeter companion
50 to man, whenever he chooses to relax himself. He carries the arguments, which he pretends to draw from the indications of nature, still further and insinuates that truth and fortitude, the cornerstones of all human virtue, should be cultivated with certain restrictions
55 because, with respect to the female character, obedience is the grand lesson which ought to be impressed with unrelenting rigour.
What nonsense! When will a great man arise with sufficient strength of mind to puff away the fumes
60 which pride and sensuality have thus spread over the subject! If women are by nature inferior to men, their virtues must be the same in quality, if not in degree, or virtue is a relative idea; consequently, their conduct should be founded on the same principles, and have the
65 same aim.
Let it not be concluded that I wish to invert the order of things…
But Rousseau, and most of the male writers who have followed his steps, have warmly inculcated
70 that the whole tendency of female education ought to be directed to one point: to render them pleasing.
"Educate women like men," says Rousseau, "and the more they resemble our sex the less power will they have over us." This is the very point I aim at.
75 I do not wish them to have power over men; but over themselves…

*flirtatious

1

Rousseau and Wollstonecraft would most likely agree with all of the following EXCEPT that

A) the radical reordering of society is uncalled for.

B) educational imbalance precludes unhappiness.

C) men are blamed for the detriments of women.

D) the claims of the opposite gender are senseless.

CONTINUE ➡

2

As used in line 13, "govern" most nearly means

A) guide.

B) manipulate.

C) influence.

D) dominate.

3

In the third paragraph of Passage 1 (lines 15-20), Rousseau suggests which of the following about women's rights?

A) Increasing the comprehensiveness of women's rights will only diminish women's reputations in the eyes of men.

B) The blurring of gender specific boundaries is unjustifiable because women are inferior to men in every aspect.

C) Advocacy for women's rights is misguided because attainment of those rights threatens female nature.

D) Broadening the scope of women's rights would upset the natural order and not produce results favorable to women.

4

Rousseau would most likely respond to Wollstonecraft's interpretation of his argument in lines 45-50 ("Rousseau declares...himself") by stating that it

A) misconstrues his ultimate goal of happiness for both men and women through adherence to traditional gender roles.

B) does not account for his point about the greater worthiness of women when they use their femininity to advance their position.

C) serves as further evidence for his belief that women are constantly complaining without taking steps towards self-determination.

D) mistakenly vilifies his intended characterization of women's roles as the caretakers and mediating forces of men.

5

Which choice provides the best evidence for the answer to the previous question?

A) Lines 5-9 ("Women, for... them")

B) Lines 17-20 ("Woman is...us")

C) Lines 28-32 ("To please...them")

D) Lines 34-37 ("Unless we...own")

6

Based on the passages, Wollstonecraft would most likely characterize Rousseau's dismissal of women's complaints as

A) deluded, because it is obscured by the male pursuit of ego and pleasure.

B) insufficient, because it neglects the history of female subjugation by men.

C) reasonable, because it accounts for the catalysts of women's oppression.

D) irrelevant, because it draws on patently debunked principles of nature.

7

Which choice provides the best evidence for the answer to the previous question?

A) Lines 39-43 ("All the...been")

B) Lines 45-50 ("Rousseau declares...himself")

C) Lines 50-54 ("He carries...restrictions")

D) Lines 58-61 ("What nonsense...subject")

8

What is the purpose of the second paragraph of Passage 2 (lines 45-57)?

A) To censure Rousseau for his chauvinistic attitude regarding the nature of women.

B) To show Wollstonecraft's deconstruction of Rousseau's claims and her corresponding objections.

C) To further Wollstonecraft's reasoning regarding gender norms by invalidating Rousseau's.

D) To delineate Rousseau's argument and the assumptions upon which it rests.

CONTINUE

9

As used in line 57, "impressed" most nearly means

A) encouraged.

B) instilled.

C) enforced.

D) internalized.

10

A central argument in Passage 2 is that women's education should

A) render women worthy of male respect in intellectual and practical matters.

B) promote women's autonomy rather than a reversal of the gender dynamic.

C) make gender relations agreeable while expanding the influence of women.

D) adopt the aims of male education while still retaining a feminine approach.

STOP

Please turn to next page for answer keys and explanations.

Answer Key: CHAPTER TEN

10.1	JFK	10.2	Garfield	10.3	Gorbachev	10.4	Bryan	10.5	Émile
1: D	1: A	1: D	1: C	1: B
2: C	2: B	2: B	2: C	2: C
3: B	3: A	3: A	3: A	3: D
4: C	4: B	4: C	4: B	4: A
5: C	5: B	5: C	5: B	5: D
6: B	6: C	6: D	6: C	6: A
7: B	7: D	7: A	7: B	7: D
8: D	8: B	8: D	8: D	8: D
9: C	9: B	9: B	9: B	9: B
10: B	10: C	10: A	10: B	10: B

Answer Explanations

Chapter 10

Chapter 10.1 | JFK

Question 1: D
Choice D is the best answer because Kennedy first dedicates the speech to the "memory of Robert Frost", thus establishing the speech as a eulogy. Kennedy then emphasizes the importance, or "crucial value", of art and artists to the flourishing of a democratic society: "I see little of more importance to the future of our country and our civilization than full recognition of the artist" (lines 59-61). Choice A is incorrect because Frost merely serves as context for Kennedy to discuss the role of artists as a whole; in addition, Kennedy implies that Frost has already been "much honored" (line 51) in his lifetime and therefore will likely be remembered after his death. Choice B is incorrect because Kennedy considers art to be a balancing force to power, but does not indicate that it is stronger than power. Choice C is incorrect because Kennedy does not state that Frost alone was the "spirit which informs and controls [America's] strength" (line 23), but indicates that he was one of many artists who performed this role.

Question 2: C
Choice C is the best answer because Kennedy describes Frost as making a great "contribution" (line 11) to the country's "national strength" (line 16); if Frost took part in the creation of national strength, he can be defined as the strength's "origin". Choices A and B are incorrect because "informants" and "references" are sources of information, not power. Choice D is incorrect because "springs" provide a literal source of water, while Kennedy describes a more metaphorical source of strength.

Question 3: B
Choice B is the best answer because "disinterested" describes the nature of the "questioning" done by poets and artists, who have no interest in gaining power or usurping it from others themselves. Because they have no involvement in the game of creating power, their questioning can thus be characterized as neutral or "unbiased". Choice A is incorrect because "equitable" describes the result of actions influenced by poets' and artists' questioning, which Kennedy does not consider. Choices C and D are incorrect because the "men who question power" (lines 18-19), and by extension their questions, are not "indifferent" or "apathetic"; this is evident in the fact that they are passionate enough to question forces of authority in the first place.

Question 4: C

Choice C is the best answer because Kennedy argues that the artist "establishes...basic human truths" (lines 41-42); these truths then become the "touchstones" of a nation's "judgement" (line 43). Since the artist puts forth the truths that eventually influence society for the better, he can be described as "guiding" and "nurturing" civilization. Choice A is incorrect because Kennedy does not describe society as susceptible to vague "truisms" without the influence of artists; instead, he depicts society as easily falling prey to "arrogance" (line 37) and corruption (line 41). Choice B is incorrect because Kennedy does not delegate the responsibility of divorcing creation from propaganda to the artist. Rather, he indicates that it is the duty of a democratic society to ensure that artists do not become "engineers of the soul" (line 66). Choice D is incorrect because Kennedy characterizes artists as protecting the "individual mind and sensibility" (line 45), not the "state"; in fact, he depicts "an officious state" (line 46) as a source of the corrupting influence of excessive power, rather than a victim of it.

Question 5: C

Choice C is the best answer because lines 41-43 explain that art establishes truths that influence "our", or society's, judgments; these lines thus describe the important contribution of artists to the "national community". Choice A is incorrect because lines 25-26 discuss Frost's role in society, not that of artists as a whole. Choice B is incorrect; while lines 37-38 describe the significance of art in the national community, they do not match with any of the choices in the previous question. Choice D is incorrect because lines 64-65 specify the roles that artists do not play and are therefore off topic: "in free society art is not a weapon".

Question 6: B

Choice B is the best answer because Kennedy indicates that the artist "must often sail against the currents of his time" (lines 49-50) in pursuing his "personal vision of reality" (line 44). Because this duty makes the artist the "last champion of the individual mind and sensibility" (line 45), the artist can be described as occupying a "singularizing" role. Choice A is incorrect because Kennedy does not depict the artist as feeling the emotion of loneliness; moreover, the singular position occupied by the artist results from his creative work, not his "lifestyle". Choice C is incorrect because Kennedy uses the archetype of the "solitary figure" to outline the role of artists in general, as opposed to Frost in particular; in fact, discussion of Frost's personality, including his introversion or individualism, is not present in the passage at all. Choice D is incorrect because Kennedy does not indicate that the artist is the only force that upholds a nation's culture and justice.

Question 7: B

Choice B is the best answer because lines 43-46 portray the artist as "the last champion of the individual mind" who is "faithful to his own personal vision"; these references to individuality and independence are relevant to Kennedy's discussion of the artist as a "solitary figure" and therefore match the topic of the previous question. Choice A is incorrect because lines 9-12 are off topic: Kennedy introduces Frost as a unique and important contributor to society, but does not indicate that his artistic achievements have made him a "solitary figure". Choices C and D are incorrect because lines 50-53 and 53-54 describe the unpopular yet influential role an artist occupies in society, but do not suggest that such a role is singular or isolating.

Question 8: D

Choice D is the best answer because Kennedy establishes the importance of society to "set the artist free to follow his vision" (lines 62-63) before illustrating against the fate of "the nation which disdains the mission of art" (lines 71-72) and fails to "set the artist free" in lines 73-74. In the next paragraph, Kennedy discusses the benefits that will come from a nation that does not restrict its artists and "will steadily raise the standards of artistic accomplishment and which will steadily enlarge cultural opportunities for all of our citizens" (lines 86-90); therefore, lines 73-74 can be seen as a transition to this description. Choice A is incorrect because the "hired man" (line 72) does not refer to a literal worker employed by Frost; moreover, the "fate" that Kennedy considers in lines 73-74 is that of a nation, not of a specific person. Choice B is incorrect because Kennedy does not focus on "mere fact" throughout the last paragraph, but instead on the idealized depiction of an artist's role in a democratic society. Choice C is incorrect because Kennedy argues against the path that is described by Frost—that of a nation without pride or hope; in addition, Kennedy does not attempt to teach, or "offer a didactic adage", but to inform and warn the reader.

Question 9: C

Choice C is the best answer because Kennedy indicates that "when power leads man towards arrogance, poetry reminds him of his limitations" (lines 37-38). Because poetry prevents man from becoming too arrogant and provides a check against power, it can be seen as a restricting or "qualifying" guide which prevents corruption. Choice A is incorrect because Kennedy indicates that critique of power is an important effect of poetry, but not that it is a motivation or obligation of poetry. Choice B is incorrect because Kennedy only depicts the limitations of power (as moderated and tempered by poetry) but does not imply that poetry itself has limits. Choice D is incorrect because Kennedy does not state that the subject or content of poetry is power, or borne out of man's desire for power. In addition, Kennedy does not believe that man's desire for power is "insatiable", since it can be productively restricted by poetry.

Question 10: B

Choice B is the best answer because Kennedy continually makes reference to an America to which he looks forward throughout the last paragraph: "I look forward to a great future for America" (line 75), "I look forward to an America which will not be afraid of grace and beauty" (lines 78-80), "I look forward to an America which will reward achievement in the arts" (lines 84-85). Because Kennedy focuses on the "future" of America, which he believes can be reached through the encouragement of artists and free expression, he can be described as emphasizing its "foreseeable potential". Choice A is incorrect because "failings" does not match the positive tone of the final paragraph; moreover, Kennedy believes that the situations described are achievable, as he "looks forward" to experiencing them. Choice C is incorrect because Kennedy does not reference specific works of literature, art, or media and therefore does not make any allusions. Choice D is incorrect because Kennedy describes the yet unrealized future of America, and thus cannot be depicting the beauty and strength that America currently possesses because of Frost's work.

Chapter 10.2 | Garfield

Question 1: A
Choice A is the best answer because in the beginning of the passage Garfield asserts that the bill has benefited all Americans by "[giving] new inspiration to the power of self-help in both races by making labor more honorable to the one and more necessary to the other" (lines 13-16) and it has had negative repercussions: "this great change has caused serious disturbance to our Southern communities" (lines 19-20). He then points out that one claim made against the bill is that "in many places honest local government is impossible if uneducated negroes are allowed to vote" (lines 44-46) and goes on to enumerate the ways in which this issue, in the broader context of all uneducated citizens, affects the country. He finally states that "it is the high privilege and sacred duty of those now living to educate their successors and fit them...for the inheritance which awaits them" (lines 90-93). Choice B is incorrect because in the second half of the passage, Garfield does not focus on the impact on white Americans, rather he is concerned that lack of education will impact all citizens present and future. Choice C is incorrect because Garfield does not mention laws made by Southern governments, only that they "resisted the change" (line 22). Choice D is incorrect because while Garfield does praise civil rights afforded by the recent political change, he does not enumerate obstacles; in fact, the entire discussion of the latter part of the passage is focused solely on the evils of ignorance and the responsibility of the people to remedy that issue.

Question 2: B
Choice B is the best answer because while Garfield does say in lines 8-9 that the emancipation of slaves has "added immensely to the moral and industrial forces of our people", that does not indicate that more people have joined the workforce--only that those people are improving. Choice A is incorrect because Garfield states that "[emancipation of slaves] has freed [America] from the perpetual danger of war and dissolution" (lines 6-7). Choice C is incorrect because Garfield states that "[emancipation of slaves] has given new inspiration to...both races" (line 13). Choice D is incorrect because Garfield states that "labor [has been made] more honorable to the one and more necessary to the other" (lines 15-16).

Question 3: A
Choice A is the best answer because Garfield states that there "is no middle ground...between slavery and equal citizenship" (lines 23-24), indicating that his position on a "middle ground" is that it is not possible. In the following lines, 25-29, he expands on that idea, saying "freedom can never yield its fullness of blessings so long as the law...places the smallest obstacle in the pathway of any virtuous citizen" (lines 26-29). This statement contends that unless all citizens are free, no one can experience the full expression of their freedom Choices B and C are incorrect because they wrongly assert that the middle ground is positive when Garfield clearly asserts that "there was no middle ground... between slavery and equal citizenship" (lines 23-24), clearly stating that he is not in favor of this idea. Choice D is incorrect because there is no compromise happening. Garfield is firm that "There can be no permanent disfranchised peasantry in the United States" (lines 25-26).

Question 4: B
Choice B is the best answer because in the lines referenced in question 3, Garfield states that there "is no middle ground...between slavery and equal citizenship" (lines 23-24), clearly implying that it is not possible to find a middle ground slavery and freedom. In the following lines, 25-29, he expands on that idea, saying "freedom can never yield its fullness of blessings so long as the law... places the smallest obstacle in the pathway of any virtuous citizen" (lines 26-29). This statement contends that unless all citizens are free, no one can experience the full expression of their freedom. Choices A, C, and D are incorrect because they wrongly address the topics of positive effects of emancipation (choices A and B) and Garfield's power to protect emancipated slaves under the law (choice D).

Question 5: B
Choice B is the best answer because Garfield addresses the next generation in sixth paragraph, insisting that this generation must not "come to its inheritance blinded by ignorance" (lines 73-74) or "the fall of the Republic will be certain and remediless" (lines 74-75). This indicates that their primary mission is to rid themselves of ignorance to fulfil their duty of preserving the country. Choice A is incorrect because while Garfield does endorse participation in political processes, that participation suffers from "corruption and fraud" (line 67) if those participating are not educated. Choice C is incorrect because the primary concern of the passage is civic education and rights, not economics. Choice D is incorrect because removing literacy prerequisites at the ballot box, while a helpful initiative, fails to resolve the primary issue of "ignorance in the voter" (lines 60-61).

Question 6: C
Choice C is the best answer because in lines 74-75 Garfield states that "the fall of the Republic will be certain and remediless" if the next generation "comes into [the] inheritance [of America] blinded by ignorance" (lines 73-74), which is an explicit warning of an imminent negative consequence brought on by lack of education. Choices A, B, and D are not the right answers because they incorrectly refer to Southern governments (choice A), school systems (choice B), and laws (choice D) which are not mentioned in any of the lines reference in question four.

Question 7: D
Choice D is the best answer because Garfield clearly denotes one consequence of ignorant citizenry: "the fall of the republic" (lines 74-75). Choices A and B are not the right answers because they incorrectly address either the position of Garfield's opponents (choice A) or bad local government (choice B). Choice C is incorrect because while Garfield does say that it is dangerous to have uneducated citizenry in lines 64-67, he does not say what the consequence of that danger is until later in the passage.

Question 8: B
Choice B is the best answer because of the key phrase earlier in the sentence that "the voters of the Union...can transmit their supreme authority" (lines 68-71) only to the "coming generation of voters" (lines 71-72), which indicates that later when Garfield says the coming generation are the "heirs of sovereign power" he means that they will be the recipients of this legacy. Choice A is incorrect because while "beneficiaries" refers to something passed down, it incorrectly implies that being the "heir of sovereign power" is an advantage gained by future generations when in actuality it is a duty because the "destinies of our governments" (lines 69-70) hangs upon the citizens' will. Choice C is

incorrect because future generations are not administering sovereign power; rather, they are gaining it from past generations who will "transmit their supreme authority" (lines 70-71), indicating the word in question has to do with acquiring authority over the government. Choice D is incorrect because while the next generation of voters are the replacements of the past generation, they are not the "replacements of sovereign power".

Question 9: B

Choice B is the best answer because Garfield states earlier in the previous sentence that the whole United States is responsible for "removing the illiteracy which it has added to the voting population" (lines 83-84) and that the people can only fix it by getting "all the constitutional power of the nation and of the States and all the volunteer forces of the people" (lines 86-87) behind the issue to bring education to those who need it. This supports that he is urging the people to mobilize behind the cause. Choice A is incorrect because "to relinquish" the people to meet this danger indicates they're giving up, but he wants the opposite, for the people to take responsibility for this issue. Choice C is incorrect because while the people should be united for the cause, they don't necessarily have to be together to solve the issue, they just have to be taking action. Choice D is incorrect because similar to choice A, if the people renounce the cause, they are giving something up, not putting their energy towards a cause.

Question 10: C

Choice C is the best answer because in lines 96-97 Garfield is reinforcing the point made at the beginning of the paragraph that "those now living…[must] educate their successors and fit them... for the inheritance which awaits them" (lines 90-93). Choices A & D are incorrect because the point Garfield is making in the passage is about "how dangerously the tide of illiteracy has risen among our voters and their children" (lines 77-79) which includes all voters, not just "black citizenry". Choice B is incorrect because "moral righteousness" is not the solution to ignorance of voters, education is.

Chapter 10.3 | Gorbachev

Question 1: D

Choice D is the best answer because Gorbachev argues that "[f]urther world progress is now possible only through the search for a consensus of all mankind" (lines 13-14) and that, for this to be achieved, the United States and the Soviet Union must "learn to live side by side while remaining different and not agreeing with one another on every issue" (lines 35-37). Choice A is incorrect because while Gorbachev does insist throughout the passage that the United States and the Soviet Union must cooperate, he does not indicate that either country needs to diversity its interests; in fact, he implies the opposite in paragraph four: "we are not giving up our convictions, philosophy, or traditions. Neither are we calling on anyone else to give up theirs" (lines 38-40). Choice B is incorrect because Gorbachev's point in the passage is that the entire world community benefits from improved relations between the two countries, but he does not only want that relationship to be preserved so that other countries do not bear the consequences; the United States and the Soviet Union would also bear the same consequences. Choice C is incorrect because Gorbachev would disagree that global peace and prosperity need only to be maintained; his primary point is that the countries should continue to make progress so as not to allow "[t]he inheritance of inertia of the past [to] continu[e] to operate" (lines 91-92).

Question 2: B

Choice B is the best answer because in lines 22-26, Gorbachev insists that the world community no longer desires to get ahead at the expense of others, and he goes so far as to say that mindset "is impossible" (line 26), or obsolete. Choices A and C are incorrect because while Gorbachev does say the world community has become more inclusive (choice A) and that "we are not giving up our convictions, philosophy, or traditions" (lines 38-39), he does so in the fourth paragraph, which is not referenced in question three. Choice D is incorrect because "systematic elimination" indicates an intentional endeavor but Gorbachev does not imply anywhere in the passage that things are happening according to some grand scheme or plan.

Question 3: A

Choice A is the best answer because by saying "development 'at another's expense' is becoming outdated" (lines 22-23), Gorbachev indicates that it's no longer necessary for countries to make their own gains at the expense of others. Choice B is incorrect because while in lines 28-31 Gorbachev does state a result of recent changes, "increasing varieties of social development" (line 29) is not an option in question two. Choice C is incorrect because lines 54-58 reference future possibilities, not results. Choice D is incorrect because while in lines 63-66, Gorbachev insists that "the world has changed" (line 63), he does not state a result that has happened because of that change.

Question 4: C

Choice C is the best answer because throughout the passage Gorbachev states that there "should be no exceptions" (line 28) to freedom of choice and that it is "universal" (line 27) before discussing "increasing varieties of social development in different countries" (lines 28-29). This indicates that he believes that freedom of choice is important for societal progress. Choice A is incorrect because Gorbachev never indicates that any country or countries are infringing on each other's freedom of choice. Choice B is incorrect because this is a tenent of "both capitalist and socialist systems" (lines 31-32). Choice D is incorrect because freedom of choice is an aspect of social relations, not economic relations.

Question 5: C

Choice C is the best answer because in lines 49-51, Gorbachev calls on the countries in his audience to not allow their differences to get in the way of their relationships with each other. Choice A is incorrect because Gorbachev states that countries should retain their individual convictions, philosophy, and traditions, but not that these varying qualities contrast each other. Choice B is incorrect because while Gorbachev does claim that each country should "prove the advantages of his own system" (line 46), he does not say that they need to advocate or prove the legitimacy of these systems. Choice D is incorrect because while Gorbachev does communicate that countries should not ask each other not to change their own ideologies in lines 38-40, the phrase "calling on" does not mean demand, and he does not indicate maintaining sovereignty in those lines.

Question 6: D

Choice D is the best answer because in lines 49-51, Gorbachev calls on the countries in his audience to not allow their differences to get in the way of their relationships with each other, stating that while they have "an honest struggle of ideology" (line 49), or differences in their convictions, philosophy, and traditions, "[this ideological struggle] must not be carried over into mutual relations" (lines 49-51). Choice A is incorrect because Gorbachev merely advocates for countries to not change their beliefs, which does not match any of the answer choices in question five. Choice B is incorrect because in lines 40-42 Gorbachev is stating a belief he has about Russia, not about individual countries in general. Choice C is incorrect because while Gorbachev does present a belief he has regarding individual countries, none of the answer choices in question five match that countries should "prove the advantages of his own system, his own way of life, and values...through real deeds" (lines 46-48).

Question 7: A

Choice A is the best answer because Gorbachev states that spiritual impoverishment would result from "shut[ting] [them]selves up within the range of [their] values" (lines 40-41), indicating that they would become limited, or deprived in their options for their "convictions, philosophy, [and] traditions" (lines 38-39). Choice B is incorrect because it refers to being deprived of something concrete or physical and, therefore, cannot refer to spirituality. Choice C is incorrect because while the situation in question might lead to general distress for the countries that are impoverished, they would not have "spiritual distress". Choice D is incorrect because while Gorbachev is implying that countries who shut themselves up within their range of values would have less development, he does not go so far as to imply they would be completely devoid of those things.

Question 8: D

Choice D is the best answer because Gorbachev first states that "throughout the world people were able to heave a sigh of relief" (lines 67-68) before saying that it was because the U.S.S.R. and the U.S. recognized that they have a responsibility to the world to life their banner of confrontation and agree to reduce weapons. This indicates that the two countries had a duty to allow the rest of the world to ease their tension. Choice A is incorrect because while the U.S.S.R. and the U.S. did take accountability, it does not fit in the placement of the word "responsibility" in the sentence. Choice B is incorrect because calling the responsibility of the two counties their "authority" indicates that they are controlling or enforcing others to do something, whereas in this case they are cooperating to reach a common goal. Choice C is incorrect because "charge" implies that they have been bestowed this responsibility by some other entity when in fact they took it upon themselves.

Question 9: B

Choice B is the best answer because Gorbachev argues that, despite the move toward disarmament and peace, the progress being made "has not become irreversible" (line 81) or "secured its position forever" (line 84), which suggests that such progress is precarious and could still be threatened. Choice A is incorrect because, while Gorbachev does say that complacency is a real possibility, it does not necessarily constitute a "threat to global security". Choice C is incorrect because Gorbachev states that "striving to give up confrontation in favor of dialogue and cooperation has made itself strongly felt" (lines 82-83), indicating that their progress is believed to be genuine, not mere niceties. Choice D is incorrect because to weaken resistance to continued progressive dialogue would not be a threat to global security-- it would be neutral at worst.

Question 10: A

Choice A is the best answer because in the last paragraph, Gorbachev makes a distinction between a "more useful and productive" (line 102) relationship between the U.S. and Russia if they have "conditions of respect for freedom of choice and a balance of interests" (lines 100-101) and one that is defined by the arms race in which "rivalry will be fatal" (line 105). Choice B is incorrect because while Gorbachev does imply that the arms race is contained, he does not mention spreading to other territories; in fact, he only mentions other countries to discuss the general idea of word development and people in the world understanding the relationship stated in choice A. Choice C is incorrect because, while Gorbachev references the "socioeconomic and political systems" (lines 96-97) and "the arms race" (lines 104-105), he does not distinguish between a rivalry centered on one versus the other; the dichotomy he actually creates is between "sensible competition" (line 100) and "the arms race" (lines 104-105). Choice D is incorrect because while Gorbachev does mention the "formation of a peaceful period" (lines 94-95) and later of a possible catastrophe when he says "rivalry will be fatal", he is not talking about the world, just about relations between Russia and the U.S.

Chapter 10.4 | Bryan

Question 1: C

Choice C is the best answer because Bryan posits that entering into bimetallism would benefit the "commercial interests and the laboring interest and all the toiling masses" (lines 91-92). Choice A is incorrect because Bryan explicitly states in lines 9-10 that "Democrats…are assembled now, not to discuss, not to debate, but to enter up the judgment rendered by the plain people of this country." Choice B is incorrect because, according to Bryan, the opposition party "[has] made too limited in its application the definition of a businessman," (lines 20-21) and therefore, does not so much lack a genuine interest, but is too narrow in its views. Choice D is incorrect because Bryan's main argument is not that the opposition isn't taking into account the needs of the people but that it is "crucifying mankind upon a cross of gold" (line 95) in refusing bimetallism.

Question 2: C

Choice C is the best answer because he writes that "[he] has been brought into conflict with those who are now…on the other side" (lines 15-16) and aligned means to be in support of a cause – in this case, the cause directly in opposition to his own. Choice A is incorrect because revealed contextually means Bryan hadn't seen or known who was on the opposing side, which wasn't the case. Choice B is incorrect because outfitted means that the opposition was now equipped with something it didn't have before, which is not contextually supported. Choice D is incorrect because there is no contextual support that "those who are now…on the other side" recently enlisted in the opposition.

Question 3: A

Choice A is the best answer because Bryan states that the opposition's "definition of a businessman" is "too limited" (lines 20-21) and then goes on to list various occupations that fall under the "definition of a businessman" that the opposition did not take into account: "the man who is employed," "the merchant at the crossroads store," "the attorney," "the farmer," and "the miners" (lines 21-32). Choice B is incorrect because he does not enumerate the various classes, but the various occupations of businessmen. Choice C is incorrect because Bryan does not mention any duties and goals of the various occupations and, furthermore, to say he is trying to elicit sympathy would be an assumption. Choice D is incorrect because Democratic leaders are not mentioned anywhere in the paragraph.

Question 4: B

Choice B is the best answer because Bryan asserts that the opposition is too "limited in [what it includes under] the definition of a businessman" (lines 20-21) and the scope of something is the extent of it – in this case, "the definition of a businessman". Choice A is incorrect because the opposition isn't limiting putting into effect the definition. Choice C is incorrect because it is not that the definition of a businessman isn't relevant to the businessmen Bryan describes; it's simply not encompassing of those businessmen. Choice D is incorrect because the opposition is not limited in the way the definition was produced.

Question 5: B

Choice B is the best answer because Bryan writes, " Our ancestors…had the courage to declare their political independence…shall we, their descendants…declare that we are less independent than [they]?" (lines 77-81). Choice A is incorrect because to say Bryan is trying to guilt Republicans would be an unsupported assumption. Choice C is incorrect because Bryan is arguing for increased independence of business (bimetallism), not of thought and action, as he writes, "Is this nation able to attend to its own business?" (lines 75-76). Choice D is incorrect because Bryan mentions American forefathers in the sixth paragraph to reject the ideas that his opponents favor "secur[ing] an international agreement for the adoption of bimetallism" (lines 56-57); he claims instead that as the forefathers intended, America should be independent of any other nations' aid or consent. Therefore, it's not necessarily an international stance he's citing, it's a domestic stance.

Question 6: C

Choice C is the best answer because Bryan states that if the government "leaves [the] farms [of "the masses" (line 47), [it] will help the "cities [of every city] spring up". Choice A is incorrect because these lines address the opposition and its impact on businessmen directly. Choice B is incorrect because these lines include the sentence about what the opposition desires and not about acting in the interest of the nation as a whole. Choice D is incorrect because this line reference talks about independence in legislation and not the relationship between the interest of toiling masses and the interest of the nation as a whole.

Question 7: B

Choice B is the best answer because the line reference in which these words appear, Bryan states, "with their demands for a gold standard…[England] shall not press down upon the brow of labor" (lines 92-94). Choice A is incorrect because these words are not direct references since they are not literal thorns or an actual cross. Choice C is incorrect because although those words are religious references, they do not sanctify the Democratic opinion. Choice D is incorrect because the crown of thorns or being crucified on the cross is not meant to relate to the worker as much as it is to show what the outcome will be if bimetallism is not adopted.

Question 8: D

Choice D is the best answer because in lines 40-42 (choice B of the paired evidence question number 9), Bryan advances that the opponents of the gold standard are not "aggressors" or trying to engage in a "war of conquest" (lines 40-41), but that they are simply trying to defend their families and the future generations of people, "posterity" (line 42), thus suggesting a moral cause and the only choice paired with a line reference in number 9 about a collective future. Choice A is incorrect because the opponents of the gold standard, while they believe in more inclusiveness in their opponents' definition of a businessman (something similar to equality), they are not suppliers of equality. Choice B is incorrect because, although choice D in number 9 is about independence and so a possible match, the "ancestors" in lines 77-79 are not necessarily the opponents of the gold standard; furthermore, that line reference does not mention anything about isolationists. Choice C is incorrect because, which it can be argued that the opponents of the gold standard think they are the voice of the people and the executor of their will, there are no choices in number 9 that support this choice.

Question 9: B
Choice B is the best answer because this line reference ends with the word "posterity," which is supported by the correct answer choice D in the paired question number 8. Choice A is incorrect because this line reference, while it is on the topic of those who are in opposition of the gold standard, is about being in conflict with those who oppose bimetallism, which is not supported by any of the choices in number 8. Choice C is incorrect because is about Democrats and not all Democrats are necessarily opponents of the gold standard, making the choice off topic. Choice D is incorrect because it does not support any answer choice in question 8 fully.

Question 10: B
Choice B is the best answer because in lines 82-86, Bryan writes, "instead of having a gold standard because England has, we shall restore bimetallism, and then let England have bimetallism because the United States has." Choice A is incorrect because it would be an assumption to say that Bryan thinks that an "international agreement for the adoption of bimetallism" (lines 57-58) would never be achieved, as he never says this. Choice C is incorrect because Bryan states that "we shall declare that this nation is able to legislate for its own people on ever question without …[the] consent of any other nation on earth" (lines 70-73), so what he's saying is a declaration – not a call to action. Choice D is incorrect because in lines 60-63, he writes, "[the government] has tried to thirty years to secure an international agreement, and those are waiting for it most patiently who don't want it at all," suggesting that it has simply not happened yet; therefore, there is no support that he thinks the gentleman's view is weak or lacking proper initiative since there has been an attempt for thirty years.

Chapter 10.5 | Émile

Question 1: B
Choice B is the best answer because only Rousseau thinks that the unequal educational system is crucial to the creation of happiness for both men and women, as he argues that "the whole education of women ought to be relative to men" (lines 27-28) and that, if that rule is disregarded, "all the precepts we give them will accomplish nothing either for their happiness or for our own" (lines 36-37). Choice A is incorrect because both authors believe that the order of society does not need to be uprooted; Rousseau states that "[a]ll the faculties common to the two sexes are not equally divided; but taken as a whole, they offset one another" (lines 15-17), suggesting that society is already balanced, and Wollstonecraft states, "Let it not be concluded that I wish to invert the order of things" (lines 66-67), suggesting that, despite her overall point, she does not mean to suggest a social revolution. Choice C is incorrect because Rousseau states that women "blame us for the faults

we attribute to them" (lines 8-9), and Wollstonecraft states that the male writers have "contributed to render women more artificial, weak characters, than they would otherwise have been" (lines 42-43), thus each suggesting that men are or should be blamed for women's shortcomings. Choice D is incorrect because the authors are in general opposition and each believe the other is mildly insane-- Rousseau exclaims "What stupidity!" in response to his perceived view of Wollstonecraft and other women, and Wollstonecraft exclaims "What nonsense!" in response to her summary of Rousseau's opinions.

Question 2: C
Choice C is the best answer because Rousseau suggests that the more women attempt to be like men, the more they will lose their ability to influence or hold sway over men. Choice A is incorrect because it implies too direct of an approach, as Rousseau actually seems to suggest that it is because of women's feminine wiles that they are able to influence men, not their outward guidance. Choice B is incorrect because it carries a negative connotation while, in the context, Rousseau implies that this ability of women is a positive aspect that they should work to protect and cultivate. Choice D is incorrect because, while Rousseau clearly suggests that women have a way of gently controlling men, he still believes that women are there "to make life agreeable and sweet" (lines 32-33) to men, and therefore would not suggest that they do or should dominate men.

Question 3: D
Choice D is the best answer because Rousseau argues that women's attempt to "usurp" (line 19) the rights of men will only keep women "inferior" (line 20), which supports the idea that giving women greater rights will not be as beneficial as women had hoped. Choice A is incorrect because women's reputations as specifically perceived by men are not the pertinent issue, but rather women's reputations in general. Choice B is incorrect because it is too extreme as Rousseau actually believes that the faculties of men and women, "taken as a whole,...offset one another" (lines 16-17), suggesting that he believes women to be equal or superior as long as they remain in their own sphere. Choice C is incorrect because Rousseau argues that women's usurpation of rights from men is the negative action, not the mere advocacy for more rights.

Question 4: A
Choice A is the best answer because Rousseau ultimately argues that all his views on how men and women should act and how their actions should be relegated, as summarized by Wollstonecraft in the cited lines, are in the sole service of everyone's happiness. He argues, in the evidence for Question 5, that unless "we are guided by this principle...all the precepts we give them will accomplish nothing either for their happiness or for our own" (lines 35-37). Choices B and C are incorrect because Rousseau states that women remain inferior when they attempt to gain more rights (lines 19-20); therefore, he would not suggest that they should "advance their position" (Choice B) or take "steps toward self-determination" (Choice C). Choice D is incorrect because, while Rousseau believes that women should "counsel" and "console" (lines 31-32) men, he doesn't go so far as to suggest that women should moderate men, or that that is something men would ever need.

Question 5: D

Choice D is the best answer because the answer to the previous question states that Rousseau's main goal is to allow happiness for both men and women, which is supported by lines 34-37. The rest of the choices are incorrect because they only state that women blame men for their faults (Choice A), that women are worth more when they remain in their sphere (Choice B), and that women should cater to men (Choice C), but fail to connect those discussions to Rousseau's greater point of establishing lasting happiness through conformity to established gender dynamics.

Question 6: A

Choice A is the best answer because, in the evidence for Question 7, Wollstonecraft responds directly to Rousseau's ideas by exclaiming "What nonsense! When will a great man arise with sufficient strength of mind to puff away the fumes which pride and sensuality have thus spread over the subject!" (lines 58-61), which suggests that she views men as being misled or deceived by their own emotions and pride. Choice B is incorrect because Wollstonecraft does not bring situate her or Rousseau's discussion in the greater context of feminist history. Choice C is incorrect because, while Rousseau does account for the reasons that women are oppressed, even if he doesn't call it oppression, he would not be considered reasonable by Wollstonecraft, who emphatically calls his beliefs senseless. Choice D is incorrect because, while she does question the validity of his appeal to nature by stating that he "pretends to draw from the indications of nature" (lines 51-52), she does not claim that such indications have been proven to be false.

Question 7: D

Choice D is the best answer because the answer to the previous question states that Wollstonecraft believes men are duped by their ego and emotion, which is supported by lines 58-61 as they reference the "fumes" of "pride and sensuality" that cloud men's judgement of the subject. Choice A is incorrect because it only argues that men have made women lesser members of society, but doesn't say why. Choices B and C are incorrect for similar reasons as they merely present a critically tinted summary of Rousseau's ideas, but fail to mention directly what Wollstonecraft herself thinks of those ideas and their origin.

Question 8: D

Choice D is the best answer because Wollstonecraft's primary motive in Paragraph 2 is to present Rousseau's ideas so that she can refute them, but in that specific paragraph she does not actually lay out her refutations. Choice A is incorrect because it implies that Wollstonecraft is expressing her severe disapproval of Rousseau and his ideas, when that disapproval is actually demonstrated later. The rest of the choices are incorrect for similar reasons as they both suggest that Wollstonecraft actually launches her defense against Rousseau in Paragraph 2 by suggesting that she presents her "corresponding objections" (Choice B) and invalidates Rousseau's reasoning (Choice C), when in reality that doesn't begin until the next paragraph.

Question 9: B
Choice B is the best answer because Wollstonecraft says Rousseau believes that obedience must be firmly established in the character of women through their education, and the word "instilled" suggests that something is being gradually ingrained. Choice A is incorrect because it is too weak and too positive, suggesting that women are being motivated to be obedient. Choice C is incorrect for the inverse reason as it suggests that women have to be forced to be obedient, when the point Rousseau is making is that it should be taught to them from a young age so that enforcement isn't needed. Choice D is incorrect because it puts the action of instilling obedience on the women themselves, suggesting that they are unconsciously assimilating to this standard rather than openly being taught to adhere to it.

Question 10: B
Choice B is the best answer because Wollstonecraft sums up her whole argument by stating that she does not "wish [women] to have power over men; but over themselves…" (lines 75-76). Choice A is incorrect because it insinuates that Wollstonecraft believes education should help women gain respect in the eyes of men, which she seems to contradict with her above statement that women's education should be for women. Choice C is incorrect because, while Wollstonecraft does state that she does not "wish to invert the order of things" (lines 66-67), she also doesn't claim to be a peacemaker, and would presumably disregard any social turmoil that came of the expansion of women's education if it meant that women gained autonomy as a result. Choice D is incorrect because, despite the fact that she would like women to have the same educational goals as men, she says nothing about how women's education should be conducted or approached, and could easily be imagined to argue that it should be approached in the exact same way as men's education is.

Made in the USA
Middletown, DE
30 June 2020